A Parcel of Ribbons - The Lee Family Letters

The correspondence of an eighteenth century family in England and Jamaica

Transcribed and edited by

Anne M. Powers

ISBN 978-1-105-80974-3

Cover: Francis Cotes (English, 1726-1770), Portrait of Miss Frances Lee, 1769. Milwaukee Art Museum, Gift of Mr. and Mrs. William D. Vogel M1964.5. Photo by Larry Sanders. Cover design by Ali Powers.

For my mother without whom I would not have gone in search of the Indian Princess and found the Lee Letters

Acknowledgments

The Lee letters were initially preserved by Robert Cooper Lee, maintaining the link they provided with his home in England while he and his brothers spent a quarter of a century in Jamaica, and later by his children, particularly Richard. Together with the letters of other descendants they are preserved in a private family collection, and I am incredibly grateful to their custodians for access to the collection and permission to make digital copies.

I am also grateful for permission to use images of the various portraits of the Lee family, and of Marchant Tubb, held in private collections.

Permission from the Milwaukee Museum of Art to reproduce the portrait of Frances Lee is gratefully acknowledged, as is permission to reproduce transcriptions of the letters written by John Lee held at the East Sussex County Record Office at Lewes.

Photograph of Bedford Square courtesy of Wikimedia Commons (c) Steve Cadman, steve@stevecadman.me.uk, Creative Commons Attribution Sharealike v2.0

Thanks are due to Professor Linda L. Sturtz and Dr Daniel A Livesay for their help and encouragement, and a shared enthusiasm for eighteenth century Jamaica.

Last, but by no means least, thanks are due to my family and especially to my husband Professor Jonathan Powers for help and support during the preparation of this book.

Abbreviations

TNA The National Archives, Kew

ESRO East Sussex County Record Office, Lewes

Editor's Note:

The letters have been transcribed retaining as far as possible the original spelling, punctuation, capitalisation, underlining (shown by italics), and paragraphing. Any obvious slips of the pen have been silently corrected, abbreviations such as yr., or Hond. have been expanded as have names and titles; the word 'and' has generally been substituted in place of an ampersand. An initial capital letter is used at the start of sentences even if not present in the original. A full stop has sometimes been added where in the original there was a dash, in order to improve readability. Occasionally a paragraph break has been introduced for the same reason. Sometimes a portion of the letter has been damaged, for example when a seal was torn in opening the letter, and missing words or illegible sections are shown in square brackets. Square brackets are also used to enclose text deduced in place of missing or illegible words. A place and date line has consistently been put at the top of the letter even when it appears at the bottom of the original, date format has been standardised, months have been expanded in full, and for letters written prior to 1752 when the modern calendar was adopted dual dates are shown between the 1st of January and 25th of March. The salutation is followed by a comma although in the original there may have been none or an alternative. Names in signatures are expanded where necessary to make clear the identity of the writer. Where text was added to a letter, no matter whether at the end or elsewhere, it has been placed at the end and preceded by 'PS' for consistency. Names of ships have been rendered into italics.

List of Illustrations

Contents

Prologue

As a child, I grew up with the story that we had an ancestor who was an Indian Princess. It was very many years before I had time to try to find out who she might have been.

My grandmother's grandmother Charlotte, whose mother had eloped in 1806, was brought up by distant cousins on her mother's side of the family in a story reminiscent of *Mansfield Park*. Charlotte had left a note about her ancestors that listed two sisters called Jaques, a Richard Lee and his sister Mrs Bevan, and mentioned a father who had 'married a creole'. My great-aunt Alice added a further note that her father said creole, but she had always heard Indian Princess.

The Indian sub-continent seemed possible but unlikely. A grand detour round the early history of Virginia led to a much greater understanding of its Lee family founders, but no Pocahontas of our own.

Eventually I came across a Richard Lee in the 1851 census who, much to my surprise, had been born in Jamaica. From his Will I discovered that he had been the one who fulfilled a promise I had been told was made to Charlotte's mother's family, to care for them for three generations.

But why did they need to be supported, and why had Richard Lee been born in Jamaica?

The note had said that Richard Lee's sister Mrs Bevan had a daughter called Mrs Mortimer, famous for writing the children's religious primer *Peep of Day*. I found a history of the Bevan family, written in the early twentieth century, that referred to a collection of Lee family letters. Many months of research led me to the current custodians of the letters, who with incredible generosity allowed me access to copy them.

It turned out that the bare bones of the note we had been left were correct but the relationships between the people named had become muddled. This was hardly surprising. Charlotte was an old lady when she wrote it and was writing of events that happened sixty years before she herself was born.

In the mid eighteenth century, in an age before childhood had been invented, Robert Cooper Lee had began his adult life aged barely eleven, as a midshipman in the Royal Navy. He saw action on the *Grand Turk* and the *Ranger* before the crews were paid off less than two years later, leaving him the possessor of £20 in prize money and without employment.

So in 1749 at the age of thirteen he set off on a new adventure. Taking with him a parcel of ribbons for sale, he joined his older brother John in the booming British sugar colony of Jamaica. He was expecting to pursue a career as a planter attorney for Francis Sadler, hero of the most recent war against the Maroons – free men and escaped slaves who lived in Jamaica's tropical interior. A considerable shock awaited him when it was discovered that Francis Sadler intended to put him to work on his plantation in an inferior position with few prospects. John's employer Dr Fuller came to the rescue and in due course Robert rose to prominence in Jamaican society as a respected attorney.

Back in England multiple tragedies struck the family leaving sisters Frances and Mary Charlotte, and their youngest brother Joseph Lee, unprovided for. After the death of Frances, Joseph joined his brothers in Jamaica and together they supported their one remaining sister in England. It was she who would become my five times great grandmother.

John and Joseph Lee both died in Jamaica, but after two decades away Robert Cooper Lee returned to England a wealthy man, bringing with him his mixed race children and his brother's mixed race sons. The children went to the best schools and the family moved in high society, members of the Prince of Wales' social circle. Richard Lee became a successful merchant and a director of the West India Dock Company. The marriage of his sister Favell into the Bevan family produced descendants among the founders of Barclays Bank. Cousin John Lee became a General.

The mother of Robert Cooper Lee's children was called Priscilla. She was known as Priscy (easily mis-heard by an imaginative child), and she was a mixed race Jamaican creole – I had found the Indian Princess.

Anne M Powers

2012

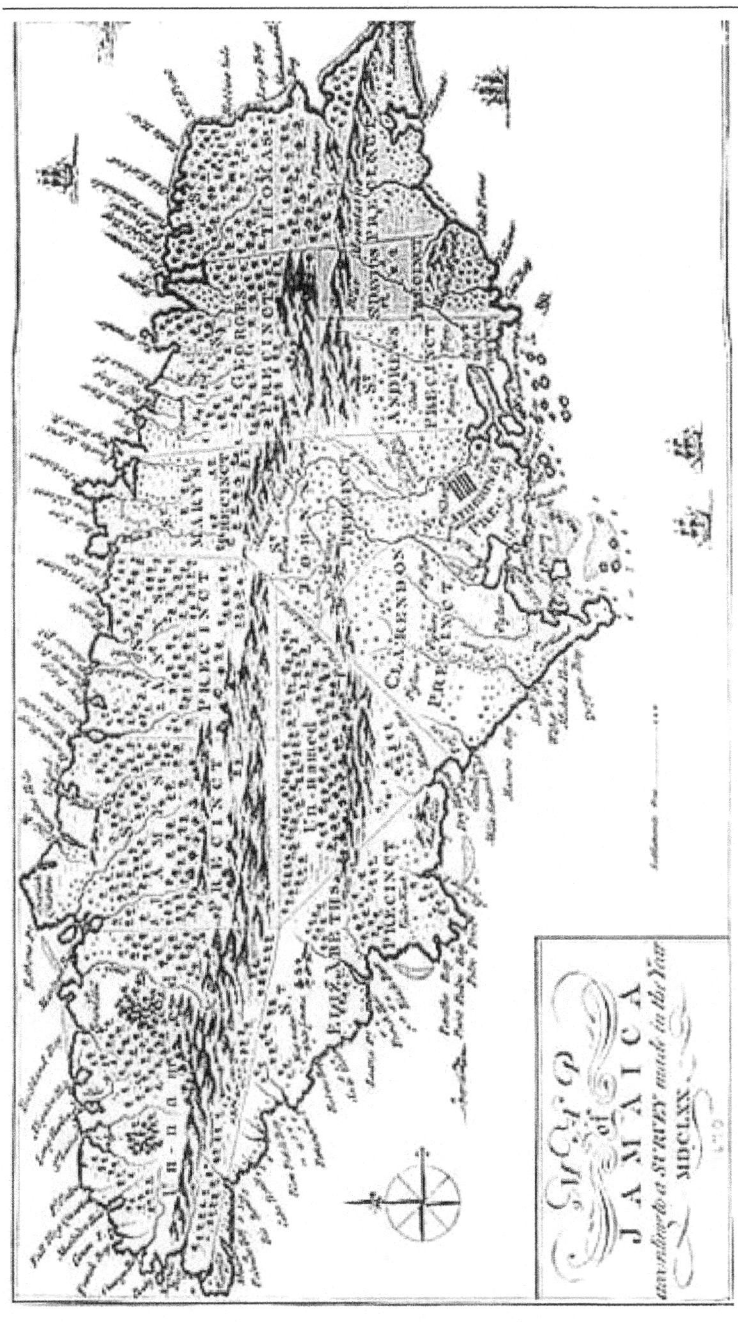

Jamaica about 1670

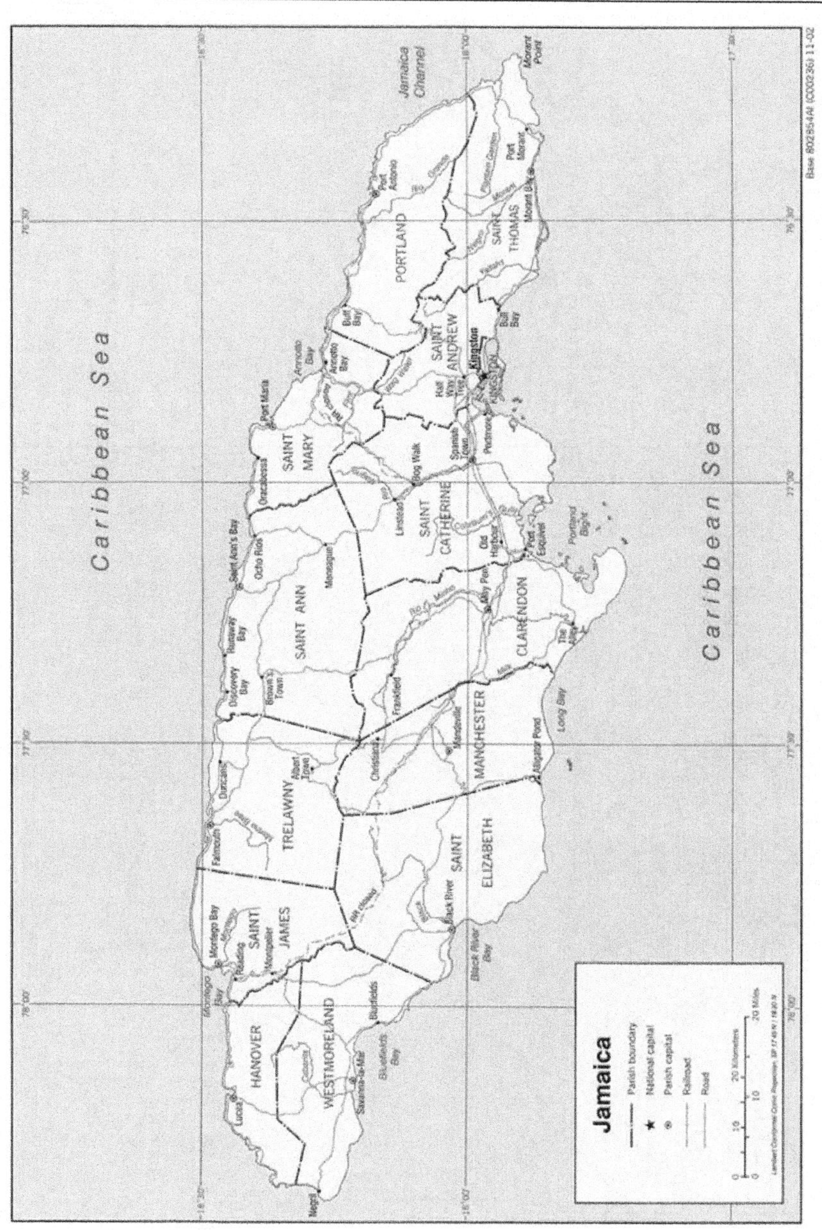

Jamaica 2002

Credit: Central Intelligence Agency (CIA) from www.zonu.com

Why go to Jamaica?

When Joseph Lee decided in 1746 to send his eldest son John to Jamaica he knew that this was a land in which his son could, if he was lucky, prosper and make an exceptionally good living. England was just barely recovering from the shock of the Jacobite invasion, with the Scots having reached as far south as Derby before turning back in December 1745. Had they but known it there was panic in London and on Black Friday the 6th of December stocks fell and people wondered whether to flee. By the spring of 1746 the Jacobites had been defeated at the battle of Culloden and stability was once more restored to the markets at home. Abroad Britain was rapidly expanding its empire, an empire which offered huge opportunities to the ambitious, and particularly to single young men.

Jamaica first came under British control in 1655 when an expedition led by Admiral William Penn and General Robert Venables seized the island on behalf of Cromwell. Penn and Venables had been sent to capture Hispaniola but had found the Spanish defences too strong, and so it was a rag tag force severely weakened by disease that came upon Jamaica in May 1655 and found it much less well defended. In fact the total population of Jamaica including women, children and slaves was only about 2,500 whereas the invading force numbered three times as many. It was not long before the Spaniards sued for truce, many of their slaves were freed or escaped to the hills, later becoming known as Maroons, probably from *cimarron* meaning wild. When the British entered the island capital of St Jago de la Vega now called Spanish Town, they found that most of the inhabitants had fled taking with them everything they could carry. The frustrated troops ransacked the town and within a short space of time found themselves short on shelter and being picked off as they foraged for food in the surrounding countryside. Dysentery, guerrilla attacks and starvation rapidly reduced their numbers, but although the start of the colony was so inauspicious the British managed to retain this toehold in the Caribbean.

The ensuing years have sometimes been described as Jamaica's Wild West period with privateers and pirates operating out of the town of Port Royal and the many small bays and coves around the coast. One of the great attractions of Jamaica was the huge natural harbour formed by a long narrow spit of land on which the town of Port Royal was built. Recreating the architecture of an English trading port, houses several stories high were built in brick and timber, and defensive forts were constructed to protect against raiding Spaniards. The town rapidly developed to be one of the richest in the Americas, trade and plunder combined to fill the warehouses that were crowded along the wharves, and hard drinking, hard living inhabitants lived short and often violent lives.

Large quantities of livestock, particularly cattle, had been abandoned by the Spanish and provided an easy income for the first arrivals who rounded them up for their meat and hides. The first planters experimented with a variety of crops including tobacco, corn, pimento, indigo and sugar. The first sugar plantations in the Caribbean had been established on Barbados and in due course the cultivation and processing techniques developed there arrived in Jamaica. Those bringing them also brought with them their own African slaves.

The changing politics in England, with the restoration of the monarchy in 1660, and the ever present attraction particularly for younger sons of being able to make a fortune abroad, resulted in a flow of young men to Jamaica. Often these included groups of brothers, such as the sons of Thomas Rose of Mickleton in Gloucestershire. Dr Fulke Rose and his brothers Thomas and Francis were granted land in Jamaica from 1671 onwards, their brother John a merchant in London ensured a flow of supplies and labour to them and a ready market for their produce, and their brother William an apothecary in London acted as sometime banker. Among the cargoes carried to Jamaica by John Rose were indentured servants selling their labour for a term of years in the hope of being able to acquire land at the end of it, and convicts captured and sentenced to transportation following the Monmouth Rebellion in 1685. Family networks among settlers were very important in providing mutual support particularly given the many disasters that struck Jamaica.

In 1692 Jamaica suffered its worst ever earthquake which hit the island just before noon on the 7th June 1692 and changed the geography of the island for ever, setting its progress back by many years. The timing of the earthquake was recorded by survivors and confirmed by the discovery of an early pocket watch, made about 1686 by Frenchman Paul Blondel, during an underwater excavation in the twentieth century. The watch had stopped at 11:43 am.

Looking at a 1670 map of Jamaica and comparing it with one drawn nearly a century later, you can see that a huge area in and around Port Royal simply ceased to exist. Port Royal was described as the wickedest city on earth, but this was mostly after its destruction when people were explaining the disaster as God delivering a just punishment on a sinful people.

About two thirds of the town of Port Royal disappeared in the quake, much of it because of liquefaction of the sandy soil on which the town was built. Brick buildings and wooden warehouses collapsed and slid into the sea. According to Robert Renny in his *An History of Jamaica* of 1807, "All the wharves sunk at once, and in the space of two minutes, nine-tenths of the city were covered with water, which was raised to such a height, that it entered the uppermost rooms of the few houses which were left standing. The tops of the highest houses, were visible in the water, and surrounded by the masts of vessels, which had been sunk along with them".

In the triple shocks of the quake the liquefied soil flowed in waves, fissures opened up and then closed again trapping victims as the sand solidified, some left with just their heads visible. In the tsunami that followed most of the twenty or so ships in the harbour were sunk or carried right over the town and many people who had survived the initial quake were drowned. The horror of the survivors at the huge number of corpses floating in the harbour was increased when they realised that many of these bodies had been washed out of the town's graveyard. Looting began almost at once, with the looters even hacking fingers off the dead in order to obtain their rings, and goods were stolen from the remaining wharves and warehouses.

The earthquake, which modern estimates suggest was about 7.5 in magnitude, was not of course confined to Port Royal. A huge landslip occurred at Judgement Hill. At Liguanea, the site of modern Kingston, the sea was observed to retreat for 300 yards before a six-foot high wave rushed inland. Most of the buildings in Spanish Town were destroyed and serious damage occurred all across Jamaica.

Worse was yet to come, for the survivors then had to endure a series of epidemics, particularly of yellow fever and malaria. Sir Hans Sloane had spent time on the Island and had stayed with Fulke Rose before returning to England. A correspondent wrote to Sloane on the 23rd of September, "We have had a very great Mortality since the great Earthquake (for we have little ones daily) almost half the people that escap'd upon Port-Royal are since dead of a Malignant Fever, from Change of Air, want of dry Houses, warm lodging, proper Medicines, and other conveniences." Another wrote "The Weather was much hotter after the Earthquake than before; and such an innumerable quantity of Muskitoes, that the like was never seen since the inhabiting of the Island."[1]

Perhaps 2,000 of the 6,500 inhabitants of Port Royal perished in the quake, many more died across Jamaica in the following few years. The island was over-dependent on imported food and goods from England, and disruption to its main harbour, loss of ships and warehousing brought about shortages of essential goods and reduced the ability to export.

The Jamaican Assembly, the island's parliament, removed from Port Royal to Spanish Town and rebuilding began almost at once, but it has been suggested that the progress of the colony was set back by twenty years as a result of the devastation. Port Royal itself was so much reduced in area, and further devastated by fire in 1704, that it never recovered. A new settlement grew up across the bay at Kingston, planned in Enlightenment grid fashion around a central square or parade ground housing wells and the powder magazine. Two years after the quake Dr Fulke Rose returned to London with his family in order better to plead the cause of the island. He died there in March 1694 and his widow Elizabeth married Sir Hans Sloane.

Fulke Rose left most of his property in Jamaica to his daughters Elizabeth and Ann. Elizabeth married John Fuller a land owner and iron founder from Sussex, and Ann married Thomas Istead. In 1733 John Fuller sent his second son Rose, by now trained as a doctor, to manage the Jamaican plantations on behalf of the Fuller and Istead families.

Rose Fuller found the plantations, at a time when sugar production in Jamaica was struggling, to be much in need of improvement. Not always in agreement with his father about the best way of doing this, he nevertheless invested in new buildings, equipment, and techniques, and over a period of two decades brought the estates into great profitability. In doing so he worked in partnership with his brothers Stephen and Thomas Fuller, merchants and sugar bakers in England.

On the 27th of February 1736/37 he married Ithamar Mill whose father Richard owned the Grange plantation. She was just sixteen, and within little more than a year both she and their stillborn son were dead. Although Rose Fuller appears to have contemplated remarrying[2], he did

---

[1] *Philosophical Transactions of the Royal Society*, 1694, 18, pp.78-100.

[2] David Crossley and Richard Saville, *The Fuller Letters*, p.164.

not do so and instead had a long-term relationship with his housekeeper Mary Johnston Rose.

Mary was a free mulatto[3], the daughter of Elizabeth Johnston a free negro who died in 1753. Mary may have been born as early as 1700 There is the baptism of a Mary Elizabeth daughter of Elizabeth Johnston 'a negro wench' on 5th July 1700. If this is the right identification of mother and daughter then Elizabeth was probably a house slave at the time and later freed. It seems probable that Mary's father was one of the Rose family, possibly Francis Rose (1656-1720), or William the son of Thomas Rose.

Mary was literate but there is no record of how she acquired her education. That she did so at a time when most women, whatever their colour, were illiterate suggests that she had a favoured upbringing at the hands of her father. We know that Mary had two sons by different fathers – Thomas Wynter who was born about February 1729 and was probably the son of Dr William Wynter; and William Fuller - born on the 28th of January and baptised on the 18th of April 1735 - who was the son of Dr Rose Fuller. From a letter written by Mary's nephew Robert Kelly to Rose Fuller in 1758[4] we know that William Fuller was sent to England to be educated at his father's expense, but as nothing further is heard of him it seems he probably died young. Robert Kelly was the son of Mary's sister Ann Rose, and his father was one of the five Kelly brothers from Galway who had sought their fortunes in Jamaica a generation after the Rose brothers.

Thomas Wynter and William Fuller were classified by Jamaican society as quadroons and as such did not have the same rights as white people, although having a mother who was free meant they too were free. However in 1745 Mary applied for herself and her sons to be accorded the same rights as whites, and in 1746 the English parliament confirmed an Act of the Jamaican Assembly granting those rights.

---

[3] Racial mix in Jamaica was categorized: Mulatto – a person with one negro and one white parent; Sambo - a person with one parent a negro and the other mulatto i.e one quarter white; Quadroon – the child of a white person and a mulatto i.e. one quarter black; Mustee, Mestee or Octaroon – a person who is one-eighth black i.e. with one black great grandparent; Mesteefeena – a rarely used term for the child of a white parent and a mestee. If one-sixteenth black, they were legally regarded as white and free.

[4] East Sussex County Record Office, ESRO SAS-RF/19/167

"At the Court of St. James 17.12.1746. Present the King's Most Excellent Majesty in Council. Whereas the Governor and Commander-in-Chief of His Majesty's Island of Jamaica with the Council and Assembly of the said Island did in 1745 pass an Act which hath been transmitted in the words following viz An Act to Intitle Mary Johnston Rose of the Parish of St. Catherines in the said Island, a free mulatto woman and her sons Thomas Wynter and William Fuller begotten by white fathers to the same rights and privileges with English subjects born of white parents. The Act was confirmed, finally enacted and ratified accordingly."

This was not a wholly unusual event, there were a handful of such Acts each year from the early eighteenth century onwards, but the proportion of all the mixed race adults and children granted such rights was very small and it does indicate that Mary had some influence over her own position, albeit presumably through the fathers of her sons, both of whom were members of the Assembly at the time.

Mrs Rose, as Mary Johnston Rose was known, nursed Rose Fuller through a number of serious illnesses, managed his household and like many mixed-race 'housekeepers' was a wife in all but name.

Into this household in 1746 arrived fifteen year-old John Lee, fresh from London, well educated and carrying his father's hopes for the family's future. His father Joseph Lee, the son of a London tailor, was a Turkey Merchant – someone who traded in luxury goods from the East. John's mother Frances, first cousin to his father, was the daughter of silversmith William Jaques, the only watchcase maker ever to become a Master of the Clockmakers Company[5].

There were five surviving children in the Lee family - Frances, John, Mary Charlotte, Robert Cooper and the youngest son Joseph. Two sons bearing their father's name had died before the youngest son eventually survived to grow up. All were baptised in the parish of St Michael Bassishaw in the City of London, and at the time the first surviving letter was written the family were living in Starr Court off Bread Street, just south of Cheapside. While seventeen year-old Frances was at home with her mother Frances and grandmother Mary Lee, and Charlotte and Joseph were at school, their brother Robert Cooper Lee had gone to sea in the Royal Navy aged about eleven.

---

[5]J.A.Neale, *The Case of William Jaques*, Antiquarian Horology, Vol.20, No.4, 1992, pp.340-355.

London and Jamaica 1746-1761

John Lee from his father Joseph Lee

London, 25th October 1746

Dear Jacky,

Wee have been in daily Expectation of hearing from you for some dayes past, that might know how you was in your voyage and how you like Jamaica, and that you are settled to your mind there – which wee heartily hope for, which makes us impatiently expect the Packett[6] of Captain Harman who is reckoned a missing ship, but as the Winde has been fair for her these two dayes, hope she will soon appear that may have a letter from you.

Wee were all glad to hear from your Unkle Jere that you was well at [missing] and pleased he made you a present.

Your Brother Bob has been at home with us about a month, and went from about 5 weeks since, his Captain has got the *Grand Turk* and [missing] will be a Stationed Ship at your parts, so hope you'll have [missing] Oportunityes to see Each other, the Convoy is ordered for your parts in a months time.

Your Brother Joe is at Mr Rodery[7], that Good man tooke him very soon after Bobby had left him – your Sisters Fanny and Charlotte are very well and give their kind love to you, your Grand Mama her blessing and all friends their Love. Mr Causton[8] and I often drink your good health, and doth Master Charles. Mr Rodery often enquires after you, as doth every One that knew you.

---

6 Packet boats were small ships carrying mail, and passengers throughout the colonies on regular scheduled services.

7 The Reverend William Rothery (1704-1759) kept a private school at Turret House, Paradise Row, Chelsea and was Lecturer at Chelsea Church.

8 Thomas Causton was a London merchant and close friend of the Lee family, 'Master Charles' was his eldest son.

Your Mama gives you her kind Love and blessing, her prayers are never wanting to Almighty God, to guide and direct you in your Youth and bless you in all parts of your life, she will write you the next packett. Thank God, my dear Jacky, he has recoverd me from my great disorder and I am as well as ever I was, and have had the rest of our furniture from Hadley, it is a good house and furnished as were used to do, and by God's providence wee live hapily. I am in the hopes of getting better business than when you left England, being concerned in an Office of Assurance on Ships and Merchandize have done some business and most of my Friends Turky Merchants promised mee their and I have a prospect of my Estate at Cairo turning out better than I expected or at least gave it in, so it will please everyone and but a profitt to mee besides the Great Satisfaction of doing Justice, and as you come into Lyfe I hope by the blessing of God I shall be able to give you some [illegible].....I will do all for you that [illegible] My constant prayers are for you

and I am Dear Child your affectionate tender Parent Joseph Lee.

Perhaps because of the illness he had suffered from, Joseph Lee's business had not been going well and the sale of the property in Cairo was probably intended for the settlement of debts.

John Lee to his brother Robert Cooper Lee in London

Spanish Town in Jamaica, 21st June 1748

Dear Bob,

I received your agreable letter of the 6th November last and am extreamely pleased to hear of your health and Prosperity.

As you have been already so successful in your Voyages I make no doubt but you will be in time a great Man, I am certain you will not be wanting in your Care of obeying Captain Kerley's[9] Commands which will gain you his favour, the Esteem of the Officers and the Love of your Friends.

Fortune has placed me, I thank God, in a very advantageous way of living of which I Suppose my Dear Papa has informed you, therefore I shall not

[9] Anthony Kerly Captain of the *Bristol*, the *Weazle* and the *Grand Turk* in 1746, the *Ranger* from 1747. Possibly the son of John and Hannah Kerly, baptised 19 Aug 1714 at Maker, Cornwall; died c. 1764, Will probated 1765 PCC PROB 11/914.

trouble you with a long Account of it but shall only tell you that it would be a very great Addition to my Happiness to see you here of which you give me some hopes.

You see how we are separated and scattered as I may say up and down in the world how great an happiness it would be for us to see each other were it but for an hour! but alas! We are separated by the Sea and such an happiness is more easily desired than obtained, but I hope we shall one day enjoy it with much satisfaction.

In the meantime I heartily wish you your health and desire you would be assured of the Love, Affection and Good wishes of

Your most affectionate Brother John Lee.

Robert Cooper Lee was at sea for less than two years. With the cessation of hostilities he found himself back in London by the summer of 1748, and the recipient of £20 prize money.

R.D. Laugharne to Robert Cooper Lee

To Mr Robert Cooper Lee at Mr Joseph Lee's in Bread Street, London.

Portsmouth, 26th July 1748

Mr Lee,

I received yours and it will be proper for you to have a £20 [torn] Attorney attested by the Lord Mayor with your Papa in order to receive your prize money when payable, I wish it was ended, and hope youl meet with good success and believe me to be

Your Sincere honourable Servant

R.D.Laugharne.

John Lee to Robert Cooper Lee

Spanish Town Jamaica, 12th November 1748

Dear Bob,

I received your agreable Letter of the 14th of June last and am extreamly glad to find by it that you enjoy the happiness of a good State of Health.

The success you have had in taking so many Prizes is very agreeable to me tho' as there is now a Peace you will not be able to continue your Conquests, therefore I hope what you have taken will turn out greatly to your Advantage.

I observe you have changed your ship the *Grand Turk* for the *Ranger* which is, I suppose ship of greater Force than the other and will not, I hope, be put out of Commission as many Men of Warr have, as I have heard, lately been.

I am glad to hear of Mr Cox's health and desire when you see him again you would remember my Compliments to him.

I was in hopes to have seen you in Jamaica before this time but am afraid I must now despair of so doing, for as there is a Peace the Government will not send out any more Ships of Warr than what we have already here.

I heartily wish you all the Health and Happiness which this Life can afford, and am Dear Bob

Your most affectionate Brother John Lee.

After a delay of several months during which Robert Cooper Lee decided not to return to sea, it was agreed that he should travel out to Jamaica on the promise of a job with Francis Sadler[10], a kinsman of Dr Rose Fuller. He left in the Spring of 1749 at the age of thirteen, travelling on the *Landovery* with Stephen Blankett an experienced Captain on the Jamaica run, and taking with him a parcel of ribbons for sale.

[10] Francis Sadler, later Francis Sadler Hals (c.1711-1753) son of Mary Rose (daughter of John Rose) and John Sadler. He was second cousin to Rose Fuller.

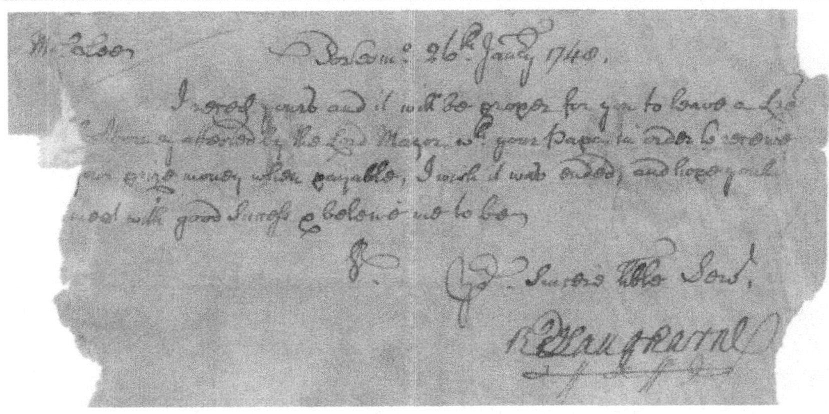

Mr Lee   Portsm.o 26th Jany 1748.

I recd yours and it will be proper for you to leave a Letter of Attorney attested by the Lord Mayor wth your Paper in order to receive your prize money when payable, I wish it was ended, and hope you'll meet with good Success & believe me to be

Sr   Yr [illegible] Servt,

[illegible]

Robert Cooper Lee's Prize Money

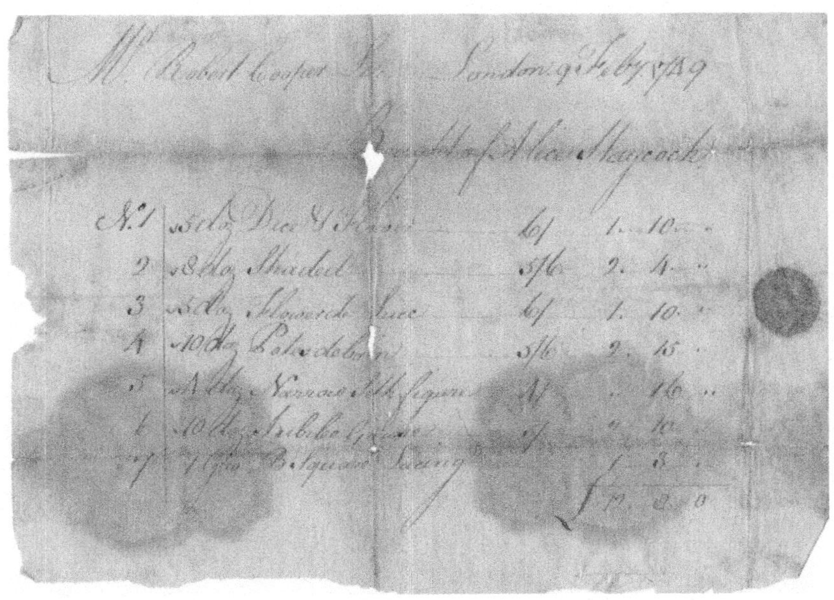

Mr Robert Cooper Lee   London 9 Feby 1749

Bought of Alice Haycock

No.	Item	Rate	Amount
1	5 doz [illegible]	6/	1. 10. ..
2	8 doz Shaded	5/6	2. 4. ..
3	5 doz [illegible] Lace	6/	1. 10. ..
4	10 doz [illegible]	5/6	2. 15. ..
5	4 doz [illegible]	4/	.. 16. ..
6	10 doz [illegible]	[illegible]	.. 10. ..
[illegible]	[illegible]		1. 3. ..
			£10. 8. 0

Receipt for ribbons from Alice Haycock

Robert Cooper Lee from his father Joseph Lee

London, 31st March 1749

My Dear Bob Cooper,

I have with pleasure received yours dated the 30th instant and Observe your waiting the Captain coming on board which I hope he did very soon after you wrote as he departed London yesterday Morning. It was only for your Good my Dear that I have parted with you for your Behaviour since you have been at home has been always Agreeable to mee and every Body speaks very kindly of you and I am glad the same reasons reconcileth you to going.

I heartily wish you a Good Voyage and a happy meeting with your Brother Jack, from whom I have received no letter, upon your arrival youl consult with him about the disposall of your Ribons, and also those for Mrs Haycock[11] which he will do with pleasure and I hope they will sell for much more than she has charged them at, the more they sell for, the more will be your advantage, as you are only to remit her the first cost and your Brother will easily get you a Bill for it.

I saw Mr Zemenes[12] this day and told him you were gone, he sayth as soon as he receiveth letters from Jamaica, he will send you some Goods and I will continue our to your Brother Jack so as you shall have a profit. I was with Mr Causton on Monday and yesterday when we drank to your good health and prosperous Voyage.

Thank God your Grand Mama is somewhat better and desires her blessing and sister desires her love and I will deliver your salutes to Relations and Mr Causton and his family.

In about ten days the *Queen Ann Snow* may depart for Jamaica by whom I shall write you under cover to your Brother Jack.

---

[11] Alice Haycock born Alice Wharam at Wentworth, Yorkshire in 1720, was the wife, and probably by 1749 the widow, of Benjamin Haycock, a merchant in Bread Street who sold silks and ribbons. He died after a period of illness and she remarried to Thomas Skinner in 1750. In her Will of 1766 she left instructions for the final settlement of her first husband's debts out of her own estate.

[12] David Zemenes was trading as a merchant in Mansell Street, London, listed in various directories from 1779, this may have been his father.

I write this to meet you in the Downes, from where if you have an oportunity I should be glad of a letter from you.

My kind love and blessing together with my daily prayers are for your guidance, health and prosperity for I am with a sincere affection My Dear Bob Cooper

Your ever Loving Parent Joseph Lee.

To Mr Robert Cooper Lee On board the Landovery Captain Stephen Blankett bound for Jamaica. In the Downes.

If sailed this to be returned to Joseph Lee in Starr Court Bread Street London.

It was common for ships to anchor in the Downs between the Thames Estuary and the straits of Dover, protected on the eastern side by the Goodwin Sands, while awaiting a favourable easterly wind to take them out into the English Channel. The Downs were also a permanent base for warships patrolling the North Sea, and a mustering point for newly built or refitted ships from the naval dockyards at Chatham. Robert Cooper Lee was probably already familiar with the area from his short time in the Navy, and his father would have sent and received goods from ships coming in or leaving England via the Downs. Crowded anchorage in the Thames in London often meant ships waiting many weeks, or even months, before being able to load or unload, until the problem was eventually solved at the end of the eighteenth century by the building of specialist docks on the Isle of Dogs and at Rotherhithe. As ships were often anchored in the Downs for some considerable time they were regularly serviced by smaller boats bringing supplies and the mail.

There are records from the 1740s of Stephen Blankett and the *Landovery* having to wait many months for a convoy to escort them to Jamaica with vital supplies for the island, but by the time Bob left for Jamaica peace meant that a naval escort was no longer necessary.

The ship's cargo would have been a mixed one, mainly designed for resupplying the colonists on Jamaica with the many items that they could not, or did not, produce themselves. This included barrels of salt beef and pork, salt fish, butter from Ireland, beer and wine, oil for lamps, clothing and shoes, rolls of Osnaburgh cloth for slave garments and fine silks and cottons for ladies, pots and pans, powder and shot, copper stills for rum making, iron collars and shackles for restraining slaves, agricultural tools for working the plantations, high quality ready-made carpentry such as window frames for planters' mansions, and luxury items such as furniture, silverware, oriental silks and porcelain.

Whatever was contained in the *Landovery's* cargo, however, it appears from the next letter that cheese and butter for the passengers was not included.

Robert Cooper Lee from his father Joseph Lee

London, 20th April 1749

My Dear Bob Cooper,

I received yours of the 5th and 6th instant I am pleased that you wrote mee as I desired you, and that you was in good health and the captain was very civill to you, had I known that you would want, Cheese and butter, for I thought the captain was to find it I would have suplied you here I wrote you 31th March to meet you in the Downes and am glad my letter came to your hands, as the Pilott who conveyed you Down, told mee on the Exchange, but that you had wrote your letter to mee, before you received mine. God send you a quick and safe Voyage, as I hope it will be as the Wind continued Easterly 8 days after your departure from the Downes, who hoped, carryed you as far as the Madeira Islands and there you come into the trade Winds. I often think of you and when at Mr Causton want you to walk with mee home, but it being for your good I embraced the offer'd occasion of sending you and I doubt not your success in time which I will endeavour to promote as much as lyes in mee.

I hope this will meet you safe arrived at Jamaica and that you will have a hapy meeting with your brother Jack - who writes me he should be glad to see you and will make Jamaica as agreeable as he can to you.

As soon as you arrive write mee, for I shall want to hear from you and by every ship write mee how you go on and how the Country agrees with you I doubt not but Mr Sadler will see you Civilly, as he is a gentleman of great honour and a near Relation to Mr Rose Fuller from whom your brother Jack has received so many great favours.

Your Behaviour here My Dear has gained you the Love of every One and I am sure you'll do the same in Jamaica you know your Duty and be always carefull to perform it to God and you may be sure his blessing will ever attend you and though at present you are too young to receive Goods yet I will continue some Advantage to you in those that shall be sent to your Brother. Mrs Lucas[13] desires her Service, you'll write her upon your arrivall for in the Goods she may send she intends you a proffit. Write also your Aunt Marlton for she loves you very well, she and all her family desires to be remembered to you your sisters Fany and Charlotte desires their love GrandMama her blessing. She is very well, and thank God, I my family Mr and Mrs Causton are and desire their Love, wee always drink to your good health and hapy Voyage.

My Constant prayers are for your preservation and Guidance, my kind Love and blessing always attends my Dear Bob Cooper for I am

your most loving parent Joseph Lee.

PS Mr Rothery was married 4 dayes Since.

The Rev. William Rothery was the schoolmaster with whom Joseph Lee's youngest son Joseph, studied at Turret House, Paradise Row in Chelsea. He offered a comprehensive education and young Joe's neat and articulate letters are testimony to its value. He married Lydia Rooker, whose older sister Frances was married to William Perrin a wealthy West Indian planter.

Chelsea was then a pleasant village lying alongside the Thames away from the hurly burly and pollution of London. The school was close to the Physic Garden, which had been founded in 1673 by the Worshipful Society of Apothecaries and also to the Chelsea Royal Hospital founded under Charles II for retired servicemen - the Chelsea Pensioners. Paradise Row is now known as Royal Hospital Road, and Paradise Walk which in 1750 led directly down to the banks of the Thames, is now separated from it by the Victorian houses that front onto the Chelsea Embankment, but in 1749 the Thames was wider and shallower than now, much of the land next to the Thames was marshy and there were extensive osier beds at Chelsea.

Robert Cooper Lee from his father Joseph Lee

London, 29th April 1749

My Dear Bob Cooper,

---

[13] Elizabeth Lucas sent a number of items of lace, presumably made by herself, for the brothers to sell in Jamaica. It is likely that she had been the Lee children's nurse.

I wrote you the 20th instant by the *Nancy*, yet I would not omitt this opportunity to express my sincere Love and Affection for you and to assure you that my parting from you was only for your Good which I doubt not but by God's blessing you will find in due time, and you may depend I will do all in my power to Serve you.

I hope this will meet you safe arrived at Jamaica, and that you will find your Brother Jack in perfect health, to whom I have wrote very fully about you and I doubt not but you'l be comforts to Each other and that you will find him a Loving Brother ready and willing to assist you in everything pray write mee as often as you can and also to Mrs Lucas who [illegible] now and desires her Service to you in her Adventure which she intends to send as soon as shall hear from your Brother I will [illegible] you shall have some profit.

Mr Causton and I often drink to your Good health, last week wee walked together with Mr Charles to Hampton, I walked on our road from Hampton to Putney, and the sixth instant wee saw the Fireworks [set] off in the Green Parke on account the Peace, and intend to go to H[ighate?] with him for Whitsun hollidays. All the family desires their service [torn] doth Miss Polly. Mr Willson[14] desires his Service he has sent three puncheons of Canisters filled with [illegible] to your brother Jack on the *Nancy* Captain Gl[?]

It is a great pleasure to me to hear [illegible] that know you [illegible] and I am assured that you will behave [three lines damaged and illegible] love and blessing together with myself Earnest prayers to God are always for you for I am My Dear Bob Cooper

Your ever tender and Loving Parent Jos. Lee.

PS Mr Rothery was married last weeke.

Thomas Causton, who had property in Highgate, was a prosperous merchant and long standing close friend of Joseph Lee. His children Sarah, Charles, Mary (known as Polly), and Theodosia (known as Doshi) were much the same age as the Lee children.

---

[14] A tea merchant, looking to expand his business into the Jamaica trade.

Robert Cooper Lee from his father Joseph Lee

London, 6th May 1749

My Dear Bob Cooper,

I wrote you the 29th Aprill last by the *Godolphin* and the 20th of said month by the *Nancy*, and as the *Vernon* is on departure for your place I send this by her that you might have letters from mee by every ship as I know it will be a pleasure to you to hear from mee. I hope by this time you are near your desired port, have had a good Voyage and a happy meeting with your Brother and a kind reception from Mr Sadler which I should be pleased to hear therefore I desire you'l write me by every ship that you have an Opertunity to send mee a letter for it will be alwayes acceptable to me to hear from you. There is no other ship at present put up for Jamaica but the *Vernon* [illegible] that my next letter to you may be [illegible] which I advise you in case it may so happen, though you may be assured I will embrace every Opertunity to write to you, for I have a Sincere Love for you and will do all in my power to Serve you.

Thank God I am in perfect health, as are brother and sisters, Grand Mama All Relations and friends and desire their kind Love, your brother is come home for the Hollidayes and Mr Causton and his family desire to be remembered to you as doth Mrs Lucas. We often drink to your good health. My kind Love and blessing together with my Constant prayers are always for you I am My Dear Bob Cooper

your most affectionate parent Joseph Lee.

It was a regular practice to send two copies of a letter by different ships, and a merchant's habit to list at the beginning of a letter the dates of previous correspondence so that the recipient would know if any had gone astray. It was not uncommon for ships to founder and correspondence to be lost. So we almost always find the dates of previous correspondence referred to at the beginning of the Lee letters and it is clear from the occasional draft copies that have survived that a letter was usually drafted in rough and then copied in a fair hand. In the case of business correspondence, the letters were often also copied into a letter book. One such letter book belonging to the Fuller family has survived and is held in the East Sussex County Record Office in Lewes.[15]

[15] East Sussex County Record Office ESRO:RF 15/25.

Also in the collection of Fuller family papers there are several letters written by John Lee, which are included here.

Robert Cooper Lee's mother Frances died on the 11th of June 1748 and was buried at St Mary's Barnes where her infant daughter Sarah Maria had been buried in January 1732. The following letter, written in a clear but childish hand, shows the delay that could occur in correspondence travelling between England and Jamaica, since the news that John had recovered from the shock of hearing of their mother's death had obviously not arrived in London until after Robert Cooper Lee had left for Jamaica.

Robert Cooper Lee from his younger brother Joseph Lee

London, 2nd June 1749

Dear Brother,

This comes to lett you know, my sincere, and hearty wishes for your health and prosperity, not doubting but by the Blessing of God you will enjoy them as my Brother does, who has some time ago recovered of a violent fit of illness occasioned on hearing of our irreparable loss but to Leave this mournfull subject My Papa is I thank God very well as also are both my Sisters, who Joyn with me in love to you. Mr and Mrs Marlton are very well as are Mr and Mrs Sayer and Master Jacky who all give their kind love to you, my Grandmama is also recovered of a fit of illness which she had some time ago, and is now perfectly well considering the infirmities of her age. I make no doubt but that you have by this time seen my Brother which was certainly a very Great pleasure to both of you, but to conclude I shall take every opportunity to tell you that I am Dear Brother

yours most affectionately Joseph Lee.

The letters often refer to various members of the extended Lee family. Mary Marlton was sister to Robert Cooper Lee's mother Frances and was married to a tobacco merchant called Thomas Marlton who traded from premises in West Smithfield. Uncle Thomas was to play a significant part in the lives of all the young Lees.

Mary Marlton's sister Hester Jaques was married to Thomas Atkins a stationer and bookseller and their daughter Jaques Atkins still lived with them. The Marlton's daughter Sophia was married to John Sayer, also a tobacconist, and during the early days of their marriage they lived with her parents. 'Master Jacky' referred to by Robert Cooper Lee's brother

Joseph was probably Sophia's younger brother John Marlton then aged about eighteen.

Robert Cooper Lee from his father Joseph Lee

London, 5th June 1749

Dear Bob Cooper,

I have already wrote you by this ship *Godolphin*, but she staying longer than I expected gives mee an Oportunity to write this I hope long before this time you have had a happy meeting with your Brother and that you find him a good friend and agreeable Companion, and that Mr Sadler has given you the kind reception, and I doubt not your good behaviour will be Agreeable to every One, in due time I shall be glad to have a letter from you which I hope I may in two months or thereabouts.

Mr Causton and his family are well and desire their Love as are Mr Marlton and his family and Mr Willson desires his Service to you.

Your Sisters are both well and Joe is now with mee but goes to School in a day or two and desire all their loves Grand Mama desires her blessing. I am to hear your Ribons will sell well as your Brother adviseth mee and has wrote for the same sort, so it pleaseth me to think it are fortunate in so little an Adventure.

Thank God I am in perfect health as I hope this will find you and that the Country may agree with you are my Sincere prayers which with my blessing I am My Dear Bob Cooper

Your most Loving Parent Joseph Lee.

At the end of June Joseph Lee received news that Bob had got as far as Montserrat on his journey to Jamaica. Joseph's footnote to the next letter that his son might need to cut his hair implies that during his career in the Navy he had worn it in a pigtail, as was the general practice, however it was more fashionable for men to cut their hair extremely short and to wear a wig or peruke. In the Jamaican climate short hair would have been a great deal cooler, although a wig would not.

Robert Cooper Lee from his father Joseph Lee

London, 21st July 1749

Dear Bob Cooper,

My last to you was 5 June and on the 30th of said month I received yours of 15 May dated of Montserrat which gave me a great pleasure to hear you was so well all your voyage to that time, and that you was so punctuall to write mee the first oportunity for nothing is more agreeable to mee, than to hear from you.

I hope you soon arrived safe at Jamaica and had a happy meeting with your Brother which I shall be very glad to hear for he writes mee very affectionately about you and will do all in his power to make Jamaica agreeable to you and I am sure you will continue that good behaviour there which you had here that did gaine you the Esteem of every Body, so I doubt not but you will be mutuall comforts to Each other, which God grant. I am pleased Captain Blanket has been kind to you I chose you should sail with him as he is a good Natured Man.

Thank God I continue in good health, and often drink your good [health] with Mr Causton, who desires his Service with all his family, Mr Willson desires his, Grand Mama her blessing, Brother and Sisters their kind love. Charlotte is at home with me and behaves very well. Mrs Lucas desires her Service your Unkle and Aunt Marlton, Mr Sayer and Mrs Sayer, all Mr Atkins family desire their Love.

My kind blessing is together with my constant prayers always for you being my dear Bob Cooper

Your most Affectionate and tender Parent Joseph Lee.

PS I have desired you Brother to write mee if it was necessary for you to cut off your hair, in such case I would send you a peruke which I will the first Opertunity if there is Occasion for you shall ever find mee ready and willing to promote your Interest. Inclosed is a letter from Little Joe. Mr Willson desires his Service.

View of Port Royal and Kingston
(from Edward Long's *History of Jamaica* 1774)

Robert Cooper Lee arrived in Jamaica on the 21st of May 1749. As the Lee letters provide only one side of the family conversation we know nothing of his reaction nor that of his brother John to their first sight of Jamaica.

The *Landovery* probably docked at Kingston which was then one of the largest and most important ports in the Americas, more important than Charleston in the Carolinas. Kingston had the largest slave market in the world and Britain held the contract for supplying the Spanish settlements in the New World with slaves, as well as shipping them to its own American colonies to work on the tobacco and cotton plantations of the Carolinas and Virginia, and in the fields of New England.

Bob would have had time to get used to the heat as the *Landovery* had sailed south and into the tropics. As they approached Jamaica he would have seen its mountains with their thickly wooded slopes grow slowly larger on the horizon. Ships entered Kingston harbour negotiating the shoals at the entrance to the huge bay, sometimes signalling for the aid of a pilot, and leaving Port Royal and its fortifications to the right. Ahead rose the lush, tree-clad hills, to the left were Musquito Point and the entrance to Hunt's Bay where the Passage Fort guarded the Spanish Town Road. Perhaps the scent of early summer flowers drifted towards the ship as they headed towards the town. More likely, however, depending on the direction of the wind, they would have been assailed by the stench of Kingston.

When the hold of a slave ship was opened on arrival the smell was overpowering. Bob was used to the stink of London privies and the smells of slaughter and fresh and rotting meat at Smithfield, but this was something quite different. The human cargo had been sealed below throughout the middle passage from West Africa and they were now brought up, chained together and blinking at the bright sunlight, to be roughly washed down with buckets of sea water and herded on shore to await being sold. The slavers might oil the bodies of some of the young men to make them look stronger and more attractive, and forcibly cork others to conceal the sufferers of dysentery – the bloody flux. Not all would remain in Jamaica, some would be joined by those being sold off by masters who did not want them or who found them troublesome, and would travel on to the Americas. Others would be going no further, their dead bodies pulled up from below and thrown to one side to await burial in the Negro Graveyard to the west of the town next to the Burial Ground for Strangers. Those who had died at sea had been tossed overboard without ceremony, their names unrecorded and unremembered, only their overall numbers were noted so that the insurance on the cargo might be claimed.

Kingston owed its beginnings to the aftermath of the 1692 earthquake and it had been laid out in grid fashion as a classic eighteenth century city with aspirations, however it was particularly unhealthy, situated as it was between two swamps. In an epidemic of yellow fever in 1747 shortly before the arrival of John Lee, it was said that more than a third of Kingston's population had died, and visitors to the island were appalled to note that few of the tombstones in the town's churchyard commemorated anyone over the age of 32. Like any seaport it was full of sailors and the many lodging houses, taverns and brothels that catered for them. The defence of the island against external enemy, and the possibility of slave uprising from within, also required the presence of the Army, and the many soldiers added to the transient population of the town.

Despite its disadvantages Kingston was a great trading port, its streets accommodating warehouses, counting houses, and elegant mansions occupied by rich merchants and some of the island elite. If Bob walked inland up Orange Street from the harbour he would have come to a large square, which still exists, known then as Dickers Wells and housing the powder magazine. From there he could have turned west along Beckford Street or perhaps east along Queen Street to the Windward Road between which and the sea were a large number of lots that had been marked out but not yet built upon when he arrived.

How long Bob remained in Kingston we do not know, but his eventual destination, which he must have been eager to reach, was Spanish Town, still often known by the name of St Jago de la Vega. He may have travelled there by road, or been rowed across the bay to the Passage Fort where a shorter route led inland to the island capital. He probably thought the town rather less imposing than Kingston, for it was not laid out on a grid pattern having evolved next to a native Taino Indian track and the Rio Cobre River, and it had grown organically. Spanish Town retained many of the buildings of its Spanish founders, which had proved more quake-proof than the English brick buildings. The former however tended to be single storey and not particularly imposing, although better designed for the tropical heat.

We don't know where Bob stayed when he first arrived in Spanish Town, but it is likely that it was with his brother John. Whether at this stage John had his own house, he certainly did so by 1754 when the Spanish Town census shows him as owning a modest house worth an annual rent of £10. Probably at first though, Bob was looked after by Mrs Rose, perhaps in Rose Fuller's house, although in 1754 Mary Rose owned a house in her own right worth £30.

Bob was in daily anticipation of taking up his post with Mr Sadler.

Robert Cooper Lee from his father Joseph Lee

London, 10th August 1749

Dear Bob Cooper,

I have answered your letters of 15 May wrote me off Montserratt at Sea and yours of the 24th of said month dated Spanish town Jamaica. My last was the 31 ult. wrote you and your Brother jointly, yet I would not Omit this Oportunity to let you know my great pleasure in hearing of your safe arrivall and hapily meeting with your Brother in good health, who I am sure you have found has a true regard for you and will do you all the Service in his power and I am satisfyed your behaviour will gaine the Esteem of Every One.

The Gentlemen of the Custom house and East India house often enquire after you and are glad to hear of your safe arrivall as is Mr Willson, Mrs Lucas and all Friends and desire to be remembered to you.

Your Sister Charlotte behaves very well and is now at Mr Causton to spend a weeke where I was last night, where we all drank to your Brother and your good health, the whole family desire their kind love, as doth your Unkle Marlton, Mr Atkins and Mr Sayer.

I hope I shall soon have another letter from you to hear how the Country agrees with you, for the oftener you write mee, the more you will please me for this is my Seventh letter wrote you to Jamaica, some of them I hope are come to your hand before this time.

Thank God I continue in perfect health, as are Brother and Sisters who desire their kind love, Grand Mama her blessing, my kind love and blessing together with my constant prayers for your health, Guidance and preservation alwayes are for you I am My Dear Bob Cooper

Your most Loving and tender Affectionate Parent Joseph Lee.

Joseph Lee had taken great care to send his son to Jamaica with a ship's captain whom he trusted, and in expectation of profitable employment with Francis Sadler. It is not clear what that anticipated employment was, but it is very clear that the next news from Jamaica was most unwelcome.

Francis Sadler was related to Rose Fuller through his mother Mary Rose, a niece of Fulke Rose who had married first Thomas Hals and after his death John Sadler. Francis Sadler owned two very large plantations one of which centred on Halse Hall in the parish of Clarendon, probably the oldest plantation great house in Jamaica, which he had inherited after the death of his half brother Thomas Hals. The other, called Montpelier, he had acquired following his role in obtaining a peace settlement after the uprising of the Maroons, the community of free blacks and escaped slaves whose attacks plagued the white settlers, in the 1730s. Montpelier was at some distance from Halse Hall and there is no particular evidence that Francis Sadler ever lived there[16] although the plantation was gradually being developed at the time when Robert Cooper Lee arrived in Jamaica.

[16] B.W.Higman, *Montpelier Jamaica: A Plantation Community in Slavery and Freedom 1739-1912*, University of the West Indies, 1998, p.16.

Clearly the Lee family had expected Bob to be placed in a similar training position to his brother John with opportunities to learn the trade of merchant, factor or planter's attorney and to handle business in the sugar trade. The work under an overseer that Bob was now being offered was much inferior employment.

There was a hierarchy of positions in plantation management – under the owner or planter came his factor or planting attorney who handled legal matters and saw to shipping of sugar and importing of supplies; the factor would liaise with the plantation manager and on a large plantation there would also be a separate overseer; under the overseer were one or more bookkeepers - these were not as we would now think accountants or clerks, but white supervisors of the black slave drivers and often barely literate. Although there were some well-run plantations, many of the overseers and bookkeepers had a well-deserved reputation for extreme violence and drunkenness. Poor young men who travelled from Britain to Jamaica in the hope of making their fortune and who found themselves employed on such plantations, if they survived the harsh conditions at all, found it very difficult to progress.

Robert Cooper Lee from his father Joseph Lee

London, 2nd October 1749

My Dear Bob Cooper,

My last was 14th August, on the 20 next I received yours of 24 June with a Bill of Exchange on Messrs Barclay and Fuller[17] for £10 sterling which is accepted, also a letter inclosed to Mrs Haycock which I sealed and delivered her and have accepted your Bill on mee for £10 2 shillings sterling payable to her. She is very well pleased with your punctuall correspondence and quick remittance of her money and whenever you send mee any bill of Exchange I will take care to send you the Goods you may desire.

I am much concerned that Mr Sadler should entertaine any thoughts of setting you to be under his Overseer, it is what I never expected from him, neither would I have consented to your going on such termes. I am much obliged to good Dr Fuller for his kind promise to see you settled in

[17] The brothers George and James Barclay from near Peterhead in Scotland were planters and merchants in Jamaica. Indentures of co-partnership between George Barclay of London, merchant and Thomas Fuller of London, merchant were signed in 1745. East Sussex Record Office ESRO: RAF/F/13/6.

Spanish Town and I hope your next letter will bring mee the agreeable newes which I impatiently wait for. I am sorry you have been indisposed but thank God you are perfectly recovered. The 15th ult being your birth day, we all thought of you and drank to your good health, wishing you many hapy ones.

Your Brother Joe continues at Mr Rothery's and your Sister Charlotte is at home with mee where I intend to have her, she behaveth very well and both your Sisters agree very well and I am desirous and do all in my power to make them as pleasant as I can with mee.

Poor Miss Green died about 14 days since after a fortnight illness. God long preserve you.

Your Brother and Sisters desire their love Grand Mama her blessing all Relations their love as doth all Mr Causton's family and friends my kind love, blessing and prayers are alwayes for you I am My Dear Bob Cooper

Your ever tender loving Parent Joseph Lee.

Joseph Lee to John Lee in Jamaica

London, 2nd October 1749

Dear Jack,

My last was the 24 August, on 21st ult I received yours of 18 June by Master Rennall from whom had the pleasure of hearing of your and your Brothers Good health, which please God to Continue. I have advised Mr Willson with the Sale of One Chest of his Bohea [illegible] which he aproves of, and also of your intention to send him returnes in Sugar, which would turn to account and I doubt not but youl give him early notice for Insurance, and as the *Nancy* arrived 23 June with his Canisters, I hope your next will advise the Sale of his other Chest of Bohea, and bring him Compleat account sales of the whole. I am concerned to find by your Brothers letter that Mr Sadler intended to send him to be bound to his Overseer though much obliged to Good Dr Fuller for his promise to see him settled in town, which I should be very well pleased to hear, as I had fully wrote you about him by the *Charles*, but I advise you make no mention of your Brothers affairs to me in your word before mee. Mr Marlton I hope to persuade to send you some Tobacco and snuff and Mrs Lucas would have sent by your ship but was disappointed in a bill sent her from Ol England, which is returned protested for non Acceptance[18] you may be assured I will remind on. I am sorry you are disappointed in making punctuall returnes for your first consignment and I hope you will be able to procure Sugar and Rum to send Mr Willson, if not bills and I desire youl send what you can procure the Soonest. Under the 20th March last you advised mee you would soon reimburse mee what I might advance for your account your £25 bill [illegible] and although I find 3000lbs Sugar entered by B and F[19] from your place which presume may be Dr F. yet the times have prevented you making your remittance or even mentioning anything about it, therefore I am willing and do hereby concern my self one half in the adventure sent you by the *Charles* which will be ½ in 44 17 security besides the ring ½ in pistols[20] and [illegible]

£22 8 6

17 6

£23 6

which I desire may be disposed of for my most advantage and returnes sent mee in Sugar Rum or bills of Exchange as expeditiously as you can and now your account stands with mee £24 1 6 for ½ said adventure and the Mourning ring & 6[?] £25 by bill remitted mee this method I intend to take whenever you send for goods more than you remit Cash for I will send what I can tho I concern myself therein that you shall not be disapointed.

I doubt not your care in disposing of this my first Adventure to my most advantage and making mee returnes in Goods or bills as expedit as you can.

Thank God I continue in perfect health as doth Brother and Sisters who desire their love, Grand Mama her blessing, all Relations and Mr Causton family his Service. My Blessing and prayers are always for you being Dear Jack

Yours very affectionately Jos. Lee

---

18 Bouncing cheques it seems are nothing new!

19 Presumably Barclay and Fuller.

20 Several currencies operated in Jamaica, pounds Sterling, Jamaican pounds and also Spanish pistoles. Joseph had apparently also given John a family mourning ring to pledge as security.

PS The letter you mention to have wrote Mr Willson is not come to hand may always advise me the prices of Hyson, Green and Bohea tea and the sorts you recommend, if you can sell them with or without Canister. Sugar continued high and Rum 3/6 a Gallon.

Your sister Fanny has got your worked waistcoat ready, and will send it by first Oportunity and then will answer your and your Brothers letter. I think you should write your Grand Mama.

The next letter is torn, water stained and damaged along the folds but is worth including because it indicates that Rose Fuller had managed to obtain Robert Cooper Lee's indentures from his cousin Francis Sadler without which Bob would be unable to work for someone else.

Robert Cooper Lee from his father Joseph Lee

London, 18th October 1749

My last was the 2d inst. by the *Ruby* and copy by the *Pompey* on the 10th ditto [recd. Yours?] of 17 July with [three?] Letters inclosed [torn] I delivered and they were very agreeably [illegible] to your Grand Mama, Charles Causton [torn] Jack Marlton at your leizure it is always a pleasure to mee to hear from you and you'll find the *Godolphin* stayd longer than expected that I had an Opertunity of writing you by her under the 5th June last so shall continue to do by every Conveyance.

[Torn] observe the whole Transaction between you and Mr Sadler and much Obliged to Good Dr Fuller, who writes mee he has your Indentures up from Mr Sadler and will take care [missing] advantageously, I can't sufficiently acknowledge my Great Obligation to that [missing] for his trouble, care and great kindness to you, I doubt not my Dear Bob, but you will always show your Gratitude by faithfull, diligent and Obliging behaviour [missing] shall think fit to place you with always [illegible] Dr Fuller [illegible] to you. Let this be your [illegible] with whom you may be with. Endeavour to make yourself usefull and then you will be regarded.

Mr Moore[21] called on mee just as I received your last and enquiring about you I told him the affair and he seemed surprized at Mr Sadler's intention

[21] Not identified, but possibly the apothecary or doctor who attended Joseph Lee.

and said he was sure Mr Saville[22] never [intended] any such settlement for you. However that be, thank God your Indentures are delivered and Worthy Dr Fuller will take care of you so the affair has very providentially turned to your advantage for which I bless God and shall be very well satisfied and pleased with whatever he doth concerning you.

Your Brother writes me very affectionately about you and that he has and will serve you all [missing] may Brotherly Love and true regard [illegible] continue between you. You must ever recall that Jack is the eldest and [illegible] to his advice I don't write this [illegible] apprehension of your doing otherwise, but as I am absent from you, I can't omit giving my best advices.

Grand Mama desires her blessing, Brother and Sisters their love, Mr Causton's family all friends and relations their Love and Service, my kind love and blessing, together with my constant prayers are for you Dear Bob Cooper Your most Loving

[the remainder of the letter is missing]

The next letter refers to a consignment of hats sent by Mrs Haycock and suggests that they were not selling well. Sales of goods sent to Jamaica were often paid for not in cash but in sugar or rum, both of which were fetching a good price in London.

Robert Cooper Lee from his father Joseph Lee

London, 25th November 1749

Dear Bob Cooper

My last was the 18th ult. And on the ninth instant I received yours of the 6 September it was very Agreeable to mee to hear of your Brother and your health and the oftener you write mee the better I shall be pleased.

As you wrote your Aunt Marlton before the receipt of mine there was no Occasion to write her so soon again, poor Mrs Lucas has been very ill but is now a little better I hope that she will soon be fully recoverd when I doubt not of persuading her to send a Consignment. I am sorry your hatts stick on hand, hope your Brother will dispose of them for you, that you might send Rum here, which will turn better to account [missing] bills

[22] Possibly the same Mr Savill of Threadneedle Street whose letters are included in the *The Fuller Letters* edited by David Crossley and Richard Saville, Sussex Record Society, 1991.

of Exchange, and when I can send any more Goods to your Brother I will speak to Mrs Haycock and hope to prevaile with her to send you some more Good, as she was so soon Paid the amount of what she [torn] you [I am pleased] your Brother is so Good to you and I have not the least doubt of the continuance of your Good behaviour.

Grand Mama desires her blessing, Brother and Sisters their love, all relations their love and Service, my kind love, blessing and constant prayers for you both I am My Dear Bob

Your tender and Loving Parent Joseph Lee

The following letter from Robert Cooper Lee's twenty year old sister Frances, like other letters written by their sister Charlotte, shows that although literate and educated both girls were less fluent in their writing, and their spelling was more idiosyncratic than their brothers. Annotation by Bob also shows that correspondence written in November in London was not received in Jamaica until five months later.

Frances Lee in London to Robert Cooper Lee

London, 30th November 1749

Dear Brother,

I reaceivd Yours of the 26th May Last Wereing you enform me of your safe arrival at Jamaica and Happy Meeting with my Brother in perfect Health. Which I am Satisfied must be a great joy to you Both. I was extreamly Concerned to hear of Mr Sadlers usage to you and I think it was so Cruel an Action as I cant help Saying he must be a Savage and no Man – but on the Other Hand Good Dr Fuller exceeds as far beyond our expectations as the other as fell Short and doubth not but he will settle you to your likeing which shall rejoyce to hear in your next.

I delivered your Letters to my Cosins which seemed to give satisfaction but they desire there love to you and will answer in the next return but they [illegible] sick [torn] sometime my [torn] a fever and then my cousin Jacky ill for almost two months and Mrs Sayer is but just recoverd of a violent Cold and Slight fever. Last September Miss Green died of a fever and her Mama is quite inconsolable.

Grand Mama is pretty well in Health but very Lame She desires her Blessing to you, and Mr Atkins family desire to be rememberd to you. Charlotte is come from Mrs Foster and lives at Home and at present we go on very well I have nothing more of News to tell you but that Mr Rothery was Marryd Last May to that Lady at Chelsea with 3 thousand pound fortune but hope that will be no Hindrance to Brothers being there. I have no more to say but that you will except my best wishes for your Health and happiness and be assured I am

your affectionate and loving Sister till Death. Frances Lee

Robert Cooper Lee from his father Joseph Lee

London, 12th December 1749

Dear Bob,

My Last was the 25 ultimo by the *Caesar* since have received yours of 8th August and 10th September which is very agreeable to mee to hear often of your health I have formerly advised you and now confirm that I very well approve of what Dr Fuller has done in regard to your affair with Mr Sadler, I have wrote him a letter of thanks for his great kindness to you, I also approved and thanked your Brother for his care of you and affection to you.

I have received no letter from Mr Sadler, neither do I expect any, but if he should think proper to write mee I shall duely consider the Content and write a Suitable reply.

If please God Dr Fuller should take you himself which your brother and you give me hopes of I should esteem it a very kind providence to you and should approve of it far beyond your being settled with Mr Sadler in any [illegible] yet in whatever manner Dr Fuller *he* shall dispose of you I shall gratefully acknowledge his favour, and I don't doubt my Dear Bob but youl do all in your power to make yourself acceptable.

I delivered your letters to Mr and Mrs Sayer, Mr John Marlton and Mr Charles Causton who all seemed pleased with [illegible] the last has answered you by the *Clarenden.* I have spoke to Mr Zemenes and possibly may prevaile with him to send you something, all which shall hear further, when I have disposed of your Brothers Rum, and send him returns, then I'll see about Mrs Lucas and Mrs Haycock and will Serve your Brother and you what is in my power.

Grand Mama desires her blessing, Brother and Sisters their Love, all Relation and Friends their Love and Service Mr Causton and I often drink to your Brother and your health my kindest Love, blessing and prayers are always for you [remainder torn]

Rose Fuller did indeed take Bob under his wing and in due course he was to receive training as a lawyer. There was never any shortage of business for attorneys in Jamaica where frequent sudden death among the colonists often led to inheritance disputes. Although Jamaica had its own legal system, the final Court of Appeal was in London, and the British Parliament had to set its stamp of approval on all Jamaican legislation. The drafting of Wills and the tracking down of land ownership deeds provided the bread-and-butter work for Jamaican attorneys. Most also supplemented their income as planters, by trading as merchants, or in some combination of these. Those who had amassed sufficient capital would also lend out money to others who were setting up in business or to planters needing money for new buildings, equipment or slaves.

There is some confusion over the date of this next letter from Charlotte to John Lee, which was probably written in January 1750. The establishment of the New Year in January as opposed to March did not occur until 1752. The letter to her brother Bob appears to be contemporary and I have placed both in January 1750 new style.

Mary Charlotte Lee to John Lee

London, 22nd January 1750

Dear Brother,

I received your kind Letter datted July 18 of 29 of December and hope that you was then in good health as you mention nothing otherwise I think myself very much obliged to you for your kind advice to me in regaird to my behavour to wards my Sister which I shall be very studious to follow and neglict nothing in my power to contribate to her satisfaction it gives me very great pleasure to hear you mention that you are in hopes of returning to England once more after a long Course of years and enjoy the fruits of your Labour as tis as great happiness as is posoble for me to injoy in this wourld that has that must be a woork of time writing is our only comfort for so long a separation which I shall indulg myself with by all opertunitty I think I can acquant you with no news but young Mr Bingly is married a very agreable young Lady I wish you a happy new year and a great manny and I sincerly wish you all the health and happiness as is possible for you to enjoy my grandmama is as well as can be expected considering her great age and desires her kind blessing to you and dear

Bobby and her Dayly prayers are for your health and prosperity all Freinds are well and desire their kind Love to you my kindist love to my brother bobby and pleace to accept the sam yourself

I am my Dear Brother your most affectionate Sister Mary Charlotte Lee.

Mary Charlotte Lee to Robert Cooper Lee

London, 26th January 1750

Dear Brother,

I received your Favour of the 24 May by which you acquaint me with your safe arrivall on the 21 of that month and your happy meeting with my dear brother it gave me very greate aneasiness when I heard you was gone but when I considered it might have been an addition to your sorrow to have taken your live of me I made myself easy. I was very much concerned to hear of your indisposition but was very glade to hear it was so short I am very glade to hear that you think you shal continyue with Dr Fuller as a happiness you coud not have thought on to have ben in the same House with my brother. I have been at home ever since July last and my sister is very kind to me and I think myself therein happy in so indulgent other Father whose greatest Care is For his Children's welfare my granmama is well and desirs kind blessing to you all Friends are well and desire the kinds love to you with your kind acceptashon of mine which is all

From your ever loving Sister Mary Charlotte Lee.

PS. Mrs Lucas and Mr Killican's[23] desire the Compliments to you, and are very glad to hear of your safe Arrival in Jamaica.

Eliza Lucas to Robert Cooper Lee

Islinton , 27th January 1749/50

---

[23] It has not been possible to identify David Killican with certainty, although two letters written by him to Robert Cooper Lee in the 1750s survive. He was also a friend of Charles Causton and so perhaps worked with or for the Caustons. A Merchant of the East India Company called David Killican, Alderman of Calcutta in 1765 and Mayor in 1775, is recorded as dying in Calcutta, India in 1785.

Dear mr Robert Lee,

I with pleasure received your letter of July 18, 1749 and was exceeding glad by mr John Lees of May 26 to hear of your safe arrival and the same by yours which was very agreeable to me and also that you think it will be more advantageous than was expected. I have been very bad with a Pluratick fever and now keep my Chamber so that it is near three months since I have been in the City. Nor have I seen Mr Lee since as he has been indisposed with colds by my letter to your Brother I have mentioned my delivering 5 peices of lace to your father to be sent to Mr John Lee to dispose of the best for my advantage and am sorry it did not sute me to send some thread and tapes but hope another time to be able to send a larger quantity if them now sent sells well or any other of lace or prises if you let me know particular. And the next as I send if it would be agreeable to your Brother for you to have a part with him of the commission money as I have not yet heard however you may have liberty of receiving consignments and I should be glad you should have some advantage by what I send the next time: as you was so ready to do what was in your to serve me which I shall not forgit. I am glad you like the countrey so well and hope all things else is agreeable to you which I shall be glad to hear and that you injoy a good state of health or any thing of news as you think will be exceptable. If you see mr Whitehorn[24] if you please to let him know mr Burtons Daughter of Islinton enquires after him and his family and if his mother is alive as I have not seen nor heard of her this year and half my compliments waits on your Brother and self and I remain

your Constant friend and humble Servant Eliza Lucas.

This same batch of family letters included one from the Lees' cousin Sophia Sayer, daughter of Mary and Thomas Marlton, two years older than John and eight years older than Robert Cooper Lee.

[24] Possibly Samuel Whitehorne of Jamaica, owner of the Landovery estate in the parish of St Ann. The Whitehorne family were early arrivals in Jamaica in the late 17th century and had settled the estate in 1674. It appears that Samuel Whitehorne's son James Risby Whitehorne subsequently lost the estate in a card game.

Sophia Sayer to Robert Cooper Lee

London, 7th February 1749/50

Dear Bobby,

I received your letter which gave me a good deale of pleasure to hear of your safe Ariaval and must tell you that you was very good to write to me so soon, and shall desire you will use the Apotacarys rule, the Same often repeated – was very sorry to hear of your disappointment you met with from Mr Sadler but on the other hand was much rejoyced to hear of Dr Fuller's Extended goodness to you and am firmly assured he will never be wanting to encourage those whom I am sure will always make it there study to return it in there most greatfull Acknowledgements.

I hope you have had your Health better than your Brother though we was not in such care for you has him for you know we often told you that you was a Seafared young Rogue and therefore the better able to go thru the World I hope in your next I shall hear you are Settled to your liking.

Master Lilly[25] often asks after you he is just the same Reble has when you left him. Mr Sayer will write you with your Brother.

All Freinds join with me in kind Love to you I Remain

your Loving Cousin Sophia Sayer.

Joseph Lee to Robert Cooper Lee

London, 17th February 1749/50

Dear Robt Cooper,

My last was the 12th December, on the 31 ultimo I received yours of 9 15 and 26 November and it gives me the greatest pleasure to hear you are so hapily settled with good Dr Fuller and the country agrees so well with you I hope God will bless you with a long continuance of Good health.

I am sorry Mrs Haycocks Hatts stick on hand, I think the sooner you can dispose of them would be the better even at the best price attainable. Enclosed is a letter from her whereby you will find she has sent you £12 8s in ribons and laces, they are packt in the Case that consigned to your

[25] Probably a brother of Hannah Lilley whose marriage is referred to in a later letter.

Brother by the *Argyle* Thomas Meathle [?] God send said ship to you in safety, and you [will] observe the order she gives about their disposall which are to send the amount to her and the profitt is to be yours.

Your letter to your Brother I have sent him to Chelsea and in Case by the *Argyle* are letters for you from your Brother Sisters Lucas and Mrs Sayer

Grand Mama desires her blessing, all Relations and Friends love and Service my kind love and blessing and prayers are always for you I am Dear Bob

Your most tender Parent Joseph Lee.

Although this letter was written after the preceding ones they were received a week later, having been packed in the box of goods referred to in this one.

Robert Cooper Lee from his father Joseph Lee

London, 2nd May 1750

My Dear Bob Cooper,

My last was by the *Argyle* on which ship Mrs Haycock sent you Ribons amounting to £12 8 which I desire youl dispose of and send her a Bill for [the] amount as soon as you can the profitt thereon is to be yours.

I received yours of 18 December and am glad you enjoy a perfect State of health which I pray God long to Continue to you my health is but indifferent at present but hope the Country Air where I am going may restore it.

All Relations and Friends desires love and Service my kind love and blessing with my prayers are Constantly for you I am Dear Bob

Your most tender and affectionate Parent Joseph Lee.

Bob kept the invoice for the ribbons which included, 5 dozen Dice and Flower, 8 dozen Shaded, 5 dozen Flower de Luce (a pattern of irises or fleur-de-lis), 10 dozen Potes debrin (possibly striped ticking or hemp), 4 dozen Narrow Silk Figure, 10 dozen Jubilee Gause, and one gross B Square Lacing.

There would have been a ready market in Jamaica for ribbons and laces, and not simply as ornament. At a time before zip fastenings and Velcro tape, clothes had to be tied, pinned, buttoned, buckled or laced. Sleeves would be gathered through a narrow hem and tied, forming ruffles. Dress bodices and stays were laced to fit tightly, with the laces threaded through numerous small round eyelet holes at the back, sewn around the edge with neat buttonhole stitch. Stays were worn by children of both sexes and sometimes by men as well as women. They were made of two layers of stiffened linen or woollen cloth into which narrow strips of whalebone or other stiffening were sewn with rows of tiny backstitching. For a woman the front, which dipped to a point in the centre, could then be covered with fabric to match with or in contrast to her dress, and the front could be recovered with new fabric to match a new skirt. Sometimes the stays had sleeves attached. In many respects stays were more like a jacket than an undergarment and they could even be made of leather[26], which nevertheless still requiring to be laced into place. The stays were worn over a knee length chemise of a fine fabric, linen or later cotton, gathered with a ribbon drawstring to follow the neckline of the stays. Skirts were spread over hoops known as 'false hips' which again were fastened with laces or ribbons, and in their most extreme form extended over two feet either side of the wearer providing a six foot wide 'canvas' of embroidered or ornamented fabric to display the owner's status. The overall impression was rather like a steam-rollered crinoline, flat at front and back and projecting hugely to the sides. Getting through doorways or travelling in a coach or sedan chair could provide real challenges and the hoops were hinged to allow them to move upwards at the wearer's sides. The various parts of this structure were tied around the waist from where they were suspended with more tapes, and repeated use must rapidly have worn the tapes out. Even shoes were often tied with tapes, when not fastened or decorated with buckles.

Robert Cooper Lee from Eliza Lucas

London, 25th September 1750

Dear mr Robert Lee,

I with pleasure received the favour of your letter of May the 10th and one from your brother at the same time of your receiving mine sent January 27 with the five pieces of lace which by this time I hope is sold and shall receive a good bill in return.

---

[26] Lisa Picard, *Dr Johnson's London*, St Martin's Press, New York, 2001, p.217

I am exceeding glad to hear you have the good fortune to be with your brother and that he consents that you shall have half the commission money on what I send. So now by this Ship shall send with Mr Lee a parcell of threads and tapes which comes to £21:8:4 and shall have them insured as I will not run the risque of the sea and wish I may have good success in the sale of them and have [torn] double the quantity your brother mentioned as I hear it is a comodity as sell well and that it may be the more advantage to you when the goods are sold I hope you will send me a good bill which then I hope will incourage me to send again – I return you thanks for mentioning of mr Whitehorn. I have not since heard whether his mother is alive or his Son as used to be a weakly child if you see mr Whitehorn pray give my compliments to him when you write I should be glad to know what family he has. I need not acquaint you about mr Lee or the rest of the family as they will write to you, at present I have a bad cold, but have been indifferent well since my last illness I hope the countrey agreas with you and that you injoy a good State of health and that all things may be agreeable to you is the sincere wish of your constant friend and humble Servant Eliza Lucas.

I am now living at Hummerton [Homerton] in Hackney

The next letter from Frances to her brother Bob hints that he had heard from others that she might have marriage in mind. There was, as it turned out, a considerable irony in her concern that she might "have reason to repent at my leisure".

Frances Lee to Robert Cooper Lee

London, 30th September 1750

Dear Brother,

Yours received 9 June which brought me the agreeable News of your good Health and Happy Settlement at Dr Fullers whos grate Goodness ought ever to be had in remembrance by us all and doubth not whatever returns you can be capable of giveing you will never be backward in performing. I think you are very full of your jokes upon me Concerning my Altering my name, but apresent see very little hopes of doing it Suitable to my inclination, and therefore must not be too hasty lest I have reason to repent at my leisure. I thank God Pappa is in a better State of

Health then he as been in for some time. Grand Mama is as well as can be expected, she desires her Blessing, there has been a little disagreement in my Uncle Marlton's family and Mr and Mrs Sayer is come to live in Watling Street they desire their kind love, pray give my kind love to my Brother and when he has time I shall be glad to hear from him beg you will Except my Best Wishes and believe me to be

your Loving Sister Frances Lee.

There is no indication as to what the falling out in the Marlton household had been, whether simply the difficulty of living with the in-laws, or possibly a foretaste of the financial troubles John Sayer would later suffer from.

Charlotte Lee to Robert Cooper Lee

London, 9th October 1750

Dear Brother,

I received your kind Favour of 9 June 14 August and am extremely glade to hear you enjoy your health in Jamaicaia which god long grant you may it gives me very grate pleasure to hear of your happy situation with Dr Fuller and the goodness of heaven in delivering you from that meloncally prospect which was before you on your first arrivall and own that that alwise providance that always takes care of them that trust in him has protected you in a most wonderful manner. I for my own part am fully convinced of the goodness of gods providence for me and makein me senceable of my [illegible] in the goodness of providace and not thinking that the afflictions we meet with in this Life is for the good of our souls and [illegible] us of this desitful wourld. I am very happy in my situation at present and am extremely contented and whant nothing to make me happy that the best of Fathers can indulg with nothing cane give me so much pleasure as to hear of your health and happiness and to think I shal in term of years se you once again which is the greatest happiness I cane desire in this wourld. I delivered your letter that you sent Mr David Kilicain to Mr Charles not having an opertunity to give it him myself and not going to Mr Wenders now had no opportunity to give it him Mr Lucas enquired very much after you and said he would do himself the pleasure to write you by a ship that was goin at that time [missing]

[Grandmother] as well as can be expected considering her great age and desires her Blessing to you and Brother Jacky Mr and Mrs Marlton is well and desire their kind love to you Mr and Mrs Sayer are well and desire Love to you as it is also Mr John Marlton and Mr Atkinsis family who desire to be remembered to you I [illegible] my kindist Love to my Brother Jacky and aquant him I should be very glade of the pleasure of a letter from him when ever he has an opertunity to write to me I wish you much health and happiness and shall take all opertunity to Lett you know that I am my Dear Brother

Your most Loveing and affectionate Sister till Death Mary Charlotte Lee.

It is not clear whether the Lee brothers in Jamaica had noticed that the letters from their father had become shorter and more infrequent, and that he had on one occasion referred to his health being less good. However it is evident that Joseph Lee prevented any member of the family from telling them he was ill again, or letting them know the seriousness of his illness. Therefore it must have come as a very great shock to them to learn that their father had died. He had in fact been ill for many months, his medical treatment had been expensive and his business neglected. He left a Will making Mary Marlton his executor, much to her surprise and distress, and leaving her and her husband Thomas with the responsibility for the five Lee children and the settling of Joseph Lee's debts.

That these many difficulties were compounded by the behaviour of Frances and Charlotte becomes clear in the series of letters that were exchanged in 1751 and 1752. The first is from fourteen year old Joseph.

Joseph Lee to his brother Robert Cooper Lee

[undated 1751]

Dear Brother,

The irreparable loss we have all sustained by the Death of him who was as dear to us as our lives and whom we lov'd as ourselves makes me write this to you hoping that you will comfort yourself under your unexpected affliction for alas you had not the warning that my sisters and I had He having been afflicted with a great purging upward of 16 Months which carried him into a Deep Consumption which ended at last in Death.

The loss that I sustained was indeed very great being quite unprovided for: Here I cannot sufficiently admire the peculiar eye that Providence has over those that are afflicted in providing for me the most Indulgent

Master and Mistress that ever any body had. I mean Mr Henshaw the Lawyer who married Miss Betty Weak[27] who is extremely kind and uses me as her Son. The circumstances in which my Dear Papa died Obliges My Two Sisters to go out into the World wherefore when you write which I desire may be soon please to Direct to me att Mr Henshaws Cooks Hall[28]. My Sisters are very well But my Grandmama sinks under her affliction which I too much fear will end in Death.

My sisters give their kind love to you and accept the same Dear Brother

Your Most Loving and affectionate Brother Joseph Lee.

Eliza Lucas to John Lee

London, 13th June 1751

mr John Lee,

I received the favour of your letter dated January 12, 1750/51 with the bill inclosed for £15:2:10¼ on mr Lee who died several weeks before I received it. yesterday Mr Costen paid me the money for it and took up the bill for which I return you thanks I am very sor that your fathers affairs turned out so indifferent at his death as not enough that by the stock goods plate china and houseall goods being sold their was not enough to pay every body so that your sisters at present are unprovided for your brother comes sometimes to see me at Hackney. I am very glad to hear he is so happily placed at Mr Hanshaws. I have not yet received a letter from mr Robert Lee as you mentioned he would send one by the next conveyance but I am glad you received mine of the 25 September last and that the threads came safe and I hope you will do your best endeavours to dispose of them and to send me a good bill in return. I return you thanks for disposeing of my lace sending me a Bill and the account: and the death of mr Lee must be a great loss to you in your business as well as in a father but wish mr Costen may continue to assist you he told me he should write to you soon their family and all your friends are well as far as

---

27 The widowed Robert Henshaw had married Elizabeth Wheake in August 1746, he is listed in various London trade directories as an attorney. At the time of this letter he had one surviving child and another on the way.

28 Cooks' Hall was on the east side of Aldersgate Street, in Aldersgate Ward Without, opposite Little Britain. It had escaped the Great Fire of London, but was burnt down in 1771 and not rebuilt.

I hear. I hope yourself and brother enjoys a good state of health and it will always be a pleasure to hear from you and of your having good success in business which with my compliments am with the greatest respect

your sincear friend and humble servant Eliz Lucas.

PS I hope you have received my letter of last March.

Joseph Lee was just fourteen when his father died but he was already a fluent correspondent, his handwriting and spelling demonstrating the superior quality of his education when compared with his sisters. As a clerk to Robert Henshaw he would expect to get plenty of practice.

Joseph Lee to Robert Cooper Lee

Cooks Hall London, 22nd July 1751

Dear Brother,

I received your kind Favours of 16th February and 3d of May much about the same time therefore hope you will excuse me if I make but one Answer to them both and not impute it to the want either of Love or respect to you.

As to what you mention in your last concerning our Dear Fathers Affairs they are indeed in a deplorable Condition; You are likewise as you mention Intitled to a Part of what our Dear Father left behind him and that you may understand the whole matter I shall give you a short Sketch of his Will which is to this Effect, first He Bequeathed the Sum of one Guinea to my Dear Brother John to buy him a Mourning Ring After which he Gave Devised and Bequeathed All and every his Personal Estate (which was but very small) Goods, Chattels and Household Furniture to him belonging to my Sister Fanny, my Sister Charlotte, You and I one fourth part to each of us and of this his said Will he Constituted and Appointed my Aunt Marlton Executrix, the Goods now appraised and if there will be enough to pay all those Debts he has Contracted in Trade we shall be very glad if we are not obliged to Compound. For his long tedious Illness which was very lingering lasted for near Seventeen Months and for the last four months of his life he did not stir out of the House.

The Generous Offer of Dr Fuller is so great that I am at a loss how to express my Gratitude and was I not Provided for, I should immediately set sail for that happy Island where (as you mentioned) the Starrs of Fortune may be more favourable than in my Place of Nativity.

It is with great Joy and Satisfaction that I find my Letters are of any Pleasure to you which I assure you shall be repeated as often as Opportunity offers.

The Happy Situation I am now in makes me in some measure forget the Severity of Fortune in separating me from the best of Parents Mr Henshaw is to me the best the Indulgencest of Masters whose kindness I will never be able to reward. My Grandmama is as well as can be expected considering the grief she has Undergone and desires her kind Love to you wishing you all the Comfort you can enjoy in this World.

I am extremely glad to hear that after all the Vicissitudes and changes you have experienced you are at last settled in so Fine away.

The Continuation of your health and Happiness is my Daily Prayer which I hope Heaven has granted having heard nothing to the Contrary and hope after some short stay there you will come once more to England and end your days in Peace and Plenty among your relations which is the sincere wish of Dear Brother

your ever loving and affectionate Brother Joseph Lee.

PS My Grandmama desires to know whether you are grown since you left England and should take it as a particular favour if you would send me over your measure.

From Joseph's account we learn that after their father's property had been 'appraised', that is an inventory had been made, they were likely to have to compound with his creditors, coming to an agreement to settle with each for part of what was owed, if the whole amount could not be found.

When the news of Joseph Lee's death reached Jamaica Rose Fuller offered to find a place there for young Joe as well. In the postscript we are reminded that although John was now of age being over twenty-one, Bob and Joe were still just growing teenagers. What is not clear from Joe's description of the Will is whether John had already received part of his inheritance when he first went to Jamaica or whether he was due to inherit his father's real estate, since only personal estate is mentioned in connection with the other four siblings. Unfortunately the Will does not seem to have survived.

Joe's reference to Bob being 'settled in so Fine away' may refer to the fact that on the 9th of July 1751 Robert Cooper Lee was admitted to the Inns of Court in London. Since by that date his father was already dead this suggests that Rose Fuller, or possibly his uncle Thomas Marlton, had made the arrangement on his behalf and that he was already studying law in Jamaica.

The news of their father's death had come as a complete bolt from the blue to John and Bob in Jamaica and it is clear from the next letter that Bob had written to young Joe to say so.

Joseph Lee to Robert Cooper Lee

London, 5th August 1751

Dear Brother,

Your kind Favour of the 24th of May came to hand the 2d August Instant wherein you take Notice of your having had no advice of the Illness of our late Dear Father in the Answer to which, It was his desire for I considering what a dreadful Shock it would be to come at once had wrote Letters to you mentioning the dangerous way in which he was but he would not lett them go Saying it would only give you disquiet and he might recover adding that it would be time enough for you to know when there was no hopes left which followed but too soon after, for on Wednesday the 6th of February last he departed this Life to our Irretrievable Loss and Irrepressible Grief; He was (according to his desire some time before his Death) Interred in Bread Street Church[29] being his own Parish in a Vault in the Church and had the last Duties paid him with all due Solemnity, my Eldest Sister and me with my youngest Sister and a Gentleman who has been a Lodger and who has a sincere regard for him following him with Sorrow to his Grave.

You very justly take Notice that this World has been World of Vexation to him and I may truly say that Death was welcome to him and Life was grown tiresome when he had not health to enjoy it with. He has thrown off this earthly body this Lump of Clay and his Soul has took its flight to those everlasting Mansions of the blessed where Pleasures wait and Joys abound ever more and has doubtless had this Blessed Sentence

[29] All Hallows, Bread Street was in the City of London on the south side of Watling Street and was rebuilt after the Great Fire, but demolished in 1878 after the move of much of the population out to the suburbs. It was only a very short walk from the Lee home in Starr Court.

pronounced, Enter those Righteous into the Joy of thy Lord, which that we may all receive is the sincere wish and hearty desire of Dear Brother Your ever Loving and affectionate Brother till death Joseph Lee.

PS Miss Lilley[30] is married

Sophia Sayer to Robert Cooper Lee

London, 9th August 1751

Dear Bobby,

I am very glad to hear by your letter I received from you dated May 10, 1750 that you enjoy so good State of Health which pray God Continue and that you are so Happyly situated, which must always have been looked on as a great Blessing, but much more now as its please God to deprive you of those on whom your dependence rested, but it's in vain to lament but I hope you will remember you have Father in heaven which is both able and willing to make up for all [illegible] and disappointments which he shall think fit to try as with if we will but trust in him and endeavour to follow his commands as far as we are able and then we shall have little reason to fear of being happy here and hereafter. I shall be very glad to hear from you whenever you have an Oppertunity and be Assure had I am with Great Sincerity

your Loveing Cousin S. Sayer.

Mary Marlton [to John Lee?]

[London], 9th August 1751

I have received Both your letters on the melancholy Subject of your Dear Father and my Brother Death whom I as Sincerely Lament as I did at the lose of your Dear Mother but you must reflect on their Happy Change which will be the only way to asswage our Greif and do our endeavour to follow there examples that we may arrive at those Happy Mansions where they are gone before. I would not miss this Opportunity of writeing to you though it will not be to your Satisfaction, your Uncle being upon the

[30] Probably Hannah Lilley of the parish of St Sepulchre who married Thomas Vincent of the parish of St Dunstan in the West by licence at St John the Baptist, Clerkenwell on 21 July 1751.

journey [I] Cannot give you the pertickulars the bills being lockd up but as far as I now will send you as follows. Your Dear Father was lingering about a Year in which time we would have perswaded him to have Cast up Shop and have Settled his Affairs but never could prevail with him but to be sure he was at grate expenses the time of his illness so believe Poor Man he was fearfull of the Consequence of it made him drive it of, to my grate surprise found after he was dead he had left me Executrix and what greatly aded to my trouble was I could find nothing to pay the depts but his Houseld goods and Shop wich is but a trivial to what he owes, as to the Will it was of Small Consequence he only desired me to make the best of every thing to pay his debts and if there was any thing left to see it divided amongst his Children but that was made a Year before he died and believe at that time he was comeing in to pritty Business in the ensureing way if please God to have continue him in his health, as to the monney you desire me to pay Mr Coustin for your Sisters is out of the Question but hope you will Continue your Good design by some other means for do assure you it will be very exceptable. I am sorry I have no better Account to give you of them both, as to your Sister Fanny she was married three months before your father died to a Purcer of a man of War he whent abroad a fortnight after my Brother died he left her with Child we none of us new anything of it tell she could hide it no longer. She is about a month to recon[?]. She as never heard from him since he as been gone so fear She has made a bad Bargin he told her he was going to new England but fear she has nothing to depend on but her own industry wich before this oversite was Praised and valued for, as for Charlotte your not unsensible of her grate spirit wich makes this trobel go the harder with her we have got her into a very good place but being the first time of her going out could not submit to it but believe she would now be contented was she in the same situation. I shall do all that lies in my Power for her and believe She will take my advise though at present her enclinations are for going abroad and Perticular to Jamaica wich I shall by no means Consent to till I have your advice what She proposes is to come with a family, I hope what I have wrote will forward your good ententions as you mentioned in my Letter and Bless you that has put it in your Power to help them that is so Dear to you.

Joe is very well and I hope happyly fixt they give him a very good caracter and I dont doubth but that he deserves it for I must say he seems to tread in both youre Stepts and trust he will meet with the same success I am but very endifferent for I cannot help commisaring with all of you in your troubles but hope time will wear em of.

My best Whishes Attends you Both and be assure I am

your Sencere and affectionate Ant M. Marlton.

John Sayer to Robert Cooper Lee

[London], 9th August 1751

This letter is damaged and very hard to read, but offers conventional condolences on the loss of 'a worthy and good Parent'.

The same batch of letters included one from Charlotte which gives the fullest account of their father's illness and agonising death. She wrote it in haste in order to catch the post and did not have time to copy it out in a fair hand. Spelling and punctuation have been edited in order to aid readability.

Mary Charlotte Lee to Robert Cooper Lee

London, 9th August 1751

Dear Brother,

I received your kind letter of the 10 of february last as also of 24 may and am greatly obligd to you for the latter in condoling with me for the loss of our dearest Father I am realy ashamed that I did not write to you before but have been so much taken up since my dearest fathers death having been in a family as I have aquanted my brother with that I hope that will plead for me. But how shal I discrib my loss and in what manner shal I give my grive vent for its impossible to paint my distress to you in a true light but shall first give you an account of the maner of his death.

The august after you left england he was taken with a violent purging which distemper he was always subject to that we was not aprehencive of it being of any dangerous condition(?) it continued on him eight weeks before we could prevail [on him] to have any advice in which time it wekened him very much. We got him to have Mr More who atended him some time but found no benefit by it. The february after we got him to go to Islinton for air which he found great benefit by we got him to stay there two mounths and we was in hope he was pretty well got over it but he still grew worse and worse till at length we got him to have a doctor who ordered him the air and to drink the Islinton waters. We immediately took lodgings at Islington and he drank the waters for three mounths but found no relive by it doctor levever attended him but did him no good for they said it was the decay of nature though he was never apprehencive of his death. When his purgin left him which was not till the september following it left such a wekness in his inside that he brought away his inside in his watter and was in such pain when he made water that you might hear him scream out all over the hous and confined him to the house for three mounths before he diyd. The pain he went through he never could bear the thoughts of death but hopd that god would spar his life for the sake of us his poor Children and he knowd but too well the great trouble and distress his death must [illegible] throw us into.

He lingered in this miserable Condition till the beginin of February. He kept his bed about ten days before he diyd and lay in such violent misery that you might hear him Cry out the moment you intered the hous but was easy for about 24 hours before he diyd. He was sencable to his last moments but never thought he should dy and dreded death extremely. His head run of my dearest mama very much towards his later end and he told us the night before he diyd that he could dream of nothing but my dearest mama.

The afternoon before he died my aunt came and we persuaded him to get up he having lain a week in his bed without so much as getin up to have it made he got up about eight o'clock but was so extremely week that it was as much as three people could do to take him up and we was afraid he would die before we could get him to bed but we got him into bed and my aunt took her leave of him, he lay composed about half an hour and then never closed his eyes again. He lay and talkt to himself all night and called out what can't I be saved shan't I be saved for when his spirits faild him which was very seldom he mistrusted being saved and the thoughts of death put him in such agonies that it would have grieved a heart of stone to see him. He lay till about four o'clock in the morning and prayd to himself and talkd of my mama but was sencible to the last moment and said half an hour before he diyd that he hoped he should get over it and he complained of being very faint (?) and called for a spoonful of rum for he had not the strength to lift his hand to his mouth and the moment he had drunk it sank down in his bed diyd.

I was [illegible] in my senses when I heard he was dead for I left him but at twelve o'clock for he insisted I shant sit up and nobody but my poor auntie was with him. This was on the wednesday morning the 6 of February and he was buried on the sunday following at bread street church he having said in his illness he would be buried there.We three went to his Burial and followed one of the best of fathers though the wourld is wicked enough to say a great many ilnatured things in regard to his misfortunes but I am certain he was a very just man and would have been glad to have paid everybody their own before he diyd.

I am very much obliged to you for your kind wishes as to my welfare but have given my brother a full account of my unhappy curcumstances so shall not troble you. My grand Mama received your kind letter in condoling with her after my papas death and desires her kind Blessing to you and her dayly prayers are for your being supported under this great trouble and affliction. I should give you a more perfect account of myself but the letters are to be put in the bag today so shall defer it to the next opertunity tears prevent my writing Legable but hope you will be able to read it I will write the next better and by the next opertunity. I am my Dear Brother

Your most affectionate Sister Mary Charlotte Lee.

It may seem odd to anyone who knows Islington in the twenty-first century to think of someone from London going there to be in the country and to take the air, but eighteenth-century Islington was not only an area of recreation for Londoners it was also noted for a number of spas. Water was plentiful, with the recently engineered New River bringing fresh water in from Emma's Well in the parish of Amwell in Hertfordshire to supply the City. Next to the basin where the New River terminated in order to distribute its water across London was the Islington Spa, also known as the New Tunbridge Wells. The source had been rediscovered in 1683 by a Mr Sadler who had just opened a house for musical performances. It was an iron rich spring known in monastic times but later closed up, and re-opened by Sadler at a time when 'drinking the waters' was becoming fashionable. The area is known today as Sadlers Wells and there is still a theatre on the site. The conditions that Richard Sadler claimed the waters would cure included 'dropsy, jaundice, scurvy, green sickness and other distempers to which females are liable - ulcers, fits of the mother, virgin's fever and hypochondriacal distemper'. Sadly whatever the cause of Joseph Lee's 'purging', the waters of Islington did not provide a cure.

Following the death of Joseph Lee and the sale of his property the family were split up. We know that young Joseph went to live with the Henshaws, but it is less clear where the others were. After a failed attempt to place Charlotte out to work in a family she went to live with her cousin Sophia Sayer. Frances moved into lodgings in Turnagain Lane off the south side of Holborn and not far from the Marltons. Whether their grandmother Mary Lee went with her or moved in with the Marltons is not recorded.

The family was not yet done with tragedy. Following the news from Mary Marlton that Frances was pregnant and her sailor husband apparently missing, the brothers in Jamaica received letters from both Joe and Charlotte, the latter as usual much the more informative, if still perpetually taken up with her own feelings.

Joseph Lee to Robert Cooper Lee

Cooks Hall, 23rd September 1751

Dear Brother,

I have taken this Opportunity to acquaint you of the Health of all our Relations to assure you of the inviolable love that I bear you As I have wrote at large to My Brother concerning the death of my dear Sister Fanny I shall not wound your ears with the sad Tale only desire you to Comfort yourself as well as you can at this unexpected loss and do not let Grief get the better of your Reason. Do not Dear Brother torment your mind with Grief that is Useless to her and hurtfull to yourself. It's true she was Niped in the Bud and cut off in the Prime of her Days yet you must at the same time Consider that she is the sooner Happy therefore, Dear Brother, given not way to Grief but consider that the same God that Gave her took her away and that he took her from this Sinful World to place her in Glory where she now is free from Care and Worldly Vexation where I make no doubt we shall all meet and follow her. I take every Opportunity to Subscribe myself Dear Brother

Your most loving and affectionate Brother in Affliction J. Lee

Charlotte Lee to Robert Cooper Lee

London, 24th October 1751

Dear Brother,

I cold wish it was in my power to administer the real comfort you so much stand in need of at present on account of poor dear sister whose death you have heard on before this comes to your hand I fancy but also my heart is to full with grive to be able to give you any consolation for so greater sorrow so greater misfortune so soon after the death of our dearest father has drove me almost to despair and my Life is a burden tu heavy for me to bear but that great god who has relesed her from all her misfortunes will one day release me from all my misery and calamitys I trust. As to the maner of her [death] my brother I fancy has given you an account but in case he shant will retell [?] it again. She was married 10 November last unknown to any of her friends and she concealed it as long as Nature would lett her till she was big with child.

In June she [illegible] her marrig and the 5 of september she was brought to bed of a fine boy and was in a fine way to do well for some days but she not suckling the child and having a great deal of milk throwd her into a violent fever which continued on her for a fortnight during which time we had all the advice that was nedfull but all in vane her time was come to depart out of this wicked wourld and on the 5 of September death put an end to all her woes. As for my part my hole comfort is upon you and my dear brother and the pleasure of seeing you once more would doubly repay me for all the afflictions I have undergone the providance has showd itself in a most [illegible] maner to me as I have wrote to my brother to begd his concent to come over as it is impossible for me to continue in this land of all my woes and have my grive dayly staring me in my face made me aply to my dear brother who I hope will take into consideration what I have said and intended till I cold hear from him to take a room and try what I could at plane work but good Mr Sayer who I shall be bound to pray for as long as I have life made me the offer of being at his hous for and take in my work there and to board me for 4 shillings a week which is a smaler sum than what I can get at my work if please God I can have imployment a kind or generous ofer from so distant relation requires more acnolidgment than I have words to expres. I desire to hear from you as often as you can and belive me to be dear brother

Your Most Loving sister in affliction Mary Charlotte Lee.

Frances Lee had married William Page secretly on the 10th of November 1750. That it was a Fleet marriage compounded her disgrace within the family. Although marriages had been to some extent regulated since the Marriage Duty Act of 1696, it would not be until 1754 that strict requirements on age, the presence of witnesses and the calling of banns or obtaining of a licence would come in. By an odd legal quirk the area around the Fleet prison had been excluded from the 1696 regulations and by the 1740s nearly half of all London marriages took place within the area known as the Liberty, or Rules, of the Fleet, close to the prison. It was area in which marriages were performed around the clock, for a fee, for anyone requiring to marry clandestinely or in a hurry. Not all such marriages were invalid or for fraudulent or criminal reasons. Many men like William Page were leaving for service in the army or navy and had no time to wait the three weeks required for the proclamation of banns in a parish church. There were even batch weddings of soldiers and sailors wanting to make provision for their partners should they die in service. Some brides like Frances could not obtain a parent's permission, a few in a time when divorce was very expensive and almost unheard of married bigamously. William Page was a purser in the Royal Navy but further information about him is lacking, other than that shortly before the birth of his son news reached Frances of his death.

Joseph Page was born on the 5th September 1751 in Turnagain Lane, baptised at the church of St Sepulchre on the 18th and buried at St Andrew's Holborn on the 20th. Frances was buried at St Brides Fleet Street on the 26th of September 1751 three weeks after the birth of her son. From the description in Charlotte's letter it is reasonable to assume that she died of postpartum infection. Family disapproval, the stress of dealing with her father's creditors and her grief at the death of her husband must all have contributed to her inability to recover.

Meanwhile in Jamaica Bob's career had received a set back.

Joseph Lee to Robert Cooper Lee

Cooks Hall, 11th February 1752

Dear Brother,

Yours of the 9th October came to hand the 1st February instant which gave me great Satisfaction as nothing is a greater pleasure to me then hearing from those whose presence I am deprived of as likewise for that six long months has passed without one Letter from you which has greatly perplexed not only me but also all your Friends in England which was greatly heightened by an Account of a great Storm and Sickness in your Island (the former of which you have taken Notice of). I leave you to judge of my fears on this Occasion when no letter came to inform me of your health tho' several Ships arrived here you mention you're not having received a Letter from me which I impute to the badness of the Weather for I assure you I have lett Slip no Convenient Opportunity of writing to you in hopes of having the pleasure of some Letters from you in answer to them. I am surprized you have not received my Letter where in I acquainted you of the State of our Dear Fathers affairs at the time of his Death as I wrote it the [torn] August last.

I heartily condole with you on the Death of Mr Monck[31] and Mr Stone[32] but more especially on the Death of the latter as he was by your Description one with whom you could have served your Clerkship with Pleasure and trust that the same God that gave him to you will likewise give you [illegible] should be very glad to hear you were happily settled of which I beg you would inform me by the first [missing] happy but God has embittered my happiness not only with the loss of the best of Parents but likewise with the Death of the best of Sisters as mentioned in my last. All Friends join in love to you with me who am Dear Brother

Your ever loving and affectionate Brother J. Lee.

PS present my kind love to Brother.

Joseph Lee to Robert Cooper Lee

Cooks Hall, 2nd March 1752

Dear Brother,

I want no motive to gratify your Request of hearing often from me, especially as your Letters always give me a Particular pleasure, they revive in my mind the agreeable hours we have spent together and make me long for those when we shall not be deprived of the pleasure of each other's company.

I hope our Family will be once more settled after the Changes it has experienced this last year. I have already informed you of my situation which is far above what I could ever expect and my Sister will I hope be reconciled to England she now intends to be a Milliner, when I make no doubt but by her good Conduct she will be enabled to get her living in a genteel and honest way.

Since my last no alteration has happened in our family and my Uncle Marlton is much better with his legg which (as I informed you before) he had the Misfortune to break. All Friends are in good Health, long may they continue so. Present my kind love to Brother Jacky and accept the same yourself from Dear Brother

---

31 Probably William Monck, Deputy Register for the Admiralty, buried Kingston 24 June 1751.

32 Possibly William Stone buried in Spanish Town 13 August 1751.

Your ever loving and affectionate Brother J. Lee.

NB my Grandmama desires her Love to you as also all Friends.

Joseph Lee to Robert Cooper Lee

Cooks Hall, 11th May 1752

Dear Brother,

I received your kind favour of December last as likewise yours to our Sister whose eyes were Closed in death some time before the receipt of your Letter of whose death you must before now have been acquainted I beg you would not grieve too much after her it is true we have lost a Sister but I do most severely miss her as I have now none remaining in England who would do me the least good office or even wishes me well except sister and Mr and Mrs Henshaw who have a real esteem for me.

You mention our friends unkindness to our sister Fanny it was that which did greatly hasten her death. She could not bear up against those afflictions which came so fast upon her, her Husband's death and the disapproval[?] Of friends added to the weak condition in which [torn] things which few have strength to resist.

I am very much obliged to you for your kind wishes for me which I do assure you are as warm on my side and shall continue so long as life remains which I hope will be sometime and it will intirely compleat my happiness once more to see you and my Brother but I must wait with Patience till that time comes in the mean time I beg you would not defer writing to me as often as oppurtunity serves [missing] must necessarily be a great addition to my happiness to hear from you who have so few friends in England. My kind love attend Brother and you [torn], concludes me to be Dear Brother

Joseph Lee to Robert Cooper Lee

Cooks Hall, 12th June 1752

Dear Brother,

The Grief you express at the Death of our dear Sister Fanny is indeed very Comendable the mention of her Name reminds me of the happiness I once enjoyed in having her for a Sister in my greatest afflictions she comforted me and would soon beguile my Sorrows but God would not suffer me to enjoy such a blessing long he took her to himself. She was too good to stay with us. It is the Severest Shock I have yet met with for when my Papa died I lost in him the best of Parents nay more was exposed to want and Poverty but then I had my dear Sister Fanny alive to whom I could unburthen myself as nothing is a greater pleasure than to relate one's Misfortunes to a friend but now she is gone I have none left even to speak to except my Sister Charlotte who tho' she loves me as much as possible yet the Wide difference there is in their Tempers makes me regret my dear Sister Fanny more and more but to leave this Malancholly subject which only renews those Tears you have already shed to her Memory you have not yet acquainted me in what manner you are situated. It gave me great uneasiness to think you should lose all the Gentlemen you workd to in so short a Time therefore should be glad to know how you are settled.

I am much obliged to you for your kind wishes for me for which I can return you nothing also but my most hearty thanks and sincere wishes for your Welfare which I do assure you shall never cease, believe me there is no pleasure so great as for me to hear from you and my Brother or the thoughts of seeing you once more and telling you my thoughts by word of mouth is what Transports me beyond myself and makes me almost forget my other misfortunes.

Present my kind love to Brother and accept the same from Dear Brother

Your ever loving and affectionate Brother J. Lee.

Joseph Lee to Robert Cooper Lee

Cooks Hall, 10th November 1752

Dear Brother,

I received your agreeable favour of the 2d July the 9th November instant am very glad to hear of your health and well doing which pray God to continue than which nothing can give me greater satisfaction obliged to you for your kind wishes and intention and do assure you my greatest concern is that Words are all the Testament I can at present give you of my sincere affection for you and am very sorry your Merchandize have not turned out to more advantage (as you mention it has not).

As to my dear fathers affairs I shall answer all your Queries in as Brief a manner as I am capable of and I first I must inform you that when our dear father died there was very little money left in the house the Goods were sold about 2 months after his decease and the money was delivered to my uncle who was then going on a journey and therefore gave Mr

Causton the money which was but £50, desiring he would distribute it among the Creditors and took his Receipt for it Mr Causton [illegible] as it still [illegible] to deliver it up and there is not a penny of the debts paid as yet this is at present the state of affairs and I shall now inform you that as to the Creditors my Sister Fanny well knew all their demands and settled them before she died.

I do not believe there was above £20 owing to him which was on account of what my Sister sold and the debts due from him well likewise on the same Account thus all his Goods and Effects made up between £70 and £80 I can assure you it has not been diminished by me for all I ever had of his (since his death) was a few of his cloaths such as would serve to make up for me and half a Guinea in money this was all I had and with this I was sent (as it were) to seek my fortune in the wide world and without my Brothers Goodness I know not what I should have done this I mention to lett you see that I have had but little of his effects and I shall now give you an Account of what debts were due from him. Mr Causton says his is £100 though nobody else knew there was a shilling due to him. Mr Wilson £ [illegible] and there are some other debts which I hope will soon be perfected for it has been a long while about. I suppose you know already that Charlotte is not gone to a Milliner no doubt to your great disappointment for when she received the money she did not think it necessary to settle to anything but to live on what my Brother was to have allowed her pursuant to her own inclinations my Uncle looked out lodgings for her in the country if she has not done right in this you must remember Nemo omnibus horis Sapit but I could have wished that she had gone about to her friends for where ever I go they are always glad to see me but she did not go to see any of them but since they heard of my Brothers goodness they have all behaved as well as could be wished. My Aunt is at present in an ill state of health but will I hope soon get over it all our other friends are well with self which blessing I hope you and my Brother enjoyed the same to whom I desire you would present my kind love and accept the same yourself from him who is and ever will be Your ever loving and affectionate brother J. Lee.

PS I wish you would communicate the contents [illegible] to my Brother as I have not given him an account of the within Mr and Mrs Henshaw's compliments attend you and Brother J.L.

Young Joseph was in a difficult position. John was sending money to Uncle Thomas for Charlotte's support while Joe was clear in his own mind that Charlotte should have been content to become a milliner. He was also concerned that their relatives were not keeping him fully informed about what had happened to the money left after the sale of their father's goods and that John and Bob might think he had taken advantage of being in London to gain an unfair share. Since he was still only fifteen, and the youngest, his Aunt and Uncle may well have felt he should not be concerning himself with the details or were simply too busy to keep him fully informed. He was also becoming increasingly concerned about his own prospects.

Joseph Lee to Robert Cooper Lee

Cooks Hall, 30th January 1753

Dear Brother,

I received yours of the 5th November, but never received my Brothers letter of the 30th of September which you take note of, my last from him was of the 20th of June and your last to me, was of the 2d of July, since which I have not heard from you which makes me imagine some Letters have Miscarryed, particularly my Brothers of the 30th of September and yours of the 27th of July, which cannot but give me some uneasiness as to hear from you and of you is the greatest pleasure I can enjoy. I am surprized at Mr Causton should so far deviate from the Rules of Friendship and Honesty as not to return you your own. I think his Actions have sufficiently [illegible] his intentions to you. As to my Sister Charlotte she is now at Boarding in the Country she thought at first when she received my Brother's bounty that there was no occasion to do anything, but that an Annual Supply of that would be sufficient to maintain and therefore went into the Country where she still continues waiting for an Answer from our Brother. I have already given him my Opinion thereon which is that he do take no Notice of a Letter which he will receive and which is signed by a great many (which I could not see before it went) but send his directions for Charlotte to be placed out to a Milliner.

I own myself obliged to you for your Concern for me which I shall endeavour to repay by taking all Opportunities of testifying my regard for you and according to your desire shall inform you of the State of my own affairs and first I must inform you that all the Supply I have ever had or am likely to have is from our Brother, it is that which till now has kept me in Cloths and is now [illegible] I believe it has been managed with the most prudent Economy as it has been in my Aunt's hands who would not encourage me in any Extravagances. And as to any future prospects you must Consider the most advantageous I can (at present) propose (if I continue in England) would be to wear out my life in being a hired Clerk to some Attorney as I have nothing to begin the World with and it is with some Concern I observe that Mr Henshaws Name will not be any great Honour to me when I begin the Work. I own my obligations to him and her and believe they would do many more kindnesses to me, but they want the power, though great changes may happen before I have served my Clerkship out, but this is at present my case. And as to the Law it intirely suits me and if it did not I should endeavour to make myself easy in whatever station of life God shall be pleased to place me, as it is Content which sweetens the bitterest draughts of Affliction. I shall endeavour to possess myself of that In virtue which I am fully convinced is so necessary in all Stations of Life.

I come now to speake of our relations with whom I live in very good correspondence and they are very civil to me I am afraid I have tried your Patience with this long Letter my papers scarce allowing the room to tell you how sincerely I remain Dear Brother

Your ever loving Brother Joseph Lee.

Joseph Lee to Robert Cooper Lee

Cooks Hall, 30th March 1753

Dear Brother,

I received yours of 30th December last and heartily thank you for your kind professions to me and do assure you that the many happy days we have once passed together will never be thought on by me but with the greatest pleasure and at the same time hopes of living to see you once more which will be an ample recompense to me for the many Misfortunes I have met with.

As to our Sister I have before sent you word that she is in the Country the Motive of which was this she thought an annuall supply of my Brothers Bounty would be sufficient to maintain her I urged the [illegible] which you have so well and so strongly and I wish I could say so effectually recommended but to no purpose she said she would follow my Brothers directions and would do as he advised her.

I have herewith sent a Letter to my Brother Jacky the occasion of which is Malancholly but I hope the event will be happy. My desire is to come over but yet my desire is not without foundation my Situation here is very bad I being at present with a person with whom it is no Credit to live with whom if I continue ever so long I shall never learn my business his practice being so very little But I do assure you I would not come to be a Burthen to either my Brother or you. No! Far be it from me I flatter myself these hands can earn sufficient for the maintenance of this Body it's true I propose to myself great even unspeakable Satisfaction in the Conversation of 2 Brothers so dear to me that life itself with them would be Miserable the long time we have been separated the cruel absence we have suffered. These I say are Motives which as I must change my Situation determine me to fly for Refuge to the Arms of the nearest Relations I have on Earth 2 of the dearest Brothers that perhaps ever existed at the same time for how laudable soever Brotherly love is accounted yet it is seldom very seldom that we see it practised I mean in the full extent of the Words.

I have acquainted my Uncle and Aunt Marlton with my resolutions who approve of them much but when I first informed them of my Condition and that I was determined not to stay with Mr Henshaw they though they could not but approve my reason yet did not propose any other remedy for me than writing to my Brother which I am now obliged to do in hopes to find in him that Asylum that I cannot obtain here. I see one Motive for their being so much for my coming over is for fear I should be any Burthen or expense to them of which they seem greatly afraid for I do assure you I have not received any shilling from them since our dear Father's death nay though my Brother in his letter of June last when he wrote to them and me was so good to desire him to disburse Mony for me an he should see occasion yet they have not thought fit to advance a Shilling although they know I at present have occasion for some for Necessarys this was what I little expected more especially as they have latterly behaved very well to me in Words.

I think there can be no impediment to my coming over as I am very clear that I can be discharged I don't rely on my own Opinion but on the Opinion of a very able Practitioner in the Law whom I have consulted about it. I have not yet acquainted my Sister Charlotte with my Intention neither shall I till I hear from you for fear it should revive in her Mind her desire of coming over I likewise hope she will not be an Obstacle for I make no doubt but she will be happily settled before she knows of my intentions.

Mrs Lucas has received your Letter and likewise the Bill of Exchange inclosed which is accepted she desires her compliments to you and when she has received the Mony will write to you she is yet in a very bad state of health with which she has been afflicted a long time.

I have nothing further to add but to let you know that my Grandmama takes your Letter exceeding kind desires you would excuse her not writing and assures you you are never out of her thoughts but that she continually prays for a blessing on all your endeavours. I hope her prayers will be heard and that you may enjoy health and happiness to your hearts Content which Concludes me Dear Brother

Yours affectionately J. Lee.

PS my last to you was in January last.

There are two letters in the collection from David Killican to Robert Cooper Lee. Killican was clearly a good friend but it has not been possible to identify with certainty who he was. The first letter refers to the wreck of the naval frigate *HMS Assurance* which was lost off the Needles on 24 April, 1753. A Customs report was lodged relating to a small amount of Rum and other goods saved from the wreck.[33] The Governor of Jamaica who survived the wreck of the *Assurance* was Edward Trelawny who had been Governor from April 1738 to September 1752. It was under him that peace had finally been achieved with the Maroons, and his term as Governor was one of the longest and most successful of 18th-century Jamaica until failing health necessitated his return to England. During his time in Jamaica his tact and natural diplomacy largely brought an end to the squabbles that had characterised the Jamaican Assembly. With his departure this accord sadly came to an end. He arrived back in London four days after the shipwreck and died at Hungerford Park on 16th January 1754.

David Killican to Robert Cooper Lee

London, 25th May 1753

Dear Sir,

I fear you never received my last Letter in Answer to yours of 11th of December 51 for I am sure I should have heard from you by Mr Spragg[34] had you received it. I should be extreamly sorry if the Miscarriage of our

[33] 22 August 1753 In order to your command signified by Mr Freemantle in his letter of 18th inst. we beg leave to Report that the Rum & and other sundry Goods saved out of the Assurance, Man of War, stranded on this Island were first brought by the persons who took them up floating in the sea to the Custom House & delivered to Mr Wilkinson as a perquisite of Admiralty in case they should not be claimed but as there was not then room in our Warehouse to contain them we lodged the said Goods in a Warehouse hired of Mr George Mackenzie at 12/6 per week http://www.customscowes.co.uk/1753-1764.htm Collector to Board Letters Book 1753 – 1764 National Archives ref:CUST 61/2

[34] Possibly James Spragg, a business associate of William Foster in Jamaica.

Letters should give the least room to doubt of the Sincerity of our Friendship and Esteem for each other; on my part I am determined it never shall, nor will it I am persuaded on yours. I have seen Mr Spragg since his Arrival at London and have heard his unfortunate Account of his being Cast away on Board the Assurance, just at the Lands End he lost everything but his Life but most of the Money and all the Governor's Effects were sav'd. Now I mention your excellent Governor I cannot but Condole with you for the great loss you have sustained, in the want of so good and worthy man at the head of your Affairs. I hope your present Governor will take him for a Pattern The great Character I receiv'd of him from Mr Spragg who thinks his absence will be very sensibly felt in the Island. But the greatest Pleasure Mr Spragg afforded me was the Account he gave me of your great Proficiency in your Profession and the present happy Situation you are in, and the great probability there is of your becoming an Ornament to your Profession all which gave me the highest Satisfaction as it confirmed me in the good Opinion and favourable Sentiments I always entertained of you, for there is no greater Pleasure than to be informed of the Happiness of those whom we Love and Esteem, because the Mind is incapable of Ease and Contentment when it is conscious of the Misfortunes and Miseries of those whom Friendship and the knowledge of their real worth has rendered dear to us. I congratulate you on your fixt and steddy Resolution to persevere in the Cause you are engag'd notwithstanding the Accidents others have met with in it, nothing is more worthy a brave and noble Soul than to surmount and conquer Difficulties and Obstacles others could not overcome.

You seem possessed of every thing requisite to make you happy in yourself and useful to others, go on and bravely persue the glorious Cause you have undertaken, my good Wishes shall always attend you and if I am capable of assisting you in it to the atmost of my Power you may command me with Pleasure. But I would send you some News if I could hear of any worth your Notice, there has been a Bill talk'd of this Sessions of Parliament for the better peopling your Island with Whites, but I believe it will come to nothing. The Master of the *Assurance* has been Tried by a Court Martial, and is only to suffer Three Months Imprisonment. A Bill passed both Houses of Parliament the 22nd Instant for Naturalizing Jews, that is, they are now by this Bill capable of being Naturaliz'd which they were not before by reason they would not receive the Sacrament, but this Bill dispenses with their Receiving it, and any foreign Jew after he has been in England Three Years may be Naturaliz'd and Purchase Lands though not Livings of the Church this is a very great Point the Jews have gain'd though they have paid well for it to those in

Power, the whole City and indeed great part of the Nation were absolutely against it. The Lord Mayor and Common Council presented a Petition against it as did likewise all the Merchants except those who were under the Influence of the Ministry, but all to no purpose. The House of Commons sate until Eleven a Clock at Night and the Debates were extreamly hot on both Sides, but the Ministry carried it 96 against 54 though Sir John Bernard Spoke several Hours against it. You have heard the Story of the Gypsey and Canning no doubt, the King has given the Gypsey a free Pardon.

My Brother desires his Love to you and is glad to hear you were happily Situated, Mr Spragg likewise desires his best Respects to you and with theirs except of my sincere Wishes for your Health and Happiness and believe me to be with Love and Esteem

Your most Obedient Servant and faithful Friend David Killican.

The 'Story of the Gypsey and Canning' referred to by David Killican was a *cause celebre* of the day, news of which would undoubtedly have reached Jamaica. On the first of January 1753 eighteen year-old Elizabeth Canning had been visiting her aunt and uncle just off the Ratcliffe Highway near the Tower of London. They had walked her home as far as the junction of Aldgate and Houndsditch after which she completely disappeared. Her whereabouts were advertised for by her mother:

Lost, a girl about eighteen years of age, dressed in a purple masquerade stuff gown, a white handkerchief and apron, a black quilted petticoat, a green under-coat, black shoes, blue stockings, a white shaving hat, with green ribbons, and had a very fresh colour. She was left on Monday last near Houndsditch, and has not been heard of since. Whoever informs Mrs. Canning a Scowrer , at Aldermanbury-Postern, concerning her, shall be handsomely rewarded for their trouble.

When Elizabeth Canning turned up four weeks later ragged, miserable and half naked she alleged kidnapping for prostitution and identified an old gypsy woman as the offender. She told an elaborate story, backed up by circumstantial evidence, which was at first largely believed. However in May 1753 the gypsy, Mary Squires, was pardoned on the basis of an alibi and in 1754 Elizabeth Canning was convicted of perjury and sentenced to transportation to the New World where she later married and settled down. Such was the public involvement with the case, with everyone taking sides for and against Elizabeth Canning, that when she was transported it was in the greatest comfort supplied by admirers and supporters.

There were always problems with correspondence between Jamaica and London, ships could be lost, as shown by the wreck of the *Assurance*, and items mislaid. The anxiety this could cause is shown both in the next letter from Joseph Lee and in the correspondence of Mary Charlotte Lee who was particularly isolated staying near Sible Hedingham in Essex, about forty miles from London, with relations of her uncle Thomas Marlton. Joe was at least in London and able to access some of the Jamaica news there.

Joseph Lee to Robert Cooper Lee

Cooks Hall, 4th July 1753

Dear Brother,

The last Letter I received from you was dated 30th December 1752 since which I have not received any Letter either from you or Jackey. I must confess it is the longest silence you have ever been guilty of for six Months have already elapsed since that time. I think I have not been remiss in troubling you with Letters but have punctually kept my word in taking every Opportunity of writing to you you certainly cannot but remember you have one Brother left in England – was your Affection so warm as you mention in your former Letters you would never suffer so much time to escape without writing at least one Line to inform me of your health – you cannot conceive the uneasiness your long Silence has occasioned – you might certainly in all this time have found Leisure to have writ one line to let me know your whole self was well. Excuse me dear Brother but as it is impossible for time to [torn and one line missing] greatest pleasure to hear from you. Consider there is but for four of us now left two in Europe and two in the America altho' the seas parts us yet we are enabled to send our thoughts to each other in writing then why should we not keep up with the most strict correspondence, certainly did but your thoughts correspond with mine there would be [no] occasion for these complaints but I hope to receive a Letter from you long before this reaches you.

I must now inform you no doubt to your great surprize that our dear father's affairs are not yet settled I have spoke to my Uncle who promises from time to time to insist to have the money from Mr Causton but has not yet done it I hope I shall soon inform you that the Mony is divided among the Creditors. I would send you over an Account of the Creditors and [account book?] of his Estate but cannot get a sight of the Books to draw up such Account. My sister is down in the Country and will continue there till she hears from Jackey which she is in daily expectation of. All other friends are well which blessing I hope both you and Brother enjoy my kind Love and best Wishes attend you both and am Dear Brother

Your ever loving Brother Joseph Lee.

Hardly had Joe written to his brother than he finally received a reply from Jamaica in which Bob told him he had sent funds for him through the Fullers in London.

Joseph Lee to Robert Cooper Lee

Cooks Hall, 20th July 1753

Dear Brother,

Since my last I have received yours of the 20th February last, which has made ample amends for the long silence complained of in mine.

Upon receipt of yours I went to Mr Fuller to know whether he had received the Letter you mentioned, when to my great surprize he told me he had not, therefore I have not yet received the expected supply.

I am much obliged to you for your good wishes and kind intentions towards me, assuring you at the same time that while life lasts they will be constantly as warm on my side, and indeed it is with the greatest pleasure I reflect that the time will soon come when we shall see each other for it rather alleviates the Misfortunes of this life when there is such mutual love between Brothers.

I with great joy lately heard of the Promotion[35] of your most worthy Patron Dr Fuller whose goodness to you, the more I reflect on it, the more it amazes me, certain I am the Almighty will never suffer such Virtue to go unrewarded but will Crown him with success in this World and Glory in that which is to come. My sincere wishes and kind love attend you my Brother, may health and happiness wait upon you both – I hope you will not be remiss in writing and believe me to be Dear Brother Your ever loving Brother J Lee.

[35] Rose Fuller was appointed Chief Justice for Jamaica in 1753, but shortly afterwards fell out with the new Governor Admiral Knowles over the question of moving the island capital from Spanish Town to Kingston.

In the autumn of 1753 Joseph Lee finally travelled to Jamaica to join his two older brothers. What the problems were that had beset the Marlton family is not clear. We know that Thomas Marlton had broken his leg and that relations between Mr Causton and the Lee family were strained. Relations had also been strained between the Marltons and their son-in-law John Sayer, possibly in relation to the way he was managing his business. Illness was an ever present threat, and that had certainly contributed to the lack of correspondence between Mary Marlton and her nephews. However she finally found time to write in October 1753.

Mary Marlton to Robert Cooper Lee

London, 18th October 1753

Dear Bobby,

Tho I have neglected writeing to you before, would not Let this Oppertunity slip, to assure you it has not been for want of Love to you, but since your absence have meet with so much trouble that has brought me into so bad a State of Health that to often I am hardly capable of Lookin to my Family. Its been a great trouble to us to hear of so many disappointments you have meet with in the Regard to your Settling in Business but I hope they are all at an end and that you are fixt to your mind. By your Brothers Letter I live in hopes of seeing you in England. I heartily wish you a Happy Meeting and dont doubth but Joe will bring you a sufficience of News to help of with your Winter Evenings.

Your Uncle joyns with me in kind Love to you

I am your affectionate aunt M. Marlton

Charlotte, isolated in Essex, was now left alone in England and had sunk into a deep depression. References to the difference between her temperament and that of her older sister leave the impression that Fanny was much the calmer of the two, which had probably exacerbated the reaction of their relations to her secret marriage and pregnancy, seemingly so out of character. Charlotte on the other hand, the much indulged youngest daughter, had reacted very badly after the death of their father to any attempt to set her to work. Whether the indiscretion she refers to in her letter was anything worse than a series of teenage tantrums is unclear but it seems likely from subsequent letters written by the Marltons that her offences were not nearly as great as she imagined.

Mary Charlotte Lee to Robert Cooper Lee

Sible Hedingham, 6th December 1753

Dear Brother,

I hope before this time you have received my letter by my brother Joe who I hope is arrived at Jamaica before this time I make no dought that it was a great pleasure to see [torn] satisfaction after so long at sea and to be informed of [torn] England since you left us as there has been so melancoly and alteration since in our family within the few years that you have been gone that I am senceable your joy at meting must be greatly dampt by reflecting of the dear relations you have lost since you see each other and I cold almost wish I was among the number of the dead than to be left without father mother Brother or sister or any freind to impart the pangs of my mind to and have the fear of being abandoned foresaken and forgot by the dearest relations I have on earth who may condem me for my indiscret Conduct and leave me to want and poverty. But give me leave to hope my dear Brother if my further behaviour is discreat and to your liking you will think me once more as your sister which by your long siylance I am afraid you have forgot she that you once called sister. Therefore beg that you will let me have a letter from you though it be an unkind one as you may justly be angry with me after what you have heard from our relations conserning my bad conduct which I am senciable you have heard in the blakist maner and as much to my disadvantage as possible but before you have this you will be satisfied by my brother Joe that there was fault of both sides of our relations side as well as mine. I hope your goodness will pardon if there is anything amiss in this Letter but beg the favour you not to mention to our relations in England when you write to them that you have received this letter from me and am Dear Brother

your most affectionate Sister Mary Charlotte Lee.

John Lee, as the eldest of the family, was in correspondence with his uncle Thomas Marlton about settling his father's affairs and, in the absence of any assets in his father's estate, was sending money to his uncle for the support of both Charlotte and Joe until Joe left for Jamaica. Thomas Marlton kept careful account of what the expenses were, itemised in this letter of which are two copies, presumably sent by separate ships. Whatever the deficiencies Joe had found in his uncle's attitude towards him earlier, it is clear that Thomas Marlton fitted him out for his life in Jamaica, paying the bills to his tailor and barber, organising the things he would need and providing him with a suit of clothing from his own pocket. It is interesting to note that Joe was not required to clean his own shoes, and that his books were bought from his uncle Thomas Atkins.

Thomas Marlton to John Lee

Pye Corner Smithfield, London, [undated,1754]

Mr John Lee to Thomas Marlton Dr.

To Miss Charlotte Lee

boarding and money she has had	£49 9s
Paid Joe's Taylor for last year's Bill	£1 12s
paid his Barbers ditto	£4 4s
paid his shoe Cleaner	2s 6d
Cash let him have	£1 16s 6d
paid for Books, Chest etc	£19 6s
paid for a Seal	£1 2s
paid Mr Atkins for Books	£2 15s 6d
	£80 7s 6d

Received a Bill from you £30

Received two Bills from Bobby £40

Dear Jacky

The above is our Account. I have charg'd you with the money gave Joey and the money he was indebted to his Barber and Taylor which is as abovemention'd. As for fitting him out I shall not charge him or you anything, but wish you all happiness. Mr Causton tells me you owe him £3 5 shillings so I had nothing to receive of him. I have balanc'd with Charlott's Mistress up to Midsummer 1754, and have given Charlott money for her expenses till Midsummer; so you'll have but one quarter to pay for till Michaelmas 1754. I have not compleated your orders in the Books but shall as soon as convenient the reason you'll [see] in the booksellers Bill. I am sorry your Brother sent too late to me for

Ticketts[36], whatsoever is in my power to do for you command me and it shall be done in the best manner I can. Your Grandmother gives her suitable respects to all and she is as hearty now as she was 70 years ago. We all join with suitable respects, and shall be glad to see any of you in England. I am lame in my hand excuse what you see amiss.

Yours to serve Thomas Marlton.

PS I shall be glad to hear from any of you when it suits you. I have enclosed the Bills. What is here mentioned is shipt in the *Peter Beckford* Captain Lovelace the Charge of shipping is ten shillings. We are likely to receive your present and return you many thanks

Mr Sayer gave Joey ten shillings and sixpence for you to buy Candied Ginger which please to forward first opportunity.

[A note to Bob about the lottery tickets was added at the bottom of the letter to John]

Dear Bobby,

Your Bill came too late to hand they had but 2 or 3 days to draw, and none to be sold after they had began to draw according to Act of Parliament, so could not buy any for you. Yours with due Respect Thomas Marlton.

About the same time as this account from Thomas Marlton arrived in Jamaica Bob received another letter from David Killican. Although several of the letters written at this time refer to Robert Cooper Lee being expected to travel to England there is no evidence that in fact he did so. It is possible that whatever business he was going to be sent on was taken care of by Rose Fuller who returned permanently to England in 1755 following the death of his older brother John.

David Killican to Robert Cooper Lee

London, 15th April 1754

Dear Sir,

[36] The Lee family were regular purchasers of lottery tickets throughout the century.

Your kind Letter dissipated every disagreeable Reflection I could possibly entertain from so long a Silence and afforded me the most sensible Pleasure, as I began to despair of ever hearing again from one for whom I had always preserved the greatest Esteem and most sincere Regard and in whose Friendship I thought myself happy; such was my Concern and Regret for the loss of one I loved and esteemed when your friendly and affectionate Letter happily removed my vain and groundless Tears and convinced me how unjustly I had violated the sacred Ties of Friendship.

I am pleased with the Thought of our one day enjoying the Company of each other, after so long a Separation I hope nothing will interrupt the pleasing Prospect, the Accidents of Life we must submit to, but what is in our own Power to bring about that happy Period, let us steadily adhere to and ardently pursue.

I am still in the same Situation in which you left me, my Brother and I live with an Old Gentleman who is upwards of eighty years of age; he is possessed of a very large Fortune which at his death the greatest part of it will be my Brother's as he intends to make him his heir; for myself, I hope to have sufficient to live with independent of the world, which is my utmost Ambition.

If I may judge from your present happy Situation I think there is not the least fear of your attaining the utmost of your Wishes in a short time; for give the Liberty I am going to take it 'tis this, to avoid if possible the Incumbrance of a Wife, that imprudent step will marr all your other Acquisitions, and put an end to all your future pleasing Wishes. I hope you will pardon my touching upon a Subject so delicate and tender and not think I distrust either your Prudence or good Sense; no, I have sufficient Testimony of both; nor would I have you think me an Enemy to Matrimony for no one entertains a more favourable Opinion of it than myself but 'tis engaging in it at an improper time that is the Fault; thus much Friendship induced me to say upon a Subject (as Portius says in Cato) where most our Nature fails.

You have no doubt heard e'er this, of the death of our Prime Minister Mr Pelham whose place is at present possessed by his Brother the Duke of Newcastle but how long he will continue in it is very uncertain for his greatly inferior to his Brother in all respects. It happened at a very critical Period just at the Dissolution of the Parliament which was the 7th Instant; the continuance of the Duke at the head of the Treasury will very much depend on the Disposition and Temper of the new Parliament when they meet, for there are several who expected preferment but are disappointed, in particular Mr Fox the Secretary at War, who it was generally believed would have Mr Pelham's places; he together with the Duke of Bedford,

Earl of Sandwich and several others are strong opposers of the present Measures not for the good of the publick, but their own Private Interests, not because those who have the Direction do wrong for themselves would do the same, but because they are not shares with them; therefore we may see what a weak and ridiculous thing all Party is and from whence it has its rise.

We have lost our Lord Chief Justice of the Kings Bench Sir William Lee[37], which is filled by the Attorney General and the Solliciter General is made Attorney, and Sir Richard Loyd Solliciter. The whole Kingdom is at present in a great Fermentation – bribery and corruption [illegible] the Means most used on their Occasion. Drunkenness and Idleness are conspicuous enough throughout the kingdom, the Proclamation for the Dissolution of the Parliament is not unlike the Proclaiming Bartholomew Fair in Smithfield which is no sooner done, than the whole place is a Scene of confusion and disorder.

Mr Beckford[38] will certainly be chose for the City of London the Livery being almost unanimous for him; his Brother Richard Beckford who is coming from your Island is a Candidate for Bristol the second city for Trade in England but he is strongly opposed by one of the Court party; thus much for News at present.

Mr Sprag's Expectations from the late Governor have all come to nothing, since his Death he has waited upon his Lady but without any better Success; he is now Clark to a Merchant and I make no doubt will do very well, as he is a very sober careful young fellow. I have not seen him for this Month past but he is well I believe and was extreamly glad to hear of your Welfare. My Brother desires his Compliments to you and would be glad to see you in London. I remain Dear Sir with great Sincerity

your faithful Friend and Servant David Killican.

---

37 The Lee family seem to have been related to the Lees of Hartwell, who included Sir William among their number. The connection was acknowledged by William Lee Antonie some years later, but the detail of how they were related has not been established and probably goes back to the mid sixteenth century.

38 William Beckford (1709-1770) enormously wealthy Jamaican planter, born in Jamaica and educated in England, he managed the Beckford's huge landholdings in Jamaica for ten years after the death of his father Peter Beckford. He returned to England in 1744 and pursued a political career as MP for Shaftesbury and then London, becoming Lord Mayor twice. He used his fortune to acquire a large estate at Fonthill where his only legitimate son William Thomas Beckford built the gothic Fonthill Abbey.

In late August of 1754 Charlotte finally heard from her brothers and discovered that she had not been forgotten, but that a whole series of letters had gone astray. Her tone is still melancholy, but her handwriting and spelling are more mature and she seems resigned to her loneliness.

Mary Charlotte Lee to Robert Cooper Lee

Sible Hedingham, 3rd September 1754

My Dear Brother,

I receivd your kind Letter dated May 11 the 22 of Last mounth and find by Looking over your Letters the last I have of yours beside this I am now answering is dated March the 20th 1752 and therefor I never had the happiness of receiving that Letter dated July 27 1752 as you mention in yours belive me it gives me great concern that these three Letters of yours never came to hand as nothing gives me so much pleasure as receiving Letters from my dear brothers and I will take care for the future never to neglect writing you by all opertunitys

As I am never so happy as when I am reading over your Letters or writing to you as it gives me great pleasure to recall my thoughts to you by pen and ink as I cant by word of mouth. I still continue in Hedingham by Mr Marlton's choice where I spend my time as agreeable as I can for one in my situation not as I'd have you think I am discontented in my manner of Living no I Bless my dear Brother for his goodness in enabling me to live as I do but being so far distant from you and the rest of my dear brothers who are my only comforts on earth gives me inexpressible grief but when I reflect it is for your advantage to stay a few years Longer and the just reason you give me in your last Letter I had much rather submit to a short and painful separation than see you dependent on any person in England, for I assure you absence has rather increased my Love and regard for you and I prefer your happiness so infinitly to my own that if I do but hear you are happy and prosper it will suport me under the many difficultys I may meet with. For as I am convinced there is no sure happiness in this wourld I will endeavour make my self contented and Look Forward that where there is eternal happiness where I hope we shall meet if dont in this. I return you many thanks for your kind advice which I will endeavour to follow. For believe me my dear brother since you do and will continue your love and tenderness to me I cannot be unhappy, the meeting with many misfortunes that I have done has given my mind a melancholy turn I can not easily conquer and I am too apt to make my self uneasy for the slights I am subject to. Mr Marlton called to see me about a week ago and behaved very kindly. I am afraid I shall tier your patance with my long Letter but will conclude with my sincere wishes for your health and happiness and am with greatest esteem My Dear Brother

Your most affictionate Sister Mary Charlotte Lee.

Eighteenth-century letters are full of references to the health of the correspondents and their hopes that the intended recipient is still in good health. Robert Cooper Lee seems to have been particularly lucky in not succumbing to the many, frequently fatal, illnesses which afflicted Jamaican colonists, although there was a reference to his having been ill when he first arrived, and also that at some time in 1754 he was severely ill. He may have been nursed back to health by Mrs Rose but in any event he made a good recovery. There is evidence from Rose Fuller's Will that Mary Rose had nursed him through several dangerous illnesses, and it seems probable that having been born in Jamaica she had early learned the skills needed to treat common illnesses. Moreover as the housekeeper and companion to two of the island's doctors she may have learned from them also. It is known that she applied her skills to treating some of their slaves.

Major epidemics killed white settlers and slaves alike, with regular outbreaks of yellow fever, plus measles, smallpox and yaws all of which were highly infectious. Yellow fever had probably arrived in the West Indies from Africa by the mid seventeenth century. Like malaria it is dependent for its transmission on mosquitoes breeding in stagnant water, both then present in abundance in Jamaica. The clay pots used in sugar production when broken were cast down and provided small pools of water; hurricanes and earthquake tsunami created larger bodies of water ideal for breeding. Where a cause of death is recorded in early burial registers, 'fever' is by far the most common. Death from fever was not always the immediate outcome and malaria, which causes recurring episodes of fever, is very debilitating even when not immediately fatal.

Among the other causes of recurring illness among Jamaican residents were gout and the dry bellyache. Gout was largely the result of a diet over rich in protein and including turtle and shellfish. The dry bellyache was in fact lead poisoning caused by the use of lead in the equipment for distilling rum. Although this cause was known from the mid-eighteenth century and acted upon in North America, nothing seems to have been done in Jamaica. Benjamin Franklin 'wrote about lead poisoning on several occasions, in particular about a disease known as the dry-gripes (or dry-bellyache) that had plagued Europe and the colonies for years….in

1723 the Massachusetts colonial legislature passed a bill outlawing the use of lead in the coils and heads of stills. Observance of this law led to vastly decreased incidence of the dry-gripes, as the population drank less and less lead-contaminated rum.'[39] In 1745 Thomas Cadwalder had drawn attention to the extreme cases of colic 'West India dry gripe' that were caused by the use of lead piping in rum distillation, but it seems nothing was done and it is not clear when the use of lead was reduced in Jamaica, with large scale illness and death among the garrisons and in the navy still occurring at the end of the eighteenth century. The better off colonists avoided the worst of this by drinking imported claret, brandy or Madeira as well as rum, but excess use of alcohol leading to liver damage further weakened their ability to withstand illness.

The following letter from Charlotte is badly torn.

Mary Charlotte Lee to Robert Cooper Lee

Sible Hedingham, 22nd February 1755

My Dear Brother,

I received your letter dated September 22 and likewise received yours dated October [illegible] of the former and must beg pardone for not answering [torn] before which I ought and should have done had [missing] prevented by one unlucky accident or another and [missing] hindred me from so doing till now. It was with the greatest consern that I heard of your Late dangerous illness and indeed was in continual pain and uneasiness till I had the happiness of hearing by your Letter of October that you was perfectly recovered which afforded me much [missing] satisfaction and I hope through the [goodness of God?] you will for the future enjoy the blessing of health which in my opinion is the greatest this wourld can afford. I return you many thanks for your kind present though am [concerned?] to take from you so young a begener and put you to so much expense though you are pleased to mention it as a trifle I esteem it as a great sum as I assure you my [missing] it was more than I desired. I according to your kind [missing] sent the Bill up to London

[39] Lisa Gensel , *The Medical World of Benjamin Franklin,* Journal of the Royal Society of Medicine, Vol. 98, No 12, pp. 534-538

inclosed in a Letter to Mr [missing] who paid the mony immediately and which [missing] was of great service to Mee as I was in great want of all sorts of Linen having bought none nor indeed had [missing] since I have been in Hedingham as I was [obliged by?] reason of my bad state of health to lay out [missing] the mony I received from my Uncle Marlton in paying apothecaryes bills and was willing to make [missing] clothes as much as possible and put my brother [to as] Little expense as I cold as I am sensible of [missing] charge I am to him so therefore I cant but [illegible] I was in great want of real necessaries of cloaths which your goodness has enabled me to supply myself with and for which I return you my most sincere thanks and indeed I am so much obligated to you for all your kindness and tenderness that I am at a loss for words to express myself and cold I flatter myself I should one day see you again and in person thank you for all your favours I should esteem myself truly happy but that joyfull day I fear is at a great distance if ever.

I daresay you have heard before now of the death of our poor grandmother who departed this life the 11 of December Last altho by course of years it cold not be expected she could Live a great while [illegible] being no ways informed of her illness and hearing of her death in so sudden in manner [affected me] extremely tho as her great age made her incapable of injoying any more happiness in this wourld and she had undergone so many afflictions it would be cruel for her sake to wish her back in this vale of misery again as I make no doubt she is now happy and free from all her cares and troubles as she was [torn] and an extrem good Liver and allways for her troubles and afflictions with that pious patance and resignation to the will of God, never murmuring when in her deepest distress for which doubtless she has received a crown of Life and is entered into the [illegible] of her Lord and that we may all follow her good example [torn] blesst place god if his infinite mercy grant [torn] think

I understand from my uncle Marlton's letter that she left what little matter of affects she had to brother Joe and you which I am sincerely glad of and wish it was four times as much as 'tis for your sakes as I am certain you deserve all the good fortune that can befall you in this wourld. [I am at] present at Mrs Bridges in Sible Hedingham but believe [I will not] stay much Longer her family being encreast [since I] have been with her that 'tis ill convenient for her [missing] but please still to continue to direct your Letters as before till I inform you to the contrary and as soon as [missing] the place where my uncle will think fit to fix me I [will immediately] acquaint you with it. I according to your [request] Directly acquainted my ant Marlton with your kind present [missing] and I daresay in her heart she was sorry for [.. I will not] tier your patance any longer with my Long scribble [when I] sit down to write to my dear Brother I know not when to leave off as I allways knoe at the conclution of my Letter many more things to say as I cannot well by writing wholy disclose my mind to you but will conclude with my sincere wishes for your health and happiness and am My Dear Brother with the greatest esteem

Your Most affectionate Sister Mary Charlotte Lee.

Mary Lee was buried at St Michael Bassishaw on 13 December 1754 thirty-eight years after the death of her husband Joseph Lee who was also buried there 'in woollen' - a measure designed to encourage the English wool industry. She may have been over ninety years old and had outlived all her generation[40]. She left £26 19s 10d to her two younger grandsons, a sum worth today about £3,190 relative to retail prices or £43,500 relative to average earnings.[41]

While Charlotte was boarding out at Sible Hedingham, and Joe and Bob were learning to make their way in Jamaica, John continued to work as a factor for Rose Fuller. However in 1755, following the death of his older brother John, Rose Fuller returned to England to manage the Sussex estates and iron foundry, and also to lobby on behalf of the faction he was aligned with in Spanish Town against the attempt by the Governor, Admiral Charles Knowles, to move the island capital to Kingston. Between 1754 and 1758 a controversy raged, with the Island divided into two warring groups - the merchants of Kingston against the Planters and Lawyers in Spanish Town. Francis Delap, Provost Marshall of Jamaica, who was suspected of trying to influence the votes in favour of the Spanish Town lobby was jailed and held in irons in Port Royal, by the Governor Charles Knowles who favoured the Kingston party. Rose Fuller testified in London on behalf of Delap, who was eventually released. The site of the island capital was only finally settled when the Board of Trade in London recommended the Commons to rule against the move on a technicality.

With Rose Fuller's departure John Lee was left with much greater responsibility for managing the Fullers' affairs in Jamaica. Already he was

---

40 She was born Mary Graby (or Graybee) in the 1660s, the daughter of a wealthy cooper called Richard Graby who owned property in Little Old Bailey. Her sister Hester married a wealthy goldsmith called Anthony Nelmes, and her sister Sarah had married William Jaques a noted silversmith and watch case maker. Hence Joseph Lee and Frances Jaques were first cousins when they married in 1720.

41 Source: http://www.measuringworth.com

extremely familiar with the growing and processing of sugar cane which was by now highly organised. To be profitable it required relatively large plantations and a large labour force – generally with a ratio of one slave to every two acres of land. The large labour force was needed to clear the land, dig trenches, plant out cane shoots, manure and weed the crop and then cut and cart it to the boiling houses for processing into muscovado and molasses. A system of taxes on clayed (refined white) sugar designed to protect the British based sugar bakers, meant that most of what was sent from Jamaica to London was the darker unrefined muscovado. Work in the boiling houses was particularly gruelling and often dangerous, as was operating the huge vertical grinding rollers in which slaves were often maimed or killed. An axe was usually kept by the rollers to cut off a trapped limb before the slave was dragged into the mechanism and crushed.

The canes were usually planted between October and December when rainfall encouraged rapid sprouting, the crop then took sixteen months to mature to its full height of eight feet. To maximise the production on an estate canes were planted in rotation so that the harvesting season could be extended over the ripening months from January to May. Harvesting was back breaking work carried out in extremes of tropical heat by the strongest male slaves. Once a field had been cut the plants were left in the ground and sprouted again to produce 'ratoon cane' which matured more quickly but yielded less sugar. Jamaican planters often ratooned two or three times before replanting with fresh cane. The rate of expansion of plantations in Jamaica was extremely rapid, from 57 sugar estates in 1673 to nearly 430 by 1739[42]. During the time the Lee brothers were in Jamaica the island was not only England's largest sugar producer, it was the world leader.

The letters from John to Rose Fuller, preserved at the East Sussex County Record Office, give us a small insight into his working life.

John Lee to Rose Fuller[43]

Spanish Town Jamaica, 25th July 1755

Honoured Sir,

---

[42] Clinton V. Black, *History of Jamaica*, Longman, Group UK Ltd., 1991, p.68
[43] ESRO: SAS-RF/21/20

I should have wrote to you by Captain Lundin, but was, at the time of his sailing incapable of holding a Pen occasioned by a Whitlow on my finger of which I desired my Brother Joe to acquaint you.

By that ship I sent you five hogsheads[44] of Sugar, which was all we had at that time in the Store viz. three of Knollis and two of Hoghole. I thought to have made up four of Knollis but on examining found that three of them was so much sunk that we were obliged to make use of a great part of the fourth to fill them up.

Since your Departure the River Road has been extreamly bad was impassable for even mules three weeks and still continues to be so for wains[45], and Mr Kay[46] has been very ill which accidents have prevented our getting down the Sugars time enough to send by Captain Hamilton, they were to be shipt on account of my Lord Londonderry, but not being yet brought down I could not ship them agreeable to your directions. As Mr Kay is much on the Recovery and the River Road is very good for mules to pass I shall press him to send them down as fast as possible and propose to ship 10 hogsheads on board the *Two Sisters* Captain Wilson, who it is said will certainly sail the first ship for account of my Lord Londonderry, of which I have by this Conveyance advised Mr Lawes (His Lordships Receiver) and I hope what I have done will meet with your approbation.

Inclosed I send you Copy of the Title Deeds of Hoghole and of Thomas's Bond and Note, Mr Peete's[47] accounts are just compleated and will be sent you with the other papers you ordered by the *Two Sisters* which is the first ship that will sail after this.

---

[44] A hogshead was a very large wooden barrel holding about 54 imperial gallons. A hogshead of sugar weighed about 1,600 pounds (about 725 kilograms). However barrel size and packed weight varied considerably and so barrels would be weighed and recorded on the Bill of Lading for insurance purposes.

[45] Wagons drawn by teams of up to a dozen oxen carried large loads but their weight damaged the roads and they could not be used after periods of flood or heavy rain. As mules could not carry the large hogsheads the sugar would have to be repacked before shipping.

[46] Peter Kay managed the Hoghole plantation on behalf of Rose Fuller.

[47] William Peete M.A. St. George 1749, St. Andrew 1742 and 1745 – these were the accounts following his death in 1751. The delay in dealing with them is quite typical of how long it often took to wind up someone's affairs.

Mr Marriot[48] has been very ill which has prevented my obtaining the Certificate so as to get the Books from him, no Court of Chancery has been held since you went away therefore no Application could be made, the Accounts relating to Mitchell & Co I have drawn out of the Account Current Books and Mr Mills Books [are] left with the Master therefore and expect to have them delivered to me the first time the Chancellor sits.

Mr Alpress[49] has been up to your Estates and I suppose he has given you an account of the agreeable order he found them in.

Everything at the Penn is well, the Cattle in very good order, and Plenty of Guinea Grass[50] and Fodder for them.

There has been an accident happened to little Tom, Nelly's Son, who as he was leaving the Cattle fell down and the wain run over him and broke his Leg, he was not far from town when the Accident happened and was immediately brought there. Doctor Worth set the Leg and he was very hearty for thirteen days, on the fourteenth he was seized with spasms and dyed on the fifteenth notwithstanding all the Care imaginable was taken to save him both by the Doctor and Mrs Rose.

Since you have been gone we have lost Mr Baldwin[51], Mr Halked[52] and Mrs Taylor the Widow of Patrick Taylor[53], and last night Mr Henry Byndloss[54] the Attorney General of a very short illness it is said Mr Richards is soon to be Attorney General.

I have nothing further to add but that I hope this may find you safely arrived in England when I begg leave to wish you a long Continuance of

---

[48] Sidney Marriott, a Master in Chancery at Kingston (Jamaica Almanac 1751).

[49] George Alpress, listed as landowner in 1754 of 125 acres in Clarendon and 51 acres in Vere. Rose Fuller took charge of the arrangements for the education of his son Samuel Alpress in England.

[50] Guinea grass had been accidentally introduced from Africa after being brought in as bird seed, it provided better feed than the native grass and soon spread extensively.

[51] William Baldwin, buried Spanish Town 18 July 1755

[52] Richard Halked, buried Spanish Town 13 July 1755.

[53] Martha Taylor, death recorded as Maximilia Taylor, buried Spanish Town 21 July 1755. Patrick Taylor was a Member of the Assembly for St George 1753, and father of Simon Taylor (1739-1813), Ann Taylor who married Robert Graham and Sir John Taylor who married Elizabeth Goodin Haughton.

[54] Henry Morgan Byndloss (c.1703-24 Jul 1755, buried Spanish Town the following day.)

Health and Happiness. I am with the utmost Respect Honoured Sir Your most obedient and most obliged humble Servant John Lee.

PS Mrs Rose is in the Recovery and desires to be remembered to you.

Early 20th century postcard showing an ox train carrying sugar and rum, a method of transport largely unchanged since the eighteenth century

John Lee to Dr Rose Fuller[55]

Kingston, 1st September 1755

Honoured Sir,

Inclosed I send you, agreable to your directions, Copys of Mr Peete's Accounts as well as of the Ferry[56] with his Executors which I have examined and found right. I am now copying the Inventory and making a Calculation of what is due to and from the Estate which I hope I shall have compleated in a fortnight or three weeks at furthest, when I shall forward them to you together with my Lord Londonderry's Papers. By

[55] ESRO: SAS-RF/21/23

[56] In 1736, an Act of the Jamaican Assembly was passed empowering William Peete to keep the Ferry and erect a Toll Gate between St. Catherine and St. Andrew, and to take up runaway negroes. In 1749, the Toll was vested in Trustees for repairing the Ferry Roads.

my Letter of the 25th July last I advised both yourself and Mr Lawes that I should ship 10 hogsheads of Sugars on account of his Lordship on the *Two Sisters*, Captain Wilson (the Ship by which you will receive this) but I'm sorry now to acquaint you that I could not comply with that Engagement on account of the smallness of the Crop on Hoghole, which I was not apprized of, as Mr Kay is not very communicative. You made at that Estate this year One hundred and seventeen hogsheads, 115 of which are come to hand and two are still on the Estate, they have been disposed of in the following manner

60 Sent to Mr Stratton before you left the Island

37 Shipt by your directions before you left the Island likewise

2 Shipt on the *Britannia,* Captain Landin, since your departure

10 Sold Lost and Smith since ditto

6 Sold Solomon Abrahams since ditto

115

and 2 still on the Estate

117 Hogsheads in all.

I imagined from the whole Tenor of Mr Kay's discourse that you would have made upwards of one hundred and fifty hogsheads at Hoghole which was my Motive for writing to you in the manner I did, but for the future I shall be extremely cautious in that respect and I hope you will excuse this Disappointment.

I came to this Town in order to have had the affair between Mrs Greenlees and yourself heard, but Mr Marriot is at the Bath and the Books are all lockt up so that nothing can be done to his Return, as the Books were order'd still to be kept by him, notwithstanding the application to have them deposited with Mrs Johnston, which was strongly opposed by the other Party, for fear (as George Lewis said) that any of them should be lost in the Removal.

Since your Settlement with Mr Bayly[57] I have found the Bond in which you was Security for John Basnett[58] to Mary Hutchinson which was

---

[57] Zachary Bayly, perhaps best known as the uncle of the Jamaican historian Bryan Edwards. Bayly was a highly successful merchant and owner of the adjoining Tryall, Trinity, Roslyn and Brimmer Hall estates amounting to over 4000 acres.

[58] Possibly the John Basnett who owned 890 acres in the parish of St Mary, but had died by 1754.

entirely discharged by you, there are two Payments endorsed off the Bond that were not charged in the Account to you settled, one is in your own Writing for £114 14s 7d and the other is in the Writing of one William Addenbrooke for £187 2s 1d making in the whole the Sum of £301 16s 8d. I have shewed the Bond to Mr Bayly and have taken up your Note to him for £35 14s 6½d and he has promised me the remainder in two or three months.

Every thing is well. The Court is now holding up at the Free School House, the old Court House having been found by Experience to be too hot. I Beg leave to remain with due Respect Honoured Sir

Your most faithfull and most obliged honourable Servant John Lee.

The hot springs in the parish of St Thomas in the East were named after the town of Bath in England and were resorted to by the inhabitants of Jamaica for similar reasons. There is some evidence that prolonged immersion in the water would have relieved the symptoms of both gout and the dry bellyache, by increasing excretion of lead[59].

John Lee to Rose Fuller[60]

Kingston, 13th September 1755

Honoured Sir,

We have obtained an Order from the Court of Chancery to have the Books that were deposited with Mr Marriott[61] delivered immediately to Mr James Barclay, and on Monday I propose to carry the Order into Execution by conveying them to Mr Barclay's Penn.

By the Direction of Mr Straton I have this day drawn on Messrs Barclay and Fuller in favour of him for one hundred Pounds Sterling which I have with his approbation received in order to pay off some of the Demands and in particular the three quarters Deficiency[62] which the Collecting

---

[59] Rolls, Roger, *Spa Therapy through the Ages,* Bath and North East Somerset Council.

[60] ESRO SAS-RF/21/29

[61] Sidney Marriott was co-owner of the *Britannia* with John and Alexander Harper, Thomas Stretton, James Barclay and William Jameson,

[62] The Jamaican Deficiency Acts imposed a fine on any plantation owner who did not maintain a required ratio of white employees to slaves. Rather than result in the

Constables must get in before the 23rd Instant, the Assembly being appointed to meet on that day; there were some other small demands likewise. I hope you will not be displeased at my making use of this liberty which gave me conditionally, and you will be quickly convinced of the necessity of it by looking over your Cash Book (a Copy of which you will have next week) where you will find the poor price Rum has sold for and the great difficulty there was to sell any at all, and to this Mr Ellis[63] has not been up yet therefore the Coach has not been paid for, Mr Hay[64] has not paid for the horses and Mr Provost discounted the amount of the Chariot in part of his [illegible] and so there has been nothing but the Rum to pay everything with, but of this you will be a better Judge when you see the Accounts, which you shall have next week, if I can get home to Spanish Town to copy them.

I hope soon to hear of your arrival and that you enjoy your health perfectly well, and that you may longer do so is the ardent Wish of

Your most faithful and most obliged humble Servant John Lee.

Back in London Uncle Thomas Marlton was doing his best to keep on top of his own business and the accounts of his nephews and niece. The inheritance Bob and Joe had from their grandmother was accounted for, as was money sent by John for the maintenance of Charlotte, and the cost of a lottery ticket. Throughout their lives the Lees bought lottery tickets, even when they had become wealthy, but they always seem to have avoided the worst evils of the 18th-century craze for gambling.

The letter from Thomas bears every sign of having been written in haste, his flourishing handwriting and frequent use of abbreviations compressing what he had to say.

Thomas Marlton to John Lee

London, 29th September 1755

Yours received with a bill on Earle and Ferrers value Thirty pounds and have placed to your account. Likewise to Twenty pounds Bobey sent to

importation of more white colonists as originally intended it simply became an additional tax.

[63] Possibly William Beckford Ellis who married Susanna Addenbrooke (widow of William) in 1757. Alternatively his brother John Ellis.

[64] Probably Thomas Hay who was Secretary of the Island and Notary Publick, he was listed in the 1754 census of Spanish Town as being also a planter.

buy a Ticket, and the Twenty Six pounds nineteen shillings and Ten pence left to Bobby and Joey by there grand mother. So with the above-mentioned and what you have sent the Ballance stands in your favour Six pounds which is in my hands and all Expenses for your Sister is payd up to the [illegible] Date and your Sister have in her hands Two Pounds 16. Wee are all pretty well and in great Hopes of seeing you and dear Bobby please to give my best respects to hope you will excuse me not writing to [torn] I have me too much on my hands at present.

I am Sir Your [?] Thos. Marlton

John Lee to Rose Fuller[65]

Spanish Town Jamaica, 30th June 1756

Honoured Sir,

I wrote to you on the 15th Instant since which I'm not favoured with any of yours. Both Mr Browne and Mr Siddall sail (with Mr Ellis's approbation) in the Ship that brings you this, as you will have an account from themselves of the Reasons for their Conduct in leaving the Island, I shall not trouble you with my Conjectures on the Occasion, only this much permit me to say that neither of them had any real occasion to act in so unbecoming a manner.

You will have forty two hogsheads of Sugars more from your own Estates shipt to you as soon as ever we can procure freight for them, which I believe we shall do on Captain Hill but of this I cannot as yet be positive but shall let you know by the Packett who will sail in all next week.

Inclosed you will receive Invoice and Bill of Lading for forty two Tierces of Sugar received from Mr Lamb on account of his Mortgage and shipped you in the *Ellis*, Captain Kitchen, I fancy I shall shortly get another Payment from Lamb to effect which no Pains shall be spared.

Mr Fearon[66] tells me he is not certain whether he can spare you any Sugars this year but if he can, he will let you have twenty hogsheads. I

[65] ESRO: SAS-RF/21/48

[66] Probably Thomas Fearon who owned large estates in Clarendon, St Thomas in the East, Vere and St Dorothy. In 1755 he wrote to Rose Fuller asking him to find a suitable tutor for his son. ESRO SAS-RF/21/34

shall apply to him shortly again for them and shall then acquaint you whether you may expect them or not.

Mrs Greenlees's Affair is quite dormant and I am of opinion that they will not go on with it, I do not hear that they have taken any steps relative to a hearing before the Master.

I have delivered Mr Mordaunt's Letter to Mr Atkins in the manner you directed, he tells me that some time since he did actually execute the Resignation you mention and that he transmitted it to Mr Mordaunt attested by the Secretary as a Notary Publick. I find on enquiring at the Secretary's office that what he told me is a fact, I have made an affidavit of Transaction which you will received by the next conveyance.

Your Friend Dr Worth[67] dyed about three weeks agoe after a few days Illness and you have lost Sukey who had been in a declining way ever since you went off; your two Girls Fanny and Kate Strachan are brought to bed of a Boy each; Mr Almeyda[68] has applied to me to write to you about his purchasing Fanny's Child and the mother if you will sell her, in order that he may manumise them, the Child's name is Stephen and he says he will give you any sum for the Freedom of it that you shall desire.

Mrs Rose desires to be remembered to you, Permit me to tender my Brother's Compliments and to assure you that I am with the greatest Respect Honoured Sir

Your most faithful and most obliged honourable Servant John Lee.

While John Lee in Jamaica was managing affairs for Rose Fuller, his uncle Thomas Marlton in London was struggling to manage his own business, cope with the death of his only surviving son, and deal with a proposal of marriage for Charlotte. In a scrawled note to Bob he listed various accounts handled on his behalf.

Thomas Marlton to Robert Cooper Lee

London, July 1756

Mr Ebenezer Michells Bill £33 8s 0d

---

[67] Dr Samuel Worth, buried Spanish Town 30 May 1756.

[68] Probably Daniel Almeyda who died in 1774 aged 56 and was buried in Kingston.

Edward Vayles Bill	£7 17s 6d
Burkett Fenns Bill	£19 10s 0d
Came Shoemaker Bill	£4 4s
	£69 18s 6d

The other charge I shall send in my next.

Dear Kinsman

I have sent you as above mentioned and have done the best I can and hope will give Satisfaction. I shall be glad at all times to Serve you as Fare as in my power. I am at this time in Great Trouble my Son John is Dead I hope you'll excuse me writing any more than what is needfull my Suitable Respects to all of you always to command Thos Marlton

I sent a letter to your Brother John about your Sister and hope for a Speedey Answer.

Tea	£3 10s 0d
Canisters	£0 2s 0d
Box	£0 4s 0d
	£3 16s 0d
	£69 18s 6d
	£73 14s 6d

[Noted in RCL's writing]

£73 14s 6d

£5 11s 9d

In Mr M's hands £20 13s 9d

£100

I received your Bill on Drake and Long value £100 TM

I wish you had Sent one Stocking and one Shoe

Presumably the correspondence had included a request for new shoes and stockings without adequately representing the necessary size!

The next letter from Thomas Marlton to John Lee shows the affection that he had for his niece Charlotte. His spelling strongly suggests that his connections with Essex (he was born in Ashen) extended to the way he spoke, writing girl as 'garle', sterling as 'starling' and 'citled' for settled. He also used 'kindman', the rather archaic form of kinsman.

Thomas Marlton to John Lee

London, 6th July 1756

Yours received by Captain Britt [?Brett] and my Spous[?] give you thanks for your entended present but have not yet received it. Since I received yours I have received a letter from Robert Cooper Lee with a Bill value one Hundred Pounds Starling, and shall dispatch his orders with care please to give my suitable respects to him and Joey and Lett him know I have received Letter and Bill. Now to the great poynt in hand that is your Sister which I find is your care and have been mine Sum time poor Garle She have not citled all together so well as I could wish and I finding She had nobody to Look on her her grand mother give her up, but I considered her Age and how Left to a wide world have taken all the care in me Lies and now she's become a woman of good Sense and behaver. She is at a Kindmans of my at Dines Hall in Essex are very Good and Sober Familey who by my privet direction care great care of her but now to the matter in hand. Since she have been there one Mr Morley who Live about one mile from my Kindman have taken a Liken to her who is a very Sober man and a Brewer and a man about £150 a year who have been with me and I want down to see how the afaire ware and I found all things right. So if you will give her £500 pounds he will have her which will be a great Match for her if this is not complyed with I dread the consiquance and faire will undoe all I have been doing for there is a great respect I think of both sides. Sir you are to answer [?] She will cost you £30 a year and this will take of our Great Care from you if it dose not suite you to Lay all the money down Send me your Bond and I'll Lend you £200 till it suite you to pay me. I have had a great care of her so shall be glad to see the Good afacts of it. Your answer is required directly. Sir I am desired by acquaintances of Mr Fuller's to writ to Mr Fuller every opportunity you have I hope you will excuse my Freddom who wish you as well as myself. Thomas Atkins have been dead about 3 months my son John Marlton have been dead about a week. Excuse all you find a Miss wee all Joyn with Suitable respects to all Yours always to command Thomas Marlton.

The offer that Thomas Marlton had received for Charlotte was a good one. It may seem very cold-blooded to us now that John Morley required a dowry of £500 before he would marry her, but it has to be recognised that a young girl with few friends or relations in England and no money was not a very marriageable prospect.

John Morley was the grandson of 'Butcher Morley' of Halstead in Essex who had been a land jobber for the Earl of Oxford, and was said to have earned £10,000 for arranging his marriage. Butcher Morley always acknowledged his humble origins and made a point once a year of killing a pig in a Halstead marketplace. The house where he was born at 11 Chapel Hill in Halstead still exists, as does the rather grander Blue Bridge house. On his death he left considerable property to his large family, and his younger son Edward received 'all my goods and chattels which shall at the time of my decease be in or about the Messuage or Tenement Malting Office Outhouses Yards Gardens therunto belonging in Little Maplestead in the said County called Starch House'. It was this property that had passed to John Morley and formed the basis of his marriage proposal Charlotte. His supposed income of £150 a year was not a huge fortune but was more than respectable, equivalent today to £251,000 relative to average earnings. With Thomas Marlton offering to lend the money for the dowry if the Lee brothers could not immediately provide it there was no obstacle in the way of Charlotte's marriage.

John meanwhile, unaware as yet of his sister's improved prospects, was busily engaged on behalf of Rose Fuller. He was struggling with familiar problems, trying to find ships in which to transport the sugar to England at a reasonable cost, and chasing up debts owed to his employer.

John Lee to Rose Fuller[69]

Spanish Town, 24th July 1756

Honoured Sir,

I wrote to you on 30th June last since which have not been favoured with any of yours, I have endeavoured to get freight for your Sugars but could not prevail on any Captain to take less than ten shillings which is a Sum

[69] ESRO: SAS-RF/21/52

Mr Ellis would not give and therefore your Sugars still remain here. I shall use my Endeavours to procure freight for them as soon as possible at the same rate as the Ships have taken at Old Harbour and the other Ports, which is seven shillings and sixpence, I hope we shall have a sufficient number of Vessells here next year to carry away the Sugars for I assure you, Sir, it is entirely owing to the scarcity of Ships that the Captains have made so extravagant demands for Freight.

Mr Lamb promises a Payment immediately, I shall not fail to call upon him for it next week.

Inclosed I send you Mr William Browne's letter to Mrs Rose[70], by order of Mr Alpress, you will perceive by it his Reasons for not continuing here. Mr Ellis will write you, I believe, about Mr Siddall who went in the *Hinde* Man of War with Browne.

I have again applyed to Mr Fearon and hope he will make you a Payment this year of twenty hogsheads of Sugar in part of his Interest money, and the rest of your money I shall endeavour to get in as fast as possible, I have wrote to Mr Dunbar but had no answer, I can get nothing from Hewitt therefore must press him agreeable to your directions.

I think you need to be under no apprehensions about Mrs Greenlees who seems to be quite easy about her suit, it stands referred still to Mr Ducommun but they are quite dormant in the matter and I doubt not but she will soon have her Bill dismissed for want of Proceedings.

The Land over the River is run out for Johnny who is very well as soon as my Brother gives me the Bill of Sale I shall forward it to you to be executed. I am with the greatest Respect Honoured Sir

Your most obedient and most obliged humble Servant John Lee.

Charlotte wrote now from Dynes Hall near Maplestead where she had been staying with relations of Thomas Marlton, having left her previous location when Mrs Bridges' increasing family and consequent lack of space forced a move.

70 William Browne was desperate to return to England for the sake of his health and had written to Mary Rose begging that he should not be prevented from doing so. - William Browne, *Albinia*, to Mrs Mary Rose, Spanish Town ESRO SAS-RF/21/53

Mary Charlotte Lee to Robert Cooper Lee

Deans Hall Mapplestead, 3rd August 1756

My Dear Brother,

I received your kind letter dated May the 1 with very great pleasure and am greatly obligd to you for your kindly expressing so much regard for my wellfair and happiness which you have from your most tender years testified to me by all your actions in the most affectionate manner. I cannot help taking notice of your kindness in that part of your Letter whering you mention an affair that I have intirely got over some time but your tender exprestions and good advice give me a fresh proof of your Love and regard and I do assure you my dear brother that poverty nor the realist distress that cold befall me cold be capable of making the guilty of an action inconsistent with virtue and honour and I cold submit to the Lowest station of Life rather than bring a disgrace and stain on my family and hope I never shall give you any reason by my conduct to make you repent your indulgence nor act unworthy of being your sister. By this time I make no doubt you have receivd information of my removal and situation so I write you word very fully on that head Last [time?] And I daresay you have been informd before by my Brother John [torn] Uncle Marlton and I wrote so in June last concerning an offer that has been made me which I shall give you a full account of. At my first coming to Deans Hall I became acquainted with the young gentleman a common brewer farmer and grazer of good family fortune and unblemished carricter who immediately professed a regard for me. I for some time gave very little attention to what he said till I was convincd by his behaviour and the extrem good carricter he bore he was a man of too much honour to make any of them proposals if he was not in ernist. I then acquainted him with my affairs and withall that I would keep up no such correspondence without my uncles knowledg he immediately went to London to my uncle who promisd to be down in a short time which he accordingly was and was so kind to enquire about him and found him to be a man [illegible] great [illegible] by all who knowd him when my uncle found it was so greatly to my advantage he promisd to promote it all in his power by writing to my Brother and acquainting him with Mr Morley's proposals and the very great advantage it would be to me cold he without injuring himself comply with what was promised and I flatter myself my dear brother you would do all your powers for me in this affair as I am convinced of the Love and tenderness you have for me so am certine you would be glad to have me so advantageously and happily setled as I assure you if so happy an event can be Brought to pass I make no doubt I shall be extremely so and as I think soberity and good sence is to be preferred before anything in a companion for life and which I assure you he is possest of in a very great degree as twas his merit [illegible] that. . .

The remainder of this letter is missing but it is clear that Charlotte was in favour of the match and thought John Morley would make a good husband. A marriage Licence dated the 28th of September 1756, and a marriage bond for £200 signed by John Morley and Thomas Marlton made possible the wedding which took place at Great Maplestead on the 30th of September 1756. Charlotte had not been told about the bride price of £500 paid by her brothers and did not find out about it for some time. Jack and Bob had gone to some trouble to raise the money and Uncle Thomas Marlton had done everything he could to further her happiness.

The same month that Charlotte was writing to Bob about her impending wedding Sophia Sayer replied to a letter from him.

Sophia Sayer to Robert Cooper Lee

London, 19th August 1756

Dear Cousin,

I am much obliged to you for your kind letter and hope you will excuse my long silence, which by the way is not very common in Woman, and I promised amend for the future as oppertunity offers.

I give you joy of your settlement in Business and heartily wish you good success and the continuance of Good Dr Fuller's favours to you. I find by your writeing we must have no thought of seeing you in England, as indeed it would be unkind to wish it, it being out of every bodys power here to put you in the like good situation as you now enjoy, and God knows your relations dwindle away so fast here in England that it is but poor encouragement for you to run the hazard of the seas, tho I think we have one chance of seeing you, and that is your Sisters marrying which perhaps may demand a visit from one of you. I fancy from the size of your stocking you are a good deal grown and therefore much altered.

I wish I could entertain you with some agreeable news, but really its not in my powers, my Mother has given you an account of the death of my poor Brother so shall not detain you on so dismall a subject only to tell you the sorrow is changed from a living to a dead one.

I thank God Mr Sayer Self and little Boy enjoy a good state of health, and joyn in kind love to you all, and assure your self I ever shall be glad to hear of your wellfares, which concludes me Dear Sir

Your Affectionate Cousin Sophia Sayer.

PS please to direct for us at my Fathers in St Johns Lane Clerkenwell

The loss of Sophia's brother John Marlton was a considerable one. Her father had lost his only surviving son and heir, and the family had lost a young man of considerable courage and energy. Six years previously, at the age of nineteen, John Marlton had been riding to Oxford when he was held up at gunpoint by a highwayman and robbed of his money and his watch. He rode after the highwayman, who fired at him but missed, and tackling him hand-to-hand John overcame him and took him into custody. The *Derby Mercury* of the 15th of February 1750 reported that the highwayman was being held in Reading jail.

Sophia and John Sayer had been married in 1745 but their son James, the baby referred to in this letter and the first which seems to be recorded, was not born until ten years later after which they had seven more children, the youngest of whom was born in 1765, the year in which John Sayer went bankrupt.

Evidence of the rapid progress that Robert Cooper Lee was making in his legal career, now aged twenty-one and having served his articles, comes in a letter from Rose Fuller addressed to Mr Robert Cooper Lee Attorney at Law and written from his Sussex estate at Rosehill.

Rose Fuller to Robert Cooper Lee

Rosehill, 17th September 1756

Sir,

The Bearer Mr Gordon[71] is a Gentleman bred to the Business of an Attorney and proposes to practice as such in your Island, he hath been recommended to me by Mr Oswald of the Board of Trade, as a very

---

[71] The brother of John Gordon, an indigo planter of Greencastle in the parish of St Ann. It has not been possible to identify which branch of the Gordon family they came from.

honest man and knowing in his way and such I do not doubt you will find him I take the liberty of introducing him to your acquaintance and ham(sic) Sir

your most Obedient Humble Servant Rose Fuller.

John Lee to Rose Fuller[72]

Spanish Town Jamaica, 21st December 1756

Honoured Sir,

I wrote to you on the 14th November last since which have not been favoured with any of yours no Vessell having arrived from London.

Agreeable to what I wrote you I have been under a necessity of drawing in favour of Mr Kay for two hundred Pounds Sterling there being upwards of that Sum due to him for Salary and Disbursements and he alledges you promised to pay him in England. I have been also obliged to draw in favour of Mr Straton for one hundred and eighty Pounds Sterling in order to pay Mr Harvie's. I imagined they had been paid the Beginning of the Crop by Mr Straton to whom I sent the Hoghole Sugars for that purpose, but to my great surprize he wrote to me the other day that the Harvies had refused to take Sugars and insisted on Cash which it was impossible to raise and desird me to send him Bills for the above Sum, I did not chuse to do it but being pressed both by him and the Harvies very much I was obliged at last to comply, at which I hope you will not be offended as it was out of my Power to comply with their Demand in any other manner. You may be assured Sir, that this is the last Trouble you will have of the kind.

I have by this opportunity sent Messers Thomas and Stephen Fuller Invoice and Bill of Lading for twelve hogsheads of your Knollis Sugar, signed them on your account in the *Cranston,* Captain Rutherford, on whom I advised you some time agoe that you would have that quantity that you might insure if you judged necessary, I hope they will arrive to a good market. The Scarcity of Vessells this year has been the sole reason that your Crop was not shipt you much earlier. I hope the ensuing year that you will engage freight on board of Vessells Sufficient to get your Sugars home in much better time. There have been two or three

[72] ESRO: SAS-RF/21/90

Meetings here of the Principal Shippers in order to fix the Freight for the ensuing year but nothing has as yet been agreed upon, nor I believe will be till after the Arrival of the Fleet from England about whom the People here are in great Pain fearing that they may have been taken, especially as we have advice of four French ships of Force cruizing off Cape Tiberon in order to intercept them.

We have been a good deal harassed with Marshall Law which has been in force from 6th of November last till yesterday, the Fatigue[73] has given me a very severe fit of Sickness of which I am just on the Recovery.

Mr Manning[74] is dead and has left Mr Spencer[75], Mr Paplay[76] (and I hear Mr Hume[77]) his Executors, so we must file a Bill of Revivor for Recovery of Tyndall's Debt which will be done as soon as possible.

Every thing both that your Estates and Penn are well, your Negroes in good health and you have a very good Prospect of the ensuing Crop.

I hope soon to hear from you and am with the utmost Respect Honoured Sir

Your most obedient and most obliged humble Servant Jno Lee

John Lee to Rose Fuller[78]

Jamaica, 15th March 1757

Honoured Sir,

I take this opportunity to advise you that you will have fifty hogsheads of Sugar shipt you in the *Britannia,* Captain Lundin, I wrote you on the seventh to which have nothing to add but my best wishes for your Health and am Honoured Sir

Your most obedient and most obliged humble Servant John Lee.

---

73 Probably a recurring bout of malaria.

74 Edward Manning died 6th December 1756 aged forty-six. He held over 6000 acres of land in Jamaica. He had married Elizabeth Moore from whom he was divorced by special Act of the Jamaican Assembly in 1739 because of her affair with Ballard Beckford.

75 Charles Spencer, a Kingston Merchant and Justice of the Peace for Kingston

76 George Paplay was a Kingston Merchant who died about 1769.

77 Benjamin Hume, a Kingston Merchant, Privy Councillor and Custos for Port Royal.

78 ESRO: SAS-RF/21/97

Two copies of this note were sent and received in London, one went on the Royal Navy ship the *Biddeford*, and the other on the *Duke* packet with Captain Dillon.

In England the newly married Charlotte was discovering that she enjoyed a considerable change in her status in Essex society. Having become part of a family with a good name locally she had suddenly acquired a raft of new friends, relations and acquaintances.

Mary Charlotte Morley to Robert Cooper Lee

Starch house Mapplested, 28th April 1757

My Dear Brother,

I have nothing from you since My Last of June but notwithstanding could not any longer forbear troubling you with a Line as I am assure you nothing affords me greater pleasure than writing and hearing from you which beg you will pleasure me with oftener for the future and I am sure I will not be behind hand in answering them as I am sure no sister can Love and prize Brother more nor none ever yet had so great reason the convincing proofs you have given me of your tenderness and the great regaird you have for my wellfair makes me certine it will give you pleasure to hear I am so happyly and so advantageously married which make no doubt you have been informed off before now by our Brother Jackys Letter, as I am certine I never imagined so happy station would ever have fallen to my Lot, tho was determind never to allter my condition unless I had a prospect of Living in a pretty maner, but could never have thought to be setled in the manner I am. Besides the happy alteration in my curcumstances I have the pleasure to have the friendship of my relations which gives me more satisfaction than I am able to express. Mr Morley's relations likewise behave with the greatest civility immediately visited me and treat me as a relation of their own. Nay even those very people that shund me and took advantage of my helpless situation now [illegible] me and court my acquaintance such is the way of the way of (sic) the wourld and so difficult it is to find a friend in need but how than can I prize those enough who when I was destitut of all wourldly comforts shewd more Love and tenderness than ever for me you might Dear Brother was one of those friends whose kindness and goodness has been unpairald and for which I shall always think on with the greatest gratatud. Mr Morley desires his Love to you and hopes one day to have the happiness of knowing you, which is the only thing I want to make my happiness compleat. I hope my dear Brother you will excuse all faults in my writing as I am a Little in hast being agoing to London to morrow and am not willing to Lose the oppertunity of puting the letters in the coffe house. But belive me my Dear Brother I am with the greatest esteem

Your truly affectionate Sister Mary Charlotte Morley.

It was nearly another year before Charlotte wrote to her brothers, having by then discovered the extent of her financial obligation to them. By this time she had given birth to a daughter, named after her, and as usual her letter was full of news of family and friends.

Mary Charlotte Morley to Robert Cooper Lee

Mapplested Essex, 13th February 1758

My Dear Brother,

My Last Letter to you was of april Last since which I have received your kind favour of 20 of January. In my Last Letter to you I informd you that I was marrid to Mr Morley but at that time did not know my obligations to you was so great as I have since found from my uncles Letter and from yours to me in regaird to the same, you gave on my marrige so great a proof of the sincerity of your regaird is hardly to be paralleld and clames my utmost Love and tender gratutud as belive me my Dear Brother it is beyound what ever I could have expected or even desired of you, and it is not without regret that I am obliged at you for selling out, to take from you so greatly and indeed the obligations I lay under to you is so great that my whole Life will be too short to discharge them. I can only say your goodness has made me compleatly happy and I desire nothing more in this wourld than the inexpressible pleasure of once more seeing you again which I most sincerely hope and ardently pray for and Live in hopes that in a few years you will be able to return to England to the pleasure of those who know you and to the joy of your sister who can not express how dear you are to her.

In one of your Letters you desired me to inform you of our relations and acquaintance but at that time was not able to give you a very perfect account, but when I was in London Last April I had the pleasure of seeing several of our old acquaintance. Mr Causton's family in particular who received me with the greatest markes of friendship inquired very much after you and my Brothers and expresd great pleasure at my being so happily setled. I see all the family but Miss Polly who was at Bath and am told she is a very fine young lady. Mr Charles Causton is an extreme sober young gentleman. Miss Causton is quite an aimable young Lady and Miss Doshe is grown a fine girl. All our relations are in perfect health but poor Mrs Atkins who has lately Lost the use of one side of her with the dead palsey from which it is feard she can never be cured. Mrs Sayer has got a fine son and daughter and soon Lays in again. I have the pleasure to acquant you Likewise that I have happily increast my famuly and have got a Little girl which my uncle and ant did me the favour to stand for. She is of my name and is indeed a sweet Little creature and I often please myself with the thoughts that she is Like her dear uncle I then imbrace her with a double tenderness and fondly wish I cold see the dear resemblance. It gives me great concern to hear by my Brother Jackys Letter of your illness. I hope before this time you are perfectly recovered and that I shall soon have the happiness of a Letter from you I am afraid I shall tire your patience with my Long Letter and so will conclud with my sincere wishes for your health and happiness and am my Dear Brother

Your most affectionate sister Mary Charlotte Morley.

Poor Charlotte, her happiness was to be short-lived. She wrote again in September of 1761, excusing the long gap in correspondence on the grounds that she had expected to see John in England, and having given birth to two more children she had been kept busy at home. It is clear from the letter that her marriage was already in trouble, both personal and financial.

Mary Charlotte Morley to John Lee

Mapplested, 6th September 1761

My Dearest Brother,

I received your kind Letter of May 25 with great pleasure and which in some measure relived the anckciety of mind I was under at not seeing you in England agreeable to your kind letter of May '60. I was frequently under the most dreedfull apprentions on your account fearing sickness or something more than ornerry had happened to you your idea was allways before me and sleeping and waking you was the chief of my thoughts. I often compared our Long separation to Joseph and his bretherin and thought our first meeting would be almost like his for near a twelvemounth I flattered myself with the most agreeable expectation of seeing you in a short time those thoughts sapported me in my most unhappiest hours and I thought the anexpresable pleasure of seeing you again would make me ample amends for all the troubles and disappointments that I threw the whole course of my Life have meet with and comforted by your kind Letter earnestly hopes that nothing will prevent your coming to England next year which is the greatest happiness I desire in the wourld and I am truly concerned to hear by your letters of the frequent indispositions you have been troubled with and ardently hope that you will for the future enjoy the most valuable blessing of health without any interruption without which wee are incapable of injoying any thing in this wourld. And that your country may be blest with peace and quietness and hope you never more will be obliged to hazard your health on any such ocation again.

It was the earnest expectation of seeing you in a short time was the reason of my not writing to you for so Long a time as indeed ashamed to own the date of my Last but hope your goodness will in some measure excuse it as I assure you it has not been owing to any un-mindfulness of you as time not any trouble of mind I can ever meet with will ever make me forget a Brother who is truly dear to me and whose uncommon goodness has left lasting impresition of gratutud on my heart and it is with unspeakable concern when I reflect that [illegible] fortune has put it out of my power to show the gratfullness of my heart to you.

I flattered myself when I first married with the pleasing ideas of having it in my power to show my dear Brother by some acknowledgement how truely senceable I was of his tenderness but was too soon deceived in this most agreeable expectation and found I was not that happy person I fondly imagined myself to be and was soon convinct I was still to be the sport of fortune. Myself was my least concern but when I reflected with how much tenderness you had strove to make me happy and had with unpaireld goodness supplyed the part of that dear father I had lost then what unuterable sorrow must it give me to wound your piece with my fresh troubles. I thought at first I would ever conceal it from you but then I thought in all probability my relations would acquaint you with it and make it worse than it realy was which was the reason that I acquanted my dear Brother Boby with it in March '59 and which I make no doubt you have heard of it so will not trouble you with the milancoly resitall. And give me leave to assure you that had it not been for my dear babies whom I then lookt on with unuterable sorrow to think they must be the innocent sufferers with me in my hard fortune otherwise as to my own part I shold have submited to it with the greatest patience as that high spirit which was ounce so great is so much brought down that I cold have been content in the Lowist station if I was to be the only sufferer. But will use my utmost indeavours not to let my spirits sink under it wighty cares and hope by the blessing of the Almighty wee shall by our industry which shall never be wanting in nithere of us we'd be enabled to make some little provision for our poor Little ones which is the utmost of my wishes.

It gives me real pleasure to hear by your Letter that you and my Brothers are so near each other and that you can so frequently enjoy each other's company I often wish with tears to see you but for one hour I shold think it the greatest happiness this wourld could afford me and hope that happy day is not far of when I shall injoy that pleasure and for some time and heartily wish it may be in your power and your inclinations when you come to England to end your day there.

The beginning of the year I flattered myself with the pleasure of seeing you mounth after mounth and got my house in readyness for you and laid fires in the romes thinking the coldness of the climat as you had not been uset to it for so many years would make you at first very tender, and am still in hopes that some of them will be there ready for the dear wellcome guest as I hope you will be so good when you arrive to take our home for your home and look upon it as your own in every respect as be assure had I never shall think I can show anough regaird and tenderness for you. But it shall be my constant study and I am sure my [illegible] inclinations to make everything as agreeable as posoble to you as shall esteem it is the happyest time that I have seen since our Long separation.

My little famuly which now consist of three children are all very well my eldest little girl Mary Charlotte is four years next November she now begins to be pretty company for me and buy her ingageing innocent prattle often diverts me many a dull hour and she frequiently talks of her uncle Lee and often asks me when you will come to see her. She desires her duty to you and all her good uncles. My other little girl Frances is three years old next February and she begins to talk any thing she stands by me and desires her dutty to you. My little boy John is two years old next April and can just begin to walk alone he is a charming little boy and it is some pleasure to me to have him of your name.

Mr Morley is very well and joins me in sincerely hopeing that nothing will prevent your happy voyage and desires me to assure you that nothing would give him more pleasure than to have the happiness of seeing you in our country. He desires to be remembered to you in the tenderest manner and accept the same My Dearest Brother from her who is with the warmist love and sincerest regaird

Your truely affectionate Sister Mary Charlotte Morley.

PS pray let me hear from you soon and Lett me know when you think I may expect to see you.

John's return trip to England had been postponed more than once, and Charlotte, busily laying the fires in every room in Starch House to keep him warm, would in fact never see him again.

John died in November 1761 and was buried in Spanish Town, without ever having received this last letter.

What the nature of Charlotte's latest troubles was we do not know exactly since her letter to her brother Bob written in March 1759 has been lost. However it is clear that by one means or another John Morley had wasted not only her £500 dowry but had also been spending beyond his means, and eventually he ended up in prison for debt.

The Starch House property should have been perfectly adequate to support the couple and their three children in comfort. It is described in some old deeds as a 'messuage formerly called Panymers, now called Starch House, with malthouse, brewhouse, barns, stables, yards, orchards, gardens and land (28 acres)'. The county of Essex was, and still is, great grain growing country, the barley providing the basic ingredient for brewing, and as ale was always in demand and was a staple drink, brewing should have provided a regular income. The straw left after the barley was threshed was used in the making of straw hats, an industry introduced by the Earl of Oxford to help the poor. John Morley's inheritance should have provided him with a good living.

It seems clear also that the marriage had broken down. Charlotte had three children in quick succession, but after the birth of her son John there were no more. It is perhaps significant that in this last letter to her brother John she refers to her son as being of his name rather than being named for his father.

Two views of Bog Walk Gorge Jamaica

Jamaica 1761-1768

There is a hiatus in the collection of letters between this last one of Charlotte's and the series written by Joseph Lee when he returned to England on an extended visit in 1768, and it seems likely that a bundle of letters has been lost. We can however fill in from other sources the events of the brothers' lives during that time.

John Lee does not appear to have left a Will, or not one that has survived, and his property would automatically have gone to his two brothers in Jamaica. He left no legitimate children, the only child of his recorded was a daughter called Mary Ann Lord baptised on the 3rd of December 1748 when he was just eighteen and before Robert Cooper Lee arrived to join him. She died the following February and there is no other record of her mother Mary Lord. The baptism did not record the colour or status of Mary Ann or her mother.

That John Lee should have fathered an illegitimate child is not at all surprising. The ratio of single white males to females in Jamaica was extremely unfavourable to the establishment of white families. The image of sexual abuse of slaves by the white colonists has probably been somewhat distorted by the extreme case of Thomas Thistlewood, who in his diaries documented every one of hundreds of couplings, consensual and otherwise, but wide abuse was endemic. For young men in a position to employ a housekeeper, the position was sometimes different. Young, free, mixed race women often became wives in all but name, and their children if acknowledged might be well provided for by their fathers when they died or left Jamaica. It can be difficult to track such children through the parish registers. Some, such as Rose Fuller's son William, were baptised and recorded under their father's surname and with both parents named. Often however only the mother was named, and sometimes only the name of the child is given. Depending on the whim of the particular vicar, colour might be recorded.

The categories of colour used in Jamaica were: Negro – a black person with two black parents of African origin, but who might have been born in Jamaica and hence referred to as a creole; Mulatto – a person with one negro and one white parent; Sambo - a person with one parent a negro and the other a mulatto, i.e one quarter white; Quadroon – the child of a white person and a mulatto, i.e. one quarter black, with one grandparent of African origin; Mustee, Mestee or Octaroon – a person who is one-eighth black i.e. with one black great grandparent; Mesteefeena – a rarely used term for the child of a white parent and a mestee. If one-sixteenth black, they were legally regarded as white and free.

These distinctions would in due course have personal significance for Robert Cooper Lee, Joseph Lee and their children, for in 1761 the Jamaican Assembly passed an Act (ratified in London the following year) entitled 'An act to prevent the inconveniences arising from exorbitant grants and devises, made by white persons to negroes, and the issue of negroes; and to restrain and limit such grants and devises'. Basically this restricted the amount that a white person could give a negro, mulatto or illegitimate person to £2000. Norwood Witter, Edward Clarke and William Wynter lodged an objection on the grounds that

As it seems to oppress a quiet and peaceable people who have ever shown themselves true and faithful to the White Inhabitants, and some of whom were employed under an Express Act of the Legislature of this Island in the suppressing of the late Rebellion of the Slaves, We think it unreasonable.

As we apprehend it lays the Penalty on the innocent, We deem it severe

As we apprehend it tends to depopulate the Country, it is impolitic

As we apprehend it takes away the Right of Free Born Britons, it is unconstitutional

And as it lays a restraint on the parental affection it is unnatural

And on the whole we think it equally Inconsistent with Liberty, sound Policy, and pure Religion[79].

but their objection was unsuccessful. Thereafter, until the Act was repealed, any rich white man wishing to leave a substantial inheritance to his children would have to petition the Assembly.

Joseph Lee fathered a mulatto son called William Brown of whom nothing further is known, and one of the Lee brothers may have been the father of Charles Rose Lee baptised in Spanish Town in 1757 and buried the following year, described variously as a quadroon and a mulatto.

By the late 1760s however both Robert Cooper Lee and Joseph had set up home on a more permanent basis with free mixed race women, Joseph with Sarah Lewis and Robert Cooper Lee with Priscilla Kelly

Priscilla Kelly's origins are obscure. Family tradition[80] had it that she was the illegitimate daughter of Dennis Kelly, who was Chief Justice of

[79] ESRO: SAS/RF 20/66

[80] Gamble, Audrey Nona, *A History of the Bevan Family*, p.67.

Jamaica in 1742 and owner of over 4000 acres there in 1754. He and four of his brothers had come to Jamaica in the first part of the eighteenth century, Dennis Kelly being the only one to survive to go home to Ireland. He had married Priscilla Halstead, who died leaving one legitimate daughter Elizabeth who was about five years older than Priscilla. When Dennis Kelly died in 1758 he left £500 Jamaican Currency[81] in his Will for a daughter in Jamaica called Margaret Wright, who was born in Kingston in October 1738. Her Jamaican trustees were Matthew Gregory and Rose Fuller and she was to receive the money at the age of eighteen, her education and maintenance being provided for till then. She may indeed have lived in Rose Fuller's household, since the 1754 census of Spanish Town recorded that four free negroes or mulattoes lived in his house. As Priscilla Kelly was said to have been born in October 1738 it is plausible to assume that she and Margaret Wright may have been one and the same. In the baptism record for one of her children Priscilla herself is described as a quadroon, but her children are described variously as 'a quadroon', 'a white illegitimate child', and illegitimate. The significance of this will become apparent in due course.

In the period between John's death and Joseph's trip home in 1768 the two surviving Lee brothers became well established in Spanish Town society and in their careers. That Robert Cooper Lee in particular had become a respected island attorney is evidenced in the letters of Simon Taylor, agent to Chaloner Arcedeckne, and one of the island's most prominent citizens. In 1767 he wrote 'Dr McGlashan has brought an Action on your Father's Administration Bond against you. Dr Gregory sent it to your Mother who sent it to Robert Cooper Lee as your Sollicitor. I think she was very right in applying to Lee in preference to McCulloch and Wharton for he is infinitely cleverer than they. . .' [82]. In 1764 Robert Cooper Lee was appointed Crown Solicitor for Jamaica, and he was acting in a variety of legal matters for many of the most wealthy Jamaican planters. He was also investing in property on his own behalf. He and his brother Joseph were in partnership with the Scot John Allen who was also working as an island attorney. Other close friends included Richard Welch, who in 1768 was Jamaica's Attorney General; Scudamore

---

81 In 1774 Edward Long gave the currency conversion rate as £1 Sterling = £1.8s Jamaican.

82 Betty Wood and Martin Lynn, eds., *Travel, Trade and Power in the Atlantic 1765-1884*, Camden Miscellany XXXV, Camden fifth series volume 19, Cambridge University Press 2002, p.38.

Winde, a wealthy Kingston merchant; and Thomas Wynter, son of Mary Johnston Rose.

Although life in Spanish Town where the Lee brothers lived was generally peaceful an example of the risks faced by white settlers, hugely outnumbered by their slaves, came with Tacky's Rebellion in 1760, and then in November 1765 Simon Taylor wrote to Chaloner Arcedeckne.

'We about a fortnight ago had an Alarm of a Rebellion in St Marys when Matt. Byndloss[83] and my Overseer were both murdered by a parcel of new negroes belonging to the Overseer of Whitehall and Ballards Valley, who about two o'Clock in the morning on the 25 of November last sat fire to the Trash houses of Whitehall on which the Overseer ran down there in his Shirt to endeavour to putt out the fire and ordered a Boy to bring him his horse. Matt Byndloss and Ballard Beckford's widow who were in the House got both up on the alarm of fire soon as which fourteen or 15 Coromantees broke into the house and killed Byndloss. Mrs Beckford saved herself by running down to the works whence she got among the canes and was carried to Nonesuch where Bayly[84] happened to be.'[85]

The Coromantees had the reputation of being the most warlike of the Africans and the incident was apparently triggered by some newly arrived slaves who had anticipated an impending uprising. They were hunted down and five killed themselves rather than face capture, while three others were killed and one who was captured gave evidence against the plotters. The whole incident illustrates the constant threat, perceived and real, faced by the white population and the divisions among the slaves, some of whom preferred status quo and the possibility of manumission if they helped their white masters, and others who wanted to rise up against them.

Life for the white settlers could be physically tough as well and both Robert Cooper Lee and Joseph had to travel around the mountainous island, collecting legal papers, obtaining signatures and supervising the probate of estates. Roads were bad or all but non existent and fords often dangerous or impassable. In June 1766 the newly married wife of Cholmondeley Dering was drowned returning from Spanish Town to

[83] Matthew Byndloss b. 1721, came from a Sussex family that had arrived in Jamaica with the first settlers.

[84] Zachary Bayly, uncle of the historian Bryan Edwards, was the owner of Nonesuch.

[85] Wood and Lynn, op.cit., p.29.

Withywood, and in 1816 Samuel Risby Whitehorne was drowned fording the Rio Magno on his way to attend the Assembly in Spanish Town.

During the sitting of the Assembly in Spanish Town planters travelled in from their estates to meet, attend the Assembly and to socialise. There were horse racing, theatre, concerts and balls to attend, and the period when the Lees were in Jamaica also saw a building boom in Spanish Town as it created the civic buildings that befitted an island capital, and were designed to ensure its continuing supremacy over Kingston.

An Archives building had been constructed in the 1740s. Set around a large open square, by the 1760s other new buildings housed offices for the Island Secretary, the Provost Marshall, the Registrar of the Court of Chancery and the Clerks of the Court and the Grand Court[86]. These were all people with whom the Lee brothers would have had regular contact. Spanish Town also had a garrison presence for defence against external threats from the enemy of the moment or internal uprisings of slaves. This force could be bolstered by the declaration of Martial Law which closed the Law Courts and required every able bodied man between sixteen and sixty to bear arms. Although there is mention of Martial Law in the Lee letters there is no indication they ever had to bear arms or ever directly experienced slave uprising.

---

[86] James Robertson, *Gone is the Ancient Glory*, pp.105-6.

Civic Buildings in Spanish Town 1774 (from Long's *History of Jamaica*)

The trip home – Joseph Lee 1768-70

There are a numerous records of Jamaican colonists leaving the Island in the hope of improving their health - many did not make it. Of the eight children of the Rev William May, Rector of Kingston, only one lived to grow up. A memorial in Kingston records his

SIX SONS AND TWO DAUGHTERS, FIVE OF WHICH ARE ENTERRED UNDER THIS STONE, VIZ. PETER,WILLIAM, ELIZABETH, GEORGE, AND ITHAMAR. TWO DIED AT SEA GOING TO BOSTON FOR YE RECOVERY OF THEIR HEALTH, VIZ. RICHARD, ON YE 28'th OF AUGUST, 1745, IN YE 21st YEAR OF HIS AGE, AND FLORENTIUS, YE 4th OF JUNE,1747, IN YE 16th YEAR OF HIS AGE. HIS SON, ROSE HERRING MAY, IS THE ONLY CHILD THAT SURVIVED HIM.

Adults did not fare much better, and many suffered from recurring bouts of malaria. With sudden death an ever present threat to the white colonists of Jamaica, and with his brother John's death in mind, Joseph Lee quit the island in haste in April 1768.

He left behind him his companion and housekeeper Sarah Lewis and two young sons, John who had been born about 1765 and William Robert born about 1767. Sarah, often referred to as Miss Sally, was a free mulatto who was only about seventeen when John was born.

Robert Cooper Lee and Priscilla Kelly's first child Frances was born in October 1758, and their first son John in September 1761. It was around the time of John's birth that the household was joined by Elizabeth Harrison, who probably came to the family as nursemaid at the age of about eleven. She remained an integral part of the family until her death nearly sixty years later. Robert Cooper Lee junior was born in 1763 and Richard in 1765. Sadly little John died in May 1764, and there may have been two more children who died before they could be baptised, as there is then a gap of five years until the birth of Matthew Allen Lee in 1771. Frances Lee was sent to school in England some time before Joseph left Jamaica, placed in Russell House School at Streatham, run by Mrs Eveleigh and her sisters.

So when Joseph departed the island in such haste he left behind him in Jamaica two growing families and a brother who had become an important member of the Jamaican establishment.

Joseph Lee to Robert Cooper Lee

St George in Bermuda, 2nd May 1768

My Dear Brother,

I embrace the Opportunity that now offers of writing to you, I hope yourself and your little ones are in as good a State of health as when I left you, a Confirmation of which under your hand will give me the most agreeable satisfaction, and my warmest wishes attend you for a Continuance of it.

You will with reason be amazed at our being in this part of the world, the reason of which is this, Captain Bickerton has been Indisposed with a disorder of the Bowells almost ever since he left Jamaica, which increased so much as to oblige him to put into these Islands where we have been for a week past. Captain Bickerton has now got the better of his disorder so that we shall proceed on our Voyage in a few days.

For myself I recovered very much by the Voyage from Jamaica here altho' not so as to be perfectly well, but I have found great benefit by being ashore on this Island for this week past. It being now their Spring the Climate it is extremely agreeable being a happy medium between the extremes of heat and Cold and I have taken what exercise on horseback I could Since I have been here, but the Island where I am and where the Capital Town is is very small and does not afford a ride of more than 14 miles, indeed all the Islands here which constitute the Bermuda's or Somers Islands do not as I am informed contain more than twelve thousand acres of Land so that you may Judge the Smallness of their extent.

I beg you will present my Compliments to Mr Welch[87] and Mr Winde[88] and all friends and give my little ones a kiss for me. Adieu my Dear Sir and believe me to be

Your most faithfull and affectionate Brother Joseph Lee.

---

[87] Richard Welch, barrister and later Chief Justice of Jamaica (1779) and a member of Council, married Lucretia Dehany in Spanish Town, 23 January 1769.

[88] Ambrose Scudamore Winde. He seems to have dropped the Ambrose from his name quite early. He had come to Jamaica with his brother Robert on the death of their father (John Winde c.1692-1759) who probably already had connections with Jamaica. Scudamore's sister Maria Scudamore Winde married Gershom Williams in Kingston in 1755. Nothing more is known of Robert, but Scudamore Winde made a considerable fortune as a merchant in Kingston, and was a close friend of the Lee family.

As the next letter was written from Streatham it appears that Joseph had gone immediately to stay with Thomas Fuller and his wife Eleanor. Among their near neighbours were Hester Thrale and her husband, whose daughters attended Russell House School and whose regular visitors included Dr Johnson and later the young Fanny Burney[89].

Joseph Lee to Robert Cooper Lee

Streatham, 3rd July 1768

My Dear Brother,

During my Stay at Bermuda I wrote you two letters which I hope you have received. We sailed from there the 28th of May and on the twenty seventh of June we arrived att Portsmouth, the next day I got to Mr Tubb's[90] where I was received with the utmost joy for from the length of time that the Ship had Sailed from Jamaica they concluded that we were lost.

On Thursday I went to see my Uncle and Aunt they live att [Stoke] Newington and were overjoyed to see me, poor Mr Sayer has been dead about three months and has left six Children so that the Circumstances of that family are rather unhappy and my Uncle has the chief of them with him. On Friday I came down here with Mr Thomas Fuller to see your finest little daughter, she is admirably improved so that she really amazed me, upon my seeing her first I talked with her sometime to see if she could discover who I was but she did not know me. She is inclined to be fatt and in extreme good health. I have been over at the School where everything is in the utmost Order and regularity – Mrs Eveleigh has two Sisters who keep the School with her and they are all Women of the most amiable disposition. Mr Fuller and myself have been all over the School I saw the Beds and other accommodations which are all with the greatest neatness and Elegance. Fanny is now with me and desires me she present

---

89 Fanny Burney described Stephen Fuller as a 'sensible but deaf old Gentleman'. Hester Thrale's son was a close friend of Thomas Fuller's sons.

90 Marchant Tubb was a surgeon who had been born in Bath, and practised in Jamaica where he married Ann Anderson the widow successively of Stephen Morant and Samuel Wheeler. He had returned to England with his wife and stepdaughter Mary Powell Morant sometime before 1768.

her duty to yourself and her Mamma and she has promised me to answer your own and her Brothers letters in a short time. I shall stay here tomorrow in order to see my pretty Neice dance, that being one of the days the dancing Master comes to the School.

Mr Stephen Fuller is down at Rose Hill so that I have not yet had the pleasure of seeing him, I propose going there when I have seen my Sister and a few other persons. I have nothing of News to write you. Mr Wilkes[91] is the Chief Subject here, about which you have already heard every thing I apprehend long since.

I was greatly recovered whilst I stayed at Bermuda and when I came onshore here was very hearty, my time has not permitted me to consult the Faculty yet, but I shall do so in a day or two. Mr Fuller tells me he has got a letter at his Compting house for me from you but I have not yet seen it. I Long impatiently my Dear Brother to hear from you, for during the time I am absent from you nothing can give me more pleasure than to hear of you and your little ones.

Your Memorandum I will send you by the first Opportunity – pray remember me to Miss Prissy – give Bob and Dick a kiss for me. Pray let me know how my matters are going on. I beg my best respects to all my Freinds, my haste now prevents me writing more – how are my little ones I recommend them to your kind Observation – the length of my letter is I am afraid too long I will concluded by wishing you every degree of health and Felicity that you can possibly enjoy. Mr Tubbs family, my Uncle and Aunt and Mr and Mrs Fuller desire to be remembered to you in the strongest manner I am My Dear Sir,

Your most faithfull and Affectionate Brother Joseph Lee.

Joseph Lee to Robert Cooper Lee

London, 27th July 1768

My Dear Brother,

When I wrote you last under date of the third Instant I was then in great hast as the Vessell that carried it was upon the point of Sailing, in that letter I mentioned that I had had the pleasure of seeing your Daughter Miss Fanny and the day following I went to see her dance which I really

[91] John Wilkes (1725-97) radical politician and supporter of American independence.

think she performs to great perfection for her age, some of the other young Ladies at the School learn Music and drawing and upon talking to my Niece she seems very desirous to learn those Sciences (some at the same School who are as she informs me younger than her being taught them) I therefore when I waited on Mrs Brett[92] took the liberty of mentioning it to her but she was quite averse to the matter and informed me that she did not think it then necessary – I only mentioned it from the Warmth of my affection for you and I beg you will impute it to that cause only. The School I am informed by both Mr Thomas and Mr Stephen Fuller is a very good one and Mrs Fuller is extremely fond of my Niece.

My Sister hearing of the arrival of the Ship came up to Town so that I had the pleasure of seeing her here, she is in very good health and desires to be remembered to you in the tenderest manner. I have conversed with her in respect to her affairs in the cause of which I have pressed her to be very explicit. I found her about Fifty pounds behind hand of which she gave me an Account and I gave her money to discharge it. She seems to discover no inclination but rather an Aversion to Cohabit again with her Husband, he is out of Goal and upon a small farm near his former residence, my Uncle when he found he would not pay the Debt having released him, his affairs are not made up yet but are still standing against him, and from the disposition of my Sister I thought it almost needless to enquire about them. I have not yet seen the Children as my Sisters coming up prevented my going down to them but shall soon go there – the Son I propose (with the Approbation of my Sister) to send to School in Yorkshire where people who have some Substance are sometimes sent, the expense will be the fitting him out with Cloaths at first and paying ten pounds annually while he continues there for his Cloathing Diet and Education, at this School he will be taught Latin French Writing and Accounts which will qualify him to be put to some business or other when he is of a proper age and in any other part of England such an Education would be very expensive. In respect to the Daughters my Sister is desirous that they should be put out to some Boarding School, I have therefore left the Choice of that to herself and my Uncle and Aunt, and by this means my Sister will have little or no trouble left on her own hands, and I hope will then enjoy the Calm of Mind and happy Contentment to which she appears to have been so long a Stranger.

---

92 Probably the wife of Captain Brett whose ships the *Rose*, and later the *Judith*, were regulars on the Jamaica run. Frances may have been sent to England in his charge as Mrs Brett seems to have had some say in her education.

I have mentioned all this my dear Brother as the first things which have arrived upon the Interview with my Sister and shall be happy to have your Opinion and advise concerning it.

A few days since I went down to Rose Hill and saw Mr Fuller with whom I stayed at Week and am to go down again in a short time and make a longer stay. Mr Fuller received me in the kindest manner and expressed great joy at seeing me, a parent I am persuaded could not show more, he enquired very particularly after you, he is in very good health although he bears the marks of age but in every other respect he's exactly the same person as when he was in Jamaica, and is now as busily employed in the sowing of Turnips, raising of Corn and improving his Land here, as he was formerly in the planting of Sugar canes in Jamaica.

You have I suppose already heard the Decision in Hall and Laing[93]. I was in Town and attended the hearing – the Arguments were long, the two Law Lords Wilmot[94] and Sewell[95] were against you and it was owing to Lord Hillsborough[96] entirely that the Determination was in your favour.

Miss Fanny has been in Town with Mr and Mrs Davison for three or four days this Week so that you will have the pleasure of receiving from him a particular Account of the young Lady – inclosed is a letter from her to yourself and her Brother.

I have seen Captain Edwardes since he arrived and it gave me great pleasure to hear from him that he left you in good health. Captain Lee[97] I have seen several times he is extremely well and desires his Compliments to you. By Captain Kitchen who will sail in three or four Weeks I will send the several things mentioned in your Memorandum.

---

[93] Probably Jasper Hall and Malcolm Laing. Jasper Hall was a Jamaica Merchant and plantation owner who died in 1798. The Hector's River Estate was purchased in 1765 by Jasper Hall Esq., who was Receiver General and Speaker of the House of Assembly in 1778. Malcolm Laing was the agent in Jamaica for William Perrin and subsequently his son William Philp Perrin.

[94] Sir John Eardley Wilmot (1709-92), Chief Justice of the Common Pleas 1766-71.

[95] Sir Thomas Sewell (c.1710-84)

[96] Wills Hill, 1st Marquess of Downshire, Earl of Hillsborough, Secretary of State for the Colonies (1768-72)

[97] Captain William Lee seems to have been a regular on the Jamaica run but nothing else is known of him.

Two days ago I went to see Mrs Venn[98] she is in very good health, her two oldest Daughters were with her, they are amazingly grown. [The remainder of this letter is missing.]

Joseph Lee to Robert Cooper Lee

London, 7th August 1768

My Dear Brother,

I have already wrote you by Mr Davison[99], but having just now received a Letter from Fanny for her Mother, I have taken the Opportunity to Inclose it to you.

Mr Charles Causton whom I have seen is extremely well and enquired very much after you, I am just now going to spend the day with the family at Highgate and in a few days I am under an appointment to go with young Mr Rose Fuller[100] to Hadley to see our old friends there so that in my next I shall write you particularly concerning them.

Captain Locker enquired much after you and the rest of his friends in Jamaica – the time seems long my dear Brother since I heard from you, pray favour me with your letters, on my part I shall miss no Opportunity of writing you – remember me to all our friends and beleive me to be My Dear Brother

Yours most Sincerely and Affectionately Joseph Lee.

---

98 Elizabeth Jones, widow of John Venn, the former rector of St Catherines who had died in 1764. He left four daughters and instructions that the family were to return to England. The older daughters were Mary, born in 1751 and Elizabeth born in 1754.

99 Possibly Monkhouse Davison (1713-1793) or his younger brother Thomas, partners in one of the leading grocers in 18th century London, Davison Newman and Co., that imported a wide range of produce including tea, coffee, sugar and spices.

100 Rose Fuller, youngest son of Thomas Fuller was born in 1748. The Lee family had lived in Hadley between about 1738 and 1746 and the older boys had been taught there by the Reverend David Garrow father of William Garrow, later to be Attorney General. That there was a close association between the Garrow and Fuller families is suggested by the fact that Thomas and Eleanor Fuller were married at Monken Hadley in 1742, and that David Garrow and his wife named one of their sons John Rose Garrow. He was born the year Rose Fuller returned from Jamaica, but sadly died the following year.

Joseph Lee to Robert Cooper Lee

London, 15th September 1768

My Dear Brother,

By Mr Davison I wrote you which I hope you have long since received and by the Opportunity of Captain Legg who carries this I have sent you the particulars mentioned in your Memorandum except my Nieces Picture which cannot be yet finished. In the Box No.1 are two Beaver Hatts one of which I desire Miss Prissy's Acceptance of and the other's for Sally, all the other things will appear by the Inclosed List or Particular of them for I do not yet know all the prices so as to send you a regular Invoice. I hope they will all please. Miss Kelly's shoes I was obliged to get made by another maker than the person you mentioned, no such person being now to be found. Ben Kenton assures me the Porter is the best of the kind and the same as that which is sent to the East Indies.

The *Phoenix* arrived some time ago and brought me your favour of the twenty fifth June last which gave me infinite pleasure to hear that yourself and my friends were in good health, my warmest wishes are ever employed for the continuance of it.

My Sister is in the Country and by a late letter from her she has fixed on a boarding School for her Daughters at about Fifteen pounds per Annum each, to which I have therefore desired they may be sent and this will bring the Maintenance of the Children to near about Fifty pounds, and I shall soon be able to know how much will be requisite for herself, her Husband I have not seen anything of as yet.

I had the pleasure of seeing Miss Fanny a few days ago, she is extremely well and I really think her the Flower of the School, she desires her Duty to yourself and her Mother.

I am pleased and at the same time much obliged to you my dear Brother for the account you give me that matters are going on so well, and hope they will continue so, for in the hasty manner I left the Island I was under some apprehensions concerning it.

As to myself I am in every respect perfectly well and if I can pass through the Winter without an Attack of the Gout I shall then think myself very happy indeed, as it will convince me that my health is perfectly re-established – the weather is now changing very fast and the appearance of winter begins to show itself, but the coolness of the Air is very pleasing and agreeable to me.

In a day or two I am going down to Rose Hill for I spend but little of my time in London and on my return shall write you again. I have lately spent some days with Mr Tubb, his house in the Country is extremely pleasant and I was most agreeably entertained the whole time I was there, the family desire their respects to you – Captain Lee desires his Compliments I'm going to dine with him today.

I beg you will present my best respects to all friends and believe me to be with the utmost truth My Dear Sir

Your most Affectionate Brother Joseph Lee.

Deffell[101] and Brett[102] are arrived I have just seen Mr Sam Gordon.

It was not at all uncommon for one of the writers of these letters to express concern about the length of time that had passed since they had last received letters. An explanation for the long gap since Robert Cooper Lee's last letter, written in July, may be found in the columns of the *Leeds Intelligencer* of Tuesday, 20 December 1768.

A letter from Penzance, dated Dec. 8, says, "For two or three days last past, a great number of pieces (to the amount of 100 or upwards) of mahogany timber have been taken up on the stream within the limits of this port, which must come from some vessel wrecked on the coast; among other pieces of the wreck was thrown onshore, a small box directed to Joseph Lee, Esq; at Messrs Thomas and Stephen Fuller's, Merchants in London, to the care of Willes Morgan; there was also thrown on shore, a lion head of a vessel, on the breast of which is a cypher."

There is no mention in the letters of this shipwreck, and hence no indication as to whether the box eventually reached Joseph Lee, although since it was mentioned in a provincial newspaper it seems possible that eventually it did so. Since the direction on the box was still readable it had presumably been painted on. What state the contents were in of course can only be imagined, perhaps it contained preserved ginger or chocolate sealed in jars and sent by Sally Lewis for Joseph to enjoy. Bundles of papers would probably have been wrapped in oiled cloth which would have provided some protection.

---

101 Probably John Deffell, Captain of the *Augustus Caesar*.

102 Possibly Curtis Brett (1720-1784) a Jamaica merchant, but more likely Captain Brett who was on leave while a new ship the *Judith* was being built.

This next letter also suggests to us that, unlike his brother John, Joseph Lee had not bought a house in Spanish Town, but leased one.

Joseph Lee to Robert Cooper Lee

London, 23d December 1768

My Dear Brother,

Your last favour which I received was of the twenty third of July last and I have been under no small anxiety at not hearing from you since that time, and also as we have letters in London of the latter end of September but I hope soon to be releived from my uneasiness and to have the particular pleasure of hearing from you.

My last to you was from Bath of the twenty fourth of October which I hope has reached your hands before now, I staid at that place near two Months and have received very great benefit from it, so that when I have the pleasure of embracing you again I hope to be in the most perfect health and strength, and indeed I now begin to set my face towards your Western Clime however I have not yet fixed the particular time and it may probably be the whole of June before you will see me with you. I should be very glad in the meantime if between my Landlord and Landladies my house could be somewhat repaired as I must otherwise I am afraid have the trouble of moving as soon as I come – there is also another thing you know the terms of my Articles, I believe it would be better that things should go on as they are and no Alteration be made till my Arrival, it will make but a few months difference, but this Mr Allen and you will best determine.

My Sister still continues at Bury I have been down to her and her children but have not seen her Husband, from which and my former letters to you it seems that nothing can be done but to continue an Annual Allowance. I am afraid I have not by my Arrival answered the utmost of her Expectations for what she seems to desire and expect is that I should take a house and she and her family live with me which, notwithstanding the warmth of my Affection for her, you know was so entirely opposite to my plan that it was impossible for me to think of it. She has declined the proposition made by my Uncle and mentioned in my last and has not fixed on anything therefore in order to conduce to her peace and happiness is much as I possibly could, I have after conversation with upon the Subject fixed the Sum of One hundred and thirty pounds annually for her which according to her own Account will be sufficient for her and her children and is the only method after having consulted my Uncle and Aunt upon the Subject which I found could be taken. I have since my Arrival given her One hundred pounds besides the Fifty pounds which you sent her.

My Sister has three very fine Children, their ages are nine ten and eleven, the boy is the youngest, the School my Sister has chose for her Daughters is at New Markett about fourteen Miles from Bury, and her Son she has put to School at Bury, the oldest Daughter reads very well and you have had a specimen of her writing, but the other Daughter only learnt to write since I have been in England. I delivered your presents to them from which they return you thanks and desired me to present their duty to you.

Inclosed I have the pleasure of forwarding to you a letter from your Daughter which I do assure you is entirely her own diction for she sat by me the whole time of her writing it without receiving any Assistance whatever, she is extremely well and desires me to present her duty to you and her Mama.

My Uncle and Aunt are very hearty for their age, he is now in his 75th year, they are going to remove to a place in Essex near thirty Miles from London he has a lay and cannot bear the Cold in the least.

Miss Fanny is to be with Mrs Murphy for some part of these Holydays and afterwards I shall have her and my Sister with me and will then get her Picture compleatly finished so as to send you. I have taken the liberty to present her with a Winter Silk.

I wait impatiently my dear Brother in expectation of receiving a letter from you, pray present my Compliments to all friends remember me to my little ones and believe me to be with the utmost truth and regard My Dear Brother

Yours most Sincerely and affectionately Joseph Lee.

Joseph Lee to Robert Cooper Lee

London, 6th January 1769

My Dear Brother,

Although I wrote you so lately I have again sat down to write you a few lines. By Captain Aitken who arrived a few days ago I received a letter from Mr Allen which gave me the pleasing Account of your good health but my Satisfaction would I assure you have been doubled if I had had the confirmation of it under your own hand, I hope I shall not be long without that pleasure for it seems a very long time since I have heard from you. I will therefore conclude this Paragraph where a Merchant would have begun it by informing you that your last favour which I received was of the twenty third July last.

Nothing will be stirring here till the meeting of the Parliament the nineteenth Instant – I have here with sent you the last Magazines which contain the latest news and shall take the earliest Opportunity of writing you again. Captain Forrest is said to be the person to relieve Admiral Parry in the Summer.

Mr Brammer[103] delivered me a letter from Mr Craswell[104] but as he sailed for Jamaica the next day in the *Prince Frederick,* Captain Johnson, I had not and Opportunity of writing Mr Craswell then but shall do so by the first Conveyance, pray present my compliments to him.

I have frequently seen Colonel Remington[105] since he has been here who is very hearty and well, Mrs Ford[106] and her family I was with a few days ago and they desired their Compliments to you, as do likewise Mrs Hay[107] and Mrs Pallmer[108].

Miss Fanny is very well and desires her duty to you. I hope soon to hear from you and shall ever be My Dear Brother

Yours most Sincerely and affectionately Joseph Lee.

Joseph Lee to Robert Cooper Lee

London, 1st March 1769

My Dear Brother,

---

[103] Probably John Brammer of St John's, Jamaica whose daughter Elizabeth married John Price of Worthy Park.

[104] Possibly Edward Crasswell who had a son called Edward baptised in Kingston 9th June 1768.

[105] Lieutenant-Colonel Gervas Remington, 43rd Regiment of Foot 1767 (retired 1774, died London, 1780).

[106] Elizabeth Aikenhead, widow of Gilbert Ford, see also correspondence of September 1772

[107] Charlotte Hay wife of Thomas Hay, Island Secretary. He died 1769 – see the following letter.

[108] It is not clear which Mrs Pallmer this is, but certainly of the Jamaican family who owned property in St Dorothy and Clarendon parishes.

By Captain Boyd I was favoured with yours of the 10th October last, which gave me very great pleasure as I had been so long in expectation of hearing from you, and I am much obliged to you for the several matters you mention. I have frequently resolved in my Mind the Subject of my future Settlement and I really have not a desire of accumulating more than I at present have and upon my return to Jamaica shall think myself happy to wind up everything for it will not be the plan to encroach upon or lessen the Principal. I may then attempt the Practising in the Colony Affairs or to employ myself in some other way that would be an Amusement and Profit to me and these are various and easy to be found here with respect to the first Plan I have received great Encouragement from my friends here.

My health has been extremely well ever since I have been here and I have the utmost hope will continue so, and especially as I shall not upon my return put my Constitution to the tryals I have heretofore done.

Miss Fanny I have the pleasure to inform you is very well which you will find confirmed by the letters here with under her own hand. I have had her Picture drawn by Cotes[109] who is in great repute here and is considered as next to Reynolds in the Art and when it is compleated it shall be sent to you by the first safe Opportunity. The Price will be a few Guineas beyond the Sum you mentioned which I apprehend will not be disagreeable to you as it will always remain a handsome Picture even after she has outgrown the likeness.

I have by this Conveyance forwarded to you a Ring which I request your Acceptance of and flatter myself the image it will represent to you may make it acceptable and on that Account make amends for the smallness of the Value.

I shall write you again in a short time and I need not my Dear Brother here repeat how acceptable every line from you always is to me. I have nothing new here but that poor Mr Hay died some short time since.

My Sister and her children are very well and desire to be remembered to you, I hope what I mentioned to you respecting her in my letter of the

---

[109] Francis Cotes (English, 1726-1770), Portrait of Miss Frances Lee, 1769. Milwaukee Art Museum, Gift of Mr. and Mrs. William D. Vogel M1964.5. The portrait was sold by the Lee descendants in the early twentieth century and has since been in America.

23rd December last will meet with your approbation, I do not see that any thing else can at present be done for her.

Your favours by Crisp I received for which I am much obliged to you and hope the parties among you are by this time all happily adjusted. I send you herewith the address of both houses to the King respecting the matters at Boston, and some Votes of the House – the Ministry have at present a very great Majority in the house of Commons and can carry any thing.

I perceive my Dear Brother you must have been in your usual hurry of business when you wrote me last, by your inclosing a declaration and one of your Memorandums. Mr Fuller is in very good health and all his family. Colonel Remington is gone to join his Regiment at Newcastle, I dined with him and several other Jamaica Gentlemen the day before he set off where the glass circulated very freely to the health of our Friends in Jamaica. Captain Bickerton has been chiefly at Southhampton since our Arrival but is at present in Town. I had the pleasure of seeing him yesterday, he was in very good health and Spirits and desires me to present his Compliments to you and Mr Welch[110] Mr Bullock[111] etc . Captain Brett is very hearty and enjoys a year of ease while his Ship is building

Pray give my Compliments to Mr Welch, Mr Bullock, Mr Winde, Mr Wynter[112], Mr Gordon[113] and all Friends. I hope to find you all in your usual good health is upon my Arrival – remember me to Sally and her children, I am with the warmest Sensations of Love and regard My Dear Sir

Your most Affectionate Brother Joseph Lee.

The following fragment appears to be the draft copy of a letter from Robert Cooper Lee to his brother written about March 1769.

---

[110] Richard Welch

[111] Edward Bullock, a barrister in Kingston Jamaica (died about 1781) or possibly Thomas Bullock, who in 1760 petitioned against his removal from the post of Commissary and Sole Judge of the King's Court of Vice Admiralty by the Lieutenant Governor.

[112] Thomas Wynter, son of Mary Johnston Rose.

[113] Thomas Gordon, barrister in Jamaica.

. . .have determined to return. I hope it will be with such Health and Strength as will insure you against that cussed Disorder the Gout. Mr Allen tells me he has acquainted Mr Hogg[114] of his and your Resolution to determine the partnership with him at the Seperation of the Articles. Mr Hogg is very well satisfied re the Seperation and will be in good temper and without Breach of Friendship. There will be no Occasion for Mr Allen's going to Leeward till the June Assizes, when if you are not arrived I shall attend to anything that may be to be done this way during his absence. I have been on the Look out for a better House for you, and had partly engaged Mrs Sympson's[115] in which J Wallen lived, as he now resides chiefly in Kingston, but he insisted on keeping it and let to Mr Bronn and Mr Paplay[116] have each a Room. If I cannot get the present House properly repaired I will endeavour to find another to hire before your arrival.

In regard to my Sister and her Children I think you have done the best that possibly could be as matters are circumstanced and if she would endeavour herself as much as we have to make her easy and happy I am sure she would be so. I am glad my Uncle and Aunt are so hearty and should have great Pleasure in seeing them once more. So large a Family of Grand Children must be very heavy. I beg my kind Love to them and Mrs Sayer.

I thank you for Fanny's Letter inclosed in my last and for your great Kindness to her since . . .

Joseph Lee to Robert Cooper Lee

London, 24th March 1769

My Dear Brother,

By Captain Boyd I sent you some letters which I recommended to his care inclosing one from Mrs Lewing[117] which Mrs Hay requested me to send

[114] Possibly John Hogg, attorney in Jamaica.

[115] Alice Sympson wife of Archibald Sympson.

[116] Either George Paplay, a Kingston Merchant who died in 1769, or his brother James who outlived him.

[117] Probably Sarah Grace Halstead who was married to Richard Lewing. Both were legatees under the Will of Thomas Fuller of St Dorothy in 1768. Richard Lewing was Island Secretary in 1770 and owner of 100 acres in the parish of St Catherine in 1754.

to your care, since then the Pacquet has arrived but as I have no letter from you by her I am hopefull to hear from you by the Man of War which is expected in every day.

The weather is now beginning to be very fine pleasant and agreeable here and will therefore induce me to Stay two or three Months longer than I intended for in one of my former letters I mentioned being with you in June but I now think of Staying till the Summer before I leave this Kingdom, so that it will be the Month of September before I shall have the pleasure of seeing you. I have my Dear Brother frequently your Idea and those of your little Ones present to me and hope to find you all in your perfect healths upon my Arrival.

I have been attending at the Cockpit for the last week hearing the Appeals from Jamaica and the other Colonies. Pusey vs Clark the Donee[118] was reversed without an Argument being suffered to be entered into. Lindsay and Milward the Donee Affirmed upon Argument with a direction that Gardners Estate should have recourse against Mrs Beckford and the Chancellor was severely reflected on for having allowed Mr Beckford's Demurrer[119] in this Cause, and in my own Cause Mune v. Palmer and Ux[120] the Donee reversed and the Exceptions disallowed in which last matter it is worthy Observation that the Defendants Council (Norton and Forrester) did not insist upon any one of the reasons made use of in Jamaica in support of their Exceptions but only endeavoured to prove that Callendar was interested at the time he made the Affidavit by being at the time the Administrator of Campbell but when we showed that he took the Administration under a power from the residuary Divisee and was not beneficially interested the Court did not then hesitate in allowing his Evidence – they sat several days and determined all the Causes that were ready for hearing.

I have the pleasure to inform you that Miss Fanny is very well and all our Relations except our Cousin Atkins[121] (now Mrs Dawson) who is in a bad

---

[118] A legal term relating to a person to whom the power of appointment is given.

[119] Demurrer – a written response to a complaint filed in a lawsuit which, in effect, pleads for dismissal on the point that even if the facts alleged in the complaint were true, there is no legal basis for a lawsuit. A hearing before a judge (on the law and motion calendar) will then be held to determine the validity of the demurrer.

[120] Ux short for uxor, Latin meaning wife.

[121] Jaques Atkins was the fifth of ten children born to the Lee's Aunt Hester Jaques who had married Thomas Atkins. She married first Woodyatt Hodges, a Warehouseman of Cateaton Street, on the Corner of Aldermanbury, London in 1755 when she was thirty-

way and not expected to recover but my Uncle and Aunt are extremely well and are removed down to Essex. I saw my Uncle a few days ago when he desired me to present his Respects to you. My Sister is also very well I have frequently mentioned to her putting her Son to some School at a distance from her but the truth is that she is very fond of her children and does not chuse to be parted from them, which is the only reason I can assign for her keeping her son at home with her.

There is nothing of News here, Wilkes is the great Topic in the City where he has many followers among whom Mr Vaughan stands one of the foremost – he has been re-chosen for Middlesex and a third time expelled by the house of Commons. The House of Commons have refused to receive the Petitions from the North American Colonies relative to the taxes to be levied there because the Assembly being since dissolved the Bodys which proposed those Petitions are not now existing.

I beg you will present my compliments to all our Friends in Jamaica, pray present my respects to Miss Kelly – tell Sally how d'you and remember me to her little ones. Believe to be with the warmest Affection My Dear Brother

Yours most truly and Sincerely Joseph Lee.

Robert Cooper Lee to Frances Lee

Jamaica, 26th April 1769

My Dear Fanny

I send you this by Mr Moulton[122] who you may remember here, and will give you a Guinea, which is a Present from your Mama. Dr Brodbelt[123] gave me the Purse and Swordknot you sent by him, for which I thank

four. He died in 1763 and she married Thomas Dawson, a linen draper of St Martin's Lane, the following year. Both marriages were childless. Thomas Marlton was closely involved in drawing up the marriage settlements.

122 Possibly Charles Moulton who married Elizabeth Barrett and was father of Edward Barrett Moulton (later Edward Barrett Moulton Barrett) and grandfather of the poet Elizabeth Barrett Browning. Alternatively the father of Charles Moulton, also Charles. The Moulton and Barrett families owned extensive plantations in Jamaica.

123 Dr Francis Rigby Brodbelt (1746-1795), son of Daniel and brother of John, medical practitioner in Spanish Town and winner of the silver medal of the Medical Society of London in 1795. He was one of the executors of the Will of Scudamore Winde in 1775.

you, and shall regard them as your work. Your Uncle sent me the Letter you wrote me at Christmas, and I am much pleased to find you go on so well. Your Brother Bob goes for England in about 6 Weeks and I do not doubt you will love one another as you ought. Your Mama and Dickie are very well. She sends you her Blessing and will write you a Letter soon. My constant Prayers are for your Happiness I am Your affectionate Parent Robert Cooper Lee.

Joseph Lee to Robert Cooper Lee

London, 24th May 1769

My Dear Brother,

I could not omit this Opportunity of writing a few lines to you as I am persuaded although my letter is one so short, it may yet afford you some satisfaction.

Miss Fanny I have the pleasure to inform you is very well and desires her duty to you, she is very happy in the thoughts of seeing her brother here. My Sister and her Family are also very well.

I hope my Dear Brother that the first Ships will bring me an Account of your good health – here with I have forwarded to you the last Magazines – pray remember me to Miss Kelly and to Sally and her boys – excuse the shortness of this letter for I am just come out of the Country and have only time to write you this Snap, in my next I shall make amends for it – I am with the most Affectionate regard My Dear Brother

Yours most Sincerely Joseph Lee.

PS with the Magazines I have sent you a pamphlet lately published and which is supposed here to contain the best Arguments that have been made use of in favour of America respecting her present disputes with Great Britain.

Joseph Lee to Robert Cooper Lee

London, 14th August 1769

My Dear Brother,

It is now a long time since I had the pleasure of a letter from you, but upon looking back at the copies of my own letters, I must impute it to the expectation you had entertained of seeing me with you before this time which I fully intended at the beginning of this year but as I wrote you on this Subject on 26th of April I shall say no more here, however my dear

Brother although I have not heard from you, I have heard of you and indeed I have received the most pleasing satisfaction from the Account Mr Watson gives me of your good health, and I pray God you may long continue so.

In my last of 20 June I wrote you fully respecting the Clerk of the Courts Office, since which Mr Vaughan has been weak enough to write a letter to the Duke of Grafton offering him 5000 Guineas for the reversion of the Patents in the name of his Son but the Reversion is not as far as I can learn given to anyone at present, and this as all other lucrative places will only be given to some person of Influence in the House of Commons.

Our Friend Captain Lee is promoted to the Command of the *Aurora* and Sails in a few days for the East Indies, he is in perfect health and in his usual good Spirits.

Miss Fanny is very well and desires her duty, she is very anxious to see her Brother – my Sister and her Family are also very well and two or three days ago I received a Visit from Mr Morley which is the first time that I had seen him, he stayed and dined with me but nothing passed between us relative to his Affairs.

I shall certainly sail the latter end of October so that I may promise myself the pleasure of being with you at or about Christmas, that time being the coolest part of the year will make it more eligible for me to get there then, when I flatter myself with having the most agreeable pleasure at the sight of you and your family.

The Magazines I have sent you but very little news is stirring at this time of the year – I beg you will present my respects to all our Friends and beleive me to be with the warmest Affection My Dear Brother

Yours most Affectionately and Sincerely Joseph Lee.

It seems more than possible that Morley was hoping for a handout from his brother-in-law, and clear that Joseph was certainly not offering one. Many years later John Morley wrote a begging letter to Richard Lee pleading extreme poverty, so it seems he never did take up any gainful employment nor ever again supported his wife and family.

Frances Lee

Francis Cotes (English, 1726-1770) Miss Frances Lee, 1769.

Oil on canvas, 36 x 28¼ in. (91.44 x 71.76 cm)

Milwaukee Art Museum, Gift of Mr and Mrs William D. Vogel M1964.5

Photo credit Larry Sanders

Joseph Lee to Robert Cooper Lee

London, 30th Oct 1769

My Dear Brother,

Since my last to you of the 27th September and 1st October Instant I am to acknowledge the receipt of your favour of 11th June and 24 and 25th July last. I was not in England upon the Arrival of the *Preston* but upon my coming back I had the pleasure of seeing Captain Keith, and to be informed by him of your good health, and that of our Friends in Jamaica. Captain Keith I have the pleasure to inform you is very well, we lodge very near each other, so that we shall frequently have the pleasure of meeting.

By Captain Stupart I have at last sent you Miss Fanny's Picture which I hope will please, it is I assure you a very strong likeness of her, the Price to Cotes is thirty Guineas (the most usual Sum for a Picture of that Size) his price for a head is only twenty Guineas, and I thought you would imagine the other ten Guineas well bestowed to have the Picture of the Size it now is, and as the Picture well deserved a handsome frame, I ordered a neat Italian fluted one for it to be put into, so that the whole expense will be £36 8s which although more than you at first intended will be fully compensated by the resemblance it has to the fair Object it was intended for and by the other Excellencys of the piece.

Mr Alpress[124] and his Family go out in Captain Stupart and I fully purposed it, but was desirous of staying till the beginning of November for a particular reason, and I am not certain whether I shall not stay Month longer in order to return with young Mr Munro – if that should take place, I shall come in one of the Pacquetts, and of this the next letter shall inform you. Mr Alpress's coming out will occasion you the trouble of providing another house for me which is unlucky as you have so lately moved into that, but I hope you will make no difficulty in procuring one.

I wrote you upon my Nephew's Arrival giving you an Account of the pleasure I had received in seeing him and before I went to the Continent, I forwarded your letter to Mr Stephen Fuller and wrote him on the subject, leaving the choice of the School to his Judgement in consequence of which he fixed on Harrow School of which Mr Thomas Fuller tells me

[124] Samuel Alpress (1739-1784)

he has wrote you, and your son is now fixed there under the particular care of Dr Somner the Head Master, and with the parts that my Nephew is possessed of, it is the best School he could be put to, for if he had been put to Small School, he would in all probability only have lost a great part of what he has by your prudent care and attention already learned, for he is now as forward in every respect as boys of near ten years old are here. I shall in a few days carry Captain Keith to see him at the School.

Two days ago I met with Mr Gale[125] who is returned from North America he enquired after you and desired me to present his Compliments to you. Mr Blackwood[126] I saw lately he is very well and has fixed his Head Quarters near the Royal Exchange. Dr Butt[127] died a few days ago at Bath of a Nervous Fever. Colonel Remington is very hearty and desires me to present his Compliments to you and the rest of his Jamaica Friends.

I have sent you as usual the Magazines etc but they will give you but an imperfect Idea of the Confusions here on account of Politics and as the Winter advances the disputes become more violent – it is however all about the loaves and Fishes – Mr Vaughan seems to have been very unlucky in his Politics for he is to be expelled by the Supporters of the Bill of Rights, and is to be prosecuted by the Crown, become as he is, the outcast of both Partys. Our School fellow Walpole Eyre very soon withdrew from the Company of the Patriots at Mile End.

I have the pleasure to inform you that my Niece is extremely well, this moment I have received a letter from her, she is very happy upon her Brother's being in England and Bob and she correspond much together.

I beg my dear Brother you will present my Compliments to Mr Welch, Mr Bullock, Mr Winde, Mr Wynter. I hope Miss Kelly is well prey present my Compliments to her – remember me to Sally and my boys and give me leave to thank you for the particular Obligations I lay under to you on their Account.

---

[125] The Gale family were prominent in Jamaica, descended from John Gale one of the earliest settlers. It is not clear which member of the family this was.

[126] A Jane Blackwood owned 1440 acres in Jamaica in 1754 but it has not been possible to establish if there is a connection. Perhaps John Blackwood, a merchant, resident in 1772 in Soho Square London and brother of Shovel Blackwood, both being grandsons of Admiral of the Fleet, Sir Cloudesley Shovel.

[127] John Marten Butt (c.1741-1769). The affidavit on his Will was sworn by Vincent Biscoe, a merchant trading with Jamaica, whose son Joseph Seymour Biscoe was later a friend of Richard Lee.

I wrote to my Sister a few days ago but have not lately heard from her, or whether she has received the letter which you wrote me you had sent. I have and shall supply her with whatever she wants and before I leave England shall carry Bob to see her and her children. Poor Mrs Dawson died about a fortnight ago by which her Husband gets about £5000. My Uncle and Aunt are both well. I am My dear Brother with the truest Affection

Yours most truly and Sincerely Joseph Lee.

PS Captain Keith desires his Compliments to you and to Miss Kelly - pray return her my best thanks for the Chocolate.

Invoice of Sundry Goods Shipped by Joseph Lee in London on board the Fanny Capt. Legg and consigned to Robert Cooper Lee Esqr. in Jamaica.

A large Globe Lamp	£2. 2. –	
ditto Pulley & Rose	. 3. 6	
Line & Tossell	1. 11. –	
8 Globe Lamps with tin Tops	3. 8. –	
Case & Packing	. 14. –	
8 Lamp Irons	2. 6. –	
Painting	. 4. –	
Matts Packing wharfage &c	. 9. 6	10. 18. –
a Pair of Gold Shoe Buckles		11. 3. –
a pair of Spectacles		1. 8. –
a dozen pair fine thread Stockings		4. 4. –
Six pair silk do		3. 6. –
Six pair black sattin Shoes		3. 12. –
Six pair black Calamanco do		1. 19. –
Six pair Shoes for Bob		. 18. –
Do for Dick		. 11. 9
Eight pair Pumps & 4 pair Shoes		5. 2. –
one Dozen pair Stockings for Bob		1. – –
Do for Dick		. 17. –
a Hatt for Bob		. 11. 8
Do for Dick		. 9. 8
a blue Sattin Hatt & Cloak		3. 18. 6
		£49. 18. 7

The Shipping Invoice for the portrait of Frances Lee and other goods

Joseph was in London at a time of political ferment, which would lead to war with America and the independence of that country. The interests of Jamaican colonists however were rather different from those in North America, leading Jamaica to remain under the Crown.

In April 1769 Walpole Eyre had become Chairman of a 'Committee of Grievances and Apprehensions' for Middlesex, meeting at Mile End. The petition that Eyre agreed to present to the King was drawn up by John Horne. Horne, later known as Horne Tooke, was a founder of 'The

Society for Supporting the Bill of Rights' in America. By midsummer it was anticipated that such committees would be set up across the country to redress national grievances at home. Clearly by October Eyre had thought better of it! Horne Tooke later spent a year in prison for his support of those Americans 'murdered by the king's troops at Lexington and Concord', but pursued a political career, interrupted again by his trial for treason in the autumn of 1794. This time he was acquitted.

Walpole Eyre was four years older than Joseph. He was the son of Kingsmill Eyre FRS (1682-1743), Secretary of the Royal Hospital Chelsea from 1716 and a garden designer. Kingsmill Eyre designed the first gardens at Houghton Hall in Norfolk for Sir Robert Walpole some time before 1721, became an FRS in 1726 and submitted a patent for a new way of processing iron in 1736. Given the family location in Chelsea it is probable that Walpole Eyre studied with Robert Cooper Lee and Joseph under William Rothery at Paradise Walk. Following the death in 1754 of his uncle Henry Samuel Eyre, a wealthy London wine merchant, Walpole Eyre inherited a large estate at St John's Wood London, including 150 acres in Hampstead which remained in the possession of the Eyre family well into the twentieth century.

Frances Lee to Robert Cooper Lee

[Streatham?], 1st November 1769

I have the happiness to inform my Dear Papa that I am in perfect health, and hope this will find him and all the family the same my Brother is agreeably placed at Harrow by Mr Fuller: my Uncle intends sending out my Picture as soon as possible pray offer my duty to Mama and love to Brother. I am Dear Papa

Your Dutiful Daughter Frances Lee.

Following the death of Thomas Hay, the Island Secretary, the previous year Edward Long, the noted historian of Jamaica, wrote to seek help from Robert Cooper Lee.

Edward Long to Robert Cooper Lee

London, 6th December 1769

Dear Sir,

My friend Mr Winde has communicated to me a matter that alarms me greatly, the more so as it is impossible for me to return to the Island till I receive a Title to my Estate, put my Connections here on a proper footing, and my Children in a course of Education. I could wish in the meantime to have those Papers Mr Winde gave me Expectation of or at least some Grounds to proceed upon here; for I am quite in the Dark as to the particular part or Clause in the Bond upon which Law designs to lay its Finger, and as all human Judgements seperately taken are fallible, and as wisdom is to be found in the Multitude of Counsellors, so I should not chuse to Acquiesce with a determination of the Bench in Jamaica solely, upon so Nice and important a Question, in which the Ruin of myself and Family may be involved, but I Rest assured, that if any Stir is made in it, I shall not be restrained by any Rule of Court or Compromised from proceeding Home with it upon the Appeal, unless I should hereafter upon a clear State of the Case sent me and the best Opinions taken here, see the reason to act otherwise. Your Sentiments upon this Emergency would be extremely usefull and acceptable to me. I need not fear to tell you that my Debts are already so heavy that I am but ill provided with the most essential means of making Defence. Nevertheless if I should be deemed by the Bench in Jamaica liable by my Bond to the Crown to pay my share of the penalty towards repairing Mr H's[128] insolvency, it will be a matter of indifference to me what Individual I am to pay. But my own and my Family's future Well being require me to gain every Advantage in point of Time and by Appealing to fight it off, and I hope as there is matter of Equity in it, that it may in case of any Judgement be carried by Injunction into the Channel of Equity, as I build much upon this in the dernier Resort. If you do not concur with me in Opinion be so good to give me your Idea at large. I would rather wish that Mr G might be wrought upon to drop his Design, which if prosecuted cannot fail of creating much trouble to himself, and to the parties for whom he Acts; I cannot in my own mind justify his takings such an unprecedented Step; I call it unprecedented for it appears to be a Case of the first Impression, and teeming with Evils in every view. Was it in my power to hinder Mr Hay from going off when he had the Governors leave and myself absent at Bath what had any person to do with his Tickett except the Captain, who was liable to Penalty for taking him on board without one. Where are Publick Officers to find Securities to be given to the Island, if by binding themselves to be responsible to the Crown and Publick for the

[128] Thomas Hay, planter and Secretary and Notary Publick of Jamaica from at least 1754, Clerk to the Council 1761.

faithful discharge of mere office keeping, they are by *Implication of Law* to be hooked in afterwards under Colour of a pretended Construction of words to pay all the Private Debts and Contracts of such Publick Officers? An Obligation unnatural and inequitable, and what was never before extended to any similar Case, nor can be in right Reason applicable to this. For if we were to pay every shilling of his Debts, in virtue of this Notion, we should still be held liable under the full penalty of the Bond to the Crown for all Delinquencies in the Office of the Public Nature committed by Mr Hay in respect to non-Entry of papers non-Recording, and other offences of a like sort which any future Assembly may hereafter discover. And this alone I should think would furnish a good nullum Tempus Argument to obtain a *Nolle prosqui* from the Government in case a Private Action of Debt should be sued out against us upon this Public Bond. Pray my Dear Sir interest my Friends Mr Welch and Bullock in my behalf if necessary, and remember that my future happiness and peace of mind, Salvation and Welfare of myself and Family are staked on the Issue of this Matter, which already fills me with inexpressible Anxiety and seems to take its rise from a Wantonness of Malevolence, or a Zeal much misguided in the Author of it. From whose Machinations may you and my Friends (under Providence) deliver.

Your obliged and most Faithful humble servant Edward Long.

PS These Bonds I think by Cl.18 of Act 10, are to be recorded in the Supreme Court if so maybe come at. Please to observe the date of the Bond and the date of Jones's Judgement.

Upon looking into Act 21, which I suppose is Mr G's Corner Stone, It appears to me that the breach of Duty must happen by the Secretary or Deputy's *delivering* a Tickett signed by the *Governor* before the name of the *Party applying for such ticket* has been up 21 days, or (if put up the stated Time) *delivering* it without taking an Affidavit that such person (him or her) has gone by that name 1 year. And that in case neither the party's name has been up, nor such Affidavit taken by him, He is not to *deliver the Tickett* without taking good Security for the paying such persons Debts so departing. I don't see how this will attract Mr Hay's case who did not deliver any Tickett, nor put up his Name and there is no penalty laid on any person who goes off without a Tickett. This the Master of the vessel is to take care of by the first Clause of the Act, which obliges him to leave a Bond with Security of a Freeholder, not to carry off any person without a Tickett. It is very Evident that the Original Meaning and Intention of these Acts, was to prevent the Elopement of transient persons, Indented Servants and Slaves. Commerce here in England has produced an Alteration in the Ancient prerogative of our Kings, in ordering their

Subjects out of the Realm or restraining them within it. But in Jamaica the prerogative still operates with respect to Public Officers, and it is by an Express Instruction that the Governor is required to give them (for special Reasons as of Health or Business) Leave of Absence from the Island for 1 year only, without which they could not depart even with a Tickett, unless they forfeited their Office, and hazarded their Bond for performing the Duties of it. The Governor's Leave I apprehend takes Mr Hay's case out of the Limitations of the Act, which relates only to the mode of Transaction the Secretary is to pursue in respect to other Persons. The Governors Leave is a Notice, and the exeat may be taken out to stop an Officer, and this I judge to be the proper Course between the prerogative of the Common Right of the Subject. Mr Hay might if he pleased had his name put up and an Affidavit sworn of his Identity, he being expressly exempted from administering the Both (because in this case he Acts Ministerially to the Justice as Notary in attesting certifying the oath to have made in his presence, and afterwards in filing it) but if he did not chuse, or thought it unincumbent on him (being Secretary himself) to do it, I see no Clause or Law to compell him; in regard to this Law and all other Penal Laws, I have no doubt but it, like all others, will as to the penal part be construed to mean not an iota more than is actually Expressed, especially where it is to be made (*Constructively only*) to Rob one-party in order to enrich another with the Spoil. Give me leave to add that I always understood the Bond to be for the Secretaryship not for the *person* of Mr Hay; for Acts of Duty pursuant to the Both of Office, and not for Mr Hay distinct from those Junctions; since the performance of those Junctions did not depend on the Locality of his Person, as you well know, that he never attended it personally, but transacted everything by Letter of Agency for Signing his Name, or by Deputy.

Joseph Lee to Robert Cooper Lee

London, 26th January 1770

My Dear Brother,

My last letter under date of 30th October 1769 I hope you have before now received, I have not heard from you since then which I impute to your expectation of seeing me in Jamaica, and indeed you would have seen me by this time, but that my Physician Dr Fothergill[129] advised me by all means to take a second Winter in this Climate, for he assured me that one Winter was a very little Service to persons who come from a warm Climate for their Health. I have therefore taken his advice and shall stay till the Severity of the Winter is over, in consequence of which I have taken my passage in the *James Dawkins*, Captain Carter, who is expected to sail by the end of February – when you reflect on the reason of my stay I am persuaded you will approve of it.

By this Ship I have sent out a few things which I have purchased here and for which the Bill of Lading is inclosed, consigned to your care, and I trust you will excuse the trouble I give you on the Occasion.

By Captain Stupart I hope you received Miss Fanny's Picture in good Order, I have had her and her Brother with me for this fortnight past and have the pleasure to acquaint you that they are both well. I intended to have had my Sister and her little ones with me at the same time and wrote her for that purpose, but she was prevented by a small Fever, but of which she has however now got the better.

I have inclosed you the Kings Speech with a Paper published on the Ev'ning of the day on which it was spoken, containing some animadversions upon it.

Mr Gale has been confined for a long time with a violent Rheumatism contracted at North America, but he is now got the better of it, he desired me to present his Compliments to You.

Mrs John Harvie[130] seems not a little alarmed at the state of their matters and at what is said to be going on in your Island respecting them, but her delicacy will not permit her to write upon the Subject; she mentioned to me the things she had left in the Island and expressed her hope, if the affairs of the Messrs Harvies' are to be closed, that she would not be shut out from her demands, and requested me to mention it in a private manner to you.

---

[129] Dr John Fothergill (1712-1780) of White Hart Court, Gracechurch Street, London, and later Harpur Street. A celebrated Quaker physician and naturalist, he opposed the prevailing treatment which included bleeding, purging, and complex traditional remedies. Instead, he wrote, treatment should strengthen the patient with diet, cordials, clean air, and cinchona (the source of quinine) as a febrifuge.

[130] Milbrough Harvie, née Aikenhead (later McLean) - sister to Elizabeth who married first Gilbert Ford Attorney General for Jamaica and then Samuel Townsend, and to Margaret Eleanor married to Samuel Alpress. John Harvie died in Kingston in 1761 and Milbrough remarried in 1772.

Yesterday I dined with Colonel Remington who is in very good health where we toasted all our Jamaica Friends – there have been many changes about the Court within these few days – Lord Camden turned out from being Chancellor and Mr Yorke appointed who died three days afterwards, upon which the Seals were put in Commission to Baron Smythe, and the Judges Bathurst and Aston. The Marquis of Granby has also resigned as Commander in Chief of the Army and has gone into the Opposition, which has increased since the meeting of Parliament, but the Duke of Grafton still keeps his ground and has at present a Majority in both Houses. Sir Fletcher Norton is chosen Speaker of the House of Commons in the room of Sir John Cust who resigned on account of his health – our Friend Mr [Rose] Fuller stood some chance for this Office and there was for sometime great expectation of his succeeding to it.

All our Friends are well and I hope to find you and my other Friends so upon my Arrival, the time believe me will hang heavy upon my hands till I see you for I am and always shall be with the truest Affection My Dear Brother

yours most sincerely and affectionately Joseph Lee.

PS 27th January My Sister and her oldest Daughter are now with me, they are both well and desire to be remembered in the tenderest manner to you.

PS 31st January The Duke of Grafton resigned the Night before last and it is expected a general Change of the Ministry will take place.

Mr and Mrs Tubb desire their best respects to you.

Joseph Lee finally returned to Jamaica in the spring of 1770, and he must have written to his sister in May, for at the same time Robert Cooper Lee also wrote to her.

Robert Cooper Lee to Mary Charlotte Morley

Jamaica, 31st May 1770

My dear Sister,

I have just time to add to what our Brother has wrote my Wishes that this may find yourself and little ones perfectly well. I inclose you a Bill for

£100[131] Sterling and am happy to have it in my Power to contribute to your Ease and Happiness. With the second Bill I will write you more particularly and in the meantime you will excuse the shortness of this. I am My dear Sister

Yours most affectionately Robert Cooper Lee.

In September 1770 Frances Lee, at school in England, wrote to her four-year-old brother Richard in Jamaica, sending him a drawing of a bird – a remarkably competent drawing for a girl of eleven.

Frances Lee to Richard Lee

I take this agreeable opportunity of sending my dear Brother a Letter and a bird of my own drawing but I cannot say a singing one but by the time he has taught it to sing I hope I shall have the pleasure of seeing him in England which will add greatly to the happiness of his

Affectionate Sister Frances Lee.

---

131 Equivalent to £10,800.00 in 2012 using the retail price index. Source: measuringworth.com

I take this agreeable opportunity of
sending my dear Brother a Letter and a bird of my own drawing
but I cannot say a singing one but by the time he has taught it to
sing I hope I shall have the pleasure of seeing him in England which
will add greatly to the happiness of

his Affectionate Sister

Frances Lee.

Sep^{tr} 19th 1770

Later that year Robert Cooper Lee wrote to his seven-year-old son Bob now at Harrow school, and also to Frances.

Robert Cooper Lee to Robert Cooper Lee Junior

Jamaica, 31st December 1770

Dear Bob,

I send you a few Lines by Mr Ramsay[132] from whom I have had a letter after his arrival in England in which he mentioned that he saw you at Mr Fuller's and that you was very well, which I am always glad to hear and hope you have continued so ever since.

Your Letter by your Uncle is the last I have received from you, and was wrote so long ago as New Year's Day. You ought to write both to your Mama and me oftener and let us know how you are, and what Progress you make in your Learning.

Your Mama and I very well as is also your Brother. He begins to read a little, and says when he gets to England you will learn him his Book I hope you will see us all there next summer. Your Mama gives her kindest Love to you. My constant Prayers are for your Welfare for I am my dear Bob

your ever affectionate father Robert Cooper Lee.

PS your Uncle and Dickie desire their love

Robert Cooper Lee to Frances Lee

Jamaica, 31st December 1770

My Dear Fanny,

Your Letter by your Uncle and the pleasing Account he gave us of you afforded your Mama and me much Happiness. I read with great Satisfaction what you say of your Learning and the desire you express to improve in every proper Accomplishment for I have nothing so much at

[132] Possible George Ramsay, Registrar in Chancery and Clerk of the Patents in Jamaica, or his brother Peter who took on the same role in 1770.

Heart as the Welfare of yourself and my other Children. I have also received your letter from Bury. I am much obliged to your Aunt for her kindness to you and am glad you was so happy with her and your Cousins. I sent you a few Lines last May by Mrs Gordon, your Mama wrote you about the same time by Mr Ramsay who was so good to write me he had seen you at Mr Fuller's and that you was very well.

Your Mama joins me in our kindest Love to you – Dick desires his love to his Sister and says he longs to see her. We are all very well – I hope to meet you perfectly so early in August, and flatter myself I shall find you in Disposition and Behaviour such I wish you to be which will amply repay me for all my Care and Anxiety on your Account. Present your Mama's best respects and mine My dear Fanny

your truly affectionate Father Robert Cooper Lee.

PS your Uncle with whom you are a great Favourite gives his Love to you.

Priscilla Kelly gave birth to her fourth son, Matthew Allen Lee, on 22 January 1771. The removal of the entire family to England had been planned for some time, and took place in the summer of 1771, as Robert Cooper Lee had promised in his letter to his son Bob. Travelling with them was Joseph Lee's eldest son John, known as Jack, who was being sent to school in England. The family arrived at Dover on the 30th of August 1771 and by early September were living in Old Bond Street in London, from where Frances wrote to their old family friend Scudamore Winde in Jamaica. Only her draft survives.

Frances Lee to Scudamore Winde

Old Bond Street, 5th September 1771

Dear Sir,

My Mama delivered your kind Letter to me and I think myself under infinite Obligations to you for it. I will endeavour to merit and deserve the good Opinion you have of me, both by my Conduct and Behaviour, as I am sensible what a good Friend I have in you, who is so kind to concern himself about one who is so undeserving of his Goodness. I have been from school this Six Months on account of my Illness, but when I return I will endeavour to make up lost Time by being very attentive to all my Learning as I have got so good a Papa and Mama who do not deny me anything, which their goodness can supply me with. I cannot express what pleasure it gave me to see them once more in my life and it shall be my endeavour to deserve all their love and be a comfort to them in their old age. They informed me you talked of me frequently, I can assure you are never out of my thoughts, for if you were I should deem myself very ungrateful as you used to be so good to me in Jamaica, and now I have left it you have not forgot me. I have told your godson what you requested and he will write to you soon, he desires his duty to you, he is a very good Boy and fond of his Book. I was very glad to see my Dear Brothers, I think them a fine Children particularly Matt, I should esteem it a favour if you would write to me and be assured [torn] opportunity of sending you some of my scrawl [torn] acceptable to you will give the greatest pleasure to Dear Sir

your most obliged [torn].

The concern that led parents to send their children to England to be educated related not only to the lack of good educational facilities Jamaica, but also to the health risks that resulted in the deaths of so many children in infancy or childhood. Before Robert Cooper Lee had even arrived in England his friend Dr George Gordon was writing to him concerning his nephew Robert Home Gordon, the son of his brother John Gordon who was an indigo planter at Greencastle. It is clear from the letter that the parents were torn between the desire for their son's well-being and their preference to keep him with them.

George Gordon to Robert Cooper Lee

[illegible,Jamaica], 22nd July 1771

Dear Sir,

I hope long er this comes to hand you will be safe arrived in England with your family in perfect good health, and that you had a happie meeting with such of them as were there before you, which with every [illegible] happiness that can possibly atend you will afford me equal pleasure with any good event attending the subject of my own connection. The anxiety and uneasiness I am under on my nephews account induces me to beg the favour of you and Mr Grant to have him removed from his mother which however hard she may think it may be absolutely necessary for his preservation and I am perfectly satisfied from the confidence his Father has in your friendship that there is no act of yours that will be considered as weal intended as his own or mine. As you know that my Brothers sole happiness is inseparable from his Child's I shall offer no apology for giving you this trouble before you are well settled in England; Only assure you if ever and Oppertunity offers by which I can evince my Gratitude for any trouble you take in this, as well as former favours it will give rise the utmost pleasure as I will ever remain yours with the most perfect Esteem Dear Sir

Your most Obliged and Obedient Humble Servant George Gordon.

Joseph Lee to Robert Cooper Lee

Spanish Town, Jamaica, 25th July 1771

I have just time My Dear Brother to inclose you a Bill of Lading for 12 hogsheads of Sugar which I have just received from Mr Reid Jr.

This also covers a letter from Mr Wynter and another from Mr Aikenhead[133].

Captain Morse[134] after reserving in Sugars upon the Faithful Assurance of sailing on the 26th of this Month has now advised me that he will not be able to go until the first week in August – you will be so obliging to communicate this to Messrs Fuller's for the government.

Altho' I have many things to say I cannot with cheerfullness write you until I have the pleasure of hearing of your safe Arrival. May the Winds and Waves be propitious to you – Adieu My Dear Brother and believe me to be with unalterable Affection

Yours most truly and Sincerely Joseph Lee.

---

[133] Probably Archibald Aikenhead (c.1700-1777) of Stirling Castle, St Ann's Jamaica, the father of Margaret Eleanor Aikenhead the wife of Samuel Alpress,. Also in Jamaica was a William Aikenhead (d. abt 1768) whose son had been educated in the law in England under the care of Rose Fuller. See William Aikenhead, Jamaica, to RF, London ESRO **SAS-RF/21/11** 1755.

[134] It has not proved possible to identify Captain Morse, who captained the *Rose* after Captain Brett obtained the *Judith*. It seems possible he was related to the Kingston Merchant John Morse.

Joseph Lee to Robert Cooper Lee

Spanish Town, Jamaica, 29th August 1771

It is with the utmost Impatience my dear Brother that I long to hear of your safe Arrival in Old England, and of the joy which must swell your heart upon the sight of all your little Family around you.

You must already have heard of the death of Mr Gordon. Mrs Gordon acts in his Affairs, his debts are in all supposed to be pretty large, and the sale of some part of his property seems the only means of paying them – the Creditors who were indeed all his Friends have at present consented to give time and therefore I made no scruple to do the same on your part and the part of Mr Fuller, that is to see how Matters will turn out upon a thorough Examination of them.

Mrs P[hilip] Pinnock[135] and Mrs Peyton died lately and poor Mr Mune the Receiver General suddenly in a fit. His Brother Mr William Mune is appointed to the Office in his Stead many other persons of less note have dropt off. It has been the most disagreeable weather that ever I felt in Jamaica, but I am thank God very well.

The unexpected death of the late Receiver General has disappointed me in the payment which I had reason to expect on account of Mr Stephen Fuller. I shall however do my utmost with the present Receiver, and will then write Mr Fuller, I have applied to the present Receiver General, and he promised me that he will make a payment of the whole Money which is due to Mr Fuller.

In your own affairs the chief payments I have received have been Mr Lopes's Note and Mr Foulkes's bond which I have applied to the payment of Mr Wynter, Mr Ruddall, Mr Aikenhead, Mr Taffe. Mr White's Order I am in expectation of receiving which shall be applied to the payment of Mr Ramsay.

I know my dear Brother I have no occasion to say anything about my Child, the tender feelings of a Father will however Overflow, and the delicacy of your own Sensations will on the present Occasion be an excuse for mine, the eyes of my affection have followed him, and it will be great joy to hear of his being fixed, under your kind auspices, whose benevolent hand will guide and direct him.

---

[135] Grace Dakins married Philip Pinnock 1744, died 14 August 1771.

Pray remember me in an affectionate manner to Miss Kelly I hope she has before now got over every Inconvenience of the Voyage, all your children are I hope well, my best wishes will ever attend you and yours. Adieu My Dear Brother, and beleive to be what I always shall be Most Sincerely and Affectionately

yours Joseph Lee.

Joseph Lee to Robert Cooper Lee

Spanish Town, Jamaica, 3rd September 1771

The sailing of the Pacquet being postponed for a few days I take the Opportunity My dear Brother of again addressing you.

This serves to inclose the first of a lot of Bills of Exchange drawn by Edward Knowles in your Favour for £321.15 .4 Sterling. It is for the Principal and Interest of his Bond to Mr Trecothick[136] due the first Instant, but as he has drawn the Bills in your Favour, I have forwarded them to you, that you may be pleased to Indorse and give them to Mr Trecothick as I would not willingly lose this Opportunity of the Pacquet to remit them.

This Morning we had a very smart shock of an Earthquake, it happened about eight o'clock. I was just sitting down to Breakfast upstairs and felt it very Severely – the Motion was violent and continued a long time; when I had run into the Street the Earth was still in motion – it has made a crack in one of the inner Walls of your house, and thrown down several chimnies about the Town, but no other mischief that I have yet heard of.

Mr T[homas] Bullock died this Morning. Your Friends Wynter, Winde and Welch are all well and desire their Compliments to you with the warmest Sentiments of Affection and regard I shall always be My Dear Brother

yours most Affectionately Joseph Lee.

---

[136] Barlow Trecothick (1720-1774) baptised at Stepney 30th January 1719/20, son of Cornish mariner Mark Trecothick (possibly born at sea) apprenticed in Boston to Charles Apthorp, later his father-in-law. Spent seven years in Jamaica between about 1742-49 then settled in London. A wealthy merchant he obtained the Freedom of the City in 1761, became a London MP in 1768,and Lord Mayor in 1770. Owner of the *Trecothick* merchant ship. He was outspoken on American matters and what he saw as misguided despotism.

PS Pray remember me in the most Affectionate manner to Miss Kelly and your little ones, my Child Jack, my Sister and her children.

Joseph Lee to Robert Cooper Lee

Spanish Town, Jamaica, 14th October 1771

I have had my Dear Brother at last singular satisfaction of hearing from you by the receipt of your letter of the sixth of August, which gave me and everyone of your numerous friends here very great pleasure although it was not intirely complete on Account of your not being then happily arrived, however my hopes and wishes have long time since landed you in England, and I trust it will not be long before I hear from you from there. There were other letters came [by the same] Conveyance which do not speak favorably of the Monarch of your Wooden World.

Our Friend Mr Winter met with a very unlucky accident in the Country as he was riding out in a Kittereen[137] with his little boy, the horse took fright, broke both the shafts and threw both him and his Child out, happily neither had any bones broke, and he has escaped with only being confined for some time on account of his Bruises. Your other friends are all well – very fine rains have fallen and still continue which will do great good and promises good Crops.

You have inclosed the second of Mr Knowle's Bills of Exchange for his debt to Mr Trecothick.

I beg to be remembered affectionately to [illegible] and to my Niece and Nephews, I hope Matt did not feel any Inconvenience from the Voyage. I am sure my friend Dick could not. I am most truly and affectionately My Dear Brother

Yours most Sincerely Joseph Lee.

137 A four-wheeled one-horse carriage with a movable hood, similar to an American buggy. Possibly named after the town of Kettering.

England 1771-1799

On Tuesday the 1st of October 1771, just over a month after arriving in England, Robert Cooper Lee and Priscilla Kelly were married by licence at St Georges Hanover Square.

It is hard to over emphasise just how unusual this was. Many white men in Jamaica had long term relationships with mixed race women, brought up families with them and provided for their children. But almost without exception, if they married at all, it was to white women, and if there were none suitable in Jamaica they returned to Britain to find a wife.

It is not surprising that Robert Cooper Lee and Priscilla did not marry in Jamaica where disapproval would have been considerable and the effect on his career and ability to do business inevitably negative. However there were advantages in having a household presided over by the mother of your children especially where she was well educated and capable of entertaining the white elite. That Robert Cooper Lee was unmarried and living with the mother of his children of mixed race would have been entirely unremarkable in Jamaica.

A 1765 letter from Simon Taylor demonstrates the sort of disapproval that a marriage might incur when he refers to the intention of Rose Price to marry. 'I cannot forget to acquaint you there is a Report on Friday last a Licence was taken out for our friend Rose Price and one Miss Patrick a Writing Master's Daughter at Spanish [Town] and without a Shilling but that Rose sett out the next day for the Red Hills with his Black wife. I should be very sorry that he should play the fool so egregiously as there has been some coolness between his father and him for some time about other matters and in all probability this will so much incense the Old man that he will disinherit him...'[138] It is not clear whether Rose Price went ahead with the marriage since the following year he was married to Lydia Ann Fagan. Fear of 'diluting' the white elite was ever present and perhaps his father intervened to reinforce the convention that marrying a mixed race wife was just not done.

Within a month of arriving in England however Robert married Priscilla and he later set about ensuring that their children would not be disadvantaged by either their illegitimacy or their slave ancestry. There is

---

138 Betty Wood and Martin Lynn eds., op.cit. pp.24-25.

no indication that his wife's background was any hindrance to Robert in England, although it must have been well known to many of those who were his friends and business associates from Jamaica. Nor is there any indication that Priscilla was socially disadvantaged, she attended the theatre, went to Ranelagh, walked on the Terrace at Windsor and dined with and entertained on an equal footing the other women of her class.

Their friends Marchant and Ann Tubb were witnesses at the wedding and Marchant was instrumental in finding them a suitable house to live in. The family moved into number 26 Berners Street, in the newly fashionable area to the north of Oxford Street, whose lease remained in their possession for over 30 years. When it was eventually sold in 1802 the Berners Street house was described as having

lofty airy bedchambers of good proportions, servants rooms and numerous closets, lofty capacious drawing room with an elegant chimney piece and stucco cornice, a large dining room and sideboard recess, library, lofty entrance hall, and suitable attached offices well arranged, and supplied with water; standing for 2 carriages, stabling for 5 horses and dry arched cellaring

There was rear access to the stabling via Berners Mews, not only useful in terms of access to horses and carriages, but enabling the night soil men to clear out the cesspits for the privies or 'necessary houses' without coming through the house. Although there was piped water, the house probably did not have an indoor lavatory, there being little yet in the way of a public sewage system (which lead to frequent outbreaks of cholera well into the next century), and its occupants would have made use of close-stools, chamber pots and outdoor earth closets. The piped water supply probably did not flow every day, and water would have been stored in a cistern connected by a thin lead 'quill' or pipe to the hollowed elm-wood water pipes laid under the street. A turncock who did his rounds in the middle of the night turned the supply on and off to refill the household tank two or three times a week[139]. Any household that ran out of water between refills would have to send a servant to collect more from a public pump.

As for the other 'suitable attached offices' these would have included kitchen, scullery and pantries. It is just possible that the kitchen would have been fitted with one of the new closed iron ranges. Cheaper and better casting techniques were making iron fire grates common, but it is more likely that cooking was still done over an open fire with meat

[139] Picard, op.cit. p.23

roasted on spits hung above it, and any cooking requiring an oven would be sent out to the nearest bakery (a practice that persisted in some areas well into the twentieth century). Ranges with an oven to one side and a water boiler on the other as well as hotplates on top were not developed until the end of the eighteenth century onwards. Both fire grates and ranges would have required daily raking out, cleaning and 'black leading' to prevent them from rusting and keep them looking smart - a filthy task usually assigned to the youngest kitchen maid.

In London due to a shortage of wood, the main fuel had long been coal for fires in each room as well as the kitchen, the sulphurous smoke contributing to the rapidly declining air quality and frequent fogs. So bad was the pollution that the better off sent their laundry out of London to be washed so it would not be speckled with soot as it dried. The fields of Islington were festooned with the drying shirts of the well to do, and the fastidious Beau Brummell insisted on 'country washing'[140].

Berners Street was a short distance from Hyde Park to the west and an easy walk into the City of London, although the family probably did not walk much in town owing to the filth in the uneven streets. They would have used their own coach for longer journeys or hired a post chaise, and for shorter journeys would have called for a hackney or a sedan chair.

A few streets to the north of the house was the New Road from the City to Paddington (now the Marylebone Road) beyond which the land was still completely undeveloped, with open fields stretching from the village of Paddington, the hamlet of St John's Wood (much of it owned by Walpole Eyre) and the remains of Kilborn (now Kilburn) Abbey, to the village of Hampstead. At the northern end of Berners Street was the Middlesex Hospital; founded in 1745 it had moved to Charles Street in 1755 and was enlarged there in 1775. There was a busy street market in Charles Street and Oxford Market lay in the opposite direction so that the Lee family servants did not have far to go for provisions, and of course there were shops in Oxford Street itself. For entertainment in summer there were the Marylebone Gardens which were pleasure grounds like Vauxhall or Ranelagh. Pepys had walked there after the Great Fire, and visitors in the 1770s could enjoy bowling greens and entertainments, with entry by subscription. Later the gardens gradually declined and became somewhat disreputable, and with pressure on building land for an expanding city were eventually replaced with more streets of high quality

140 Ian Kelly, *Beau Brummell The Ultimate Man of Style*, Free Press, New York, 2006, p.95.

housing. In the meantime Berners Street was still a quiet, clean location on the edge of the most fashionable and expensive territory around Portman Square to the west and Grosvenor Square south of Oxford Street.

It must however have been quite a shock for Priscilla, Betty Harrison and five year-old Richard fresh from their sea voyage and with memories of a much quieter home in tropical Jamaica to find themselves amidst the bustle and noise of the second largest city in the world (only Beijing was larger). Even for Robert, who had known London and had kept up with London news, the city he came back to was very different from the one he had left.

There were two new bridges across the Thames, Westminster Bridge which had been under construction when he left was opened in 1750, Blackfriars Bridge opened in 1769. London Bridge had finally lost its jumble of houses and shops in 1757 and acquired a new and elegant Italianate balustrade. Water still whirled and eddied under its many arches however, a hazard to the river boatmen, causing the river to freeze in hard winters, and the Tudor waterwheels on the medieval bridge continued to raise water from the river into the public water supply.

In addition to the new bridges, London had been spreading rapidly outwards covering areas that were just fields in Robert's youth, and its population had grown from about half a million in 1750 to three quarters of a million two decades later. Courtyards, such as Starr Court were subject to uncontrolled infill, and gardens and open spaces were rapidly being built over. Once fashionable areas like Covent Garden had gone downhill and were now the haunt of thieves and prostitutes, their wealthy inhabitants having moved westward. It was not uncommon for buildings in the slum areas to collapse without warning; the poor and dispossessed slept where they could in cellars, garrets and stables.

In the face of increasing crime a rudimentary police service was beginning, the Bow Street Runners having been founded just as Robert was leaving England by Henry Fielding from the Magistrates Court at No. 4 Bow Street, work later carried on by his blind brother John Fielding. The impact of the Runners was still limited however, they were small in number and operated all across the country serving writs and apprehending criminals. For those who were convicted, older medieval prisons such as the Fleet remained but the Newgate of Bob's childhood was being rebuilt. The hapless offender who was sentenced to hang would be paraded from prison in an open cart along Oxford Street to Tyburn (modern Marble Arch) where the mob could enjoy a good execution, observe whether the offender met a good death and watch the body cut down to be taken for dissection. Patrolling the streets at night was still left to the Watchmen whose duties largely consisted in calling the hours and watching out for fires. Much of the old medieval City Walls had been demolished in the 1760s and fine new buildings had gone up in the City and Westminster. To provide for the expanding population new hospitals such as the Middlesex were funded by private subscription, the London Hospital was being developed at Whitechapel for the treatment of the poor 'at any hour without expense'[141], and near to Bedlam additional provision for the mentally ill had been provided at St Lukes Hospital, while private asylums catered for the better off.

As soon as he could after their arrival Robert Cooper Lee set about making contact with old friends and started to exploit the network within the Jamaican ex-pat community in London, amongst whom he hoped to do business. One of his earliest calls was on his old benefactor Rose Fuller.

Robert Cooper Lee to Priscilla Lee

Rosehill, 26th October 1771

My Dear Priscy,

I reached this Place on Wednesday afternoon tween 4 and 5 o'clock, having a good deal of Rain the last 20 miles and not the best Horses. It gave me great Pleasure to see my best of Friends, and I think him extremely well and hearty and happy beyond description amongst the most agreeable young Family. He inquired after Mrs Lee and my young Folks. I intend staying here till Monday Morning and hope in the Evening to be with Mr Long at Chichester and by Thursday Night at my own Fireside. If any thing [illegible] material you may write me at Mr Long's. I hope you have been all well since I left you. Make my best Compliments to Mr and Mrs Tubb and Miss Morant and my Love to Fanny I am My Dear

Your Affectionate Husband Robert Cooper Lee.

Meanwhile Joseph had heard of the family's safe arrival in London.

---

[141] Picard, op.cit. p.93

Joseph Lee to Robert Cooper Lee

Spanish Town, Jamaica, 3rd December 1771

It was My Dear Brother with the utmost satisfaction that I had the pleasure of receiving your agreeable favour of 14 September by the *Mary,* Captain Smith, your friends Winde, Wynter, Simpson and Cooke were drinking your health with me at the time I received your letter, and you may be assured it put us in very good Spirits.

I sincerely rejoyce to hear that you found my Niece so well as you mention for we had very disagreeable accounts of her soon after you left this Island.

When you have been longer in your old Climate I shall expect to hear your sentiments and when you have fixed your Plan (if it is to practise at the Cockpitt) your numerous friends here will be eager to testify their respect and Esteem for you by forwarding you in it.

The latter part of this year has been wet and sickly, but your particular friends have held it out very well except your friend Mr [Edward] Bullock who has had different attacks, which have made him begin to think seriously of Old England.

Poor Mr Archer died at North America, you are I hear one of his Executors. Miss Davis was lately married to Ensign Dobbins. Miss Redwood to Mr John Rodon.

I beg you will present my affectionate love to my worthy and much Esteemed Sister Mrs Lee my Sister Morley and all the little ones and my respects to every enquiring friend. I am truly and on unalterably My Dear Brother

Yours most Affectionately Joseph Lee.

PS 4th December. An action has been brought against Mr Ellis this Court (in which nothing is yet done) by William Gilchrist the Millwright upon the Act of this Island made in his favor, for Mr Ellis having erected a Mill with side Rollers above three Inches more in Diameter than the Main Roller – the Act made in favor of Mr Gilchrist having never been confirmed by His Majesty – Mr Ellis desires me to write to you to solicit the Rejection of it, and the principal argument which Mr Ellis urges for the rejection of this Bill is for that the Preamble of the Act sets forth a new Invention of Mr Gilchrist's and particularly describes it 'with large side Rollers *and* Springs in the brass blocks with Levers' whereas in the Enacting part the penalty is laid upon such persons who make Mills 'with side Rollers above three Inches more in Diameter than the Main Roller *or* the brass blocks and levers upon the aforesaid Principal and Invention of

William Gilchrist' now Mr Ellis having built a Mill with laye side Rollers exceeding three inches more in Diameter than the Main Roller but without Springs in the brass blocks with levers mentioned in the preamble of the Act and Action has nevertheless been brought against him, which Gilchrist contends that Mr Ellis has [in?ed] under the enacting part of the Law, whereas Mr Ellis insists that such enacting part is contrary to the spirit and Intention of the Law specified in the Preamble, the Preamble speaking only of one Machine with Rollers and Springs and the enacting part speaking of Machines with Rollers or brass blocks and Levers, thereby describing different Machines to those mentioned in the Preamble, which is a reason assigned by Mr Ellis for the Rejection of it.

Another reason assigned by Mr Ellis is for that this Act has never been printed promulgated or published. Mr Ellis also alledges that the having side Rollers larger in Diameter than the Main Roller was not a new invention but had been put in use before the passing of this Act – from all which Mr Ellis contends that Mr Gilchrist should and ought to have been kept and confined strictly to the Machine described in the Preamble. I have kept you too long upon this dry subject. I will conclude as before that I am most Sincerely

Your most Affectionate Brother Joseph Lee.

PS 5th December - I am much concerned to add that Mr Bullock (the Counsellor) died this Morning[142].

Joseph Lee to Robert Cooper Lee

Spanish Town, Jamaica, 12th December 1771

The Pacquet being detained some time gives Mee an Opportunity My dear Brother of again addressing you, which I wish to do as often as possible – indeed the principal purpose of this is at the desire of Mrs Gordon – the late Mr Gordon having by his Will devised his Estate in Trust to yourself, Mr Welch and Mr Bullock. Mrs Gordon has requested me to write to you to send out a power of Attorney to carry on and execute that Trust, in Order to join in such Sales of his property as she may think necessary.

---

[142] Edward Bullock, buried Spanish Town 5th December 1771.

The short space since the date of my last letter does not permit me to add much here, but I'm sorry to inform you that this short Interval has deprived us of Mr Bourke[143] who died on Wednesday Morning – he had been slightly indisposed but was very well on the Monday – on Tuesday he complained of a sore throat which terminated in a Quinsy and in a few hours brought on his dissolution. He has by his Will devised his Estates in Trust to his Brother[144], Mr [Charles] Palmer[145] and his youngest son[146] (upon his attaining his age of 21) and upon the deaths of Mr Palmer and his youngest son, he makes Mr WP Brown, Mr Welch, Mr Hall, yourself and Mr McCabe Trustees until his debts and legacies are paid, and appoints them with his first named Trustees Executors.

Our Session of Assembly has gone very smoothly. The Bill for the holding of Alternate Courts at Montego Bay and Savannah La Mar has been the principal contested matter, it however passed the Assembly by Majority of 14 Voices but its fate is not yet determined in the Councill.

I hope soon to hear from you by some of the London Ships now expected in, in the meantime except of my best wishes for your health and happiness, pray give my love to my Sister Lee and your family my Sister Morley and her children and remember me to Jack of whom I hope soon to hear a favourable Account. I am with the utmost warmth and truth

Your most Affectionate Brother Joseph Lee.

Joseph Lee to Robert Cooper Lee

Spanish Town, Jamaica, 27th January 1772

I had My Dear Brother very great pleasure on the receipt of your favors of the 5th October and 2nd and 21st November, whereby as well as by Captain Stupart, Mr Campbell and others I had the agreeable Accounts of your being happily settled. My own happiness is so much wound up in yours that I have not a Wish beyond it. It gave me a real satisfaction to hear that my Neice Miss Lee was so happily re-established in her health,

---

143 Nicholas Bourke, married Elizabeth Fearon 1748, Clarendon Jamaica.

144 John Bourke of London.

145 Charles Pallmer was married to Jane Peters Bourke, daughter of Nicholas, in 1770.

146 Edmund Fearon Bourke (1754-1812).

believe me you can have no joy of that kind in which I do not most Cordially participate.

I observe what you mention about Mr Palmer's bond belonging to Mrs Bristow, it was impossible to get anything last year after you went away, the season was late, and almost every payment that could be made engaged both in that matter as well as your own but I shall bestow myself for the present year. I had a short time before the receipt of your letter applied to Mr Pallmer, who assures me of the payment of that Bond this Crop.

I shall be very happy to render any services that lay in my power to Mr and Mrs Boyd and Mrs Murphy (to whom please to present my compliments) without esteeming it any trouble whatever, and indeed as I may find it necessary to windup matters, to retire from that extensive scene of Law Business, in which I am at present engaged, I shall then have more leisure to attend to any matters of Attorney ships.

A Judgement has been recovered in the Action upon Mr Dowell's bond (the general issue only being pleaded) and Execution is issued – in the matter of Mr Dawkins Ejectment Your Apprehension was right as to the Mistake in the Second commission, I was not at the time well enough to look at it, although I with difficulty made a shift to write the letter which inclosed it.

The Affidavit about Maurice Dawes and the copys of your Accounts Memorandums etc I will forward you by Captain Foot as they are too bulky to go by the Pacquet and Captain Foot will sail in a short time.

You have given me great pleasure by the Account of your having placed Jack so agreeably, I shall always my Dear Brother be happy and satisfied where ever you may place him as I am sure it will be for the best, and I shall not Mind any expense whatsoever on the Occasion. Propriety, Integrity and Industry are the great things which I wish to inculcate in him.

Mrs Rynes died about Christmas without giving the Mortgage to you which you directed, Mr John Rodon and Mr Curtis are her Executors who have a Power to Sell for Payment of Debts and from them I understand that there will be sufficient to pay every body. Mr Samuel Jackson and Mr Ireble are also dead, the latter within three days of his intended Marriage with the widow George Richards.

Mr Beach[147] has purchased from Mrs Sadler Hals Hall Plantation Subject to the Payment of her debts, your demand at the time of Sale I mentioned to Mr Beach, who promised to pay it this Crop, in which engagement however I am apprehensive he will fail, but you may be assured I shall attend to it very closely. A Treaty is on foot for the sale of the late Mr Gordon's house and Penn on this side the River, to Mrs Sadler for which Mr Beach's bonds are intended and offered in Payment to Mr Gordon's Creditors, but I have declined changing the Security for your Debts. I know not what the other Creditors may do. Mr Ellis has had thoughts of purchasing Roses Penn, in which case I apprehend I should follow your inclination to change Mr Gordon's security for his – now I have mentioned Mr Ellis's name I must tell you that he has another Born[148] and your Friend Mr Harrison is upon the very precipice of Matrimony with Miss Cross. Mr William Bullock has quitted his connection with Messrs Lyon and Ridge and leaves the Island in one of the first Ships.

My letter I am afraid you will think too long, but I think the length of a letter ought to bear some proportion to the distance it is to go. Shall I trouble you Sir to send me out two Suits of Cloaths (Summer colours) the Coats to be without capes and with Buttons on the Sleeves, and a Scarlett Waistcoat with a gold Lace – Lovick has my Measure, and also six pair Sattin Shoes and six pair Callimanco Shoes for my friend here, my Sister Lee's size will fit her, or John Gresham Tavistock Street Covent Garden has the measure.

Your friends Welch, Winde and Wynter as well as your other friends are quite well. I am very happy that I can assure you that I am so too.

Remember me very affectionately My Dear Brother to my Sister Lee, Miss Lee and my three Nephews, My Sister Morley and her Children, on whose Account I have a great addition to my happiness in contemplating the peace and tranquillity she must enjoy, by the pleasure of having you upon the Spot with her. My Blessing, and I hope many Blessings wait on Jack.

Adieu My Dear Brother and believe me to be

Yours most Sincerely and Affectionately Joseph Lee.

---

[147] Thomas Beach, married to Helen Hynes daughter of Jennett Guthrie by her first husband John Hynes. Jennett Guthrie's second husband was Francis Sadler (later Francis Sadler Hals) of Hals Hall for whom Robert Cooper Lee had expected to work when he arrived in Jamaica. The Beach family later changed their name to de la Beche.

[148] Charles Rose Ellis, son of John Ellis was born on the 19th of December 1771.

Joseph Lee to Robert Cooper Lee

Spanish Town, Jamaica, 26th March 1772

Captain Brett delivered me your favor of the 10th December and it was with very great pleasure My Dear Brother but I learnt from and also from your subsequent favor of the 30th of the same Month, that you, my Sister Lee, and the rest of your family were well, I most sincerely wish a very long continuance of it. We have a report here of your having a severe frost, which has frozen the Thames and detained some of our Ships, if that been the case, I hope that you or your family have not received any inconvenience from the extremity of the cold.

I have troubled Captain Stevenson with a Paquet in which I have forwarded to you the Affidavit respecting Maurice Dawes under the seal of the Island and also the copy from the Office of the Assignment of the Ferry Toll from Wallon to Campbell. The List of your Securitys and Debts, the copys of your Memorandums sent to me, the copy of your last Account Current with Mr Tubb and the copy of your last Account Current with Mr Provost wherein the Commission on Mr Venn's Estate is credited to him, the date of Mr Mickan's Bonds you will find in the same Book and also the date of Mr Breary's Bonds to Mr Stallard, but the latter Bonds I have not got. Mr Byndloss has furnished me with the dates and sums of them.

I thank you much for your kind attention to my child, it is an Obligation of the tenderest nature conferred upon me, and of which I shall always retained the deepest Impression.

I am much obliged to Mrs Ford and the Ladies for their obliging enquiries after me, will you be so kind to present my most humble respects to them. In a short time I hope to do so myself in person.

We have had a continuance of seasonable (that is rainy) weather for a long time it seems as if it would continue so for the course of this year which will do great good in many parts especially in the low lands, and the Estates in the Walks will do very well this year notwithstanding the Rain.

In one of my former letters I think I mentioned to you that Mr Harrison was again going to enter into the matrimonial State with Miss Cross, that is very soon to take place and also another Match between Mr Pinnock[149] (Clerk of the Court) and the younger Miss Dehany, this is all the News of

---

149 James Pinnock and Elizabeth Dehany were married in Spanish Town on the 19th of April 1772.

our little Circle. Mr Bristow (after whom you enquire) behaves very well, and I am satisfied will turn out to the warmest expectations of his friends, he shall not want any thing that my countenance can afford him. Mr Byndloss and Mr Davis (the latter is still with me) will I hope do very well, the business of the Law is not at present favourable to young beginner – an Extreme scarcity of cash, that evil still heightened by the Circulation of an Adulterated Coin, and the practice of the Law almost entirely carried on by advance, are very great impediments to a young person. Mr Burchall continues at the Grange, he has his Errors, but I have not any fault to find with him in the conducting of the business.

Mrs Sadler has (as I formerly wrote you) sold her Estate to the Chief Justice, and she now lives at the late Mr Gordon's house and Penn which she has contracted to Purchase at three thousand three hundred pounds including only the lands purchased from Mr Ellis.

You are now I hope agreeably settled in your new house, our friend Mr Tubb must have saved you much trouble, in the matter of the house and in other matters. I am much indebted to his kindness during my stay in England, pray make my best respects acceptable to him and to his family.

The matter of the Clerk of the Courts Office, Mr Pinnock informs me he writes you of by this Conveyance, in consequence of his intended Marriage he purposes (as he informs me) to go to the Bar, and to execute the Office by Deputy, and he has since mentioned his intention to execute the Office in the Name of some other person, but this last he has not spoke with certainty about, probably you may already have settled the matter of the New Deputation – whatever you do will be agreeable to me. I have the terms of the Agreement between Mr Vaughan and Mr Pinnock, you no doubt know them, the sum reserved to Mr Vaughan is £2900 sterling, the terms will be the same for our Moiety in a proportion. I have understood Mr Vaughan had an intention to sell his part or to purchase - our proportion by the difference of the rents is better by one half than his, our Society is so very small now that I am almost at a loss to mention any persons for the Office except those you take notice, poor Cook if he was once extricated it would be of great Service to I feel very much for his Situation. Mr Graham's disappointing him in the intended Cargo was a great Stroke against him and I am afraid it will take many years of rainy weather at Old Harbour to make him easy.

Pray remember me affectionately to my Sister Morley and her Children I wrote her by the *Duncannon* Pacquet, copy by this Conveyance. I hope she is now happily settled to her satisfaction and that peace pleasure and content attend her. I shall be desirous to do what lays in my power to add to her Felicity – pray present my affectionate respects to my Sister Lee,

Miss Lee and your Sons, to whom I most sincerely wish every degree of happiness. My kindest love to Jack – and you My Dear Brother will always command the utmost of my good Wishes and regard and I shall always be Yours most Sincerely and affectionately Joseph Lee.

Joseph Lee to Robert Cooper Lee Junior

Spanish Town, Jamaica, 16th June 1772

Dear Bob,

I have received your letter of 4 January which gives me much pleasure, and I shall always be glad to hear from you. I have also been extremely pleased to hear of your Improvement in School, and the more so as you will be a pattern for your Brothers and your Cousin, besides the pleasure it must give your Parents.

I thank you for the Account you give me of your Cousin Jack and desire you will give my love to your Sister and to your Brothers Dick and Matt.

I am Your Affectionate Uncle Joseph Lee.

Joseph Lee to Robert Cooper Lee

Spanish Town, Jamaica, 16th June 1772

I embrace the Opportunity to acknowledge the receipt of your favour by the *James Dawkins,* Captain Carter, from whom it gave me great pleasure to learn that you and your family were well, the continuance of which I earnestly wish for.

The Papers herewith are forwarded by desire of Mr Delap consisting of his power of Attorney and the perusal of which will more fully inform you of his purposes, than anything that I could say in this place to them therefore I will refer you.

Mr Nedham's Settlement I have received, and proved and recorded it. I shall also attend to what you mention respecting Mr J Williams. I have seen Mr Watt who is very hearty and well, he gave me Mr Fuller's letter and I shall therefore settle with him agreeable to that direction.

I was astonished at Dr Irving's Bill which you inclosed me. I shall write to him by the first Post, and no doubt he will replace it immediately. Mr Palmer has promised me Payment this Year of the Bond to Solomon Abrahams and I have given him a Calculation of what is due on that and also on his other Bonds your Property which he has likewise promised me Payment of – the Want of Ships at the South side of the Island for the carrying away of the Sugars has been productive of much Inconvenience, and given pretence for delays where payments have been promised.

You have inclosed two Bills of Exchange drawn by Mr Herring one for £100 sterling and the other for £30.1.7 sterling which with an Order for a small Sum in cash which he has sent me makes up the Balance due on his Bond to you, you have also inclosed a Bill of Mrs Seniors for £100 sterling and this makes the first remittance I have been able to make you. Mr Welch's Money I have not yet received but it cannot be long before that comes in, I am also promised a Payment on Mr Archer's Note, and Mr Sinclair has likewise undertaken to make a Payment, all which with such other of your matters as can be collected in by the 25th of next Month shall be transmitted to you.

I also send you enclosed Bill of Exchange drawn by Mr Harvie[150] for £100 sterling and a small one of Mr Stephen Morant's for £30 sterling on Account of my Private Account with you.

Dr Wynter[151] and Miss Ann Trelawney died lately, the death of the latter has much affected her family, the former is succeeded in his Custos-ship by Mr Sinclair. Many other persons of less Note have dropt off – Sir Charles Price is very ill and thought to be in great danger.

I will endeavour to procure the affidavit about the death of Joseph Luddington, and transmitted to you - the out of the way place in which William Lee who is the person to make the Affidavit lives is the reason I have not yet procured it.

I beg you will present my affectionate and best regards to my Sister Lee and the young folks, and to my Sister Morley and her family. May every Happiness attend you and yours I am My Dear Brother

yours most Sincerely and affectionately Joseph Lee.

---

[150] Possibly William Harvie.

[151] William Wynter, born about 1704, buried 15 May 1772 in the north aisle of the church in Spanish Town.

Joseph Lee to Robert Cooper Lee

Spanish Town, Jamaica, 1st July 1772

By the favour of Mr Mitchell who sailed in Captain Crisp, I wrote to you My Dear Brother, covering some papers from Mr Delap, and also covering the first of some Bills of Exchange.

I now take the Opportunity to forward to you the second of those Bills of Exchange, and the Duplicate of Mr Delap's papers will be forwarded to you by Mr George Gordon who sails in a few days in the *Modest.*

We have had about three weeks since a very high flood which has tore away all the woodwork of the 16 mile Walk Bridge and greatly Damaged the road, the rain was general and has done great damage in most other parts of the Country.

The Want of Ships at the South side is a new Scene of Distress which is increasing as the Season is advancing, Captain Kitchen and a small ship are the only Vessels now in the Harbour, and the whole affair loading is engaged, they sail at four shillings. I shall by them send home the whole of Mr Fuller's Complement, but great Quantities will be left here, and for the same Cause, there can be little or no Sales.

I fear Mr Beach will not pay Mrs Hals's Bond speedily, I have applied to him concerning it and have received the excuse of want of Shipping and want of Sales, and indeed I have little expectation from him for I have not been able to procure payment from him of his own Accepted Order which you left with me.

Upon Mr Harrison's marriage with Miss Cross, he has advanced a certain Sum in the payment of Mr Cross's debts by way of Settlement upon the Lady, and among others he has undertaken the payment of Mrs Bristow's demands, that is what was then due. I am in consequence to receive from him about two hundred pounds sterling this year and the remainder the next year, which will be very eligible and certain payments for Mrs Bristow – this puts me in Mind of some more Marriages which are soon to take place. Mr Scott (the Privy Councillor) with Mrs Goulbourn of Vere, and Dr Mat Gilchrist with Miss Nanny Fearon.

Mr James Pinnock has gone to the Bar since his Marriage, and I wish he may meet with success there, he is at present making his first reappearance at the Cornwall Assizes – his Name continues in the Office the Chief Justice having approved of his going to the Bar, in Virtue of a similar precedent in Mr Andrew Arcedeckne.

I have the pleasure to inform you that your several friends are very hearty, although the weather is now extremely warm. With my best and most affectionate regards to yourself and your family I am My Dear Brother

yours most truly and sincerely Joseph Lee.

In the summer of 1772 Priscilla Lee took her children on holiday to Margate. Seaside holidays were becoming fashionable as was sea bathing and Margate was an early adopter of the bathing machine, a wheeled hut drawn into the sea by a horse to provide discrete changing facilities and a canvas shielded area hiding the naked bather. At first a quick dip and a glass of sea water were taken primarily for medical purposes rather than pleasure - the Royal Sea Bathing Hospital was opened at Margate in 1791 for the treatment of tuberculosis. In 1772 the small town was rapidly developing as a seaside resort for Londoners, with convenient access by sea or road.

In 1848 *A Topographical Dictionary of England* said of Margate, 'About the middle of the last century it became much frequented as a bathing-place, from the fineness of the beach and the purity of the air; and though originally consisting of but one scattered and irregular street, it has, by the erection of new buildings at various times to meet the wants of the increased number of visitors, attained its present importance.' [152] The advent of steam packets and the railway would change the town radically in the nineteenth century, but for the moment it provided a quiet summer holiday.

Robert Cooper Lee to Priscilla Lee

Berners Street, 4th July 1772

Tho' I have expended several Quires of Paper since I came to Town, and have been at it since six o'clock this morning till eight o'clock in the Evening, half an Hour for Breakfast and an Hour for Dinner excepted, yet I must add this Sheet to the Number, assured that I cannot employ it in a manner more agreeable to myself, nor for any one to whom it will be more acceptable, tho' it is only to say I am well; Mrs Murphy and Mrs Boyd were in Town yesterday, but returned in the Evening; the former

[152] Source: http://www.british-history.ac.uk

wished you had been here to pay her Compliments to you; they and Mr Boyd desired to be kindly remembered to you and Fanny; I apprehend your Cash must be rather low; I ought to have inquired before, but any Bills you had drawn should have been honoured. Captain Hepburn sent me the Turtle yesterday. What was I to do with it? I thought it would die before it got to Margate, or you should have had a Turtle Feast. I therefore sent it to your Favourite in Lincoln's Inn Fields. I expected to have been with you on Monday, but have this Morning got Notice of a Court of Appeals at the Treasury on Tuesday, and Mr Tucker's Cause is on the List, which detains me here much against my Inclination till Wednesday Morning. I hope you my Dear, Fanny, and the Boys are well. God preserve you all to

Your ever Affectionate Robert Cooper Lee.

PS Your Letters by the two last Posts have miscarried.

There are numerous references in these family letters to turtles arriving from Jamaica for the family to feast on. Once caught in the Caribbean they were kept alive until the ship arrived in England. Their flippers were sewn together and they were turned onto their backs, as if left upright they would suffocate under their own weight. Once out of the water in England their survival time would have been limited, although they were sometimes held in large tanks to be fattened up.

On one occasion the Lees sent a present of a turtle to their sons' headmaster, which caused no little stir in the school! That such a present could be sent on the assumption that the headmaster's cook would know what to do with the creature shows how widespread was the delicacy, even if it was still something of a luxury item.

To cook the turtle it would be killed and the head removed, then the whole animal plunged into boiling water for about ten minutes to make further preparation easier, once removed from its shell, gutted and skinned, the body might be baked while the fins could be cut up and slowly stewed. The head, lights and fat were made into the much valued turtle soup. The fat of *Chelonia mydas* has a greenish tinge, which is how this species came to be called the green turtle.

Ten days later Robert Cooper Lee again wrote to Priscilla at Margate, having taken their son Richard on a trip to the dentist.

Robert Cooper Lee to Priscilla Lee

Berners Street, 14th July 1772

I thought to have presented Dick's Tooth to you this Ev'ning, but going into the City yesterday to enquire after Captain Stupart, I met with Mr Jackson, for whom and his Father in Law Mr Serocold[153], I had a piece of Business in hand some time ago, and they wanted to have it completed, which I am about doing, but it will detain me here two Days longer. I hope Stupart will be in before I leave Town; he has been out full ten Weeks. Your Yams are not to be found, which is very excusable considering how lucky we were with the Turtle. Dick was frightened at the sight of Mr Spence (Hemett was out of Town) with his Instrument in his Hand, but the Promise of another Day at home made him submit, and the Tooth was taken out without any Pain or Trouble. I have a penitential Letter for you from him, and he is to write one to his Sister in a few Days. I have eat a pound and a half of Cherries today, besides a Mutton Chop and Cauliflower. My kind Love to Fanny and Matt. No Account of Bob; his new Cloaths are in hand; light green with a white Button. No Account of Mr Tubb I sent him a long Letter by yesterday's Post. Adieu till we meet.

Yours most Affectionately Robert Cooper Lee.

Joseph Lee to Robert Cooper Lee

Spanish Town, Jamaica, 13th July 1772

In my last of the first Instant I mentioned my intention to forward to you the Duplicate of Mr Delap's Papers. I now take the Opportunity to do so, and by the desire of Mr Ellis, I also forward to you Power of Attorney from him to you to act in his Law concerns the chief Occasion of which is the renewall of his contest with Mr Adams for the land patented by Judith Jordan – Mr Ellis has brought his Ejectment against Mr Adams for that run of Land, in consequence of which Mr Adams has applied for a Commission from the Grand Court for the Examination of Witnesses in Great Britain and has also filed his Bill in the Court of Chancery here for the Examination of such Witnesses to be taken in perpetuam rei

[153] Serocold and Jackson were London Commission Agents for Jamaican planters on a par with the Fullers, Longs and Hibberts. The Serocolds were related to the Rose family by marriage (a connection going back to the beginning of the eighteenth century) as well as to the Jacksons.

Memoriam – in both those Commissions, Mr Adams, with Intent to deprive Mr Ellis of your Services, has thought proper to name you one of his Commissioners. Mr Ellis has therefore transmitted you this power that you may Act as his Attorney and Sollicitor on the Occasion, and has also made some Memorandums concerning it which you have inclosed, and the perusal of which will probably bring the full recollection of the whole matter to your Memory, Mr Ellis will himself write you in the Occasion.

The Defence of an Appeal in the Suite against the late Mr William Beckford Ellis's Estate[154] will soon be forwarded to you, a Donee has been obtained here by which the latter Deeds between Mrs and Mrs Ellis and her Trustees are established and Mr Barton's claim which he set up under the first Deed of Settlement is disallowed and the Creditors are let in for payment of their debts, from which Mr Barton has appealed and the Papers are ready to be transmitted. I have told Mr Campbell who has carried the whole on, that it will be necessary at the same time to send you a good Bill for £150 Sterling at the least or a general Order for the whole amount of the expense upon some house in London. I mention this circumstance that I may know what will be the proper Sum to be sent on Occasions of the like Nature, as it is in many cases necessary to see that the Money accompanies the papers.

Our friend Mr Winde goes to Great Britain in this ship (the *Modeste*) and will be able to inform you how well he leaves your friends on this side the water.

I have wrote to Mr Irving about your Protested Bill, but have not yet heard from him. I suppose a proper Bill will accompany his Answer.

This I hope will find you and your family in perfect health, I beg you to make my affectionate regards to my Sister Lee and your children, I hope my Sister Morley and her family are well and beg you will remember me to them.

I am always My Dear Brother

Yours most Sincerely and Affectionately Joseph Lee.

---

154 William Beckford Ellis was the brother of John Ellis referred to here as Mr Ellis. He had died in Jamaica in December 1764.

Joseph Lee to Robert Cooper Lee

Spanish Town, Jamaica, 19th July 1772

Mr Ricketts goes home a Passenger in this Ship with our friend Mr Winde – his Bond to you which is due this Month, he has desired to be indulged in till next year, which I have complied with, as I imagine you would approve of it. Altho' the 25th is so near the payments do not yet come in – Mr Palmer tells me he has 150 hogsheads to Ship ready, but has not yet been able to get them taken in, and he assures me that is the reason he has not at present, complied with his Engagement. Mr Lewing has promised me the payment of his smaller Bond which I shall no doubt shortly receive from him. Mr Reid has promised me a good Bill for the Balance of his Protested Bill. I must very soon write to you again with these matters, and therefore I will only now assure you that I am with the most cordial Affection and regard towards you and your family My Dear Brother

Yours most Sincerely Joseph Lee.

PS after a carefull search among Mr Jaafe's Papers, I cannot find any such Warrant as you mention – there is a Memorandum in your hand writing in the year 1766 of your transmitting a Certificate of his being Chaplain to the Prince Edward to Mr Jones.

Joseph Lee to Robert Cooper Lee

Spanish Town, Jamaica, 20th August 1772

Long before this reaches you, I suppose our friend Mr Winde has given you an Account of your friends here. Since he left us the death of Sir Charles Price is the only circumstance that has happened, he has by his Will given everything to his Son, and in case of his death without Issue, and without otherwise disposing of it, then to his two Nephews Mr Archbould and Mr John Price.

The Death of Mr Adams has for the present put an end to the contest in which Mr Ellis was engaged, and respecting which I wrote you on the 13th of the last Month.

You have inclosed the Answer I received from Dr Irving, I shall not I believe hasten your payment by taking any Compulsory methods, but I hope the waiting a short time will produce it. You have enclosed a small Bill I have received for your Account from the Executors of Mr Bernard Senior – the other matters remain as by my former letters.

It has been a long time since I heard from you and I have been the more uneasy at it, upon receiving the Account of your having a fit of the Gout. I long much to hear that you have got rid of that companion, and wish you a very long continuance of health and every other felicity. I am with the utmost truth and regard My Dear Brother

Yours most Sincerely Joseph Lee.

Joseph Lee to Robert Cooper Lee

Spanish Town, Jamaica, 13th September 1772

By the *Bland,* Captain Wylly, which arrived only a few days since, I have had the pleasure of your favor of the 27th May, which altho of an old date yet gave me much Satisfaction, and I was happy to find by that, that you and your family were well.

You have here with the first of four Setts of Bills of Exchange

James McLelan	50		
George Williams	151	5	1½
Benjamin Heath	37	9	6
Edward H Wynter	100		
	388	14	7½

and if I can procure Bills you shall have others by the Pacquet.

I was much surprised at the Account of your being no longer connected in the Clerk of the Courts Office, matters are in a very awkward situation in that respect, I have wrote to Mr Howell on the subject a copy of the Paragraph you have inclosed – before I left England I requested our friends Messrs Fullers to pay my part of the rent which is two hundred and fifty pounds Sterling per Annum as it becomes due, and they have Monies of mine in their hands for that purpose, but having been in daily waiting for some final settlement of the matter on your side of the water, I have never been able to come to any conclusive Settlement with Mr Pinnock on that head, nor have I received any thing on that Account, and from what you mention I am not likely to do so, and I am not furnished with any Duplicate of the Assignment or anything of that kind to show my right, in which case I might have procured Mr Pinnock to act under an appointment of the Governor and taken his Security for the Payment of the Moiety of the Rent which he now pays to Mr Vaughan – from what you mention it makes it necessary that it should be put upon some certain footing. As you are upon the Spott you will have great Opportunities of securing the Lease in case of a New Patentee and I will readily join you in any sum for that Purpose, and I am persuaded your Interest can procure it, the Securing the Lease from the next Patentee is an object I have much in View, and hope you will be able to Accomplish it. I shall always have Moneys in the hands of Messrs Fuller's to answer any purpose of that kind.

After all my application to Mr Irving I have been obliged to take a Judgement against him for your Protested Bill as there were other matters of the kind against him this Court but he has assured me that he will make a point of your Demand being paid.

I purpose writing you by the Pacquet which will sale in about 10 days. I beg you to remember me very affectionately to my Sister Lee and my Sister Morley and to all the Young folks, give my hearty love to Jack. I wish you every felicity this life can afford and shall always remain with the utmost Sincerity My Dear Brother

Yours most Affectionately Joseph Lee.

Joseph Lee to Robert Cooper Lee

Spanish Town, Jamaica, 14th September 1772

At last I have procured William Lee's Affidavit relative to Joseph Luddington which I take the first Opportunity to forward to you, and the Duplicate shall be sent by the next Conveyance agreeable to Mr Farbrace's letter to me on the subject – the expenses upon this and the Duplicate will be £9.10 shillings Currency or £6.15.8½ Sterling which Mr Farbrace writes me he will settle with you.

I have not now time to add anything but must refer you to my letter by the Pacquet. You will always believe me to be My Dear Brother

Yours most Sincerely and Affectionately Joseph Lee.

Joseph Lee to Robert Cooper Lee

Spanish Town, Jamaica, 21st September 1772

This serves to inclose you the second of some Bills of Exchange, the first of which I forwarded you by the *Ferret* Sloop, and I now transmit you a

Bill of Exchange of Mr Shickles[155] for £254.03 5½ Sterling which I apprehend to be very good.

Since my last I have your agreeable favor of the 26th of June which gave me infinite pleasure, to hear of the health of yourself and your family, May you enjoy along the continuance of it. I hope the British Climate it will continue to agree with my Sister Lee, pray make my affectionate respects to her. I am heartily concerned to hear that my Niece Miss Lee has had any return of her disorder so as to make it necessary on that account for her to take the Margate Waters, but I hope she is by this time again re-established in her health, an event I most sincerely wish for.

Had Mr Bryan Edwards[156] been on this side the Country I apprehend I should have been able to write you with certainty respecting Mr Bassnetts[157] matter, but Mr Edwards was at the North side at the time your favor came to my hands, and has continued their ever since. I immediately wrote to him upon the Subject, which I forwarded to him and am in hopes I shall have an Answer from him before the sailing of the *Anna Teresa* Pacquet which is now in Harbour you will be assured I will do every thing in my power to have the matter properly and speedily adjusted.

Mrs Ford[158] must long ago have been satisfied respecting the matter which caused her Alarm, upon Mr Trower[159] mentioning the matter to me I went into the Office and found the Patent properly recorded, and

---

155 John Shickle (1713-1782) born in London and apprenticed in 1728 to serve Fearand [?Fearon] Dawkins and Malcomb of Jamaica Merchants. By 1754 he owned over 3000 acres, mainly in Clarendon and Vere. In the year of his death he was Custos, and Chief Judge of the Common Pleas, for Clarendon and Vere. He fathered fourteen children with at least five women, four of whom were recorded as negroes. Elizabeth Martin Israel whose colour is not recorded, and her three illegitimate children all ended their days in England, inheriting considerable wealth from John Shickle.

156 The great Jamaican historian and nephew of Zachary Bayly.

157 Richard Bassnett is listed by Feurtado as a Kingston Merchant in 1726. It seems likely this is Nathaniel Bassnett a London merchant, part owner of a ship called the *Commerce* in 1761.

158 Widow of Gilbert Ford owner of Mount Sion plantation, Attorney General for Jamaica in 1760, who died in 1768. The trustees of his estate were William Nedham, Rose Herring May, Thomas Gordon and Robert Cooper Lee.

159 Probably James Trower a member of the Jamaican Assembly and father of Elizabeth Saville Trower married to Edward Bullock, also mentioned in these letters, who had died the previous year.

prepared the Deed of Conveyance from the Trustees to Mrs Ford which was executed by Mr May here and sent home to be executed by the other Trustees Mr Nedham and Mr Alpress.

I beg pardon for omitting to acknowledge the receipt of my Watch – Captain Boyd delivered it to me very safely. I have no Memorandum about the Puncheon of Rum, but Mr Davis has frequently spoke to me about it. I gave him your direction, and I think he told me he had shipt it – if he has not I will have it taken proper care of for you.

The matters you mention for my friend Mr Tubb and yourself I shall punctually attend to and if there is any other matters you will desire to have sent from here I shall receive a pleasure in procuring them for you.

I have not since seen Mr Pinnock upon the subject of the Clerk of the Courts Office, and upon looking at his Agreement with Mr Vaughan I find that he was to settle his Accounts at the end of each half-year and to make his remittances within six months afterward so that I have no immediate right to call upon him. I left with Messrs Fullers a copy of the Agreement between Mr Howell and myself, in consequence of which Mr Howell is to make an Assignment to me of a Moiety of his half, and Messrs Fuller's was so obliging to undertake to give security for me to pay one Moiety of the Rent – these things if not already done will be necessary.

I sincerely rejoice at the pleasing account you give me of our friend Mr Rose Fuller, and hope he will long enjoy the same good state of health.

I must defer writing in answer to the other parts of your letter until the sailing of the *Anna Teresa* a boy being now waiting to carry this down to the Pacquett but I cannot conclude without desiring you will remember me most affectionately to my Sister Lee and your family my Sister Morley and her family and to my child. I am My Dear Brother

Very truly and Affectionately Joseph Lee.

Joseph Lee to Robert Cooper Lee

Spanish Town, Jamaica, 1st October 1772

I take the Opportunity My dear Brother to drop you a few lines by this Pacquet, and I also forward you the second of John Shickle's Bill of Exchange for £254.3.5½ the first of which I sent you by the *Duncannon*

Pacquet, and I now also inclose you the first of a Sett of Bills of Exchange drawn by Edward Hampson Wynter[160] for £100.

At last I have procured a Sett of Bills for the payment of Mrs Murphy's rent, the first of which you have inclosed, but I have not been able to do anything with Mr Cuniffe's Protested Bill, I have mentioned it to him and have given him the Calculation of what is due upon it, but without procuring any effect.

The Appeal Papers in Campbell vs Barton were forwarded to you by the *Ferret* Sloop, I believe I mentioned something of the Cause in one of my former letters, but I will take up a few Minutes of your time upon the Subject. Upon the hearing here the argument took up a very long time and the general Defence set up by the Answers and by the Examinations[?] were the overvaluation of the Negroes, as to Mr Campbell's particular demand, and that the purpose of the Conveyance from the Trustees being to enable Mr Ellis to borrow a Sum of Money from Messrs Fullers, and to enable him to execute the Mortgage to them for securing the payment of it the Conveyance from the Trustees should not be extended any further than to the Monies actually borrowed from Messrs Fullers, these were the points they laboured to sett up preparatory to the hearing, but upon the hearing, altho' they contended as to the overvaluation of the Negroes, yet they deserted the other part of their defence and took an Objection to the Conveyance from the Trustees, for that there was no probate of the Execution of it by the Trustees, this Objection was battled for two days, but it appearing to be in the nature of a fine and recovery from Mr and Mrs Ellis, and they being the only persons interested in it, the Court overruled[?] the Objection.

I hope my Dear Brother this will find you in good health with your whole family, I beg you will remember me affectionately to my Sister Lee and my Neice Miss Lee.

I have pleasure to inform you that all your friends here are very well, with the most Cordial Affection and Esteem I always shall be My Dear Brother

yours most truly and Sincerely Joseph Lee.

PS A fact in favour of Mr Campbell is that the Original Bill was filed against Mrs Barton in her life time so that she might have come in and setup her claim if any she had, but she put in no Answer. Mr Barton's

[160] Edward Hampson Wynter (c.1750-1797), second and only surviving legitimate son of Dr William Wynter of Jamaica.

claim is mearly as Administrator, which he setts up in prejudice of Mrs Barton's own Children by Mr Ellis.

This letter was sent by the *Anna Teresa* packet as intended and Robert Cooper Lee received it on the 30th of November 1772, by which time his brother Joseph was already dead. He sent an answer on the 26th of December not knowing that his brother would never read it.

There is no record of the cause of Joseph Lee's death, which must have occurred about the 27th of October, as he was buried in Spanish Town on the 28th, and burials in tropical Jamaica usually occurred within a day or so of the death.

Joseph had made a new Will in February 1772, probably to accommodate the fact that his daughter Mary Jaques Lee had been born since his return to Jamaica, in it he requested that his body should be returned to England and buried in the parish of Barn Elms, now better known as Barnes, on the south bank of the Thames. Although his Will did not say so explicitly it is clear he wished to be buried near to his mother. His wish was honoured and Robert Cooper Lee had a splendid new brick vault and tomb created in the churchyard of St Mary's Barnes where Joseph was reburied on the 30th of July 1773. With its distinctive classical urn on top it was clearly visible in contemporary illustrations of the church.

Joseph had at least £6000 placed on deposit in London with the Fullers, and he set up a trust fund of up to £10,000 to be managed by his brother and the Fullers to oversee the education and upbringing of his three children. The executors were authorised to dispose of 'all lands, negroes and other slaves and other real estate for the most money that can be had and moneys transmitted to Robert Cooper Lee in Great Britain' in trust for John Lee, William Robert Lee and Mary Jaques Lee.

His sister Charlotte was to receive an annuity of £100 a year and £50 for mourning, and it is noteworthy that he specifically said that this was to be paid directly to her 'for her sole and separate use and not subject to the debts or control of her present or any future husband'.

He left £1000 to his brother Bob, with £100 to Priscilla and £100 each to his niece and nephews Frances Lee, Robert Cooper Lee and Matthew Allen Lee at the age of twenty-one. Richard was singled out to receive £200 – no reason was given for this and it may just be that Dick was his uncle's favourite.

One hundred guineas each was left to his friends Richard Welch, Scudamore Winde, Thomas Wynter and George Wotton, and his friend and partner John Allen was left fifty guineas for a ring.

When it came to providing for his children, we hear for the first and only time of his 'mulatto son George Brown' who was left £300 Jamaican currency to be assigned on his behalf as the executors thought fit. His other children were to receive £1000 each on reaching twenty-one. The residue of the estate was to be divided half to Robert Cooper Lee and the rest equally among his three children. Sadly Mary Jaques Lee died in December 1775 aged four.

A codicil to the Will left two negro slaves to 'Sarah Lewis, who now lives with me' and an annuity of £100 Jamaican currency, effectively treating her almost equally with his sister Charlotte and recognizing that she was likely to remain in Jamaica. Some time after Joseph's death his son William Robert was sent to England and the guardianship of his uncle. With both her sons at school in England and her daughter dead, Sarah Lewis began a relationship with Samuel Queneborough. Her daughter Ann Queneborough was born in 1779 and died at the age of three, but her son Samuel Taylor Queneborough, born in 1784 was left an annuity and £8000 sterling by his father and died in Cornwall, England in 1839. Sarah was left property in Spanish Town and an annuity of £140 Jamaican per year by Samuel Queneborough. There is a burial record for Sarah Lewis, a 'free Brown' aged 72, on the 18th of April 1819.

It is worth noting that Joseph had circumvented the 1761 Devises Act by leaving each child less than £2000, and by having transferred most of his liquid assets to the Fullers in London. Robert Cooper Lee oversaw the education of his nephews and managed their invested inheritance which gave them a very comfortable, if not overly luxurious, life style.

With Joseph dead and his children in England, the Lee family were all now firmly re-established in London. The four older boys were all sent away to school and were joined by Robert Home Gordon whose mother had finally been persuaded to part with him to Robert Cooper Lee's guardianship. Having recovered from her latest bout of illness, Frances went back to school in Streatham. Throughout their time at school Robert Cooper Lee wrote regularly to his children and they replied, often with requests for money or chocolate or looking forward to the holidays! During those holidays they spent time with other children of the Jamaican Plantocracy such as the three sons of John Scott – Jack, George and Matthew, with whom they formed lifetime friendships.

Robert Cooper Lee to Priscilla Lee

Deal, 17 June 1773

I wrote you two or three Lines yesterday afternoon from Canterbury. As there was no Machine from thence to this Place for Patty to come in I took a Coach there which brought us and her, and all the Baggage safe to our Lodgings – Barnes arrived some Hours before us, and my Horse is not the worse for his Journey. We found Mr and Mrs Tubb and the two young Ladies perfectly well, and as cheerful and busy as ever; they were impatiently looking to see or hear from us, to know how you was, and were extremely glad to hear you was so much better. I flatter myself you have continued to mend, and that I shall find you quite stout, when I return, which shall be as soon as you please, for Mr Tubb has kindly offered to take the Charge of Fanny and the Boys, and tells me I may go away whenever I will. Our Landlady seems a very obliging quiet Woman; the House is as near the Water as Mr Rowe's at Margate, and our Apartments are at least as good, and the Beds and every thing else neat and clean. Mr Tubb's House is so near us that we can talk together from our different Windows, and he is acquainted with all *necessary Folks for getting good things,* so that I think you will like our Quarters very well. Gunpowder Tea at 9/6; best Hyson at 6/6; plenty of Turtle's Eggs, Salt Beef etc. The Boys took their first Dip in the Water this Morning; Miss Morant and Fanny begin tomorrow. We have all taken a Glass of Salt Water, and only want you to pledge us or at least to drink to. My best Compliments attend Mr Mayo – Mrs Tubb is anxious to hear about Mr Morant. I wish you would request Mr Mayo to make Enquiry for Major Campbell or any of the Officers that are arrived, to know if Mr Morant is come or coming, and let me or Mr Tubb know what he hears about him. There is no such thing as an Oil Skin Cap to be got here, so that one must be got in London to bring down with us. Our Neighbours desire their Love, as do the Boys their Duty. Fanny will write at the foot of this. I expect to hear from you by tomorrow's Post. Take Care of yourself for all our Sakes; I am ever tenderly and sincerely

Your Affectionate Husband Robert Cooper Lee.

PS remember me to Mr Farquhar, not forgetting Mathew Allen Lee.

Dear Mama,

I flatter myself this will find you much better than when we left you and that in a few days we shall have the pleasure of seeing you here and be assured that I shall wait impatiently for that happy period. We met our good friends very well. On my arrival I enquired after a Con House and I can inform there is very good Milk to be had at Deal everything is plenty enough Pease at about two Shillings a Gallon Cauliflowers four pence apiece very fine ones. There are also good Flowers and I hope you will find this place perfectly agreeable. Mrs Tubb has Handkerchiefs and Silks for your Inspection. She had a piece of Muslin but at your not coming down the person who it belonged to sold it. The India Ships are not arrived. Dick and Jack join me in our Affectionate Duty to you and in hearty wishes for your Speedy recovery. Pray give our kind love to Matt and believe me to be Dear Mama your most Dutiful Daughter Frances Lee.

Below this was written in a careful childish hand

my duty to my dear Mama Richard Lee.

The 'Machine' referred to in the letter above was the public stage coach. It would be common practice to send the servants ahead of the family when they moved between properties and on this occasion we can assume that Patty was their maid and Barnes the groom or footman. There are very few references in the Lee letters to their servants, apart from the much loved Betty Harrison, and none at all to the slaves working on plantations in Jamaica in which they had a share.

Just how many servants were required to keep up their establishments is not clear. In general overseeing the housekeeping and hiring servants would have fallen to Priscilla, but with ultimately three houses to maintain (although Berners Street may have been rented out part of the time) there would have been a need for a housekeeper in the country, plus agricultural workers on the estate, a gardener, cook and kitchen maids and probably at least one footman. Some staff would have been hired in on a daily basis when the family was in residence. To maintain the stables at least one groom and a stable boy would have been required as well as a coachman. In London a footman, kitchen and cleaning staff were needed, and when the children were small there may also have been nursemaids (although Betty probably mostly fulfilled this function) and later there may have been a governess unless Priscilla taught the children their early lessons herself. Robert employed a series of clerks to assist with his correspondence.

According to Liza Picard[161] it was assumed that a family of the middling sort consisting of two or three persons would have three or four servants, whereas the Duke of Bedford employed forty in his London house alone. The Duke's French cook was paid sixty pounds a year and his footmen between six and eight pounds a year, while a head coachman got between twelve and twenty-six pounds. Footmen would expect to have a suit of livery provided, other servants would receive a new suit of clothing at Christmas and servants higher up the pecking order could expect to receive cast off clothing which they could make over for themselves or sell, in turn they would pass things on down the chain until all that remained were rags (and even these had a value), which is one reason why historically so little clothing survives.

An idea of the cost of outfitting a fashionable servant comes in a bill of 1799 from the tailor Martin Haberer for the uniform for Robert Cooper Lee junior's groom, which included 'A drab colored second cloth coat velvet collar etc £2 15s, A striped toilenait waistcoat with cotton sleeves £1 2s' and a pair of 'Corderoy breeches lined with leather' for £1 7s. Toilenait, or toilenet, was a kind of poplin, a medium weight fabric made of wool, or a mix of wool and cotton or silk and cotton. It was often used for waistcoats and this one, being striped, was probably towards the upper edge of the range – one made at the same time for Bob himself in a fabric called swan down cost only a little more.

Meals would be provided for live-in servants who could expect to eat after their employers perhaps only on left-overs, but might eat very well when the employer was away and not keeping an eye on expenditure. Washing could have been done at home for the Lees, particularly when they were in the country, and would probably not have been done more than twice a week at most owing to the cost of soap and the difficulties of finding space for drying when the weather was wet. They might have employed a washerwoman, or particularly when in town, have sent their linen out into the country for washing. Hard soap was quite expensive at a penny halfpenny a pound and the household might have used ten pounds in a week. Servants were often issued with a single bar for personal use which they were expected to make last many months. A good laundry maid would know how to wash, blue (using Jamaican indigo for whiteness), clear starch and iron, with the treatment of ruffles and lace requiring special skill.

---

[161] Liza Picard, *Dr Johnson's London*, Weidenfeld and Nicolson, London, 2000.

Working and living conditions for servants were often not comfortable, and even in a good household it was common for servants to have to share a bed in the garrets, where they might keep a small box for personal possessions, which were probably few. There was always a shortage of good servants in London, supplemented by untrained newcomers regularly arriving in search of streets paved with gold.

If a servant remained with a family for any length of time they might expect a small legacy on the death of their master or mistress. There is every reason to suppose the Lee servants were well treated, and indeed Betty Harrison remained with the family for nearly sixty years, despite at some point marrying a Mr William Pack, who presumably could have provided her with an escape route had she wanted it. Robert Cooper Lee left a legacy of fifty guineas to his clerk James Bowes, and fifty guineas and an annuity to Betty Harrison. Both Frances and Richard Lee left small legacies to servants on condition that the person was still in their employ at the time of their death, and Richard continued to pay an annuity to an old retainer of his brother Robert. Holidays would have been few, although for servants whose employers moved between different houses there would have been slack periods when they could enjoy some entertainment. Time off on a Sunday to attend church would have been expected, although the eighteenth century was not as insistent on formal observance as the Puritans of the previous century or the evangelical Victorians were, and there are no references to the Lee family attending church except for weddings and christenings.

Robert Cooper Lee to Priscilla Lee

Berners Street, 30th August 1773

At last my dear I have the Pleasure to tell you the *Princess Amelia*, so long looked for, is safely arrived at Portsmouth. Mr and Mrs Welch send their best Respects to you; they landed yesterday (one day sooner than our Anniversary of landing at Dover) after a very tedious and dangerous Passage, as Mr Welch writes me; he had not got my Letter and waits one from me. Dr Gordon and Mr McLeod[162] are also come. I have a Letter from the former, who talks of staying at Portsmouth a day or two, and calling upon Mr Long at Chichester on his way to Town. Our friend

[162] John McLeod of Colbecks estate St Dorothy. He married his cousin Margaret McLeod in Edinburgh on the 20th of November 1773.

Winde is very well and writes in good Spirits. If the Box for Mr Allen is not gone don't send it; he has had a severe Attack, and was to come Passenger in the Pacquet, as the last Resource. Poor Bristow has been very unlucky in his different Masters. Bob dined with Mr Fuller at Streatham yesterday; I went on by particular Invitation to Wandsworth to see Miss Barnes; she begs her best Compliments and your Commands, as she returns in *Stephenson.* She is looking out for a little Dog for Mrs Lewing[163]. Bob is gone off to Harrow properly. I must break off having to write both Mr Welch and Dr Gordon. Richard is very well, and longs to spend a day or two at home; both he and Bob desired their Duty to you; and Love to their Sister and Matt. With mine to them, and unalterable Affection to you I remain,

yours most sincerely Robert Cooper Lee.

The Lees' close friend Scudamore Winde visited them in England in the summer of 1772, but he later returned to Jamaica from where he continued to send them presents of ginger, cashews, chocolate and other island delicacies.

He died in Kingston in late September 1775, generous to the last. His Will included legacies to numerous god-children, £1000 to Frances Lee, and £500 to Robert junior. His lands at Fencott in Herefordshire were left to Robert Cooper Lee with reversion to Robert and Frances on the death of their father. Robert Cooper Lee was also made joint executor with their mutual friend Joseph Mayo. A note in Scudamore Winde's own hand totalled the legacies at £58,550, a significant amount of which went to his four illegitimate children, the mulatto Robert Winde and the children of Sarah Cox – Penelope, John and Thomas. Sarah Cox was provided for as was a negro woman called Patt freed by Winde and her daughter Mary. Before long both Robert Winde and his half-sister Penelope would make their homes in London where they and their children would continue the connection with the Lees.

With the loss of one of their closest friends in Jamaica, and the steady arrival in London of many others as they came 'home' to acquire property in Britain and settle into the role of absentee landlords, all the Lees except perhaps Priscilla and Frances came to regard England as their real home. It was a curious feature of Jamaican life that even third generation creoles

[163] Mrs Richard Lewing née Sarah Grace Halstead.

continued to regard Britain as 'home', something which contributed to the difficulty of establishing a permanent white community in Jamaica and which distinguished it from the other North American colonies.

Now firmly established in England, Robert Cooper Lee turned his mind to securing his children's legal status. Frances, Robert, Richard and Matthew were all illegitimate and their mother Priscilla was of mixed race and almost certainly also illegitimate, though exactly how far back her slave ancestry went is unclear.

In 1776, in a petition unique in the records of the Jamaican Assembly, Robert Cooper Lee requested protection for his children from any future claim that they fell within the provisions of the 1761 Devises Act. The petition[164] was presented on his behalf by his close friend, and Member of the Jamaican Council, Richard Welch,

That the Petitioner hath several Children, who tho' now considered as not affected by, or within the Intent and meaning of the said Act, yet as doubts may hereafter arise from lapse of time, or want of Evidence, when the witnesses may be dead who could prove their right to take any Estates, real and personal, by Deed or Will notwithstanding the said Act,

And praying, That in order to remove any such doubts, and to prevent any evil or mischief that may attend his said Children by Attempts to bring them within the Intent and meaning of the said Act, this House will be pleased to give leave to bring in a Bill to enable the Petitioner to settle and dispose of his Estate and Fortune by Deed or Will, in such manner, and to such persons as the Petitioner shall think proper, notwithstanding the said Act.

A sub-committee was appointed to investigate the background to the case consisting of Benjamin Lyon[165], Robert Richards and James Lewis, all men well known to Robert – the Lyons were close family friends. Very quickly they returned and reported that they had *inquired into the Allegations therein contained and do find the same to be true, and do report that it has been proved before them that the Children of the said Robert Cooper Lee were born of the body of a reputed white woman, and that they are not within the intent and meaning of a certain Act.*

---

[164] TNA: CO 140/56 Minutes of the Jamaican Assembly, 16-22 November 1776.

[165] Benjamin Lyon, an attorney in Jamaica, and his wife Elizabeth Ann had travelled to England shortly before the Lee family. He had returned to Jamaica leaving his wife and six children behind and he died there. He was buried in Spanish Town on the 27th July 1780. Robert Cooper Lee was one of his executors.

What is especially curious is that Priscilla is referred to as 'a reputed white woman', although frustratingly the evidence examined by the committee supporting this was not minuted. Certainly the parish priests who baptised the Lee children were confused about their status, John Venn (who died in 1764) had noted against the baptism of Frances which had recorded her as a quadroon, 'I believe a white illegit. child'. Critically if Priscilla Kelly had been a white woman, born legitimate, there would have been no reason for Robert not to have married her in Jamaica.

Whatever the underlying truth of Priscilla's racial mix a Private Act of the Assembly was granted

to authorize and enable Robert Cooper Lee late of the Island of Jamaica but now of the Kingdom of Great Britain Esquire to settle and Dispose of his Estate both real and personal in this Island by Deed or Will in such manner as he shall think proper notwithstanding an Act of the Governor Council and Assembly Intitled An Act to prevent the inconveniences arising from exorbitant Grants and Devises made by White Persons to Negroes, and the Issue of Negroes, and to restrain and limit such Grants and Devises.

No similar provision could be obtained on behalf of Joseph Lee's sons John and William Robert who were undoubtedly quadroons, but the provisions of their inheritance and the guardianship of their uncle shielded them from any prejudice they might otherwise have encountered. The children of Joseph and Robert Cooper Lee were gradually cutting their links with the land of their birth.

The Lees lost further friends with Jamaican links in 1777 with the death of Rose Fuller in May and Marchant Tubb's wife Ann in June. She was buried at Ringwould near Deal where they had spent so many happy times and a heartbroken Marchant placed the following inscription on her tomb

In the Vault beneath are deposited the Remains of Mrs Ann Tubb, wife of Marchant Tubb, Esqr. late of the Island of Jamaica. She died 26th of June 1777, Aged 55 Years. In Testimony of whose Virtues, As an affectionate Wife, A Tender Parent and a faithful Friend, This Memorial is erected By her surviving Husband Who too severely feels The Loss he records.

On the 7th of August 1777 Priscilla Lee gave birth to her sixth child, who was named Scudamore Cooper Lee and baptised on the 27th of August in the fashionable church of St Maylebone.

In September the same year we see the first signs of the extravagance that would characterise the life of Robert Cooper Lee junior in the following correspondence from Eton school. After barely two years at his first school Bob had been removed from Harrow. It is not clear whether this change of school was because of bad behaviour or simply lack of academic progress. Bob did not lack ability. When he was sent to England in 1769 his father had written to Stephen Fuller 'My eldest son goes for England in the *Jamaica* Captain Hamilton and will be introduced to you by my brother who is in London, otherwise by my Friend Mr Blackwood, a Passenger in the Ship, who has kindly taken charge of him for the voyage. He is a healthy boy, and has just entered his seventh year. I flatter myself you will find him well disposed and free of any evil habits. He is tolerably apt, and his time here has not been unemployed, as he can both read and write, and has some knowledge of figures. I would wish to give him an education, so that he may be able to do something for himself when he grows up'[166]. The adult letters of Robert junior show that he did eventually obtain an education in the classics and acquired French, but he seems always to have suffered from a streak of indolence, a habit of extravagance and a disinclination to 'do something for himself'.

J Davies to Robert Cooper Lee

Eton, 4th September 1777

Sir,

Your sons extravagance became so notorious here, that upon hearing of it, I ordered the Dame to send to me his half years bill; it is enormous; and even after deducting the extraordinary expenses at first coming, it is double what it ought to be besides this He has contracted various debts.

Where He got this habit of expense I know not; but I think it my duty to prevent its pernicious effects spreading further, for it has already done some mischief here.

It occur'd to me at first to show my disapprobation of his conduct by degrading Him at the trial for the next remove, but I thought it better to represent the case to you and desire that you would not bring him back at all.

I am Sir your most obedient humble Servant J Davies

---

166 Gamble, op.cit, p.74.

J Davies to Robert Cooper Lee

Eton, 6th September 1777

Sir,

I received your letter and since that have made farther enquiries concerning your sons expenses. I shall oblige the Bookseller, who contrary to my rules, has let him have many sets of expensive books to take them again; these I find were not sent in to Mrs Roberts, who, you think, might have check'd this spirit of extravagance but she will let you know that it was impossible and that He displayed this extravagant lush [?] in every thing immediately from his first coming and so far [illegible] Mrs Roberts having much influence, I am convinced that it is not in my power, not even in yours, I am afraid, to correct this disposition in Him.

But further He has taken no pains to distinguish Himself in his business and to deserve the place I gave Him – on the contrary He has been Idle, as his Tutor Mr Heath will inform you – therefore I will not absolutely refuse to take Him again, but I declare to you my resolution (which nothing shall induce me to alter) to keep Him back another half year in his present remove, that he may merit advancement by his application to his studies, and Reformation in other respects.

I am, Sir, your most obedient humble Servant J Davies.

By October of the same year Matthew Allen Lee had started school under Mr James at Greenwich, although it appears his appetite was not satisfied by the size of the breakfast on offer. By the following spring twelve year old Richard, who had originally gone to Mr Roberts' school in Wandsworth, was writing to his father from Harrow where he was with Robert Home Gordon.

Richard Lee to Robert Cooper Lee

Harrow, 30th April 1778

Dear Sir,

I take this opportunity to acquaint you how Gordon and I like the fourth form we have not done a Greek lesson yet nor will till Monday. (And the reason I wrote to you today instead of Sunday was because I shall be so very busy in doing derrivasions for Monday). We both like it exceedingly as much as we have seen of it and I assure you Bramley and me are as yet good pax. I hope that what you were complaining of the last time I was at home is now well and will permitt me to see you next Thursday the publick speech day. I should be much obliged to you if you would send a few things for me by the next stage that is some Chocolate that was left in the post chaise last Tuesday also my hat that you were so obliging as to promise me, my neck cloths, nankeen waistcoat and breeches, ruffled shirt and silk stockings. I hope you will not be angry with me because my wants are so numerous. I will if possible write to my Mama on Sunday but I cannot promise as I shall be so busy the [illegible] therefore I must remain (without saying half what I have to say)

your most dutiful and affectionate son Richard Lee.

NB I desire my duty to my Mama.

The next letter began with a list of all the items that Robert Cooper Lee was sending to his son Richard and to Robert Hume Gordon at Harrow in time for the Speech Day.

For RH Gordon - A suit of Nankeen, A Bean [?] Waistcoat, A ditto pair of Stockings, A ruffled Shirt, A pair Leather Breeches, And Chocolate

For R Lee - A Suit of Nankeen, Two Cravats from Frances, A ruffled Shirt, A pair silk Stockings, And Chocolate

Dear Richard,

The above particulars you and Gordon will receive by Favor Mrs Davison. Your Mama will send the Hats for each before the Speech day. The Chocolate was left at home, and not in the Post Chaise as you thought. Your Letter was not a Moment too soon. We are always happy to hear from you. Matt went off in good Spirits His additional Loaf for Breakfast is promised. No Letter from him yet. I thank you for your kind Enquiry after me I am thank God pretty well again and go about as usual and intend visiting Harrow on Thursday as I proposed. I am very glad you and Gordon like the fourth Form so well. Your Mama Sister and Brother send their Love to you and Gordon I am

your truly Affectionate Robert Cooper Lee.

NB Derivations – not Derrivasions – See the Lutia [?] Dictionary when in doubt.

Frances Lee to Richard Lee

Berners Street, 5th May 1778

My dear Richard,

To assure you your letter gave me the greatest pleasure I hope is unnecessary as I flatter myself you are sensible of the regard I bear you and the Happiness your kind Favors ever bestow. I was much pleased at the Mark of your remembrance for tho' I never once doubted your attachment tis agreeable to find that tho' absent you are in the Thoughts of the person you esteem. Whether you'll gain any advantage from my Correspondence is rather doubtful to me But I shall not hesitate to pronounce that I shall derive much pleasure from yours. I do not however expect you to write me so often as you do to my Papa and Mama. Only let me hear from you when you are at leisure to write this knowledge that you are conferring Happiness will be a sufficient Inducement. I am sorry to acquaint you my papa has had a slight attack of the Gout I am likewise happy to tell you that he has not the least remains of it and I hope he will be well enough to perform his promise of seeing you on Thursday. I have seen your Friend Long[167] since he came to Town probably he may be the Bearer of this to you for if it goes by the post you'll not receive it till tomorrow Morning and as he is to return to Harrow in the Evening a few Hours will make little difference. By him likewise you'll receive two smart Hats for Gordon and yourself. My Mama fears they will be too small should her Conjecture prove true you will return them by the first Opportunity. Matt remained with us untill Thursday he was my Beau (be assured I should have given the preference to you) till he went. Bob has walked out with me more and more since your Departure. Indeed I miss you much however as you are a gainer from the Separation I ought not to wish you here. But we do not always act as we ought and I cannot help frequently wishing for you – poor Betty often does the same – she desires her Love to you. I will not fail writing you particularly about her. I am glad Long is so kind to you. Your Excuse for not writing a longer Letter I readily accept as it was an affair of so much Importance that prevented you. I wish you my dear success in your Endeavors to gain Improvement for although a good Man is far preferable to a good Scholar it is more pleasing to find both goodness and Learning united. As for your being the first I have every reason to hope it and tis *almost* as much in your power to be the latter. Your Friends Mr

[167] One of the sons of Edward Long, probably Edward Beeston Long who was closest in age to Richard.

Tubb and Miss Morant desired their Compliments to you. I have no News to communicate – yet I have contrived to fill two pages. My Papa and Mama desire their kind Love. Bob desires his. Adieu my Dear Richard for the present, the kindest and best wishes of an affectionate Sister are always yours. Nor is her Friendship less tender than her Affection equally connected to you by both she experiences infinite pleasure in subscribing herself

your Sister and Friend Frances Lee.

From their earliest arrival in England the Lee family, along with most of fashionable society, decamped from London into the country for the summer. After their first summers spent in Margate and Deal they moved first to Sutton and later to Shredding Green near Iver in Buckinghamshire. Business still called, and Robert Cooper Lee often travelled between London and the family in the country where they frequently had a house full of their childrens' friends.

Robert Cooper Lee to Richard Lee

Sutton House, 29th May 1778

Dear Richard,

Tho' I hope to see you Wednesday next I will not on that account postpone acknowledging your last Letter. It was sent here yesterday. The Family left Berners Street last Sunday and find the Country very delightful – a good Prospect of Fruit Peas etc but at present only Asparagus, and green Apricots and Gooseberries for tarts. Your Mama sometimes wishes Gordon and you had some of them. I am afraid you will not see either your Mama or Sister at the Speeches. Little Scudamore engrosses your Mama so much that she cannot stir, and your Sister cannot go without her, besides I am sorry to say your Sister continues very poorly indeed. Gordon's Hand being hurt is I suppose the reason of his not writing to me. I hope it will soon be well again. Mr Heath's Displeasure on the Account of the Cloth is I flatter myself is over. You must always consider what he thinks wrong to be so, and that to be right he thinks so. Your Mama Sister and Brother send their Love with mine to you and Gordon.

I am my dear Richard's affectionate Father Robert Cooper Lee.

PS By late accounts from Greenwich there is certain Intelligence of Brothers Richards studying hard in the fourth Form.

There are frequent references throughout her life to bouts of ill health suffered by Frances Lee, from the first mention in her letter to Scudamore Winde that she had been away from school for six months. Whether she suffered from the consequences of some illness contracted in Jamaica or from something else is unclear. Severe debilitating pain in her side is the one symptom she mentions in correspondence, yet at other times she led a normal life riding, walking and socialising with the family.

Robert Cooper Lee to Richard Lee

Sutton, 12th June 1778

Jack has made his Election for Greenwich[168]. He comes here from Mr Augier's[169] tomorrow, and will stay with us a few days – to taste the green Pease Gooseberry fool etc. Matt spent the Whitsuntide Holidays at School the measles being much about Sutton, and your Mama is not a little afraid that Scudamore may catch the Disorder. Your Brother Bob goes to Stamford Saturday the 20th. Charles Gray[170] has left School and goes to Bristol next Monday. I hope you did not incur Mr Heath's Displeasure last Speech Day by the neckcloth – or dining at Jones's. The best Way another time will be not to use one or do the other. Your Mama is very well as well as myself. Your Sister was so all last Week but has not been so well this. The Country is very pleasant and agreeable, and I hope will soon set her up again. I am My dear Richard's

Truly affectionate father Robert Cooper Lee.

In the autumn of 1778 Frances was staying in Margate, for the sake of her health, with Dugald and Mary Malcolm who were chaperones to Elizabeth Goodin Haughton who was soon to be married to Sir John Taylor. They were shortly to return to London where the Malcolms had a house in Wigmore Street.

---

168 The Royal Military Academy.

169 It is not clear which Mr Augier this is, however there was an extensive mixed race Augier family in Jamaica descended from John Augier whose seven freed children went on to obtain the rights of whites for themselves and their own children, some of whom entered fully into white English society.

170 Later Sir Charles Gray, Commander in Chief in the West Indies.

Frances Lee to Priscilla Lee

Margate, 7th October 1778

I am rejoiced my dear Mama beyond Expression at the prospect of our so soon Meeting. I hope to find you all well – my dear little Scudamore is included in you all whose Health I shall drink to today in a Bumper may he see many happy years. I have been far from well for these two or three days past, but I hope you will think me improved and I trust that the Air of the Downs will be equally salutary with the Sea with the Assistance of both I hope to have a tolerable Winter. We are to leave this on Friday to sleep at Rochester and to dine on Saturday at Eltham when I hope to meet my Papa or in Wigmore Street whichever is the most convenient to him. I cannot say will be equally agreeable to me because if the latter I shall be another Evening without seeing you. The weather is very fine and favorable for our own Journey. Margate begins to thin (that's the Expression) Lord Galway[171] will have the Honor of being on the road with us. I was not on Mondays Ball Mrs Malcolm and Miss Haughton[172] were, I begg'd to be excus'd from accompanying them, Mr Malcolm preferring the Fire-side we remained at home together. We had a rout last night two Card Tables I assure you I played at the Commerce one. I am glad to find from my Papa's Letter that there's one from Lady Carlisle[173] in Berners Street. I really began to fear her Ladyship had forgotten me. I had a glimpse one morning at the Bathing room of poor Miss Vaughan she was attending Lady Isham[174] and her Daughter. My Papa I suppose has bought me part of the twenty Thousand pounds. I will not dispose of it as I did last year before I got it. I hope to be in time for the Turtle. I shall not surprise you in the eating Way my appetite being very little better than when I left you. I have not ventured to follow Mr Farquhar's Prescription fearing the Consequences[175]. I am going to be very busily

---

171 Robert Monckton-Arundell, 4th Viscount Galway (1752-1810) – at the time of this encounter he was still single.

172 Elizabeth Goodin Haughton married Sir John Taylor by Special Licence on 17th December 1778 at the Malcolm's house 16 Wigmore Street, witnesses at the wedding were Dugald and Mary Malcolm.

173 Margaret Caroline Leveson-Gower wife of Frederick Howard the 5th Earl of Carlisle, a Whig peer and supporter of the Prince of Wales during the Regency crisis.

174 Susannah Barret m. Sir Justinian Isham 1766, possibly related to the Jamaican Barrett family.

175 Walter Farquhar had married the widow of Dr Thomas Harvie of Jamaica. He was a close friend of General Samuel Townsend, and guardian of his daughter Elizabeth

employed in preparing for our Journey you will be kind enough to excuse the shortness of this Scrawl. Were I to write for ever I could never find words sufficiently expressive of my Affection and respect. I request you to present my respectful and affectionate Duty to my dear Papa. My love to Bob and my usual remembrance to little Scud, whom I long to see. The best compliments of this Family attend you. I remain very truly and tenderly My dear Mama

Your most dutiful and affectionate daughter Frances Lee.

By 1778 Robert Home Gordon was an orphan (his father having died four years earlier and his mother some time before that) and Robert Cooper Lee was his guardian. Gordon was at school at Harrow with Richard and it was from there that he wrote to his guardian shortly before Christmas 1778.

Robert Hume Gordon to Robert Cooper Lee

Saturday 5th December 1778

Dear Sir,

I have received the money Tea and Sugar you sent me and am much obliged to you. As I have received so many favours of you I think it is my duty to acquaint you that I have a great desire to go to sea in which I hope to meet with your approbation as I should be very sorry to do anything without your consent indeed I think that to be the most advantageous Line of Life in which I can possibly engage as I do not think that I have sufficient talents or application for the law, I should be glad to hear from you before the Holidays.

I remain Dear Sir your dutiful Ward

Robert Hume Gordon.

Robert Cooper Lee remained close friends, and regularly in contact, with the great Jamaican historian Edward Long, conducting various bits of business for him over a period of years. The following letter highlights the

Trelawney Townsend. The General introduced him into the household of the Prince of Wales where in due course he became Sir Walter Farquhar.

particular importance of irrigation to some Jamaican plantations for which dams and lengthy aqueducts were constructed and water courses diverted.

Edward Long to Robert Cooper Lee

Woolley Green, 10th May 1779

My dear Sir,

After begging you will except my many thanks for the charge you was so obliging to take of my Dispatches for the Packet, I must express my concern for the tumble you got in the mud; whether this happened by your making too much Leeway towards the Kennel, or whether I was the innocent cause of your being ex equilibris, having forgot to apprise you that the contents of my missive to Mr Wynter were of extraordinary magnitude and Weight, I condole in the fall, and rejoice at your resurrection.

I am partly of your way of thinking, that the eating ceremony performed at Domine Heath's is by no means the least pleasant act of his Exhibition; according to Cato's observation,

"Interpone tuis interdum Pastia Speechis ut propis animo quimvis sufferer Oratorem" the great pleasure in human existence undoubtedly arises from a due mixture of corporeal with intellectual entertainments; and I know of nothing worth going to see or hear, unless it ends in Eating. Hence it is that a Lord Mayor's Show, or a Charity Sermon wisely conclude with a Dinner or Supper.

If I understand the new Clause introduced by Mr Morant into his Deed of Confirmation, I am convinced, and I think I could make it equally clear to you in five minutes conversation, that it tends in its extent to render the rest of the Deed a Nullity, or something worse. I cannot conceive his reason for suggesting it; because, as we have it not in our own power, nor can possibly have it in our power, to hinder him from making any use of the water he pleases before it reaches us, (provided only that he does not divert, nor evaporate it) so I think that if we subscribe to this new Clause "permitting him to use the water of Pindar's and Juan de Bolas Rivers for *any* purposes" we shall irremediably arm him and his Successors with a right as well as a power, to expand all those waters among his Cane pieces in dry weather; or in drawing them by Cuts away from our Damhead to any part of his own Land on the opposite bank below, and at pleasure, and in short to stop our mill entirely; these consequences it leads to. - He possesses Land below our Damhead; we possess none above it; we therefore cannot possibly obstruct his *due* and *proper* use of it; what end therefore the clause is meant to answer to him, in any beneficial or cautionary sense, I do not at present in the least comprehend, but am very desirous to hear. I may perhaps misconceive the Clause, from the abridgement you have given me of it; I am persuaded Mr Morant meaning to act the part of a Friend and good Neighbour cannot view it in the light I do; and I hope and trust, that he will not tack any injurious Condition to his Indeed, nor insist on any *new point* which was never proposed at the time when with his consent (which I thought honourable and generous) I constructed the work; at which time, as Mr Gale knows, and no other Condition was required from me than that I should not cut down the wild Canes which Mr Morant's overseer was to plant on the opposite Bank or River Course for the better defence of his land.

I have no objection to such a clause, with this Provisoe "That he shall not apply it to any use injurious to us, nor tending to diminish the sufficient supply of our mill Gutter at Lucky Valley.".

In regard to "laying Materials", there can be no objection to it, *under the same proviso of no resulting injury to us.*

To the Truth my good Friend, I expected Mr [illegible] would behave like a Gentleman in this Business; but there are so many Hums! and Hahs! thrown in from time to time, that I begin to think his Intent not quite so charitable as I once believed it to be. They drive me almost mad, among them. However I am resolved at all Events, to endure patiently, and act as prudently as I can. I may peradventure see you next week in Town, so I defer the Subject till then, I will bring the map of the premises with me, and show you what course the two Rivers may be made to take. I shall thankfully receive in the meantime any news you meet with worth the trouble of communicating to Dear Sir

Your affectionate and faithful Servant Edward Long.

PS our very best Compliments to your Famille.

In 1779 Robert Cooper Lee acquired the lease of number 30 Bedford Square, London. The house had been built only a year or so earlier on the west side of Bedford Square, 'being the third house southward from Bedford Street'[176], now Bayley Street. It was an elegant house on four floors. A survey of 1914 described the front room on the ground floor as having 'a chimneypiece of white and coloured marble. The frieze is fluted, and contains sculptured figures. The front room on the first floor has its

[176] http://www.british-history.ac.uk/report.aspx?compid=74312

walls treated as large panels, and over the two doors are decorative paintings. The chimney piece is of white marble, and the flutings of the pilasters are inlaid with coloured marble. The ornamental plaster ceiling is of very delicate design. The figures in the oval medallion are modelled on classical lines, and in their delicacy are suggestive of cameos.' There was basement space for kitchens, servants and an extensive wine cellar; there were mews to the rear leading to a double coach house and stabling for five horses. It was a sign that Robert's business was prospering, and he would shortly be joined in the Square by a number of others with West Indian Connections, Thomas Hibbert and Marchant Tubb among them.

There was a large oval garden for the use of residents in the centre of Bedford Square as the individual houses did not have gardens, the rear instead giving onto the mews. The new Georgian Squares were designed with railed gardens at their heart not simply to provide pleasant private space for walking or sitting, but equally to prevent them becoming areas for fly tipping or ad hoc development as had happened in the older parts of the City. To the east of the Square were the British Museum and Bedford House, and to the north of these the land was open and undeveloped all the way to the clusters of buildings that were Sommers Town and Pentonville, with the new Smallpox Hospital where now St Pancras and Kings Cross stations stand.

Bedford Square showing No 30 second door from the right

Robert Cooper Lee to Priscilla Lee

Bedford Square, 4th October 1779

After breakfasting a second time at Bromley Welch and I reached town yesterday before twelve O'clock. At the Golden [missing] we took a Coach that conveyed us to Mr Morse's Conduit Street, and thence to the elegant Lodgings in Brooke Street, where I left Mr Welch and proceeded to Bedford Square calling in Wigmore Street to deliver a Parcel to Miss P Malcolm. I found my new House quite agreeable, and after [washing] and dressing I called in Brooke Street. Mr Dehany[177] and young Welch there. All Intreaties to dine in Queen Ann Street were vain. We proceeded to

[177] Possibly Philip Dehany (c.1720-1809) or his nephew George Dehany (1760-1806)

Mrs Schaw's in Farm Street Berkeley Square – fixed on a Chariot[178] and Horses and went and dined at the British. We parted about seven o'clock, Mr Welch for Lodgings to go to bed – I to visit the Sick – poor James Williams [in] Piccadilly; he has been very ill with an Inflammation in his Lungs, but I hope out of all Danger. This Morning before Nine O'clock Mr Allen made his appearance. He came from Barnet this Morning. He stays in Town to answer his Letters, a Pacquet going next Wednesday, after which he goes to Hants for Mrs Allen and attends her to Tunbridge Wells. I have not seen Mr Welch today. He went into the City before me. I left word where Allen and I should dine, but he would not come. The Letters from Ireland are arrived – Poor young Munro – Gordon's Cousin is dead in Jamaica and Mr Gwynn I hear is also dead. I have got your [illegible] from Mr Wynter which I will bring down with me. Mr Welch talks of returning on Friday Morning. I sincerely wish myself with you. I hope you have been quite well since I left you – and Fanny better and Mrs Welch the same – and Scudamore and the young Welchs well. My kindest Love to Fanny and Scud, and best respects to Mrs Welch [and] my little favourites[?]. Yours ever sincerely Robert Cooper Lee.

In the autumn of 1779 Robert Cooper Lee entered his eldest son at Lincolns Inn hoping for a legal career for him, hopes that never really coincided with Bob's own wishes. However it may have been the origin of the family's nickname for him of 'The Counsellor'. Priscilla Lee, who was in the late stages of her final pregnancy was out of town.

Robert Cooper Lee to Priscilla Lee

Bedford Square, Tuesday Evening 9th November 1779

The finest Lord Mayor's day since the year 1752. No News from Jamaica. The old News blown over and all safe for the present. Bob entered Lincolns Inn with great Cheerfulness. I expect him home in half an Hour. Welch sets off tomorrow morning for Bath with Mr Capper in the Bath Coach. Our friends in Town all well. I hope to dine with you on Thursday. My kind love to Fanny and Scud.

Your ever affectionate Robert Cooper Lee.

---

178 A four-wheeled coupé or cut down coach, usually seating two passengers facing forwards, usually drawn by two horses in pole gear. The high box seat would have an elaborate hammercloth and liveried footmen rode on a rearward dummy board.

Robert Cooper Lee to Priscilla Lee

Bedford Square, 11th November 1779

Don't be angry. Business must be done. Besides when I gave you Reason to expect me to Dinner today I had quite forgot it was the Jamaica Club day and I was an Absentee for at least three Months. No farther News from the West but many, concurring Accounts that d'Estaing[179] is in America, and gone to New York. A Letter for you from Mrs Boyd – it will keep – a Letter from Mr Tubb – Still on Crutches and can't say when they come up. Our Turtle by the *Latium* is arrived, and expected in Bedford Square tomorrow. Will you send the Cart for it? I don't know the Size, but if not very large we may I think as well eat it ourselves. Mr Bourke[180] and Isaac dine with us on Saturday at four O'clock. The Coach horses may come on Saturday Morning and carry Bob and me down in the Post Chaise – if I can get him leave. My Love to the Children.

Yours ever affectionately Robert Cooper Lee.

Robert Cooper Lee to Priscilla Lee

Bedford Square, 23rd November 1779

My dear Priscy

Just returned from Mr Allen's. The Pheasant was most excellent – the best I think I ever tasted. Sympson[181] and Knight of the Party – and Mr Mayo[182]. He is now musing by the Fire. We are to have Bread and Cheese and Toddy. I overtook the light Infantry at Pegs Marsh exactly four Miles from Sutton. We called at the Floor Cloth Manufactory and did the necessary. The Name is not Cole. Mrs Allen has given up all

---

[179] Jean Baptiste Charles Henri Hector, Comte d'Estaing (24 November 1729 – 28 April 1794) a French general, and Admiral who led a fleet in support of American independence. His French royalist sympathies later resulted in his death at the hands of the French Revolution.

[180] John Bourke, merchant and friend of the Lee family.

[181] Perhaps Dr. Archibald Sympson, Member of the Jamaican Assembly for Vere 1775, 1787, 1790, or more probably his son Alexander (d. London 1798).

[182] Joseph Mayo (c. 1728-1790) of Craven Street and Ramsgate, Kent.

Thoughts of seeing the King next Thursday. Remember me to Miss Lee and Scud. Send the Chaise on Friday Morning And I will bring you and Scuddy a large Piece of the Duchess's Christening Cake. Mr Mayo desires his Compliments.

Your ever Affectionate Robert Cooper Lee.

Robert had attended the Christening of Lady Anna Eliza Brydges the second daughter of the Duke and Duchess of Chandos on the 18th November 1779 at the church of St Marylebone. He handled a number of transactions for the Duke and Duchess and sometimes stayed with them at Avington Park. The Duchess, Anna Eliza Gamon, had first married Roger Hope Elletson (Lieutenant Governor of Jamaica from 1766–68) who died in 1775. She never visited Jamaica but from him she inherited the Hope Estate which she managed as an absentee landlord. So rich did her Jamaican properties make her that one press report claimed she wore £60,000 worth of diamonds to one glittering social event.

Tragically her eldest daughter died at four weeks old and her husband as a result of a freak accident when the Duchess playfully removed a chair he was about to sit on. The Duchess was so distraught that she lost her reason and her second child was brought up by guardians, although she had recovered sufficiently to attend her daughter's wedding in 1796[183].

Robert Cooper Lee to Priscilla Lee

Bedford Square, 30th November 1779

The Sutton Clock is half an Hour too fast. I quite forgot the Cash by the Coachman – it shall go to morrow by Mr Cracknell. Sir John's Coach brought me home, and I am very well. D'Estaing is certainly dispersed. His intentions were against Carolina Bermuda and Halifax. I have seen a Letter from Arbuthnot's Secretary, I mean an Original Letter. My kind Love etc. Lord Lyttelton is dead. A strange dreaming Story is told about his death.

Yours ever Affectionately Robert Cooper Lee.

---

183 See Sturtz, Linda L., *The 'Dim Duke' and the Duchess of Chandos: Gender and Power in Jamaican Plantation Management -- A Case Study,* Revista/Review Interamericana 29, 1999, http://www.sg.inter.edu/revisa-ciscla/.

Thomas Lyttleton (1744-79) was a Whig and a friend of the Prince of Wales, whose wild life had led to his being known as the wicked Lord Lyttleton. He was said to have told friends that a bird had flown into his room telling him he had only three days to live – three days later he died.

On the 27th of January 1780 Priscilla gave birth to her last child at 26 Berners Street. She was named Favell Bourke Lee, probably after John Allen's wife Favell and the family friend John Bourke.

Robert Cooper Lee to Richard Lee

Bedford Square, 5th February 1780

You have given me great pleasure, my dear Richard, by sending me two letters this week, in return for two of mine last. I am always happy to hear from you, and desire you will on all occasions let me know your real inclinations and wishes. I find there will not be the least occasion to interrupt your studies at Harrow, in the contemplation of being an Admiral; if that is your Ambition I can get your name entered in the book of a King's Ship; and it will be time enough for you to make your appearance two or three years hence, and then your time will be reckoned from being entered on the Book and you will have the opportunity of changing your mind, if you choose it without any inconvenience. And whatever your Station in Life may be you may rest assured the being well founded in Literature will be neither Crime nor Injury. I am extremely happy at your being so well with Mr Heath and the other Gentlemen at Harrow, and I trust you will continue so. I flatter myself from your Disposition, you will long make me happy. Your Mama and the youngest sister are very well; Frances la-la. Bob and Scud hearty. The Welchs, Allen and Sympson dine with me today. Your Mama joins me in kindest love. God bless and protect you.

I am your very affectionate Father Robert Cooper Lee.

Robert Cooper Lee to Richard Lee

Bedford Square, 22nd April 1780

If I made any Mistake in the Direction (for you know I generally write the Direction before the Letter) it is for Want of better Information. Is it Mr or Dr Heath? Your Brother says you write him DD. I was at Dorking this Morning soon after Nine O'Clock in time for the Rolls and Butter at full Meeting. Gordon and Jack did me the Favour to see me safe to Town, but under positive Engagement to return on Tuesday Morning. I am very well pleased with Jack's Improvement as well as Gordon's both in Latin and Writing, and Jack's Impediment in his Speech I think is less. Your Sister writes me every other day from Bath, and in the high Spirits I trust she will find Benefit in her Health as well as Pleasure by the Jaunt. Mrs Welch and your Mother are above at Tea. Gordon, Jack, Welch junior and Scuddy are round me below – drawing, joking, laughing etc. And so you like the fifth form, though the Books are difficult, and not the less for its Privileges; a reasonable and temperate Use of them you will find as in everything else to answer best and the truest Enjoyment. I will add only, that whenever you are about doing anything the Propriety of which is at least doubtful, call me to your Mind, and reflect how my Feelings are to be affected by your Conduct. Your Mother and the Youths here send their kindest Love to you. I am My dear Richard

Your very affectionate father Robert Cooper Lee.

June 1780 saw one of the most serious outbreaks of political violence experienced since the 1745 Jacobite uprising. Perhaps fearing that Irish rebellion would be triggered following the American Declaration of Independence, attempts were made to bring in measures to reduce legal restrictions on Roman Catholics. Following the first Catholic Relief Act in 1778 a Protestant Association had been formed presided over by the fanatical Lord George Gordon. Organised violence in Perth and Edinburgh took place in 1779 with the result that a promise was made that no Catholic Relief Bill should be introduced in Scotland.

On Friday 2nd June of the following year a huge procession, perhaps numbering over 40,000 men, assembled at St Georges Fields in Southwark. Wearing blue cockades and carrying blue 'No Popery' banners they advanced across the river to the House of Commons to present a petition for the repeal of the Relief Act. That evening riots broke out, with Catholic targets being attacked; windows were broken, furniture thrown out into the street and set on fire with the consequent burning of whole buildings. First to be attacked were well known embassy chapels, the Sardinian Chapel near Lincolns Inn Fields and the Bavarian Chapel in Warwick Street, which was only saved by the arrival of the soldiers. There was a lull in the violence on Saturday but by Sunday afternoon the chapels were again attacked, and again the soldiers arrived to restore order. On the Monday and Tuesday the blue cockades appeared to be taking over, the Prime Minister Lord North only narrowly escaped the mob and shops closed, passers-by were told to hand over money and people hastily hung out blue banners or pieces of blue cloth and chalked 'No Popery' on their doors in the hope of avoiding attack. The Newgate, Clerkenwell and Marshalsea prisons were set on fire and their prisoners set free, and other prisons released their inmates in order to protect the buildings, with the freed felons swelling the numbers of the rioters. On the Wednesday evening the King summoned a council and active measures were finally ordered against the mob. By Thursday the organised violence was over. Around a hundred buildings had been damaged or burnt, and there were at least 210 dead in the streets and a further 75 dying of their injuries. Trials followed with more than twenty rioters being hanged. Lord George Gordon however escaped the charge of levying war against the King, being defended by his cousin the great advocate Thomas Erskine. In 1787 he converted to Judaism and the following year was imprisoned for defaming Marie Antoinette and the administration of justice in England. He died insane in prison in 1793. Brackley Kennett the Lord Mayor of London, whose procession Robert had so admired the previous year, was convicted of criminal negligence for his conduct during the Riots during which he had failed to read the Riot Act, and he was fined £1,000.

Most of the Lee family were not in London at the time of the riots, but Robert Cooper Lee was in town and the troubles came very close to their new home in Bedford Square, with the burning of Lord Mansfield's house in nearby Bloomsbury Square.

Robert Cooper Lee to Richard Lee

Bedford Square, 10th June 1780

My dear Richard,

Mr and Mrs Allen have devoted to morrow to you. Your Brother is to be of the Party. They will tell you the unexampled Occurrences of the last Week and how your Candlesticks have been disgraced. Thank God all is quiet again. Lord George Gordon in the Tower, and many of the Rioters in Custody. I kept up Stairs the whole troublesome times, but I hope to venture down safely tomorrow. It was I assure you no small Disappointment to me, my not being with you last Speech day, but it really was not in my Power. I take it for granted the Tea Sugar etc got safe. You will hear from your Mother if you don't see her tomorrow. I hope soon to embrace you.

I am My dear Richard's Very Affectionate Father Robert Cooper Lee.

Sadly there is no further explanation as to what happened to Richard's candlesticks!

Later that summer Robert was hunting once again for a family house for the holidays. Eventually he settled on a rambling Elizabethan manor house at Shredding Green, near Iver. It was an area in which a number of West Indian families settled, the most prominent perhaps being Sir William Young, Lieutenant Governor of both Dominica and Tobago, whose home at Delaford became a regular haunt for Frances and her mother.

Robert Cooper Lee to Richard Lee

Bedford Square, 24th June 1780

My dear Richard,

It would be more pleasing to me to date my Letter from a Country Residence, but I have not yet been able to meet with one to suit us. The Family were at Richmond last Wednesday on that Business, and this Morning I took a Circuit of 20 Miles on the same Errand, but without Success. Gordon and Jack came home yesterday, the latter's Health is perfectly established their Hollidays are for five Weeks. Both Houses of Parliament met last Monday, they have declared the Fears and Apprehensions of the Petitioners on the Account of the late Act in favour of the Roman Catholics to be from Misconception of the Act and without any Foundation, the Act therefore is not to be repealed, but some new Regulations are to be made to prevent the Roman Catholics from having the Tuition of Protestant Children. The Camps in St James's and Hyde Parks continue. And there is another very near us in the Museum Gardens. The Tryals of some of the Rioters are to come on at the Old Bailey next week. The taking of Charles Town makes many entertain very sanguine Hopes of a speedy Reconciliation with America. There has been a Report this Week of an Insurrection in Philadelphia against the Congress and in favour of the British Government, but it wants Confirmation. Yet I think there is Reason to expect the Year 1780 will be more fortunate to us than any for some Years past. Thank God I am perfectly recovered from my last Attack of the Gout. Your Mother and all the young Folks are well and join in kindest Respects to you. May you Seven Years hence be as happy for that time of Life as you are now for the time present! I cannot wish you better and sure I am that every good is truly wished you by

Your very affectionate Father Robert Cooper Lee.

Robert Cooper Lee to Priscilla Lee

Bedford Square, 1st September 1780

My dear,

My Intention was to leave Town about twelve O'Clock, after seeing Lord George Germain[184], but I have just now a Line from the Duchess of Chandos[185] desiring to see me at four o'clock to take my Soup with her. If I get away in time I will return to Isleworth this Evening otherwise to Breakfast in the Morning. Remember me to all with you.

Your ever affectionate Robert Cooper Lee.

In the autumn of 1780 Richard Lee, not yet fifteen, travelled abroad to further his education, going first with his father to Brussels and later moving to Hamburg. From this period of his life he preserved a considerable collection of letters from his father and his sister Frances. Robert wrote to Priscilla who was staying at Mill Platt, Isleworth.

Robert Cooper Lee to Priscilla Lee

Margate, Sunday Morning 1st October 1780

It was about Nine O'Clock last Night when we reached this Place. The Rain set in when we got to Rochester, and continued all the Way to

---

[184] Lord George Germain was Secretary of State for the American Department. In 1760 he had been court martialled *at his own insistence* after the Battle of Minden and deemed 'unfit to serve his Majesty in any military capacity whatsoever'. His actions in relation to the military campaign in America probably contributed to British losses at Yorktown.

[185] Given the date of this supper meeting it probably related to the following land transaction described in documents held at the London Metropolitan Archives: Settlement of the estates of Anna Eliza, Duchess of Chandos ACC/0788/013 30 Oct 1780 Contents:Tripartite agreement: 1) Duke of Chandos and Anna Eliza Duchess; 2) Edward Willes, Justice of King's Bench and Robert Cooper Lee of Bedford Square, gent; 3) Henry Howorth of Lincoln's Inn and James Coulthard of Lincoln's Inn. Consideration: paid by Edward Willes and Robert Cooper Lee to Duke of Chandos 12 Oct 1780. Premises: manor house of Great Stanmore and messuages, tenements etc. in Great and Little Stanmore, etc.

Canterbury but the Diligences[186] are warm and comfortable, much more so than the Road Post Chaises and neither Richard nor myself caught cold nor feel any Inconveniences from the Journey. Mr Welch had very kindly provided Beds for us, and was admiring the Ladies dancing Cotillions when we arrived here. He had desired to be sent to when I came, and immediately made his Appearance in high Health and Spirits. I found Mr William Bullock and some others whom I knew in the Coffee house Captain Knatchbull joined Mr Welsh and me, and we had a pleasant Repast of Ham and Chicken and Brandy Punch, and after an Hour's Chit Chat retired to rest and had a comfortable Nap over a Barbers Shop – but the Bed was very good and the Sheets well aired by Mr Welch's Orders, and it was a convenient Situation to get our Hairs dressed this Morning. Two boats went for Ostend on Friday Evening. One was expected in last Night to return about Noon today. But I am afraid it is not come, in which Case if I cannot get away today I shall endeavour to pay a Visit to our Friends at Deal. The Weather is very mild and the Wind fair I therefore wish to get away. Mr Welch and Captain Knatchbull talk of taking a Hunt to morrow Morning. Richard desires his Duty and joins me in kindest Love to all. I will try to send a Letter by the return of the Boat. I ever am

Your tender and affectionate Husband Robert Cooper Lee.

PS Remember us most kindly to our Friends in Berners Street and to Mr and Mrs Kluft. I had intended to have taken our Leave of the latter, but had not time on Friday.

Robert Cooper Lee to Priscilla Lee

Ostend, Thursday 12th October 1780

Last Night I got here safe and well. The Wind is not quite fair. A Fishing Boat intends going this afternoon. I intend this by a Passenger but I do not expect to go in the Margate Pacquet, the *Emperor Joseph*, till the wind is more favourable the Weather here is tolerably good – it has been otherwise. My kindest Love and Compliments where due. I left Richard Tuesday Morning very well and in tolerable good Spirits.

Your ever Affectionate Robert Cooper Lee.

---

186 A French coach equivalent to a mail coach, so named because of its reputation for good time keeping. It seated about eight.

Robert Cooper Lee Priscilla Lee

Bedford Square, Saturday Evening 14th October 1780

It is enough to tell you that I am arrived safe and in perfect Health – and that I left Richard last Tuesday Morning very well and in tolerable good Spirits. I had a most exceeding fine Passage back, and am only thirty Hours from Ostend. I hope to find you, and our young Folks all well to morrow Noon or certainly at Dinner. The Coachman I understand is in Town. I have not seen Mr or Mrs Allen but I'm going to seek them.

Your ever Affectionate Husband Robert Cooper Lee.

These next letters from Frances to Richard were sent care of Monsieur Gobert at Place de St. Michel in Brussels.

Frances Lee to Richard Lee

Isleworth, 16th October 1780

The Pleasure my Mother and I experienced on my Father's Return was not a little increased my dear Richard by the agreeable Information of your being well and fixed in so eligible Situation where I hope you will find the Utile and Dulce United. May every circumstance, occur not only to render you the accomplished Gentleman but an happy Man. At Parting we promised to write each other regularly once the Month. I depend on the performance of your promise and you may equally rely on my Punctuality. Tho' I do not promise to write entertaining Letters yet I hope you will feel some degree of pleasure from and Intercourse with a Sister who loves you as tenderly as I do. I would at this moment give a Trifle for a pair of Wings that I might take my Flight to Bruxelles and there have a view of my dear Richard *en Robe de Chambre, en Pantoufles et les Cheveaux en papillotes,* so metamorphosed that I imagine I should find some difficulty in recognising him. Our Berners Street Friends were particularly attentive during my Father's absence. Mrs Allen was with us near a Week and Mr Allen paid as several Visits your favourite Mrs Godfrey paid us an Evening visit last Thursday. Unfortunately she was not admitted. My father called at the great House this morning and there saw the whole Family. Monsieur Richard is allowed by Monsieur son Pere to be a perfect Judge of Beauty. I shall soon be ashamed to write French as you will be shortly tout a fait un François. The most welcome Intelligence I can give you is that my Mother et toute la Famille se portent bien. Your Health is everyday drank not en vin de Bourgogne but in humble Port or Sherry. Matt is to make an Excursion from Greenwich next Saturday. He will I make no doubt be very particular in his Enquiries about your Sword and Bag. Scud often talks of you and Miss Favell shall be taught before your Return to drink Brother Richard. The Pacquet which arrived last Week brought an account of poor Mr Lyon's death. Jamaica was quite safe the 18th of August. Long may it continue annexed to the english Crown. There is very good News from America but I shall leave Politicks to my Fathers Pen. He is to fill the Remainder of the Sheet I shall therefore not engross too much of it. I have another Reason to conclude – a summons to dinner – adieu my dear Richard I am toujours

Your affectionate Sister and sincere Friend Francoise Lee.

On the same sheet Robert Cooper Lee wrote to Richard, a letter with distinct echoes of those written to him by his own father over thirty years before.

My dear Richard,

My Letters from Ostend and Margate I hope got safe to your Hand to tell you I had reached England in perfect Health and Safety. I left Margate on Saturday Morning in the Diligence, arrived in Town that Evening, and on Sunday I had the Pleasure to find your Mother and the Family very well at Isleworth. I was not so fortunate in my Diligence Companions as you and I were. They were no other than two Abigails and one of them I believe could dress a Beef Stake, however they behaved decently and we made the Journey tolerably well. I spent yesterday at Isleworth and upon my coming to Town this Morning I was made happy with your kind Letter of last Friday. The Narrative of your Morning Exercises is very pleasing. The Conclusion calls forth my tenderest Feelings. You know my dear Richard it was not matter of Choice that induced the present Separation, but I considered it as a Measure for your Improvement and Advantage, and which I am confident it will prove. I honor and respect your Feelings on this trying Occasion at the same time I know you are possessed of manliness and good Sense to reconcile you in some measure to it. My Life will be always devoted to make you as happy as in my Power, and you may be assured of constantly hearing from me. I had the pleasure of seeing Mr Campbell's Mother and Brother and made them happy in my Account of him. Remember me kindly to [him] and our other Friends at Bruxelles. The last Bell is going I must conclude. Mr and Mrs Allen desire their kind respects I dined with them today. My dear Richard I am

Your tender and Affectionate father Robert Cooper Lee.

Shortly after Robert Cooper Lee returned from leaving Richard in Brussels, news reached London of one of the most devastating hurricanes ever to hit Jamaica, indeed possibly the worst ever recorded in the Caribbean. It was the first of five such storms to hit the island in a period of seven years. This first storm caused the worst damage at the western end of the island, flattening most of Westmoreland and Hanover parishes, including the estate of Thomas Thistlewood and the gardens he had lovingly built up over decades. A huge storm surge ten feet and more high overwhelmed the small coastal town of Savanna-la-Mar, driving one ship over the wall of the fort, normally fifteen feet above the sea, and drowning over three hundred people. Hardly six buildings were left standing. The psychological effects were as bad as the physical damage and Thistlewood reported that people were afraid to go to sleep and the 'hurricane has made every body look ten years older than they did before, and the healthiest show a great dejection in their countenances – nothing looks pleasant or agreeable since.'[187]

Disease and famine inevitably followed, but this disaster was different in one respect for it resulted in one of the first ever public relief operations. The reasons for this were partly political. With the declaration of independence of the American colonies there were fears in London for the rest of Caribbean islands whose strategic and economic importance was immense and which had been complaining about lack of support from London. In addition to this there were now in London a large number of ex-pat Jamaicans with first-hand knowledge of the island, and property and contacts still there. Among them of course was Robert Cooper Lee and so it is no surprise to see his name appear on the list of the committee 'appointed for receiving the Subscriptions for the relief of the unhappy Sufferers by the late dreadful calamities in the West Indies'[188] along with every other prominent West Indian then in London.

They set about arranging banking facilities in London and requested 'All Bankers in Great Britain and Ireland . . . to open Subscription Books immediately, in order to promote an object of such importance.' In case anyone should have concerns about the management of the Fund they said that ' The Public may be assured, that the whole proceedings of the Committee will, from time to time, be laid before them, and the money

[187] Trevor Burnard, *Mastery,Tyranny and Desire*, p.66.

[188] London Evening Chronicle, January 1781.

collected applied as frugally and expeditiously as possible, for the relief of the Sufferers.'

Inevitably there were arguments about who should receive aid and how it should be distributed. Jamaica made the decision to distribute some £10,000 of aid in cash payments which arrived just when it was most needed after a second hurricane had hit in October 1781. Much of the aid did not find its way into the hands of the poorest sufferers but into the pockets of the planters. Nevertheless the reaction to the hurricane of 1780 marks a new approach to disaster relief and one with which Robert Cooper Lee was closely involved.

Frances Lee to Richard Lee

Bedford Square, 15th December 1780

My dear Richard,

Your Letter which I have hourly expected for [more] than 10 days past I now entirely given over. I confess I am rather [illegible] lest Indisposition should have prevented your writing. I am in hopes however that you have written and that the letter has by some accident fallen into other Hands. My punctuality I hope you will consider as a proof of my Regard and that though absent you are remembered by me with the tenderest affection. So you must bid adieu for some time to your gay Habiliments and be content to wear sable sacred to the Memory of her late imperial Majesty – her Death I fear will render the Carnival less gay than you expected. I hope by this time you are perfectly reconciled to your Situation I cannot say that I am so to this loss of your company which I feel now more sensibly as this was the Season of our Meeting – you are ever our constant Toast. I shall drink your Health in a Bumper on the 23rd. I anticipate the arrival of that day by wishing you my dear Richard the Enjoyment of many happy years such as you have already seen! Matthew came Home last Monday and Gordon and John are to make their appearance next Week. Mr Charles Gray was in Town a few Days since he is going in the army. Mr Green has had a Letter from our little Friend Captain J.Brett he was then in America and had some idea of visiting the West Indies. I hope you have given up all Thoughts of a naval Life. Pray let me know if you have yet resolved on what profession to follow. How goes on Musick? Captain Morse who is a great proficient recommends you to learn *the improved* German Flute if you cannot get one at Bruxelles let my Father know by what means he can send you one. Suppose you were to exchange your Instrument for the Violin it is universally allowed the only one for a *Gentleman.* Captain Morse recommends it in preference to any other. I have not as yet made my appearance in Publick - for though it is not genteel to be seen before Christmas I should not have stood on punctilios had I been well enough to go out. My Mother has been to one play. We are to have the honor of Colonel and Mrs Kelly's Company with the addition of that of Mr and Mrs Welch to dinner today. Mrs Allen has not been out of doors since the seventh of last month. Do you learn riding and dancing? Pray do both. I think them very necessary accomplishments. How I long my dear Richard for your return! I never knew the extent of my Affection until this seperation! My Father and Mother join in kindest Love as do Matt and little Scud, Favell walks stoutly. Mrs Harrison talks incessantly of her dear Master Richard. She has got a new gown to wear on your Birth day which will be remembered by us all but by none more than by my dear Richard's

Affectionate Sister and invariate Friend Frances Lee.

PS [from Robert Cooper Lee]

Frances has left me Room I will add a few lines. Matt has this Moment called on Me for a Guinea to pay Mr Astley tomorrow morning on commencing his Scholar in the Art of Riding. The Guinea is for six Lessons. Bob is to be of the Party and Mr Allen talks of accompanying them. Mr and Mrs Welsh and Colonel Kelly dined here and is just now gone. Mrs Kelly was to have favoured us with her Company but was prevented by Indisposition. Your Letter of last Friday is not yet come to hand. I hope to receive it tomorrow. I know you are well and doing well will be always the highest satisfaction to me. May every Blessing attend My dear Richard is the most cordial wish of His

ever affectionate father Robert Cooper Lee.

Philip Astley had served as a soldier in the Seven Years War and was an expert horseman. He later made use of his riding expertise to develop spectacular shows, discovering that by creating a circular ring not only could the audience get a better view of the trick riders, but the centrifugal force aided the riders in maintaining their balance. He moved his Amphitheatre to Lambeth where he had opened a riding school in 1770. A great showman, his spectacles included all the ingredients of modern circus – musicians, clowns, animals (but not wild animals), feats of riding and acrobatics - and they became highly fashionable. Although his original amphitheatre was destroyed by fire, as were several successive buildings, it eventually became Astley's Royal Amphitheatre and the circular ring at forty-two feet across became the international standard size for all circuses. For Matthew Allen Lee, not quite eleven years old, lessons with the Master must have been exciting indeed.

Frances Lee to Robert Cooper Lee

Cowley, 31st October 1781

Mon tres cher Pere,

The inclosed Letter from Mr Heath came this morning with a few lines to yourself the purport of which was to acquaint you that Mr Pott gave little or no hope of Mrs Bowes seeing again and to request you to transmit the enclosed to your friend in Jamaica and to request him to apprise Mr Bowes[189] of the melancholy accident and afterwards to deliver the Letter from Mr Heath. We were this morning at Rickmansworth and have just fixed on Monday next for having the pleasure of dining with our Friends there. On our Return was met with Mrs and Miss Baynes walking in the Village of Harefield. We alighted and accompanied them to their Demesne walked around their grounds which are delightful. We appointed Saturday next for drinking Tea there but having since recollected your Engagement to Messrs Grant we intend to dispatch a Card tomorrow morning and to mention Tuesday instead which Day we hope will be perfectly agreeable to you. My Mother is much obliged to you for your Letter this Morning and desires I will present her Love. This Day must ever be to me a Day of serious Reflexion. Among the various Blessings for which I am indebted to an indulgent Providence the having bless'd me and untill this period with such parents commands my Gratitude this most powerfully! May Heaven long continue so inestimable a Treasure is the first Wish of my Heart! An Heart which must ever supplicate this choicest gifts of the Omnipotent for the best and tenderest of Fathers. Whilst this hand can guide a pen the dearest Pleasure I can know will be of assuring you of a Truth from the Contradiction of which I hope you will experience a mutual pleasure that I am My dear Sir

Your most affectionate and very dutiful Daughter Frances Lee.

---

[189] Probably Deputy Commissary General of Stores and Provisions, and Magistrate in Kingston, Edward Bowes. His wife was called Ann.

An event which must have been of business significance to Robert Cooper Lee, but which is not mentioned in the letters, was the death of John Ellis and his wife while travelling to England in 1782. On the 25th of July a fleet left Bluefields Bay Jamaica for England, it included the *Ville-de-Paris*, which had been the flagship of the Comte de Grasse during the American Revolutionary war and had been captured by Admiral Rodney, and on board the *British Queen* with Captain James Hodge were John Ellis his wife Elizabeth and their niece Anna Maria making her first trip to England.

The *British Queen* was a ship of 350 tons with a crew of 45 and 20 carriage guns, which in 1761 had been owned by 'Peter Impaud, Elias Benjamin de la Fontain, Daniel Vialars and others of London, merchants' when she was issued with letters of marque against the French. In May 1776 she had been included in a fleet of transports taking troops and wagons to Canada, and another record refers to her making a trip to Greenland. In 1777 she had been surveyed at Deptford and found fit for service as a transport ship. In 1780 her then owners, Wilkinson and Company, offered her to the government to carry stores to Jamaica and it is possible she was returning with the fleet from this latest episode in July 1782.

John Ellis and his wife Elizabeth Palmer had two sons, John and Charles Rose, both of whom were already in England. Ellis was one of the largest landowners in Jamaica. Son of George Ellis and Anne Beckford he had inherited the Newry plantation in St Mary, half of the Sixteen Mile Walk plantation and a share in Palm plantation in St Thomas in the Vale. In 1752 he bought Montpelier from the widow of Francis Sadler Hals. When his brother George died in 1753 leaving a pregnant wife (the sister of Edward Long), he acquired about another £30,000 of property on the grounds that his brother's Will had failed to make provision for any possible children.

The route frequently taken by ships sailing back to England was heading north out of the Caribbean and up the coast of America before striking out across the Atlantic, and ships captains relied on a combination of luck and experience when it came to avoiding extremes of weather.

It seems that the fleet had got roughly to the latitude of Boston when in the early hours of the morning of the 17th of September a severe storm hit them. Initial reports in the British press during October and November concentrated mainly on the fate of the *Ville-de-Paris*.

A Captain Cox who arrived in London in early December reported having seen the *Ville-de-Paris* after the storm and that she had lost her main and mizzen masts and that the crew had thrown all the guns overboard and sealed up the gun ports. The ship had been pooped, hit by a huge wave on her stern, which had carried away a large part of the structure, however the crew had used sail canvas to seal the ship and when last seen by Captain Cox she had been heading for the Azores under jury rig. However a report in the *Leeds Intelligencer* on the 24th of December said that 'the *Sylph* cutter, which sailed to the Western Islands near two months ago to look after the *Ville-de-Paris* and the *Glorieux* men of war is returned to Spithead, without having obtained any intelligence of them'.

News of the ill-fated Ellis family was finally reported in the *Hereford Journal* on the 9th of January 1783.

'William Shotton, late servant to John Ellis, Esq of St Mary's, Jamaica, who took his passage from that island, in the month of July last, for London, on board the *British Queen*, Captain Hodge relates the following melancholy tale: That they sailed from Jamaica on the 15th of July, under convoy of the *Ramillies* ; that his said Master, together with his wife and two nieces, two boys his wards, and four servants were on board; that they met with nothing particular on the passage till the 17th of September, when at three o'clock in the morning in lat.42 there came on a violent gale of wind, accompanied by a swelling sea which strained the ship almost to a wreck, and caused her to make so much water, that the pumps were obliged to be kept incessantly going. At three o'clock in the afternoon it laid the ship on her beam ends, and carried away her mizzen mast, with various other things, off the deck, and at the same instant washed the said William Shotton overboard, and likewise his wife, who then happened to have fast hold of his clothes; but having both got hold of the wreck and entangled themselves with the ropes, they floated in this situation for near two days, and were then providentially taken up by the ship *Catherine*, Captain McLey, bound from Cork to New York. They were afterwards taken by an American priveteer, and carried to the Havannah, from whence they obtained a passage to Philadelphia, and from that place to New York, where he embarked on board the *Minerva* Captain McAddams, which is arrived at Portsmouth. Whilst they remained on the wreck, he frequently saw the ship on her beam ends: but being much exhausted and struck with heavy seas, the ship disappeared to him, so that he cannot say for certain whether she righted or sank, but is inclined to believe from her distressed state, and having six feet water in her hold, she must have inevitably sunk. He could not learn any thing of her from the *Catherine*'s people after he was recovered. He further adds, that he saw several ships founder during the gale, but could not learn their names.'

While the fate of the Ellis family was still uncertain, Robert Cooper Lee was enthusing about events relating to America. We tend to think of the declaration of Independence by the American States in 1776 as marking the key point in the events that led to separation from the Empire. However, from the British perspective at the time that merely led to several years of war, and for Robert Cooper Lee and the Jamaica interest to specific fears in relation both to the safety of Jamaica and the security of its trading links with England. So for them 1782 actually marked the more important event.

Robert Cooper Lee to Richard Lee

Bedford Square, 6th December 1782

My dear Richard,

One of the most important Events in the Annals of Great Britain has taken place. The Independency of the United States of America. On the 30th of November Provisionary Articles were signed at Paris by his Majesty's Commissioners and the Commissioners of America, to constitute a Treaty of Peace, when the Peace shall be agreed upon between Great Britain and France. This previous Step, the signing of Articles with America being an Acknowledgement of her Independence, has removed the principal Obstacle to a general Accommodation. The Parliament met yesterday, and was opened by one of the longest Speeches from the Throne that has been made for many Years; it contains great Variety of Matter and expressly declares the Dismemberment of the Empire by the Seperation of America. The Address in the House of Commons was moved by Mr Yorke and seconded by Mr Banks. There was no Amendment moved. Mr Fox Lord North and Mr Pitt spoke, but there being no Opposition to the Address it is called a Conversation, and not a Debate. All Parties seemed agreed on the Necessity of assenting under the present Circumstances, to American Independence. And equally agreed with respect to France and Spain to accept of nothing short of honourable Terms of Peace. How that can be reconciled to the Idea of giving up Gibraltar I cannot see, yet that is confidentially talked of, and that the Spaniards are to give us the Island of Porto Rico in the West Indies in Exchange. Our captured Islands to be restored to us, and St Lucia to the French. In the East Indies the French demand to be put in the same Situation they were in prior to the last War, but that cannot be agreed to on our part. The prevailing Opinion here is that a general Peace will take place. Our political Barometer the Stocks have risen five or six per cent. I would send you Woodfull's Paper with the King's Speech and the Debates on it, but I conclude you will easily get a Sight of them.

A Frigate the *Resource* from Jamaica arrived a few days ago; she left Jamaica the 14th of October, and brings to Government Intelligence that the French and Spaniards were preparing to make another attempt on that Island. Don Solana with the Spanish Ships was about proceeding to the Cape, where the land Forces intended for the last Expedition had continued; they expected to meet the Reinforcement of Ships and Troops from France that sailed in September, when Lord Howe sailed, and to make a force of 25,000 Men and 25 Ships of the Line. Admiral Piggott from America would be soon after them, and Admiral Hughes with the Ships detached from Lord Howe's Fleet shortly afterwards. I therefore trust Jamaica will escape this Danger. Have you seen Sir Edward Hughes's Accounts in the Gazette of our Engagements with the French Fleets in the East Indies?

Your Mother and the Family came to Town yesterday having left Cowley for the Winter Season. We are all perfectly well except Frances, and under the Direction of Sir Richard Jebb she is getting better. She desires me to say she has been injoined from writing or you would have heard from her, but she expected you would have opened the Correspondence before now. Mr Allen is returned from Scotland without making a Purchase there. I am just returned from dining with him, and had the Pleasure of drinking your health in a Bottle of Bruxelles Burgundy. Your Brother was of the Party. He has not yet got rid of the Ague occasioned by attending Mr Ewer the first three days of last Term[190]. What is the Price of Sugars [with] you? The Idea of Peace has sunk them 10/ percent here. Mr [missing] has taken Mr Knox's House in Soho Square for a year ready [missing]. You know it is near us. He is very well. All the Family join in the kindest and affectionate good Wishes for you.

I ever am Your truly Affectionate Robert Cooper Lee.

PS Since my last I have had the Pleasure of a letter from you and am expecting to hear from you again every day.

Sir Richard Jebb was an outspoken doctor who had gained royal favour after saving the life of the Duke of Gloucester, brother of George III, at

---

190 The Law Terms in London were Michaelmas, usually from the first week in October to the 1st of December; Hilary beginning on the 20th of January and ending before Lent (which prohibited the taking of oaths); Easter beginning two weeks and a day after Easter Sunday and ending a week after Ascension day and finally Trinity, beginning a week and a day after Trinity Sunday and ending on the 14th of July.

Trento in Italy. For this he was rewarded by the King with the lease of a part of Enfield Chase, which was broken up in 1777, and built a house there which he named Trent Place and which by a curious co-incidence many years later was bought by Frances Lee's brother-in-law David Bevan. John Coakley Lettsom a friend of Jebb wrote of him

I loved that man with all his eccentricity. He had the bluntness, but not the rudeness, of Radcliffe. He had the medical perception, but not the perseverance and temporizing politeness, of Warren. In every respect, but fortune, superior to Turton; or to Baker, but in classical learning; and yet he was the unhappy slave of unhappy passions. His own sister is, and has long been, in a madhouse; the same fate attends his cousin, and a little adversity would have placed poor Sir Richard there also. There was an impetuosity in his manner, a wildness in his look, and sometimes a strange confusion in his head, which often made me tremble for his sensorium. He had a noble, generous heart, and a pleasing frankness among his friends; communicative of experience among the faculty, and earnest for the recovery of his patients, which he sometimes manifested by the most impetuous solicitude. Those who did not well know him, he alarmed; those who did, saw the unguarded and rude ebullition of earnestness for success[191].

It would seem that whatever Jebb's treatment for Frances was it had some success since by later in December 1782 she felt well enough to write a birthday letter to her brother, the longest she had been able to write for five months.

Frances Lee to Richard Lee

Bedford Square, 23rd December 1782

I should not have waited until *this Day* to assure my dear Richard of my good Wishes had I been able to write before. A severe Indisposition ever since we parted has rendered writing extremely irksome to me. I should be sorry you had so good an Excuse for your Silence at which I must confess I have been more hurt than displeased. I do not expect any Apologies but I shall be most happy to hear from you. By your letter to my Father I am pleased to find you are so well satisfied with your Situation. I assure you (sans compliment) I miss you much and I wish most fervently you were again returned to Old England. Nothing but the persuasion that you will derive advantage from the seperation could in any Degree reconcile me to it. As I can give you no account of public Occurrences you must be satisfied with hearing of domestic concerns. In the first place all the Family (myself excepted) are well and to add to its

[191] Source: http://munksroll.rcplondon.ac.uk/Biography/Details/2414

Glory our Cousin John is going to enter his Majesty's Services. He has not yet got his Commission – perhaps he will wait till the Articles of Peace are signed that by so doing he may not give a proof of his Valour the will of his peu dame and Cousin John has ever been esteemed a prudent young Man. Gordon did us the honour of spending the anniversary of his Birth here he returned to his Castle on Saturday but has promised to visit us in the course of next Week. Your friend Captain Enri is in Town but I hear nothing of Captain Cox Wilson[192]. Mr Mayo[193] Junior dined here on Friday and threatened to write to you very soon. Mr Augustus Floyer[194] (who is going to the East very shortly) has called two or three times on Bob but they never met until last Saturday at the Opera of which Bob is as great an Amateur as ever. Mr Ross[195] and his niece Miss Colquhoun (who resembles her Brother exceedingly) are constant attendants also. For my part I do not expect to see the inside of either of the theatres this season – not from choice shall I absent myself but from necessity. Sir Richard Jebb (who is my Physician) will hardly allow my going out in the Day and to confess the Truth since this last severe attack I find I am much better by remaining quietly at home. Mrs Siddons is universally admir'd and as much the [illegible] as ever Garrick was. Mrs Abington is gone to Covent Garden. (NB these are all very domestic concerns). The Royall Coach[196] is a very grand one it made its first appearance in Hyde Park yesterday. Madame did not or did not chuse to know us tho' our Coach I assure you is far from despicable. Mr Tubb is going to Bath with an heavy Heart poor Man! I have not seen his Son-in-law. He and his cara sposa are removed only last Week from Bryanstone Street – their Mansion in Cumberland Street is *superb*. I had almost forgot to condole with you on the loss of the £20,000. My Father gave you a Ticket in which Scudamore and I were parties concerned but alas! our usual good Luck prevailed – it was drawn a Blank. Mr William Hibbert a

---

[192] Possibly George Cox Wilson, born 1763 Red Lion Square, London, Ensign 66th Foot 1781.

[193] Joseph Mayo(1764-1851), son of Joseph Mayo of Ramsgate (c.1728-22 Oct 1789) close friend of Scudamore Winde.

[194] Augustus Floyer born in Madras in 1766 to a military family; Brev Col Sir, Madras Cav; KCB; d. 17 Oct 1818 Secunderabad.

[195] Hercules Ross and the daughter of his sister Margaret Ross.

[196] The 24 foot long coach, now known as the Coronation Coach, was built for George III who sold all his father's state coaches to raise the £7562 4s 3d it cost to build.

young Man with a small Fortune (and a Brother of Mr Hibbert[197] in this Square) was fortunate enough to get one of the £20,000. It would have been as well bestowed on us.

This for me is a very long letter and more than I have written at one Time for these last five Months. The Lyon family are engaged to dine here. We shall celebrate this auspicious Day most jovially in spight of Sir Richard Jebb (who had prohibits Wine) I shall drink to the Health of my dear Richard in a Bumper of Burgundy. Whilst my heart will glow with the tenderest affection and the warmest Wishes for his happiness, as my Friendship and regard for him are inexpressibly great it must suffice him to know that he is and must ever be most dear to his affectionate Sister F.L.

PS my Father and Mother send their kindest Wishes. Betty her duty and prays you may live many Years.

The reference to Marchant Tubb relates to the somewhat precipitate marriage of his step-daughter Mary Powell Morant to the widowed Joseph Royall, whose first wife Catherine (sister of John Morse) had died just six months earlier. Mary was forty-one and had seen no need to marry before this, Joseph Royall was twenty years her senior. The relationship was not to last.

Robert Cooper Lee to Richard Lee

Bedford Square, 24th January 1783

All hail returning Halcyon Days! Once more all Europe is at Peace. Farewell the glistening Camp, the Clarion's Sound, the solemn Trumpet and the Din of War. In short the Preliminary Articles between Great Britain and France and between Great Britain and Spain were signed at Versailles on the 20th Inst the Preliminaries with Holland are not yet signed, but a Cessation of Hostilities is agreed upon. This important News was announced by a Letter from Lord Grantham to the Lord Mayor at Nine O'Clock last Night. The Terms of Peace are not yet public but I flatter myself they are as favourable to Great Britain as we could

---

[197] Thomas Hibbert leased 44 Bedford Square from 1782-1784. A third brother George Hibbert was a distinguished naturalist and collecter. The Hibberts were prominent in the West Indian lobby in London and in the building of the West India Docks.

expect. I hear that we keep Gibraltar, that the captured Islands in the West Indies are to be restored on both Sides, and the affairs of India to be on the Footing of the Peace of 1763. Trade in general I conclude must flourish from this Event, though that of the Neutral Powers will be greatly lessened by it. As an Instance of the extensive Trade under the neutral Flags I am told no less than twenty two Danish Ships are coming from India to Europe this Year. The Hollanders I believe will be the greatest Sufferers by the War; the weakest generally go to the Wall. I believe that I mentioned to you formerly our Friend Mr Boyd having been unfortunately taken by Monsr. Sufrein's Squadron. Mr Boyd was returning from Ceylon to Madras, and was a Prisoner on board the *Fin* French Frigate in the Engagement between Sir Edward Hughes and Monsr. Sufrein on the 12th of April. The *Fin* actually struck to one of our Men of War who was so much disabled that he could not take Possession of his Prize, which therefore got off, no doubt to the great Mortification of Mr Boyd, who was shortly afterwards sent away to the Isle of France commonly called the Mauritius. He was afterwards sent to the Isle of Bourbon from whence Mrs Boyd has a letter from him dated last August, and where he must remain till exchanged or the Peace is known. If you look in the Map you will see the Isles of France and Bourbon in Africa not far from Madagascar and about the same distance on the other Side the Cape of Good Hope as St Helena is on this side. Monsr. Bufoy who made a considerable Figure in India last War was at the Isle of Bourbon with four Ships of the Line and some Frigates and was to proceed to India with Reinforcement of Troops he having the Command of both French and Dutch by Sea and Land, but he could not reach India earlier than last December, and before that time much is expected to have been done in our Favor as the arrival of our Force under Sir Richard Bickerton would give us a decided Superiority.

Your Letter of 31st December I had the Pleasure to receive on the 14th Instant. We are always happy to hear you are well, and you must not be surprised at our feeling some uneasiness when the Irregularity of the Post prevents us from hearing from you. You mention an expected Rupture between the Imperial [court and the?] Turks; I hope it will not be so, as a continental War generally spreads and involves the maritime Powers, and we surely want a Continuance of Piece. The Men of War that had actually sailed from Spithead for the West Indies and India are recalled and returned into Port.

Many Enquiries are made after you and kind respects desired. Mr Tubb is still at Bath. Mr and Mrs Royall very well. George Dehany goes out in the next Fleet to Jamaica. Jack Scott in Town thinking of going out. The Lyons thinking it will be necessary for them to do something for themselves. Your Mother is perfectly well. Your Sister much better than usual and anxiously expecting a Letter from you. Matt departs for Winton next week. I should have mentioned the Counsellor but he can speak for himself. Scudamore is commenced Schoolboy at Mr Wynter's Gloster Street All join in kindest respects to you.

Your ever Affectionate Father Robert Cooper Lee

PS Mr Ross[198] is well. He dined here yesterday.

Poor Macgenise! The public as well as the Judge who tried him are much in his Favor and I believe he will be pardoned – in the mean time he remains in the condemned Cells![199]

Dr Daniel MacGinnis (Macgenise) was tried at the Old Bailey for the murder of his landlord John Harvey. He pleaded self defence, and a number of very prominent persons with West Indian connections spoke in his defence. He was defended by John Silvester and Thomas Erskine and, as he was almost penniless, his defence must have been paid for by others. He was convicted of murder and sentenced to hang, but a month later he was granted a Royal pardon and his sentence was commuted to two years imprisonment in Newgate.

Frances Lee to Richard Lee

Bedford Square, 15th February 1783

If I could I would tell you my dear Richard the Pleasure I received from your kind Letter. You will believe it made me happy as it acquainted me of your health and happiness and as it assured me of the Continuance of your regard. Your Vanity I find has suffered an Increase by the Commendations of the Ladies – pray is it the Custom of Hambro' for the Ladies to make fine Speeches to the Gentlemen? There are some of my acquaintance here who have adopted that Fashion and I daresay you have heard of the Encomiums paid to Bob, Mr Scott and Mr Lyon by certain young Ladies not a dozen miles from Delaford. But the Beaux have made so ungrateful a return that if I thought the Ladies were capable of Resentment (for you must know they are of a very forgiving Nature) I

[198] Hercules Ross of Rossie.

[199] *Old Bailey Proceedings Online* (www.oldbaileyonline.org, version 7.0, 07 June 2012), January 1783 (17830117) and *Old Bailey Proceedings Online* (www.oldbaileyonline.org, version 7.0, 07 June 2012), February 1783 (17830226).

should think they would never deign to look on such cruel Swains. They wish much for an Introduction to you. Miss Freeman having sounded your Praises. Jack Lee they think very handsome and agreeable but rather diffident. He is at present their greatest favourite. And when he once mounts his Cockade he will certainly rise in their Estimation. My father does not seem very serious about the Light Dragoons, he seems rather to recommend a marching Regiment to our valiant boy. I congratulate you (or rather Mr Lehman) on the prodigious rise in Linnens. It seems to be the Opinion of the knowing ones that the Peace will not be a lasting one, you will make what use you please of this hint. I had a most elegant Bow yesterday from an acquaintance of yours – the Baron – he had not an opportunity of enquiring after you (which he has frequently done) or of Alans *Brack* – poor Magenise! Tomorrow is the important Day. It is generally thought he will be pardon'd. I saw today in the Park your Friend Payne. He is fatter than Bob ever was. Captain Enery (who is lately promoted to a Lieutenancy, rather an Irishism but you will understand it) has din'd here once – he is still the same good-natured agreeable young Man. He joined in lamenting the state of your Friend Cox Wilson ! The Mr Hanburys[200] dined here on Monday – Mr C. Hanbury enquired very particularly after you. Mr Simon Clarke has been returned from his continental Expedition sometime. He quitted Bruxelles on account of its being too gay a place. He prefers the solitude of London! I suppose Mr H. Ross will soon be thinking of Hamburg. My Mother desires I will tell you she wishes you will make your Wishes (for any things this little place can afford) known that she may have the Pleasure of gratifying them by so good an Opportunity as Mr Ross will be. My Father is gone to drink Tea with the Royalls. Mrs R. always enquires very kindly after you and desired I would remember her very kindly when I wrote as did my Friend Dickson and Mr Lyon when I saw them last there is very little Intercourse between the families in Berners Street and Bedford Square. I have not din'd once there this Winter and my Mother only once – Madame not being in a situation to receive Company[201] our Card Parties are knocked up. I have hardly touched a Card (which with my good Luck is no great loss) this Winter. The Lyons [are] much at home – the Scotts are of my Brother's parties J. Mayo [torn] much at Ramsgate and is going to Oxford [torn] will have to be taught Whist by

[200] Possibly Capel and John Hanbury from the Quaker Banking family, also involved in the tobacco trade.

[201] Favell Allen was expecting her second child. James Allen was born on the 15th of April 1783 in Berners Street.

you when you return. I must not omit the important Intelligence of Mr Allen's having partly engaged Mr Bearcroft's House in this Square. What an acquisition! Besides which he has made a purchase in Scotland and is now Laird of Inchmartin. Lee[202] is grown a fine Boy Our Naval Officers [?] Scud improves in impudence daily. He is at last become a Day Boarder (that is to say he dines at school) at Mr Winter's in Glocester Street. I have ventured to one play since I wrote you (but not to see Mrs Siddons) the Entertainment was Rosina a very pretty musical piece the plot taken from Thomson's Palemon and Lavinia – I caught a little Cold there but for this last Fortnight I have had a dreadful Cough on the whole however I am better for Sir Richard Jebb. I must now conclude this scrawl with assuring you of the affectionate wishes of my Father and Mother as well of

your sincerely attached Frances Lee.

Frances Lee to Richard Lee

Bedford Square, 6th May 1783

I have been so engaged with Masquerades Operas Ranelagh and other fashionable places of resort that from honor I have not had it in my Power to thank my dear Richard for his last kind favor. I confess I had almost given up the hopes of ever receiving another Line from you. It is generally allow'd that 'a bad Excuse is better than none' I will not allow that it is. I therefore approve of your not attempting to make one for your long Silence and of your reliance on my Good Nature etc. But why offer a bad pen as an Excuse for the shortness of your Epistle? I cannot accept it as I daresay if you had not another pen at hand you are too much the Man of Business to be without a pen knife in your pocket. Then why not take a little Trouble to give me a great deal of pleasure? which would have been the Consequence of your adding a few more lines. I however thank you most sincerely for the Happiness I deriv'd from the assurance of your still remembering me with affection. Believe me my dear Richard I esteem you as the dearest of my friends and that your Happiness is the first Wish of my Heart. Will you believe that I have really been to a Masquerade? I was last Thursday at one – our party consisted of thirteen. The four Lyons, Mr Ross and Mrs Colquhoun, Dr and Mrs Whitefield, the Laird of Strathbogie, Mr James (a Cousin of Sir Philip Clark). Mon

[202] John Lee Allen, born the 22nd of June 1781.

Pere, Ma Mere et votre tres humble. They all went in Dominos excepting my Mother and what Character do you think she assumed? that of an old Woman with a Basket of Cakes. She was really an excellent Mask. I thought a Domino would be too warm I therefore went in a fancy Dress. There were two excellent Mungos who had been lately in Jamaica – I ventured to attack them – your Friend Captain Enery did me the favour of acknowledging me we both wish'd for you. I think a masquerade is a favorite amusement of yours. I liked it much better than I expected I should. The Company was numerous about twelve hundred and tho there [illegible] few *good* Characters (I mean well supported ones) the Novelty of the scene pleased me much. I have been once to the Opera and as often to Ranelagh (the latter has only been open'd a Fortnight). The Opera House is amazingly improved and I think much enlarged at least the pit is. I have been several times to Kensington Gardens they are as much frequented as ever. I must not omit to acquaint you I am going to have a rout this Evening consisting of the Betts[203] and Lyons (who make ten) and I expect the honor of Ensign Joseph Madocks's Company. He requested Bob would invite him not to see *me* but the Betts, so I have sent him a Card. I was in hopes Jack Scott would have made one but I am sorry to acquaint you he is very ill (tho' I trust not dangerously so) with a Fever. There are few persons whose Death would give me more real Concern than his for I am not acquainted with a more amiable young Man, he has my sincere prayers for his speedy recovery and I'm sure you will join yours. I had the pleasure of having a very good account of you lately 'that you were in good health, good spirits and kept the best Company in Hambro'. I wish you long the Enjoyment of three such good Things though I confess I had rather be the Witness of them and as it is very unlikely my taking a Trip to Hambro I hope the Day is not very distant when you will condescend to revisit old England. Their Majesties have lost another Prince – Octavius – I daresay you have seen him on the Terrace – poor little Fellow he died under Inoculation. We were much alarmed about poor Scud! Thank [torn] is now perfectly recovered from the Measles. [Torn] to the Laird of Inchmartin's Family. Mrs Allen is very indifferent. My Father received your Letter a few Days since and your Commission shall be speedily executed I have had a Shirt Buckle made for you some time expecting Mr Ross would be going to Hambro' I shall send it by the first Opportunity and I beg you will wear it for my sake. If you are not tired of my Nonsense I really am writing and I really

---

[203] The family of Samuel and Elizabeth Peachy Betts, contemporaries of the Lees in Jamaica, consisting of two sons and four daughters.

could not have written three pages to any other person than yourself. I don't know whether you will consider it as a Complement but I really mean it as one. Adieu my dear Richard. My Father and Mother send their kindest Wishes mine ever await you. I am toujours et je serai à jamais

Your most affectionate Sister and sincerest of friends F.L.

Frances Lee to Richard Lee

Bedford Square, 14th May 1783

I hope the Trifle that accompanies this will be acceptable to my dear Richard and that he will value it on Account of this Donor. Mr Hanbury I understand proposes setting out for Hambro To-morrow. I shall trouble him to deliver this scrawl to you tho' I only wrote you last Week I presume a second Letter will not be displeasing I should hope to hear from you before we leave Town (which I imagine will be in a Fortnight) I returned yesterday from Woodford where I have been spending a few Days with my friend Sophy Gardiner. In this Evening we are going to Mrs Lyons Rout. Tomorrow we dine at Sir John Taylor's on Friday at Mrs Welch's and afterwards to Ranelagh, on Saturday I am to be at Mrs Green's fourth Christening[204] – a propos of Christenings Mr Allen's *second* son was christened on Monday by the name of James (after his Grandpapa on his Father's side). I was not present the rest of the family were. My Mother chaperon'd the Miss Venns[205] to Ranelagh on Monday Evening I believe she had not been there for two years before and as a proof of her tasteful fashionable amusements she intends going again in the course of next Week. I have only been twice this season and twice more will close my amusements. I *blush* to say I have not yet seen (nor shall see till next Winter) Mrs Siddons that Unique of theatrical perfection. I can fancy she is every thing that is charming and that must suffice for the present. The Lyons are going into Devonshire for the Summer with their Mother and Sisters if the Ladies approve the Country and they mean to reside entirely there and the Gentlemen will only come to town to attend Term. Our Friend Jack Scott is still very indifferent – it is sixteen Days since he has had the Fever without Intermission. I am

---

[204] Harry, son of Edmund Green and Catherine Morse.

[205] Four daughters of John Venn (died 1764), Rector of St Catherine, Jamaica.

really much concerned about him. We hear from Matt every Week he expresses much satisfaction at his change of residence. It is however a long spell from Christmas to August to be at School. We had not the pleasure of seeing your Friend Joe Maddocks on Tuesday as I expected we were however very Merry without him – we did not part till after one in the Morning. Bob's blame from la Bett is I believe pretty nearly extinguish'd, he was however very polite and attentive to both sisters. I thought of you more than once during the Evening – for a wonder I came off a gainer at Lottery Tickets. We see Mr Tubb and Mrs Royall frequently they never failed to enquire after you. Mr Allen told me this morning he had had a Letter from you I presume it was to congratulate him on the Increase of his family. We have had very delightful Weather lately it however threatens rain to-day which will be very acceptable for the Dust is intolerable. I have at last got an horse light Chestnut 14 hands and half six years old and some Blood – am I not quite the female Jockey? I have only rode once and was much pleased with her paces (for my Horse I believe is a Mare). The Exhibition is open'd but I have not yet been I understand the Collection is a very bad one. It is however so good a Lounge that it will ever be crowded.

À present il faut vous dire adieu mon cher Frere my Budget being pretty nearly exhausted. I leave politicks for my Father's Discussion. I shall conclude with this Truth that I am invariably

your affectionate Sister and sincere Friend F.L.

PS My Father and Mother and Captain John (whose Commission is not yet purchased but who is most impatient to reach Gottingen) desire to be kindly remembered, your faithful Servant Betty says my duty and God bless *Master* Richard. Amen say I.

Frances Lee to Richard Lee

Bedford Square, 3rd June 1783

My dear Richard,

Notwithstanding you are two Letters in my Debt I cannot omit so favourable and Opportunity of assuring you how invariably my best Wishes attend you. Mr Gray has at last finished your Shoes; with them you will receive 6 pair Silk Stockings, 6 Waistcoats and a pair of leathern Inexpressibles. The inclosed piece of paper I trust will be acceptable. The Gift is indeed trifling but as Mark of my regard I am sure my dear

Richard will receive it with pleasure. Great News! The papers have this Day announced that the Duchess of Devonshire has presented the Duke with a Son and Heir[206]. Talking of great folks - We were on Sunday at Hanwell Mrs Allen is much benefited by the Country Air. And what do you think is come to pass? *Mr and Mrs Royall are Seperated* by mutual Consent – they each complain of the violence of the others Disposition. Mrs R. is returned to her Father whom she no longer calls Tubby. The marriage was concluded in such haste that I am not the least surprised at the seperation. I pity neither. Poor Jack Scott is still in Bed we have however hopes of his Recovery. Fevers are very prevalent just now as well as putrid sore throats. Thank God we have all hitherto escaped. In the course of this Week we shall fly the Contagion and breathe the pure Air of our Sabine Fields and enjoy this Converse Sweet of our rural Visitants. The Baynes's I confess stand foremost on my list and I promise myself much enjoyment in their Society (I do not except the *blue Officer*). I mean to ride a great deal provided my strength will admit of the Exercise you may depend on hearing of all my feats of activity and I shall expect to be informed of yours as I understand you have got an Horse – your poney I am told is blind. Will you authorise me to dispose of him at the Fair and I shall remit you the purchase money, or if blind poneys are in greater demand at Hamburgh than here shall I ship him by the first good Opportunity? I must for the present have done chatting being interrupted by my Friend. We are going this afternoon to a small party at Mrs Farquar's[207] you know my partiality in the family and you can therefore have no doubt of my being agreeably entertained. Gordon who always pays us flying Visits din'd here to-day he desired I would remember him very particularly to you. My Mother desires her kindest remembrance. My Father accompanied by Mr Harrison and Mr Allen are gone to pay Mr Hibbert[208] a Visit in Hertfordshire they will return tomorrow.

---

[206] In fact Georgiana did not give birth until July 12th, and then to a daughter. The Duchess's often scandalous behaviour and the fact that she had not yet produced an heir after nine years of marriage kept her very much in the headlines.

[207] Ann Farquhar was the widow of Dr Thomas Harvie of Jamaica, and after his death had married Dr (later Sir)Walter Farquhar. He was surgeon in the 19th Regiment of foot, and subsequently on the personal staff of the Prince Regent, partly due to the influence of General Samuel Townsend – also a friend of the Lee family.

[208] George Hibbert was hugely wealthy on the basis of his Jamaican estates and had settled at Munden in Hertfordshire. He was a key figure of the West Indian lobby in London, and of the West India Dock Company.

Adieu my dearest Richard with my whole heart am I

your most affectionate Sister and very sincere Friend F.L.

The Lee family were friends with the Baynes well into the nineteenth century, perhaps having met in Jamaica. Alexander Baynes (who died about 1803) was Surgeon to the Ordnance Department in Gibraltar. He married Margaret Macleod, sister of Lt.-Gen. Sir John Macleod. All their sons went into the army and his daughters married into the army. The Baynes were well connected in society as Sir John Macleod's wife the Honourable Lady Amelia Wilhelmina Kerr, was sister-in-law to Lt.-Gen. Lord George Lennox, son of the second Duke of Richmond.

Alexander Baynes' eldest son Edward Baynes (c.1768-1829) served in the West Indies and North America, and as Adjutant General to the forces in Canada negotiated the peace with America to end the war of 1812. Edward Baynes married Ann Frances Cator, grand-daughter of Jamaica merchant John Morse and Elizabeth Tyndall Augier, herself the grand-daughter of an African slave.

Frances Lee was a close friend of Ann Frances Baynes' aunt Catherine Morse who married a young barrister called Edmund Green in 1777, and whose fourth child's christening is mentioned above. He fought a lengthy battle to secure the inheritance of the Morse children against their English relatives who wanted to use the 1761 Devises Act, preventing negroes, mulattoes and illegitimate children from inheriting more than £2000, to challenge John Morse's Will. To further their case Edmund Green used the argument that since their grandmother Mary Augier and all her Augier siblings and children had been granted the legal rights of white people in 1747 this took precedence over the later Act. It was a case that dragged on for many years and after the death of the chief protagonist Edward Morse in Jamaica in 1794 was only finally settled in 1799. It seems not unlikely that Robert Cooper Lee may have advised Edmund Green in the case.

Robert Cooper Lee to Priscilla Lee

Bedford Square, 5th August 1783

Mr Bowes and myself got to Town very well about 10 O'clock. From that time till three I had a tolerable Levé. The Travellers for Portsmouth set out yesterday between one and two. Prey acquaint Captain Lee that Colonel Gordon has written to General Havilland in his favor. General

Townsend[209] who is returned to Chatham is to acquaint further in a few days. No particular News in Town. Billy Pusey[210] is gone to his long home. Capt and Mrs Gardiner[211] left their Cards here Sunday last. I have heard nothing of Frances's favourite Officer. My kindest respects to all at Cowley

Your ever Affectionate Robert Cooper Lee.

Frances Lee to Richard Lee

Cowley, 13th of August 1783

I may offer my dear Richard the same Excuse for not writing before as he pleaded in his last most welcome Letter. The Expectation of hearing again very soon from him (as my Father kindly flattered me I should) I have waited a whole fortnight for that happiness and my stock of patience being now quite exhausted I sit down - not to scold -but to assure the most beloved of Brothers that every proof of his affectionate attention is to me a source of the most pleasing gratification as well as that every Account of his being well and happy gives me an Increase of Health and Happiness. Your last letter found me in Bed and almost incapable of stirring a joint owing to the violent Bruises received in a fall from my horse – but whilst I perused those delightful assurances of my dear Richard's regard I forgot all pain. He will I am sure be happy to hear that I have been some time recovered from the consequences of my accident. Don't think however that I am intimidated by it. I would have rode the same Horse as soon as I was able but I could not obtain permission nor do I think it likely with my Mother's Consent that I shall ever ride again! You will not who are so well acquainted with the merits of the Daughter wonder that every means should be taken to preserve the Life of so amiable a Being – a much more amiable one however interests the present feelings – Jack Scott who has been with us three Weeks. I think him benefited by the change of air, but on Saturday he was obliged to undergo a most severe Operation the having a large swelling (where the fever had most probably settled) behind his Ear opened. Mr Freeman was the

---

209 Samuel Townsend (c.1732-1794) married 1772 Elizabeth Ford neé Aikenhead.

210 Colonel William Pusey, M.A. for Vere 1765, '6, '8, '70, '81. Speaker pro tem 1782. Died 1783, (St. Dorothy Parish Church) aged 42 years.

211 Possibly Captain, later Admiral Sir, Alan Gardner (1742-1808), husband of Susanna Hyde Gale (1749-1823).

Operator and his Patient bore it most manfully and thank God he has been better ever since. To esteem Jack Scott as he deserves requires only a residence under the same roof – in my life I never met with a *more* amiable young man I will not even except my Friends Dicky Dunn or Lieutenant Thomas Brett (better Men than either never lived). Tom has been with us for the last Week he talks of his friend Dick very often – nay he sometimes threatens to take a trip to Hambro' to see him and only wishes for Mr Rudhall to form the party. I think [torn] would be a little surprised to see them. I think it more likely you will see Captain John Lee – it is fixed that he is to go in the 45th Regiment. He has not however yet appeared in the Gazette of course he has not mounted his Cockade. Matt joined us about a month ago (don't think Jack and I are united in holy Matrimony and the Ceremony was performed by the Rev Matt Lightfoot the parson of our parish) after nearly six months absence. I think him much improved by his residence at Winchester. I must repair to the duties of Ma Toilette as we are going this Evening to the Terrace – on my return I will conclude this scrawl.

It is near a Week since I commenced this to my dear Richard since which I have been so troubled with a violent head and throat I have not been able to make a conclusion. We had a pleasant Walk on the Terrace but did not see any of the Royal Family. Dr Ford[212] who has the honour of being Accoucheur to her Majesty inform'd us that the Queen and Princess were as well as could be expected. The Prince of Wales's Birth-Day will not be solemnised untill March – there were some trifling illuminations at Windsor on the Occasion and the Terrace was much crowded in this Evening. My Father received your Letter on Saturday wherein you mention having written to me. I conclude your letter to me has miscarried. I hope therefore you will compensate as much as is in your power for the Loss by answering this very shortly. It is a long time indeed since I heard from you. My Friend Dickson (who has been with me for this last Month – she left me [illegible] days ago) was much [torn] with your familiar mention of her she desired I would return her [compliments]. Our Neighbours the Youngs[213] we see very often. Their

---

212 Dr James Ford (c.1718-1795), brother of Gilbert Ford erstwhile Attorney General in Jamaica. Queen Charlotte had given birth to her fifteenth, and last, child Princess Amelia on the 7th of August.

213 Sir William Young who had been Lieutenant Governor of Trinidad and Tobago bought the manor of Delaford in 1767. There is a painting of his family, in seventeenth-century fancy dress costume, painted by Zoffany, in the Walker Art Gallery in Liverpool. Sir William's eldest son would eventually join Wilberforce in opposing the slave trade.

Brother who is a Lieutenant in the 13th is an agreeable lively young Man he is at present at Delaford. The Baynes's however are by far the most to my gout of any in this part of the World. We are to have the pleasure of their Company To-morrow at Dinner and *they* are to have the pleasure of partaking of a small Turtle. A Friend of mine would gladly be of the party I am sure – not for the sake of the Turtle only that that would prove no Objection unless he has lost his good Taste for good Things. The Allens have been sometime in Scotland, they are not yet returned from thence. I expect my Friend Sophy Gardiner to spend a few Days with me very shortly. My Father had positively fixed to accompany Lord Straathbogy to Scotland to introduce him to his Friends there but his Lordship as positively declined going. He is still at Sevenoaks and I believe will continue there some time longer. I have got to the End of this third page tho' I hope not to the end of your patience as I would fain flatter myself that my Letters can never be too long for you. I know this that I am always sorry when I come to the End of yours. All here join in affectionate regards. Tom Brett desires to be most particularly remembered.

Adieu my dear Richard believe me always the most sincere of Friends as well as the most affectionate of Sisters F.L.

Robert Cooper Lee to Priscilla Lee

Bedford Square, 25th September 1783

The Turtle is to be killed tomorrow Night. You are expected to Dinner on Sunday. I will give you half of my Bed and return with you as early as you please on Sunday Morning. Mrs Deave[214] (late Mrs Powell) and her young Husband have been gone from Town these three weeks. I called this morning in Bond Street and was told they went to Bristol. Another very fine Day. I write this before Dinner lest I may be late coming home. If any thing material I will add a Postscript. My kind Love to all.

Yours ever Affectionately Robert Cooper Lee

PS Frances's Letter is come to hand. Many Thanks to her for the pleasing Intelligence it contains.

---

[214] Susanna Slatford Powell, already twice widowed, married Henry Deaves esq. of Cork Ireland, by licence at St George Hanover Square, 29th August 1783 (source:Pallot's Marriage Index). Susannah Slatford Deaves is shown as owning 144 slaves in a place called Rock Rent, Clarendon, Jamaica in 1811 and 155 slaves at Slatford, Clarendon in 1818. She seems to have become an absentee landlord after the death of her second husband.

Robert Cooper Lee to Priscilla Lee

Bedford Square, 1st October 1783

I found my Way this Morning through the Fog tolerably well, and got to Town at half past Nine. Our part of the Town is as still and quiet as Cowley. I stayed here till near five and then took a slight Repast at the Piazza Coffee house. No Letter from Richard. Matt's I suppose is at Cowley. Mrs Pringle desires her best Thanks for the Partridges. Mr Tubb is very busy with his new House and has removed sundry large Bottles etc. Mr Jacob Neufville[215] and Son called here today. Old Josiah it seems is dead very lately. Mr Jarrett[216] desires me to say Mrs Jarrett will be happy to see you when you come to Town. I lament being from the Country this fine Weather, and shall certainly return Friday. The Irish Volunteers are likely to be troublesome. Let the Captain take Care of that. My kind respects to all at Cowley. I am

Your ever Affectionate Robert Cooper Lee.

PS Two black Hats just came for Frances to chuse one.

Robert Cooper Lee to Richard Lee

Bedford Square, 9th October 1783

My dear Richard,

My Letter of this day Fortnight I hope has reached you before now. I have not since had the Pleasure of hearing from you, but am in daily Expectation of that Satisfaction. Mr Ross is returned from the Continent, and gone again to the North. His Nephew accompanied him to Paris, and was greatly pleased with the Jaunt. Mr Ross was fortunate in meeting his Friend the Comte de Grasse in Paris, and by his means he obtained every success every where; and left his Business in the best Train. I suppose Dr Ross almost despairs of seeing his Brother in Hamburg. Next year he may be more at leisure. The principal Object of his present Jaunt to the

---

215 Three members of the Neufville family, including Josiah Neufville snr, Josiah Neufville jnr and Isaac Neufville, patented land in St Thomas in the East in 1742. Jacob Neufville and his wife Margaret had a son Charles baptised in St Thomas in the East in 1757.

216 Possibly John Jarrett of Trelawney, Jamaica and London

North is a Purchase he has in View in the Neighbourhood of Montrose. The Paragraphs in the English Papers respecting the Trial of the Comte de Grasse was without the least Foundation. There is no Charge as yet exhibited against him. A Court of Enquiry upon the Conduct of the Fleet in general is sitting. The Comte is under no Apprehension of public Censure. He makes a Point of going in public every day, and the popular Clamour has pretty well subsided. Mr Ross in his Way from Paris to Versailles saw the famous Balloon that was sent up into the air in the Presence of the Royal Family. He says it fell about 4or 5 Miles from the spot it set out from. It is fortunate this Invention was not discovered before the Peace, as the Inventor would have undertaken to put thirty thousand men by means of different Balloons upon the Rock of Gibraltar. Our Cousin John is actually gazetted an Ensign in the 16th Regiment in the Room of the famous Benedict Arnold, who having only Rank in America, is some(?) creeping up in the Army. His Leave of Absence is not yet settled, but I expect it will in a few days and that he will set out for Göttingen in the Course of a Fortnight. I hope to get him Letters of Introduction from General Faucett. He will write to you as soon as he arrives at Göttingen. I'm going tomorrow into Hants to spend a Week at Avington with the Chandos Family and I shall probably see Matthew, as I shall be within four miles of Winchester.

Peace was proclaimed here last Monday as between us and France and Spain. I was not in Town. The Mob compelled Illuminations in the City. The Parliament meet the 11th November. The Irish Parliament about the same time. All our Concessions to that Country have not satisfied them. The Volunteers seem inclined to govern every thing. I hope we shall not have a Civil War there upon the back of the American one. Mr Flood the great Orator in the Irish Parliament is to come in here for Winchester.

Our Neighbourhood at Cowley is increased by the Arrival of Sir William Young from the West Indies. I have been to pay my Respects to him. He is a very polite pleasant Man.

Your Mother and all the Family are well. Your Sister has got on Horseback again upon a quiet well broke Animal. The Weather here is delightful, but rather cold. God bless and preserve you.

I am My dear Richard's Very affectionate Father Robert Cooper Lee.

Frances Lee to Richard Lee

Cowley, 27th October 1783

I should be undeserving the Pleasure I derive from my dear Richard's Letter could I suffer such a valuable proofs of his regard to remain unacknowledged six Weeks without alledging some reason for my silence. I have at present the old Excuse Indisposition to offer – indeed I have been scarcely one Day tolerably well since I was favor'd with your last kind Letter and it requires no small Exertion (since I find Writing a very painful Occupation) to thank you for it. I do not mention the Circumstance in order to enhance the value of my scrawls (for I will suppose they are in some degree valuable to you) but merely to show that it has not been for want of Inclination (but ability) that I have not before address'd my dear Brother. You will see by the Date of this that we are still enjoying rural Felicity. We shall not remove to Town before the beginning of December – so it is decreed. Have you heard of our Acquisition in Bedford Square? Mr Tubb and his Daughter (alias the widowed Wife) have taken an House on the North side[217] and I suppose have nearly got into it. The Allens are settled (at least the furniture is, for they are still at Hanwell) in theirs. Besides which I expect to have much enjoyment in the Society of my Friend Sophy Gardiner whose Brother is lately married and has got an House in the Square and I presume (if my friend's taste coincides with mine) that she will prefer a Town Residence at least for the Winter Months. I think it probable that you have not heard that our friend Charles Gray is become a Father. His Daughter must be near two months old. He has been only in Town for a few Days since his Marriage and then he comes without his Cara Sposa – I understand she is a very pretty Woman. Our military boy talks of setting out for Brunswick in the course of this Week. He has worn his Regimentals but once and that was when he pay'd his Devoirs to his General (Robertson) so I had not the pleasure of seeing them on, they are monstrous smart off. Red and Lemon Colour Silver Epaulette – very elegant Sword in short he (Captain John I should have said) is quite the Thing sans Badinage. I think the Cockade becomes him *wonderfully*. I mentioned to him what you said about Gottingen but Brunswick had been determined on before. He goes from Harwich to Helvoetsluys. Gordon is quite rusticated. He sometimes takes a drive to Town for a few Hours but he is so partial to Sevenoaks that he has not been once here during the Summer. I believe my Father wishes him to go to College but

---

217 No 13 Bedford Square

Gordon I fancy does not relish the plan that being the Case I suppose he will remain where he is for some time longer. As a young man of Fortune and *Spirit* I wonder he does not wish to go to the University and then to make the *Grand Tour.* Jack Scott is still with us and perfectly recover'd – indeed I think is stouter than I ever remember him. I believe I mentioned Mr George Dehany's being gone to Jamaica – he went last March. He made but a short stay for he has been returned about a Fortnight. As Term commences next Week I suppose there will be a general Muster of the young Lawyers of our acquaintance I think there is a pretty numerous Set. Your Friend (or rather schoolfellow) Mr East is going to be a Pupil of Mr Ewer. Young Mr Mayo is at Oxford and will I suppose be a Candidate for the Chancellorship then there are the two Lyons (who by the bye with their Mother and Sisters are settled near Exeter and who will only be in Town for a few Days during Term). The most important news in this part of the World is the arrival of Sir William Young from the West Indies. He is a great acquisition to the Neighbourhood for he is a most agreeable Man. I have not yet had the Pleasure of seeing him. My Intimacy with his Daughters has been lately interrupted by mutual Indispositions. They had both been very ill and the youngest is thought to be in some Danger. I am really much concerned for tho' the Miss Youngs are very great Originals yet as they possess a large share of good Sense and good Nature they are often very agreeable Companions and indeed to me they have been always particularly attentive and kind so that I should be ungrateful did I not feel interested about them. As I find my paper is nearly finished I must think of bidding my dear Richard adieu. My Father and Mother desire I will assure you of their affectionate regard and accept of the best Wishes of her who is most truly

Your friend and affectionate Sister F.L.

PS Mrs Boyd from whom I heard lately made kind enquiries after you and desired to be particularly remembered when I wrote as did Mr Tubb and Mrs Royall when I saw them a few Days ago. Write soon and love me always as I love you.

Frances Lee to Priscilla Lee

Woodford, Tuesday evening [undated]

My dear Madam,

I truly proposed being with you Tomorrow but from *a very particular and unexpected Circumstance* I am *obliged* to defer my return to Saturday when I hope to meet you in perfect Health. I cannot say I have been quite as well as you wish me to be I was very la la when I left Town and I do not think I have been better for the pure air of the Country. Be kind enough to send as soon as you conveniently can the enclosed Note from my Friend Miss Gardiner who with Mr and Mrs Gardiner are to be in Town to dine with Mr Robertson Saturday which is the reason for my fixing on that Day instead of an earlier for I might *possibly* be cock enough to come on Friday but then it would be giving them the trouble of coming on my account *only*. Mr and Mrs Gardiner and Miss G. Desire their kind Compliments to you and my Father. They will have the pleasure of waiting on you on Thursday Sennight if I can prevail on the good old Gentleman I will to be of the party. Give my best and affectionate regards to my Father and assure him it will give me pleasure to receive a Line to hear that you are all well. Till we meet be assured my dear Madam of the tender invariable affection of

Your dutiful Daughter Frances Lee.

PS my kind regards to my Brothers and Favell and best Compliments to the Ross's and "the Squire of Dames".

Robert Cooper Lee to Priscilla Lee

Bedford Square, 11th November 1783

Mr Allen and myself got back from the House of Lords before five O'Clock We saw every thing completely having taken our Stations within three Yards of the Throne. Mrs Allen looked charmingly in the Court full Dress. Lady Essex blushed near her. The Prince of Wales took the Seat of Edward the Confessor. He looked very well and nobly. The Speech is an excellent Performance. The Address was moved by Lord Scarborough and seconded by Lord Hampden. There was no Opposition to it, but Lord Temple in a long Philipick well delivered avowed Opposition.

I was in Westminster Hall today before ten O'Clock to attend the Cause Pinnock and Dixon. It was put off till Tuesday next. I must therefore be in Town on Monday. I hope to have the Pleasure of joining the Family at Cowley on Friday at Dinner. Jane is very anxious to get the House in readiness for your Reception, but makes no Complaint except of the Rheumatism with which she is much afflicted. I wish to know by a Line that you are well, and that Frances is better. I have not seen our Neighbours on the North side. My kindest Love to you and Frances I am

Your truly affectionate Robert Cooper Lee.

The winter of 1784 was one of the coldest on record with twenty-eight days of continuous frost reported by Gilbert White at Selbourne in Hampshire, temperatures driven down following the volcanic eruptions of the Laki Craters on Iceland the previous summer and the Japanese Asama Yama in the autumn. The Icelandic eruption had caused the 'sand summer' with a blood red sun and the 'great dry fog' of 1783, referred to in the letter from Robert Cooper Lee in October 1783. There had been severe thunderstorms with huge hailstones and a frost on the 23rd of June that damaged growing crops. Both sets of eruptions caused severe famines locally - in Iceland about a quarter of the population is thought to have died when half the sheep were poisoned by contamination of the grass. Poor harvests in France added to the social and political pressures that were building and would end in Revolution. As a result the end of the year found John Lee battling his way through snow drifts towards Brunswick. He had been given a year's leave of absence from the army during which he intended to learn German and study mathematics, the latter very useful in relation to both artillery and surveying.

John Lee to Robert Cooper Lee

Brunswick, 3rd January 1784

Dear Uncle,

After the most disagreeable journey I am at last arrived at Brunswick. I was happy to find that my constitution was so much mended for when my servant was complaining bitterly of the cold, I hardly wish'd for a covering in the cart. I stay'd but one day at The Hague where I wrote to Bob and had occasion to visit Monsieur Moliere and Co for £20 which carried me to Hanover. Travelling at this time of year is far more expensive than in the Summer. On the same day I arrived at Hanover, I had the honor of being presented to Prince Frederick and Prince William by Major General Grenville who at the same time offered me letters of introduction to Brunswick. The roads are very bad, and in some places impassable on account of the snow. I had once the satisfaction of having the two fore wheels of my cart broke down, the Horses take fright and run away: and three times the honor of being laid fast in the snow. A little jockey Hat and thin Regimental Great Coat were not suited to this climate. I have been here four days, and I can't get the Lodging in the town: there are 19 or 20 English here and more expected in the spring. I waited, the day after I arrived, upon His Excellency Monsieur Feronce[218] to whom most of the English are recommended; he says £200 or £250 is the allowance of most young men here; if they had less the inhabitants would not trust them, and as the Prison is a very damp, disagreeable place, I should be afraid of catching cold, if I was put into it. As to the manner of transferring the Bills, I suppose Sir Robert Herries will find no difficulty in it. The expense of the journey including the servant is £30 besides the note you gave me when I set out. I shall have the Honor, in the course of the next week, to be presented separately to the Duke and Duchess of Brunswick, to the Duchess Dowager, and to the Duke Ferdinand. I am extremely obliged to General Robertson for his letter to General Reidesel; 'tis quite an English House. Please to give my duty to Mrs Lee and love to all the family; you will oblige me very much by presenting my best compliments to General Townsend who I hope is well. You will not, I am sure, be at much trouble to guess that I am, my dear Sir,

your dutiful nephew, John Lee

PS Please to direct to Mr Lee

Hotel d'Angleterre

Braunschweig

While John struggled through the snow to Brunswick, Frances had been despatched to Bath to drink the waters in the hope of improving her health.

Frances Lee to Priscilla Lee

Bath, 8th January 1784

The greatest pleasure I can experience at this distance is the knowledge of your being all well. This pleasing Information I had the Satisfaction of receiving yesterday Morning and it banished for a while every disagreeable

---

[218] Jean Baptiste Feronce von Rotencreutz (1723-99), Privy Councillor (1761-) to Karl I of Brunswick, and Finance Minister (1773-) to Karl Wilhelm Ferdinand. He was admitted a Fellow of the Royal Society (UK) on June 28, 1764.

sensation, from the bottom of my heart did I bless the Almighty that I alone was suffering pain of Body. I assure you my dear Mama it has been ever the greatest aggravation to my sufferings, this conviction that they cause the sense of uneasiness to those for whom I could cheerfully resign my Being and I have ever wished for a restoration to health as much for your sake as my own. I was confined to my Bed on Tuesday. I had recourse to the pills which together with Mr Tubb's assistance relieved me after a few hours pain. Yesterday I had a tolerable Day. To-day the snow (for I feel most sensibly every change of Weather) has rendered me less so. My Cold has been rather a severe one however I am certainly quite a different creature since my arrival here. My side is so much better. Both Saturday and Sunday I was almost free from all pain. I trust in God I shall return to you if not in perfect Health at least much better than when we parted. My Father has been so good to say that he will make it convenient to come down at any Time. A Day or two ago I gave Mr Tubb to understand that I expected my Father in about Fortnight that I supposed he would stay a few Days and he would then shew us the Way to Town. Mr T. seem'd to think or gave me reason to think that he had not any thoughts of coming so soon. Now I must request as a particular favour that my Father will allow me to fix the Time of my Departure. In my last to you I mention'd the wish of being in Town by the 25th or 26th I will be satisfied to remain here three Weeks longer from the date of this and on no account can I think of a longer absence. As it must be a matter of Indifference to Mr Tubb and Mrs Royall whether they are here or in Town and as they say it was on my account only that they came here I would fain hope that we shall return together, but should it happen that they are inclined to stay when the time I propose is elapsed I must beg my Father to find some Cause for my going to Town. I shall have then drank the Waters five Weeks. I have not seen any other Friends since my last. Mrs Hall[219] call'd again on Tuesday. I could not see her. I believe I shall fix on Sunday for dining with her. Mr Ramsay call'd on Tuesday and this Morning. I had not the pleasure of seeing him – poor Mrs Delap[220] Mrs Hall thinks in a very bad Way. Mrs Royall and the old lady it seems had a Miff in Town. The former is very desirous of a rencontre. I have not been at the Pump Room for some Days – it suited Mrs Royall better to have the Water sent for and it rejoiced me to stay at Home. The Weather

---

219 Probably Mrs Jasper Hall.

220 Presumably related to Francis Delap whose cause celebre in Jamaica was supported in England by Rose Fuller among others.

however has been milder till yesterday. I have drank tea three or four times at Mrs Wignall's[221] (which is very near but I never *would* venture to walk) Miss Wignall is in a bad state of Health. The old Gentleman is very stout for his time of Life 75 and is a very agreeable Man. I am happy to hear my Father found our Friends at Newington[222] so well. I suppose Miss Morley[223] is, or will soon be in Town. The hams arrived safe for which Mr Tubb desires his best Thanks. Mrs Royall joins him in kind Compliments to you all. I beg my affectionate respects to my good Father. My kind Love to the rest of the Family. I hope to see Scud perform Friar Bacon. Adieu my dear Mama God bless and preserve you long to

your most affectionate Daughter F.L.

PS remember me kindly to Mrs Boyd when you see her.

Frances Lee to Richard Lee

Bath, 10th January 1784

My dear Richard is I trust too well acquainted with my Heart to have imagined for one moment that my silence could have proceeded from any other cause than the Inability of writing. I wished to write a long letter an I could before this have assured you by a few Lines of the Happiness your last kind Favor afforded me, indeed Richard I may truly say I never was made happier by any Letter in my Life – it contained so much about yourself (which is to me the most pleasing subject you can ever divert on) and know you are passing your Time so profitably and so much to your own satisfaction adds in no small degree to my Enjoyment. My Happiness is likewise increased by the assurances that I am so dear to you and the Concern you express at my Indisposition as well as your kind Wishes have rendered you (if it were possible) more dear to me. How much shall I value the present intended for me by Mon tres chere Frere! I hope on my return to Town (which will be in about three Weeks) that I shall have the pleasure of receiving your Representative. I told Betty you were sitting for your Picture and she said 'I hope the Man will make him just such a pretty *Boy* as he is and not such Fright as he made Mr Ross's

[221] Anne Wignall was sister to Marchant Tubb.

[222] Thomas and Mary Marlton

[223] Frances's cousin Frances Morley.

Children[224] with green Faces'. I suppose poor Creature she thinks there is only one painter in Hambro'. I hope however you have made choice of a good one and that I shall see you well represented. My Father I suppose has written you that I am here, with whom, and all about it. I shall therefore only add that I think I am better for the Change of Air, or the Waters. As for the Amusements I have not been able to partake of any. I sometimes go to the pump Room where the Company assemble about one o'clock. The Duchess of Devonshire is here but she goes little into public as she is at present a Nurse. A very extra ordinary Circumstance in these refined times. I had the pleasure of a Visit yesterday Morning from our little Friend Tom Brett who is staying at Bristol with Mr Rudhall. Tom tho' a little Fellow has a great Heart and as good an one I firmly believe as any in his Majesty's Dominions. Pray have you any Air Balloons in Hambro? Here the people are Balloon mad. The Ladies of the Ton would not be seen but in a Balloon Hat or Bonnet. When I *come out* I shall certainly mount one for they add prodigiously to the Height an object of some Consequence to such little Folks as myself. I hear often from my good Father he proposes joining us shortly and we shall return to Town together. Before my Departure I hope I shall be able to attend Mr Tysons and other fashionable places of resort. The Fire-side at present I find the most comfortable place. The Weather has indeed been dreadfully cold and I am but too susceptible of its effects. I hope yet to be *gay* before I die. I have great Dependence on your working a thorough reformation on your return. Eighteen long months are elapsed since I beheld the most amiable, as well as the dearest of Brothers, how often have I wish'd to see him during that time! I am however in some measure reconciled to a seperation, which will ultimately I trust turn out to your advantage. I remembered you on your Birth-Day (I may with truth add I remember you every Day) and I drank a Bumper to your Health at the Castle at Marlbro'. May many, many happy years be allotted to my dear Richard! Captain John set out Bag and baggage (including his Valet) the Week before I left Town. My Father writes me that he was four Days at sea which was only a prelude of the Inconveniences he was likely to undergo

---

[224] If this refers to Hercules Ross, they are his children with Elizabeth Foord, born between 1776 and 1781. The reference may more likely be to the children of his brother Colin, who was a doctor who settled in Hamburg and became secretary to the Association of Hamburg Merchant Adventurers. Among his descendents were the brothers Charles Ross, a leading landscape painter of his day, Gustav Ross, a pioneering physician, and Ludwig Ross, a classicist and epigrapher, as well as Edgar Daniel Ross, a liberal who became a prominent Hamburg politician.

before he reached Brunswick. Never was there anyone less calculated to encounter Difficulties than our Boy. I really doubt whether you would know him. The Prince of Wales is the first Man of Fashion in Town Captain John Lee the *third* and I leave to your penetration to discover who is the *second*. Your last containd a [illegible] which you must excuse my resolving not being a competent Judge of fashionable Improvements (but I desire Mr Richard you will not *blab* my Ignorance). I had proposed to myself the satisfaction of transmitting you with this a small Bill (de mes Epargnes) but this Jaunt as cut so deep in my Finances that I cannot immediately effect what I have so much pleasure in doing the contributing in the smallest degree to your Ease and Convenience. Were I possessed of thousands I could never know a Superior pleasure than that of my dear Richard's being a Share of them. It is now time to bid you adieu, which I shall not do without requesting you will write me soon. You [will] make me most happy. Yesterday an air Balloon set out from [this] place. I wish from my Soul that it could have convey'd me to Hambro'that I might have had the pleasure of assuring my dear Brother in person how truly I am

His most affectionate Sister as well as faithful Friend F.L.

PS Mr Tubb and Mrs Royall desire their kindest regards.

Frances Lee to Robert Cooper Lee

Bath, 11th January 1784

My dear Sir,

Your few kind Lines by yesterday's post afforded me much Happiness. I should have been uneasy had I not received them. I have so much Dread of the Gout. I attribute my not hearing from you this Morning as you promised to your more important engagements. I have the Vanity or rather the Happiness to know that you ever think yourself agreeably engaged whilst you are giving pleasure to me. I have been interrupted twice since I began this scrawl first by the Appearance of Mr Dehany and soon after by good Mr Ramsay accompanied by Mr Cuthbert and his Son. The latter is very much grown rather taller I think than Matthew. Mrs Byndloss and Mrs Hall have been very kind in their calls and Enquiries indeed so has Mr Ramsay this is the third time of his calling but the first of my seeing him. Mr Brownrigg called this morning and we are to fix on Day in this Week to dine with him. Mr Watt and his nephew from Liverpool were here this Morning before we were dress'd in short we have many Visitors (or rather I have). Thank God I am again pretty tolerable after rather a serious alarm about two o'clock on Friday Morning. I went to Bed with a little headache and about the time I mentioned I awoke so ill that I confess I was a little alarmed. A Confusion in my Head that I never in my life felt before. In about a quarter of an Hour I felt a violent oppression at my stomach and a copious Discharge of Bile in about two Hours relieved me. The next Day I was little more than a piece of still Life about Noon I was somewhat animated by the appearance of my little Friend the Captain (to whom I had given Intelligence of my being here) he spent two hours with me and then departed. I cannot think of any other cause - than the eating a *single* pickled oyster - of my Indisposition. I have however had no return and I am today so well that I intend waiting on Mrs Hall at Dinner. I had the pleasure of seeing my Friend Sophy yesterday she only came to Bath for a few Hours and dedicated a few moments to me. Mr Tubb's Gout only lasted one Day. The Cause I verily believe though he differs was a Draught of Bath Water. I shall exact a promise from you that you do not touch a drop. Mrs Royall has been complaining but I believe her Ails cannot be remedied. The happy Major is well. Mrs Nason[?] better. Mr Tubb's anecdotes divert both. I expected to be able, my cold being much better, to come out next Week. You shall have a true and faithful account of my proceedings. The clock strikes three (and Mrs Hall desir'd I would make my appearance early) adieu then mon cher pere for the present. Assure my good Mother of the invariable affection of her who is most truly

Your dutiful and grateful Daughter F.L.

PS Mr Tubb and Mrs Royall greet you most kindly. Remember me to all enquiring Friends. The inclosed to my dear Richard pray forward. Mrs Dehany and Mrs Pinnock have called here but I could not see them.

Frances Lee to Priscilla Lee

Bath, 13th January 1784

Miss Lee of Belmont had the pleasure of opening my last Frank and the politeness of keeping it in her possession till Yesterday Morning. The account of your being all well is truly satisfactory to me and I am persuaded you will not be less happy to hear that I think I am gaining Strength daily. My side is at times perfectly easy and scarcely ever very uneasy. I have not yet felt myself hungry but I contrived to eat a good Breakfast. I cannot say much for my other Improvements but all in good time. Sophy Gardiner thought I looked much better than when she saw me in Town. I spent a very agreeable Day at Mrs Hall's. Our party consisted of Mrs Delap, Mrs Gray and her two sons, Mrs Cargill, Mrs Hall and her three children and myself. In the Evening we had a Mrs White (a countrywoman of ours) and Bobby alias Counsellor Richards who observ'd on his Introduction to me that he could not be introduced to a Daughter of his Friend Mr Lee without a Salutation. By so near an approach he discover'd his Wrinkles which might otherwise have passed unobserved. Mrs Cargill is a very pleasant Woman and I hope to have the pleasure of introducing her to you. She did me the Favor of calling with Mrs Hall the beginning of the Week but I did not see her. Mrs Hall proposes being in Town some time next Month to make some stay and she and Mrs Cargill are to keep House together – poor Mrs Delap seems to be on her last Legs. She as well as Mrs Hall made very particular Enquiries after you and desir'd to be kindly remember'd. Jasper is a very genteel well behaved Youth, John a fine bold Fellow and Miss Hall a fine Girl. Mrs Royall I am sorry to say is very indifferent, a violent Cold has settled in her Face and she is at present in much pain, a Day or two I hope will remove a very disagreeable Sensation. We had proposed coming out To-Night going to the play dress'd. We have never yet had a Gown on a convincing proof that we were not at Mr Tysons ball, nor was Mr Tubb. The weather was too severe and I too weak to undergo the Fatigue of Dressing. My Father has made me very happy by the Intelligence of joining us (I do not mean Major N. and your humble) on Saturday or Sunday. On the strength of seeing him on one of those days we have fixed on Monday next to dine at Mr Brownrigg's. There is a small apartment under this roof which I fancy my Father will find large enough to sleep and dress in and Mr Tubb desires I will propose his being en Famille here. I think I may answer that this proposal will be accepted. I don't know if I dreamt it but I have a strong presentiment that Mr Ross will accompany my Father here. Mr Watt and his Nephew were here Yesterday the former gave Mrs Royall and myself an Invitation, not to dine, but to Bathe with him. Pray make my Excuses to Mrs Allen for not having written to her, indeed I am but a bad Scribe just now. Remember me to Miss Young when you see her. I am glad she did not write to me for I should not have been able to have corresponded with her. The Weather is thank God very mild, but too dirty for walking, excepting Sunday I have not been out for several Days. My affectionate Duty awaits you and my good Father. My kind Love to all with you. Tell Favell I hope she has learnt to pronounce Queen, Quaker and Smith. Give her and Scud many kisses for me. Adieu my dear Mama God bless you and grant me the Happiness of meeting you are in perfect Health. When you see Mr and Mrs Shluss pray offer my best Compliments as well to our neighbours and Mrs Mackay.

I am your most dutiful Daughter Frances Lee

PS The two Officers Captain Rudhall and Captain Brett are just gone. They desired I would present their kind compliments. The former will be in Town the beginning of the Week the latter means to come and spend a few Days here.

Matthew Allen Lee to Richard Lee

Bedford Square, 16th January 1784

My dear Brother

I suppose you may think it odd in my not writing to you before, or that I am a very impudent fellow in writing to you now. You know that I am at Winchester indeed I am very glad that I am, for James's was a shocking place. Our noble cousin has been gone above a month and we have only heard from him once since he has been gone, and that was from the Hague, I little thought that he would have been a soldier. Scud is at home and is grown very impudent, more even than I was to you. We had accounts from Mr Boyd about a week ago my mother is gone to Mrs Boyd's now at Hampton. Jack and George Scott are by now at Jamaica. They sailed above five weeks ago. The Dowager Lady Hume died the day before yesterday and left the great house in Portman Square with almost all her fortune to *Billy Gale*[225] Mr Farquhar's Ward who is lately gone to Jamaica, expects about 13 thousand pounds in Legacies. Jack Scott left the Black and a very good Hackney to my Brother. My mother has got a little tame canary bird which she says if you were here you would delight so to teach[?]. She received your letter and will write very soon. My sister is at Bath and is a great deal better than she was by the assistance of Waters Sir R.Jebb and Mr Tubb Bob's friend. All here desire their love to you and my good wishes attend you, believe me to be

Your ever affectionate Brother M.A. Lee

---

225 The Dowager Lady Home, born Elizabeth Gibbons in Jamaica in 1704, had married first James Gale (d.1733) in 1720 in Jamaica, and then William, 8th Earl of Home in England in 1742. He left her barely eight weeks later and died in 1761at Gibraltar where he had been made Governor. Her house in Portman Square is one of the finest examples in existence of the work of Robert Adam. She left the bulk of her estate to her distant relative William Gale. See http://aparcelofribbons.co.uk/2012/03/the-queen-of-hell-in-portman-square.

Robert Cooper Lee to Priscilla Lee

Devizes, 24th January 1784

So far well. I have had a very agreeable Journey to this Place. The Chaise was perfectly comfortably, and I did not find the Cold in the least disagreeable. I got to Reading at ½ past 12 where I took a Bit of cold Chicken and Ham by the Help of which I held out till now. I arrived here ¼ before 8, and having ordered a Veal Cutlet and a Bottle of Port, and being seated at a good Fire I cannot employ the mean time more pleasingly than in telling you I how am. I intend leaving this for Bath about Nine to morrow Morning – first dressing and taking a good Breakfast. The Distance is [twenty] Miles. I find I am in time for to Night's Post. My kindest respects I beg to Mr and Mrs Allen Mrs Welch Mr and Mrs Kluft etc. Remember me kindly to all the Bairns. I salute [missing] most affectionately

Yours ever Robert Cooper Lee.

PS I heard at the Hyde Park Turnpike Fox was again victorious. I have heard nothing here yet.

John Lee to Robert Cooper Lee

Braunschweig, 27th January 1784

Dear Uncle,

I have been long expecting to hear from England, but I suppose if you have written, the Post is stop'd by the snow; for no less than four posts are now missing. (I don't know whether to be pleased or displeased about the change in the Ministry, and as I have no opinion I think I may as well put the subject into parenthesis and say no more about it). I heard to day that something of more fatal consequence then the change was to be feared; pray be so obliging as to inform me. Brunswick is at present very unhealthy, owing in a great measure to a very bad hooping cough that is prevalent at this time. I hope Bedford Square is free from every complaint of the kind. I have at last with difficulty got into lodgings very agreeably situated in the Mog Market. The Servant I brought from England I wished to keep but as I could not prevail upon him to take more than fifty Guineas a year I thought it would be better for him to go to England. I might have saved myself the trouble of bringing so many cloaths here; for when the people here put on a new coat they never leave it off till it is almost ready to drop from their backs; but this is to be said only of the natives, the English are more civilised. Any piece of news or intelligence will always be gratefully received by one, who wishing to be dutifully remembered to Mrs Lee and lovingly to all the family, is at the same time your dutiful nephew John Lee.

Scudamore Cooper Lee to Robert Cooper Lee

Uxbridge, 21st February 1784

Dear Papa,

I received your Letter and am very sorry I cannot answer it myself, but I have got a Friend to write for me; I am very well and long to see you and my Mama with Mr Blake. I hope the Weather will soon change. Mr Rutherford will be in London next Wednesday, when he will call for you; Some of the Boys have got Chilblains, but I have escaped as yet and hope I shall not have them. Please to give my Duty to Mama and love to my Brothers and Sisters and accept the same from Dear Papa

your dutiful son S.C.Lee.

PS Please to thank my Sister for the cake she sent me.

John Lee to Robert Cooper Lee

Brunswick, 24th February 1784

Dear Uncle,

Not having heard from you ever since I left England, I am very happy to find, by a letter I have just now received from Hamburg, that you and all the family were in Health. I wish that the journey to Bath has been of as much service to you, as it has to my cousin Frances; pray be so good as to deliver to her the compliments of all her old friends at the Hague. Brunswick is at present unhealthy, on account of a sudden thaw, which dissolved the great quantity of snow that has been on the ground for these two months past, and caused an inundation or overflowing of the whole Town, no such thing as staring out of the house, nay some people go about the town in boats; as for myself 'tho, find, I amuse myself with fishing out of the window. But really it is very unhealthy and the streets are overflowed. (NB I hope you don't believe a word about the boats). The King of Prussia's Review will be in about a month, where all the English that are here will be present; and where the cash will be as necessary article as any; but I shall, with your permission, take the liberty to draw upon you before that time. After giving my Duty to my Aunt, and Love to my cousin Fanny and the rest of the younger branch, permit me, my dear uncle, to subscribe myself

your very affectionate nephew John Lee Ensign 16th Regiment Foot

PS pray give my best compliments to Mr and Mrs Allen I hope they are both well. In the summer we shall be able to keep up correspondence, but at present, on account of the snow, and contrary winds a letter may be a month or 5 weeks going to England. I was very happy to hear, that in the change of Ministry General Cosway found himself in the Ex-party; I flatter myself I shall be more successful in the next trial. I was not a little surprised on my arrival to find many of the English of 17 or 18 Captains and immediately voted myself a new made Captain. Have you heard from the Scotts since they left England? I hope the climate of Jamaica does not disagree with them. Be so good as to remember me to them, when you write. Pray oblige me by giving my best compliments to the young counsellor your son.

John Lee to Robert Cooper Lee

Brunswick, 3rd May 1784

My dear Uncle,

For fear I should forget it, you'll excuse me if I begin with telling you that I have just sent over a draught to you for £20 sterling payable to Henry Kidder or Order; it was drawn some time ago, before I received Sir Robert; I gave it to Kidder and thinking it too small to be sent over alone, I begged him to keep it till I should have occasion to draw upon him a second time; he kept it very quietly for about a fortnight, and ever since he has been plaguing me with letters, the burden of his song is Give me my money. I e'en let him have his own way for once. I am very much obliged to you for your two last letters, which I received by the same Post – your advice is always agreeable and welcome, but none more so than where you desire me to draw upon you for the future; this being the first essay, pardon me if it is not right, but with a little practice, my small genius may expand, and I may shortly be able to draw upon a more extensive plan. The £50 you was so good as to send me is devoted to the Berlin excursion; and therefore may be placed among the extra expenses. The last fall of snow we had here was on the 24th of April. Every appearance now of approaching Summer tho' the cold has not yet left us. I am happy to hear that you have been so well all the winter, I hope all the family have been the same. As for myself I have not had the slightest indisposition, notwithstanding my thin cloathing. I shall be particularly obliged to you if you will give my best compliments to General Townsend. Pray give my duty to My Aunt, and best respects to all the family and at the same time believe me my dear fellow,

your dutiful nephew, John Lee.

John Lee to Robert Cooper Lee

Berlin, 17th May 1784

Dear Uncle,

I take this opportunity of writing to you to acquaint you with the commencement of my Travell, for I have lately taken into my head to make the Tour of most of the Kingdoms in Europe and God knows where I may be the next time I write to you, perhaps at the Hague, at Paris, at Vienne, or at Belgrade, most likely at Strasbourg. If I went to Brunswick to learn the German Language it is rendered impossible almost on account of everybody speaking English; the College is a mere School, the 17 or 18 English that are in it are all very young; from 13 to 15 years old. The Masters are by no means good. I daresay you will attribute all that I have said to my restless disposition, but I assure you, my dear fellow, being of an age to think of my own advantage, I cannot consider the time that I spend at Brunswick other than as lost. God bless you, Sir, I wish to convince you. I set out from Brunswick the 9th May, arrived here 3 days after, was introduced to the Ambassador, Sir John Stepney, a very polite man; and the same day sent round 100 cards to different people of fashion here, and have received many in return not to mention Dinners, Suppers, etc etc. I was presented with many English at this Court to the Queen and all the Royal family; from thence I went to Potsdam to be present, with the permission, at the Review where I was presented to the King of Prussia, but was never so much disapointed in the ideas I had formed of the Greatest General, Statesman and King in the World; when I saw a dirty filthy little fellow step forward; the sharp eye that he was famed for, is now quite dim, his thread bare coat cover'd with snuff, and his boots, which he never suffers to be clean'd, as dirty as you can well suppose them. I have seen him frequently since but he's always the same nasty figure; but thank God, for decency sake, he washes his face now and then. After having dined with Kings and supped with Princes, etc etc I shall not know what to do with myself when I join my Regiment. I hope Dick was well the last time you heard from him; I wrote to him three weeks ago, but have received no answer; the Shop takes up his whole time, I suppose; not a moment to spare, to write to a lazy Ensign. Pray give my duty to My Aunt and compliments to all the family, and believe me, my dear Uncle,

your dutiful nephew, John Lee.

John Lee to Robert Cooper Lee

Brunswick, 31st May 1784

Dear Uncle,

I found your letter of the 4th on my return from Berlin, and was not a little surprised that you had not heard from me. I wrote to you just before I left Brunswick and one soon after I arrived at Berlin in the latter mentioning my disposition to remove from this place, for there are really so many English here at present and more coming every month that there is no possible opportunity of speaking German, and there are so few and such bad masters that it is impossible to learn anything else; now, Sir, be so good as to take these things into consideration, and send me over one or two letters of recommendation to Strasburg. Nothing else is wanting (tipple excepted) Strasburg is proper for learning both French and German besides there is a Garison of 10,000 men there. It is also famous for producing many good officers, Sholto Douglas for instance, as Light a little compact soldier, as one would wish to see. Pray be so good as to send the letters over soon for the least delay will break in upon my leave of absence. Please to give my duty to my Aunt and best compliments to all the family; to Mr and Mrs Allen. I am, Sir,

your most obedient Humble Nephew John Lee.

NB I have taken the liberty this morning to draw for £50 – this is a very extravagant place.

In the summer of 1784 Robert Cooper Lee set out on a lengthy trip, visiting first the estate in Herefordshire he had inherited from Scudamore Winde, and then travelling on to Scotland.

Robert Cooper Lee to Priscilla Lee

Eye in Herefordshire, 21st July 1784

Tuesday Night Eleven O'Clock. My paper is small, and I must make the most of it. Believe my Sighs and Tears my dear! The Sun was sunk And Old Charing Cross are all expended, and the Nightingale gone to Bed. Since Saturday Afternoon we have been here, 4 Miles from Lempster, 12 from Bromyard where old Blue keeps a very good House, excellent Cyder, and the Landlord's Daughter has a high Head. Alderman Harley is next Door Neighbour here, Cream and Anchovy meliorate Sallad, White Currants not good for Currant Jelly but make excellent Shrub [grow them] up against a Wall prevent their being bitter. Maister Parry and I have signed Articles for Lease of Fencott for Seven Years, 105 Acres in Arable 10 Acres in Hopground. The Buildings must be repaired but he is to hall to place. Six Children here. At Clarke's Croft Hester Williams Butcher and four Children, Veal 3d and 2½ per pound Mutton 3½ and 4d. Two Oak and a Bur Stick cut down last year for repairs. Two days continual rain. Some Thunder yesterday. Parry of – I forget the name of the place, but Fencott's Brother, his House fired with Lightening last Sunday Night. Half the House, all the Cheese, 100 Bushels Wheat, the Childrens' Cloaths and Dairy Utensils burnt. Damage £200. To morrow Morning we are to set off for Hereford thence to Ledbury Glocester Cirencester and Marlbro'. You shall hear from me in my business - Marlbro' you know is in Line to Wooley Green[226]. [My] kindest Love to all at Sutton. I hope all are well I am and have been since I left you perfectly so. Adieu

I am Yours ever sincerely Robert Cooper Lee.

Robert Cooper Lee was accompanied on his tour of Scotland by his partner John Allen, newly laird of Inchmartin, and Hercules Ross who had bought an estate at Rossie near Montrose where he would in due course build Rossie Castle. It is not clear who else accompanied them, but the party may have included Robert Home Gordon who owned property at Embo. The tour illustrates the number of returning Scots who used their Jamaican money to build fine Georgian mansions and 'improve' the land through schemes of building, drainage, aforestation and the introduction of new agricultural techniques.

---

[226] Home of Edward Long.

Robert Cooper Lee to Priscilla Lee
Edinburgh, 13th August 1784

Dr Carlysle met us in the Way between his house and Mr Wedderburn's as we were going to pay our Respects to him. I presented Miss Dickson's Letter to him, and which he received most kindly. We had the pleasure of his Company at Dinner at Mr Wedderburn's, and were much delighted with his cheerful and elegant Disposition, as well as his good Sense. I assure you we all left his Company with Regret, and unanimously agreed he was a Companion for Princes. Mr and Mrs Wedderburn[227] you know, Her Sister Miss Blackburn and Miss Christie (our Friend the Captain's Sister) were of the Party. The Ladies of this Country are justly remarked for their affability. The Fish and Sauce, and three young Turkies were remarkably good. We saw Lord Abercorn's a very pretty Place, and Dalkeith, upon a grander Plan. Many thanks for Frances's Letter by today's Post. The Grand Tour is altered, the Bill recommitted notwithstanding the Chancellor of the Exchequers Opposition. We go from Gartmore and Keir to Loch Tay, and being so far proceed to Inverness the West Road and return by Aberdeen, Rossie and Inchmartin. Don't write to Inverness or Perth, But till the 19th to Aberdeen, the 20th, 21st and 22nd to Inchmartin, and afterwards till the 27th to Dun's Hotel. God bless you all. Just returned from Mr Stirling's[228].

Your ever affectionate Robert Cooper Lee.

---

227 James Wedderburn fled to Jamaica with his brother John after the defeat at Culloden having seen their father Sir James Wedderburn of Blackness, hanged, drawn and quartered for treason in 1746. He returned to Scotland in 1773 a wealthy man and married Isabella Blackburn. While in Jamaica he fathered several children including Robert Wedderburn with a slave named Rosanna. He freed his son but later disowned him. Robert Wedderburn became a radical anti-slavery activist writing a bitter denunciation of the mis-treatment of his mother and grandmother.

228 Possibly William Stirling of Keir and Cawdor (1725-1793). More likely his second son John of the Hampden Estate, St James, Jamaica, who died in Jamaica in 1795. The Stirlings had an interest in the Keir and Cawdor estate well into the twentieth century.

Robert Cooper Lee to Priscilla Lee

Gartmore in the Shire of Perth, Monday Morning Six O'Clock

16th August 1784

You will receive my first Letters from Edinburgh to morrow Morning I was too late for Tuesday's Post, and Wednesday was no Post day, so they could not go till Thursday. I reckon this will reach you on Saturday Morning and find all the Family at full Breakfast. I shall then be at Inverness or beyond it. I flatter myself with the Pleasure of hearing from you at Inverness having directed my Letters that come to Edinburgh till the 18th to be forwarded on to the Inverness Post Office. On Saturday Morning we left Dun's Hotel, breakfasted at Linlithgow, then to Falkirk, near which Town the first Action happened between the King's Troops and the Rebels in 1745, turned off to Carron to see the great Ironworks there[229], some Cannon of 132 Pounders, from thence by Dunnepace to Kilsyth, and so on to Bogside[230], the Seat of our Friend Mr Finlay[231] by whom and his good Lady we were received most hospitably. Finlay is a great Improver not only in farming, but in a fine Family of eight Children – Miss Finlay the eldest, about ten years old, entertained us after Dinner with Musick vocal and instrumental very pleasingly. Miss Murray was the only Visitor besides us. She is the Daughter of the Dowager Keir who lives at Caudor joining on Bogside. Our Dinner was excellent and all, except the Moor Game, from the Farm. Mrs Lee's Health and Family's was drunk, as indeed it is every day. Mr Allen has a Story that Miss M. was much hurt at hearing there was a Mrs Lee. From Bogside we went to Glasgow, where we met some Jamaica Folks. Moses Stobs spent the Evening with us. I had the Pleasure to see George Gordon's Children, the Boy about 16, the Girl about ten, she is rather fair and pretty, they are under the Care of Mr Macintosh a very sensible good Man, in a

[229] The Carron Ironworks just north of Falkirk, powered by the River Carron and fed by locally available coal and ironstone, had opened in 1760 following the example of Abraham Darby at Coalbrookdale. They had recently developed a highly successful short barrelled naval cannon called a carronade and also produced other guns. So well respected were their castings that the Duke of Wellington trusted Carron artillery above all others. More peacefully Robert and his friends would also have seen castings for steam engines, fireplaces and stoves.

[230] Near Kirkintilloch.

[231] James Finlay, married to Helen Wedderburn (daughter of Alexander, possibly related to James Wedderburn, d.1786)

considerable way of Business, and was an intimate Friend of the Father's. Glasgow is a large opulent City, the Houses well built and the Streets well laid out. After viewing the Town, the Bridge etc yesterday Morning we proceeded to Dumbarton to Breakfast; this is a very pleasant ride through a fine Country with many Gentlemen's Seats and the River Clyde in View. From Dumbarton we went on to Lake Lomond passing Mr Graham's Estate of Ardoch[232] and having in View the Firth of Clyde, Port Glasgow and Greenock, and the distant Shore of Argyllshire. We came in View of the Lake from a high Hill, it was rather Cloudy weather up the Lake but we had a Peep at Ben Lomon Mountain and saw many of the Islands. The whole was a noble and picturesque View. We returned about five Miles along the Lake, and saw the Ends next Dumbarton crossed the Waters of Leven by a Ford, and on through a wild mountainous Country to this Place where we got at ½ past four. I saw yesterday several Views of Sixteenmile Walk[233], and I must not forget to tell you that in our Way to the Lake we saw two Preachings. I joined the Audience at one, the whole Country assembles on the Green next the Kirks. Both Men and Women stout and hearty and well clothed. There is a noble House here, well finished within, great Improvements made and making. Mr Graham entertained us in Stile. His Sons are very fine Boys, much handsomer than their Sisters, but somewhat delicate like their Mother. We go from hence after Breakfast to Stirling and to Keir to Dinner, tomorrow Mr Allen leaves us. Mr Ross goes on the whole Tour. My next will be from Inverness which you cannot get sooner than Sunday se'night, this goes from Stirling. My constant Prayers are for you and those with you. My kindest Love to all ours, remember me to Miss Dixon and Mr Brett and all friends in Bedford Square. Richard I suppose has had his Sumons. I lament the loss of Matthew's Holidays. Once more Adieu

Your ever Affectionate Robert Cooper Lee.

---

[232] Robert Graham, later Cunningham-Graham (1735-1797) of Gartmore and Ardoch, former Receiver General of Jamaica. He married Anne Taylor, daughter of Patrick and Martha Taylor of Kingston, sister to Simon Taylor and Sir John Taylor of Lyssons Hall. Graham had a distinguished political career as a radical attempting to introduce a Bill of Rights long before the great Reform Act of 1832. He was a close friend of Thomas Sheridan, Charles James Fox and Sir Thomas Dundas whom he succeeded as MP for Stirling.

[233] Sixteen mile Walk in Jamaica, so named for the sixteen estates that contributed to the building of the River Road, passes through a deep gorge with the river Cobre running through it.

PS you can't receive this I find till Sunday Morning. Excuse Mr Graham's Paper and my writing on two Sheets without filling both I wish I had time for it.

Robert Cooper Lee to Priscilla Lee

Rossie, 29th August 1784

Yesterday Morning we left Aberdeen, recrossed the Grampian Hills, and once more bid Adieu to Strawberries and Cream for this Season; we had a great Plenty of them and every other good thing at *Dunnoter's* Table. His House is fitted up almost a la Mode Mr Tubb. I came with Dunnoter in his Chaise and four as far as Stonehive on the Borders of his Estate, about 15 Miles from Aberdeen, and a run of 22 Miles more brought us here Dinner. On Friday and Yesterday there was Rain, only Showers since we left Edinburgh. My Narrative left off on Tuesday the 17th at the good Lady's of Glenquick; that Morning we set out from Keir and about six Miles from thence in the Lands of Sir Wm. Stirling we saw the Remains of a Roman Camp. It is said to be the farthest Station in the Highlands that the Romans had. In the Neighbourhood of Glenquick we met a Clergyman I should say a Minister, a Reverend old Gentleman well-dressed with two or three Ladies in Company in riding Habits; they had been taking a short Walk of 8 or 9 Miles, and upon Enquiry we were told the Living was worth not more than thirty Pounds a Year. Our Party were much charmed with the native Politeness and good Humour of Mrs Menzies. She put her homely Fare before us with great Civility and we enjoyed it much. She told us of the Distress of the Country and Losses by bad Seasons, and mentioned that two years ago she had lost eighty Sheep by the Inclemency of the Weather, and had not yet recovered the Loss, and this she told with a cheerful Countenance, and without letting the Smile once leave her Cheek.

We were obliged to walk up Taymouth Hill, and in descending it on the other Side we came in the View of Kenmure [Kenmore], a small neat Town at the Head of Loch Tay, and Lord Bredalbine's Seat close to is called Taymouth. The View is very grand and pleasing especially after coming by Glenammon [Glenalmond] and through a wild uncultivated Country. Loch Tay is about 15 miles in Length and more than a Mile broad. Kenmure and Taymouth are in a Bottom having on each Side very high Hills planted with Firs and other Trees. The Grounds at Taymouth are well laid out with Roses and Clumps of Trees like an English Park. We slept at Kenmure and next Morning embarked on Loch Tay and went up about two Miles where we landed, and walked about a Mile to a Place called the Hermitage; it is a small Wood with winding Walks, and by an artificial subterraneous Passage we came to a fine Waterfall of about 180 feet. We returned by Water to Kenmure, and the rest of the Morning was spent in viewing the Grounds, a Fort upon one of the Hills, and the House in which there are some good Rooms and several Family Pictures; particularly the Portrait of Duncan Doo (the Dove) the founder of the Family of the Macgregors, and the Estate was increased by the Masacre of Glencow.

We left Kenmure Wednesday Afternoon and had a very agreeable Ride on the Banks of the Tay, and after leaving it we crossed Tumble [Tummel] River and got into the great Highland Road from Perth and Dunkeld, and proceeded to Blair in Atholl which we reached about 10 O'Clock, having in our Way from Loggeraith [Logierait] Ferry passed Fascaly, the Pass of Killiecrankie and the Place where Lord Dundee was killed, in Memory of which there is a Stone erected. We went this Afternoon about 24 miles; the latter part of the Road was between amazing high Hills with rapid Waters in the Bottoms, and the Road made on the Sides of the Hills very high from the Waters – an awful Scene. We stayed at Blair in Athol, as you may suppose, that Night. On Thursday Morning we viewed the Duke of Athol's Seat there, but we had not time to see much of it. The House is a good Family house; the Grounds are extensive and well laid out, and immense Quantities of Wood in the Grounds and on the surrounding Hills; there is a fine Waterfall but not equal to that at Taymouth; the Grounds seem better than at Taymouth, and are laid out in a different Stile, but the Want of such a grand Piece of Water as Loch Tay I think makes the Place much inferior to Taymouth.

From Blair in Athol we went after Breakfast to Dalnacardock, from thence to Dalwhinnie where we dined, and then to Pitmain [Kingussie],, making a Journey of about 40 miles in 12 Hours. Between Dalnacardock and Dalwhinnie the Waters that before ran into the Tay, changed their Course in the Country of Glengary and run into the Spey. On Friday morning we went from Pitmain to Avemore to Breakfast from thence to Dalmagarrie to Dinner and in the evening reached Inverness; our Journey this day was about 50 Miles. At Avemore we were among the Grants and in Sight of Inverlochy Mr John Grant's Country, were told the History of Craiggallikie Mountain, and saw the Hill that produces the fine Stones like Diamonds.

At Inverness our Journey through the Mountains ended. I know not how to describe the Wonders we saw during the last two days; immense Mountains succeeded by others for near a hundred Miles; in the midst I may say at times of a thousand Mountains; not an Inhabitant Tree or the least Cultivation for Miles together; some few Spots only capable of being cultivated, but where they could be met with, the hardy industrious Native cultivated, lived in Huts made of loose Stone and Turf, and the Distaff and Spinning Wheel continually at Work. The People quite cheerful courteous and intelligent, and whilst they can procure Food happy and contented. We heard at our different Stages melancholly Accounts of their Distress for Food the last two Winters. As to our Party we met with good Fare at all the Stages, the Cookery sometimes not the best, but good Appetites dispensed with Nicety. The Roads throughout are very good, but hilly, and being obliged to take Horses from Stirling to Inverness without the Opportunity of changing we made short Stages. In the midst of the Mountains where no Tree was to be seen for Miles we found the Natives digging out of the Mossy Ground large Roots of Fir Trees that may have been there for Ages, and this Wood when greatly decayed is used by the common People throughout the Country for Light instead of Candles. The Tradition is that all the Country was once covered with Fir Trees yet in many Places now so barren no Tree would grow. At Dalwhinnie and Pitmain we saw the first Crop of Pease in Blossom; they will hardly ever pod.

At Avemore the Land grows somewhat better, and there are large Woods of natural Fir. We heard of several Partys of Gentlemen that were out shooting Moor Game, and were told they had good Sport, killing 19 or 20 Brace a day by one Person. At Inverness our Parties separated Mr Ross and Robert[234] went to Fort George Mr Gordon and I accompanied by our cousins Mr Munro and Mr Smith crossed the Ferry of Kesac [Kessock] and made a Journey of 30 miles to Dalmore to Dinner. In our Way we drank Whisky on Farrintosh [Ferintosh] Land, a Territory that belongs to Forbes of Culloden, and that has the privilege of making it without paying Duty[235]. We called at Dingwall one of Mr Fox's Boroughs[236]; it belongs to Mr Duncan Davidson who has a pretty Estate near it, a good House and

---

[234] It seems most likely that this was Robert Home Gordon, Robert Cooper Lee's ward, whose father John had died in 1774, and who later bought the heavily encumbered estate of Embo in 1790. Robert Home Gordon named a Miss Mary Munro of Dalmure in his will in 1827 along with George Munro of Fowlis and Mackenzie and Murray cousins. His cousin Colin Mackenzie, who died in Jamaica in 1841, owned the Mount Gerald estate close to Fowlis and Novar.

[235] It would appears that the duty-free privilege was withdrawn in 1784 and the distillery closed the following year, so Robert and his party were among the last ever to taste this particular whisky!

[236] The Whig Charles James Fox was the MP for the Burghs of Dingwall, Kirkwall and Tain. After Fox won the 1786 Westminster election, aided by the Duchess of Devonshire among others, George Ross held the seat, but died less than a month later.

Gardens, the Lands improved and improving. We crossed a Ford of the Firth of Cromarty, and went down along the Banks of the River ten or twelve Miles to Dalmore. On both Sides this River the Lands are very good, well cultivated, abound in Gentlemen's Seats, and make a most pleasing Appearance.

We passed by Sir Hector Munro's, Sir Harry Munro's and Lady Munro's in our Way to Dalmore. There we found Mrs Munro and her three Daughters, and with Mr Munro[237] and Mr Smith we made a company of Eight. Mrs Munro is a sensible good old Lady, has brought up her Family extremely well, and is esteemed and respected by all the Families in the Neighbourhood. You may be sure we were welcome Guests and were most hospitably entertained. On the Sunday morning Mrs Munro accompanied us to Novane; in our way we breakfasted at our Aunt Mrs Mackenzie's. Here we met another agreeable Family of Cousins three Daughters and one Son all grow up as well as the Munro's. We took a Glass of Whiskey according to the Custom of the Country before Breakfast, and then attacked the Bread and Butter, Tea, Eggs and Cheese. At Novane Sir Hector[238] received as most cordially. We had the Pleasure to find another Family of Ladies here. Sir Hector's Mother a fine old Lady of Eighty and four Sisters not very young. All too our Cousins[239]. Sir Hector insisted on our returning there Monday Evening. We couldn't refuse him, but took then an early Leave that we might not keep the Family from Kirk. Mrs Munro went with us from Novane to Cromarty about 30 Miles Crossing Invergordon Ferry near Dalmore. Our first Visit was to Mrs Smith, another Daughter of Mrs Munro, who has two Children. Mr Smith is Manager for Mr George Ross at Cromarty, and the

---

[237] The Mr Munro in the party was probably George Munro, second son of Sir Harry Munro and his wife Anne Rose of Kilravock (pronounced Kilraik). He died in Kingston, Jamaica of a putrid fever on 22 April 1802. Source:Alexander Mackenzie, *History of the Munros of Fowlis*, A&W Mackenzie, Inverness, 1898, p.145

[238] Sir Hector Munro of Novar had a distinguished, though not uncontroversial, career in the army first in the '45 and later in India. When he returned to Scotland he made extensive modifications to Novar House and carried out agricultural improvements and afforestation, planting hundreds of thousands of fir and Scots pine trees.

[239] Sir Hector's mother was Isobel Gordon daughter of Sir Robert Gordon of Embo, and his sisters were Christian, Ann, Jane and Elizabeth. His brother Alexander succeeded to Novar on his death. I can find no reference to the Lee family having Scottish blood relations and so assume that the reference to cousins is to relations of others in the party, particularly cousins of Robert Cooper Lee's ward Robert Home Gordon of Embo.

Family live very comfortably on one of [the] Farms improving under his Direction.

After taking Wine and Cake we proceeded to Cromarty House, leaving Mrs Munro with her Daughter. Just as we came to the House we met our Friends from Fort George, who had come by Water about 12 or 14 Miles, and were rather long in coming owing to the Tide and contrary Wind against them. They came in the Fort Boat accompanied by Lieutenant Whyte. We all entered the House together. Mr Gray who is Mr Ross's Nephew and declared Heir received us with great Politeness. He is a well bred Man and of the Ton as well as of Business. The House is modern built in the London Stile for Grosvenor Square all of Stone well finished and furnished and cost £4000 – good Gardens and Hothouse Policies or Pleasure Grounds, the Hills clothed with Woods, and the level Lands well cultivated and improved, upon the whole a delightful Place. It is a Pity the Climate it was not better. The Town of Cromarty also belongs to Mr Ross, and for the Employment of the Poor he has a Manufactory of Sail Cloth. I was told he has laid out Eighty thousand Pounds. We spent the day very agreeably with Mr Gray and some Friends with him. The Garden supplied Cherries Rasberries and Peaches.

On Monday Morning our Friends returned to Fort George notwithstanding a pressing Invitation from Sir Hector, but their Carriage was at Fort George, and we had a forced March to make, and more Business to do that day than we were aware of. Mr Smith crossed Cromarty Ferry with us, and we went on to Tain (another of Mr Fox's boroughs) to Breakfast. Mr Mackenzie and Mr Munro joined us here, and we breakfasted with Dr Macfarquhar's Family. Only three female Cousins appeared in this Family. From Tain we went on, crossed Meikle Ferry which divides Ross from Sutherland, passed Squelbo [Skibo], one of Mr William Gray's Estates[240], through Dornoch (another of Mr Fox's Boroughs) and reached Embo about One O'Clock. We were joined by several Gentlemen and after viewing the Estate returned all to Dornoch to Dinner. Mr Gordon was better pleased with the Estate than he expected. There is an old House in which one of the Tenants Family live with Fear and trembling lest it should tumble on them. The Grounds have been neglected and are out of Heart. Great room for Improvement. Stone and Moorland sufficient. I must stop here. Tomorrow Morning we set out for Inchmartin.

---

240 William Gray was yet another of those Scots who had made his fortune in Jamaica.

The late eighteenth century was a time of intense interest in agricultural improvement and the repeated references in the letters to improving the land, planting timber and so on show that Robert was as much interested in it as anyone of his class. Although his main income was from his London and Jamaica business he did also have lands in Herefordshire and at Shredding Green where he took an interest in agricultural production. Sadly many of the techniques that worked well further south were disastrous in the marginal lands of the Highlands, and the wholesale clearance of crofters from their ancestral lands from the late eighteenth century onwards led to much misery, depopulation and mass (often forced) emigration.

Robert Cooper Lee to Priscilla Lee

Dundee, 30th August 1784 One O'Clock

Mr Ross accompanied us the first Stage. We are now ten Miles from Inchmartin. Mr Allen is to meet us on the Road. A fine Sunny Day Frost last Night. Excuse this short Letter. You will receive this Sunday Morning. I hope to be with you in a Week afterwards. My fellow Travellers desire their kind respects to all at Cowley. My most affectionate regards also

Your ever Affectionate Robert Cooper Lee.

Frances Lee to Richard Lee

Cowley, 15th September 1784

You were not well my dear Richard when we parted. I cannot therefore be easy untill you assure me that you are quite well again. You will I am sure devote a few moments to me when you consider that by doing so you will make me happy. I shall think it a long time till we meet, accustomed as I have been of late to your Society it would be wonderful if I did not feel a blank in my Happiness without it. I have been rather la la since Monday. I however accompanied my Friend Sophy to the Terrace in the Evening, my Father and Mrs Brett formed the quarteto. The King was the only one of the Royal Family who appeared – so we were not fully gratified. My Father went Town yesterday Morning and with him my agreeable Companion. We expected the former would have returned to dinner to-day and Mr Bowes had intimated that my amant (Mrs Kluss) would accompany him, but we have been disappointed perhaps they may yet come. Gordon and Bob were off yesterday. I was confined to my Room the whole Day I therefore have seen little of the remaining Beaux. Matt I fancy will return to Winchester in the course of the Week. This is my Father's Birth-day. I have just drank to his Health in a Bumper. May Heaven long preserve him to us! I am sure you will say Amen to this prayer! You still I suppose hold your resolution of going to Pendulum Hall and Cats Hill on Saturday. Should it be convenient to call at Woodford Sophy G. desir'd I would assure you she should be happy to see you. If there should be a leisure Day in the next Week before Saturday May I not hope for the pleasure of seeing you here? To a Man of Business a long Letter must be a bore. I shall therefore make an end to this scrawl. My Mother desires I will present her kind regards. Adieu mon tres cher frère je vous aime de tout mon Coeur. F.L.

Robert Cooper Lee returned from Scotland to be confronted with a demand from his eldest son to be allowed to tour Europe. Bob's extravagant habits, first demonstrated at school were still causing problems and he continued to spend as if his father's pockets were bottomless.

Robert Cooper Lee to Robert Cooper Lee junior

Cowley, 9th November 1784

Dear Robert,

I am very glad to find that you are awakened to your own situation, which certainly calls for your most serious thoughts. Time is not to be recalled. I will therefore draw a veil over the past and only look forward. The Road is still open fair and easy for your Success, Honour and Comfort. Let me once more urge you to step into it, and to act and preserve with manliness. How many are there even of your contemporaries who would be happy to avail themselves of the prospect that courts you? Why will you spurn it? Look around and find if you can the man that has gained a desirable Situation in Life without application to make himself useful. Be assured you will never have the assistance of those who can be useful to you, unless you can help yourself, and be also useful to them. Your Conduct and Situation may incline them to pity you, but you will never have their approbation or Esteem. It may be necessary to repeat to you that it is impossible for you to have from me, whenever I may drop, more than equal to your present allowance, and should any accident rendered me unable to follow Business even that must be lessened during my life. I believe you'll find upon Self Examination that most of your present Knowledge is rather superficial and that you have much to learn. Believe me, Habits of Application and Economy are absolutely necessary for you to obtain. Each will aid the other in practise. I need not point out to you the ill consequences of Idleness and Dissipation, how insignificant and contemptible they render the Man, and how surely they lead to difficulties, meaness and disgrace. The only Foundation on which a Man can safely depend is moral Rectitude; on this with Application and Economy he may insure Success, Independence and Satisfaction. With regard to your going abroad, I think you should above all things avoid going in Company, unless with a most intimate Friend, by whom you could not possibly be interrupted in your own Plan. You do not go for Pleasure, or to visit Courts. I recommend you taking a few letters of Introduction and Servant, and a few Law and other Books. Avoid Paris if you can, if not, don't stay more than one day in it. Sit down in the some Town at a distance from the Capital, where you can perfect yourself in the language – allot a time for Study and strictly adhere to it. You will soon find company, and Amusements enough for your leisure hours. Limit your expenses, according to your Income, and let nothing make you swerve from that Rule. I will add only that you will ever have my most cordial wishes for your Welfare, and every assistance in my Power, consistent with the Duties I owe to the rest of my Family.

I am your truly affectionate Father Robert Cooper Lee.

Robert was also faced with some serious overspending on the part of his nephew which he proposed to control by having John's pay made over directly to him by the Regimental Agent, something which John took in good part. The news in the second part of his letter however came out of the blue.

John Lee to Robert Cooper Lee

Cassel, November 1784

My dear Friend,

Your last manoeuvre of taking my Ensign's pay off my Hands was not a bad one you are an old soldier I see now so you know that I had set that down on the list of my Spring manoeuvres; on my arrival in England I intended to have drawn for it and dash'd away with it still I suppose it will make no great difference if the draft is at the Top or the Bottom of the Paper.

With much reluctance

Cassel, 28th of November 1784

Sir,

Pay to Robert Cooper Lee Esq or Order whatever Monies are or may be in your Hands due or belonging to me for the Purchase Money of my Enseigncy in the 16th Regiment of Foot, or for Pay, arrears or otherwise, and the same shall be allowed by, Sir, Your humble Servant John Lee

To Agent for the 16th Regiment Foot, Dublin.

You know my good Friend that you write rather an unintelligible stick, therefore you'll excuse me if I can't make out the old gentleman's name, Colocane, Colocarni, Colicanute, or some such outlandish name; but I could not make it out; surely it was not my good Friend Colquhoon. As it is impossible for a better footing to subsist between any two persons than at present between us; I take this opportunity of communicating to you a circumstance which if you think it an error, you may the better be able to overlook; I here confess to you that it is an affair of Love. I had the honor of first been acquainted with the Lady at Brunswick. She is I assure you of as good family as any in this Place. Tho' not entirely destitute of Fortune the short time we have been united we have seen that our joint allowances will scarcely be sufficient for us even here. As it is a thing already done; too little cannot be said upon the subject, but to leave it entirely to you, commending my wife and myself to your favor?

Pray give my duty to my Aunt and Love to all the family, and believe me, my dear Uncle

your dutiful nephew, John Lee.

There is no further indication of who his new wife was, not even her name, and the suspicion arises that this was one of John's jokes. Whatever the case, only a year later he is referring to his 'poor dear Wife deceased'.

By the following summer the 'Counsellor' had been despatched to France to further his education, which if the next letter is typical was being pursued in a very desultory fashion.

Robert Cooper Lee Junior to Richard Lee

Toulouse, 9th June 1785

The Heat of this Climate positively renders a Man incapable of all Mental as well as Corporeal Exertions. The Composition of a Letter (which is an operation both of the Body and Mind) is at this Season, and in this Country absolutely a most laborious undertaking. This is my third Essay. I am resolv'd in defiance of a most profuse Perspiration to accomplish my Wish.

Imprimis, with respect to Potts affair (which has given me, in spite of my Philosophy a great deal of uneasiness) I believe that I can in some measure penetrate into his motives. Do you recollect my Mothers Conversation with *good* John Bourke? Potts recent Conduct took its [illegible], I am clear, from the Particulars of that Conference. Ma Mere has been the innocent Cause of much Chagrin to me. It is done however, and can't be helped.

How does Punch continue to make it out? You are not in all probability completely in his Secrets of Finance, and therefore will only have it in your Power to judge from appearances. Had he any Success at Newmarket? Did the Levite's accustomed good Fortune attend him? Did little Joe shake his [illegible], and to what purpose? You, I trust, exercised the Family Prudence in the only Business in which we can lay claim to that Virtue. However Equal to the 'Damnosa Nexus', we have not sufficient Courage for the 'Praeceps Alea'. May we never have!

Du Gazon has been enchanting the Toulousians with her Talents, which are, in truth, wonderful. She is more indebted to Nature than to Study. In Louisa in the [illegible] she is inimitably great. The Songs of 'Je ne desorterai jamias' and 'Vive le Nu' brought you most strongly to my mind. How many slight 'Damn you's' have I honored you with, when you have bored me with those Tunes. On the whole I think the French Stage extremely inferior to our own. In the Tragedy their Actors are absurd and contemptible. To rant is to [illegible], to bellow is to excell. 'They tear their Passions into tatters and out-herod Herod'. In Comedies of real Humour (for such Moliere's indisputably are) they are at best mediocre. Their Excellence lies in little pastoral After Pieces such as Blaise et Batet Les Chesseurs etc. The last of those petite Pieces I admire exceedingly. It is perfectly au gout Francois.

With respect to the Inhabitants at large I hold them as a warlike Nation in perfect Contempt. I once thought that the Idea of one Englishman being able to thrash three Frenchmen proceeded from a vulgar and national Prejudice. I begin to think now that there is some truth in it, and yet I am in Province that supplies France with un thers de ses Soldats. Their animal Spirits are more constantly elevated than those of the Bull Family. But they stand as little Chance with us at a real Laugh as they do at an equal Contest. They are too Heaven be thanked, at least a Century behind us in the Refinements and Elegancies of Life – and so much for the Comparison.

Believe me, Richard, I have the highest and sincerest Regard for my City Friends. If I have ever said anything contradictory to such Sentiments, it has proceeded from a Wish to ruffle the Serenity of the Temper of a Friend of mine, and to see his upper Lip rise in contact with his Nose. How do all the Youths fare? Is it Summer in Bedlam yet? Does Tom Sharpe frequently sport a Solo at Carshalton or Croydon? Harry is [illegible] in all the delights of Love and Charms of Beauty. Tom Lewes is a Blackguard. I wrote to him at his particular request and he has not deigned to answer my Letter.

How do you like Shreding Green? Who is the Goddess of the Day or rather Night? With respect to myself I have not had a Stroke since the 20th March at Paris. Je ne m'ai branlé que deux fois. It is terrible but Flesh and Blood can't help it. I mean to cool my Letch in Pyrenean Snow next Week. Your Letter will be forwarded thither to me. My affectionate Wishes attend the family at Shreding Chateau (do you remember Old Plowitz at Brussels?)

Believe me Your Affectionate Brother and Friend Robert Lee.

John Lee to Richard Lee

Cassel, 17th June 1785

Dear Richard,

I will not send you a Journal of my tour through Flanders as you may be much more accurately informed by any two penny half penny Book upon the subject. My friend and companion Thomas was very sensibly affected by the quick transition from Roast Beef and Plumb pudding to harricoes, fricasées, sour crout and sausages. It seem'd as if every Bush gave him a purging; in the same manner as some men's mentalular powers are excited by a turd. There was also a disagreement between the Rhine wein and his bowels. At Calais and Dover none of our Baggage was examined or even open; such was the respect paid to Monsieur de Lee and his Post Chaise. On road the Plan of Encampment was changed, at the Head Quarters fixed at Cassel, as the best suited for Study. Thomas is a very worthy little fellow, he is rather hot upon occasion; terribly enrag'd against the Postilions, and swore at them; which will not make them go faster, as you and I very well know and if there is any thing singular in him, it is his boasting himself a great [illegible], which you and I do not. Dick, I came away without settling with Foot, I shall be obliged to you if you will pay him twenty Pounds for me, when it is most convenient to your finances. Give my compliments to him and tell him he shall hear from me by the next post. How do the Pounds, Shillings and Pence go on? Has my Brother answer'd my letter if he has keep it for me till I come over. Do, my good friend, remind your Mother of sending some Present to my Mama with my letter. I daresay Uncle is very near Shreeding Green by this time. The weather here is very disagreeable for three or four days it is remarkably hot, then comes a thunderstorm and Rain for one or two days more etc and so forth. When I first arrived on the Continent, Rain was as much wanted as it had been in England, but we have had a great deal since. Thomas and myself have written to the Landgrave to ask his permission to Shoot here, for we have been refused by the Jäger[?] Marshall, and stand a great chance of being refused by him too but it is worth trying for. I hope you have sent my Baggage before this time, but if you have not send it as soon as possible, for till then I shall be perfectly idle, which of all things you and I detest for I have no Books with me. God bless you, Dick, and keep you out of the Fleet or any other Prison. Give my most kind duty and respects to Uncle and Aunt and compliments to John Allen and Mrs Allen, to Foot, to Punch and the Old one, to General Townsend, to Gordon, to Captain Gordon - tell me in your answer what news from Bob at Toulouse; I shall write to him if it will not interrupt his studies.

John Lee to Richard Lee

Cassel, 20th August 1785

Dear Richard Lee,

Your letter gave me much pleasure, and your punctuallity charmed me and tho' a lad not very fond of taking advice, which (between ourselves) is no good point in an Officer, I did, notwithstanding followed yours, with [illegible]. I do not know how call you that auf English. Though I assure you the thoughts of seeming to run away from young Rougé, gave me some disagreeable sensations. I received an answer from him, for my apology, in which he behaved as much like a gentleman as I had done otherwise he is the last man I should be inclined to disoblige. So Old Jack Scott is come back; if I had staid a little longer in England and should have seen him. I hope he does not come over for bad health; I believe I should say, on account of his bad health but I have almost all my English vergessen. I was just going to give you a very smart observation of my own but upon second thoughts, I'll keep it for Foot's letter. For you must know that I write 4 letters by this post, Dick, Jack Scott, Foot and

Gordon. You need not ask to see the letters, for it will be the same as this, over and over again; ditto repeated. I went the other day with my friend Strutt to a country residence of the Landgrave called Hofgeismar; where the old gentleman, who is fond of making the most of everything, has converted ¾ of his dwelling into an Inn; it is large like the Castle Marlbro' but not half so good. Over each door is written the price of its lodging from 2 grosse:6 Pfen. to 7 grosse:8Pfen. I and my friend and I wishing to appear like two dashing Englishmen took 4 grosse;4 Pfen. worth of lodging. There is a diabolical Table d'hote there, where Shoe makers and Tailors dine with their customers and sup if they chuse it; but that depends entirely upon themselves. I was compelled to dine there by necessity not being able to dine any where else, having had a quarrel with the court which often happens with me. Your Papa will tell you the particulars. If I don't finish this letter soon, I shall have nothing to say in the other three; so goodbye t'ye Dick. I have not yet received my goods and begin to think that they are gone to the bottom let me know if you have heard anything of it, but I may buy the same things again. The damages I estimate at £150 which I shall make you pay, or you will forfeit all your credit and Interest behind the counter. I'll get the Pounds, Shillings and Pence out of you. Give my Duty to Uncle and Aunt remember me to Matthew and Scud. I have met with Schoolfellow of Matthews here he is called Starkie.

John Lee to Robert Cooper Lee

Cassel, 9th October 1785

Dear Uncle,

Tho' I have not yet received from you an answer to my last letter, yielding to my natural philoscribical turn, I must trouble you with another; and at the same time I have to inform you that I have taken the liberty to draw upon you for £100 payable to my good friend Mr M.M.Berman, or Order, an Irish Pawnbroker lately imported. I am just return'd from Hanover, where I heard there was to be an Encampment and Review. I went with my friend Major Strutt. But on account of the very heavy and Incessant rains, which had overflowed all the Leina so much that all the fields with the corn on the ground were overflowed and of course destroyed. The corn is so much ruined all along the Banks of the Weser that the Countrymen will not give themselves the trouble to carry it away, but leave it there. If efforts continue to go so swimmingly, we shall have every reason to hope for a Famine. On account of all these things, three days after we had been at Hanover, orders were given out for the Camp to break up. I intended to have sent you a Plan of it, but as I have not yet received my Instruments, it is not in my power. Pray how does Shreeding Green agree with you? I hope you don't find any ill effects from the damp which must arise from the great quantity of water about your estate. Wishing you, my Aunt, and all the family a continuance of health, and change of the weather.

I subscribe myself your ever dutiful Half pay Lieutenant.

John Lee to Robert Cooper Lee

Cassel, 4th December 1785

Dear Uncle,

Your time, I dare say, is so much taken up with Shooting and Hunting that you have not had time to answer my last letter. But this will not hinder me from informing you that I have taken the liberty to draw upon you for £100 sterling. I did not immediately want the Money, but it was to oblige the German Acquaintance, who, as he sets off for England tomorrow, wishes to have a Bill upon London. Payable at thirty days sight to George Schmerfeld or Order 'tis for a friend of Georges, as he told me. But be that as it will I shall be much obliged to you, if you will give him his money when he comes for it, and take care that no Silver Spoons are in his way. If it is not too late May I beg you to purchase for me Lottery Ticket. I'll pay for it when I come of Age to inherit All my fortune. It will be nothing new to inform you of the Death of our Landgraf. But it will be to tell you something of his Successor Wilhelm 9th. I went to his first Court, and he was very polite, asked after all at Bedford Square gave us as much as we could eat and sent us home again. He has begun very strangely, by taking away 2/3 from the Officers pay both in the civil and Military. Sent away Parsons, Lawyers, Physicians, Professors of all Arts and Sciences, Musicians, players etc etc etc etc. For which he is universally abused and curs'd. Carriages and horses selling every day. If you have any Sons destined for the Military I would by all means recommend you to send them here, being finely adapted to study. With the remainder of the Portion which my poor dear Wife deceased, brought me, I intend to make a little Excursion a few days journey from here to visit a Lady I fell in love with on my way from England. What is become of my friend Bob Gordon and his Master and Mistress? And is Bob Lee still upon the Pyrenees Studying Law? Dickie is he still shooting in Leicestershire, instead of minding his Logbook and Ledger? Will you be so good as to ask my Aunt if I may take the liberty of recommending for Flavilla Lee my Music Master, who will be in England next Spring. All my shooting is finished, every thing very dull, nothing but reading, to pass the dull hours away, or smoking out of window. With once more exhorting you to beware of my friend Schmerfeld, I will finish my epistle.

John Lee to Robert Cooper Lee

Cassel, 14th March 1786

Dear Uncle,

I should not have troubled you with this second letter so soon after the first, if I had not yesterday received a letter from Berlin informing me that I must be there about the end of April; therefore I shall be much obliged to you if you are able to procure me letters of introduction to send them so that they may be at Cassel about the middle of April. One letter to the Ambassador is all I should wish for. I received your short letter the day before yesterday. I am very much obliged to you for thinking of my Promotion in the Army, if you get it be so good as to procure me leave of absence for another year for I should be very sorry to break off in my course of Mathematics. Your Authority still subsists, and ever shall. I am in the same predicament as you was on account of the Post, and I think, even with you for your short letter [remainder missing]

John Lee to Robert Cooper Lee

Cassel, 12th April 1786

Dear Uncle,

I have been waiting for some time in expectation of Letters for Berlin, but not having received them I must do as well as I can without. In the meanwhile, in order to get clear of Hesse, I have been forced to take the liberty of drawing upon you for £150 which I find will be insufficient. I am sorry to have so far exceeded the Sum you mention'd to me. The common idea we have of the cheapness of this Country does not so much consist in the low price of some few articles, as in the scarcity of many articles more common in the most civilised parts of Europe. It was more than I expected. And as it must be paid, it was much better to apply. I hope you, Mrs Lee and all the family have been well in health this Winter. Pray how are you pleased with your purchase at Shreading Green it is a great pity that there is no water there. I only troubled you with this letter to inform you that I must draw for a little more than the £150 I shall be much obliged to you if you will inform Richard Lee that I have sent a Box by way of Hamburg the England. It contains Books etc. I'll thank him if he takes charge of them, and secures them from being seized.

John Lee to Robert Cooper Lee

Leipzig, 1st June 1786

Dear Uncle,

As the poor old King was not able to be present at the Reviews, I was obliged to assist there in his stead, he is in his old age become exceedingly jealous that he would [not] permit the Prince Royal to have any command, so that he came merely as a spectator. I gave my letter of Introduction to Lord Dalrymple, but he is a droll dog, he is very melancholy and remarkably absent. He sometimes invites company to dinner but never speaks to them, except sometimes interrupting them from a strong political argument, he asks who makes their breeches. I went to the first review at Potsdam, where I was greatly entertained (for the instructive part is the manoeuvres in the Autumn) supped always with the Prince and Princess Royal. Potsdam itself is a caserne. The second review is at Berlin, and the third at Magdeburg at which last place the Army was encamped, and all the strangers Officers were encamped with them. 'Tis the first time I ever slept upon the ground with straw. Nothing to eat, except one meal at the Adjutant general's table. I mean to stay in Saxony for these three months, in order to be at hand to assist at the Autumn Manoeuvres.

Apropos. On my arrival here, finding myself rather low in cash I offer'd a Bill of Exchange upon my Uncle but as his name was not among the list of Merchants or Bankers, they would not take it, but however they say that they will send it to England, and upon its being accepted, they will pay the money, recommending to me at the same time to procure a letter of Credit upon one of the great Bankers or Merchants in London which might serve me in any place. If you could obtain such a letter for me I shall be extremely obliged to you. The Bill is payable to the Order of Messieurs Reichenbach and Company for £100 sterling at thirty days sight. These Merchants are very troublesome fellows. I am confined to my room by a violent cold and fever, which is very much the ton here everybody has it. I am under the Hands of an Apothecary, who is a perfect Sangrado, he will starve me in a very short time, my only food is physic.

The Apothecary is just gone, and he says he try some experiments upon me.

I intended to have written a long letter but I have such a violent headach that I must go and lie on the bed.

I hope my Aunt has enjoyed her health this spring, pray give my Duty; and remember me affectionately to Richard, Matthew and all Relations and Friends.

Robert Cooper Lee to Robert Cooper Lee Junior (in Paris)

Shreeding Green Bucks, 29th June 1786

Dear Robert,

The Family removed only on Thursday last from the Square. I followed them on Saturday and have hitherto preserved in my Plan of staying in the Country the whole Fortnight which I hope to accomplish undisturbed by Business. I find the Relaxation very pleasant; the weather is fine, and I pass the time in riding and walking, seeing my Hay stacked and thatched, the Stone Parlour floored, and visiting our Neighbours. The last Winter deprived us of Mr Greenwood and Sir John Coghill. In consequence of the Death of the latter Lady Charleville has sold Richings Park to Mr Sullivan, formerly a Dealer in Opium in the East, for the trifling Sum of ten thousand Guineas. The Gentleman is himself a Bachelor, but his Brother Mr Richard Sullivan, a little Nabob, and his Lady reside with him. I have as yet seen the Lady only, a very agreeable Woman, and the Gentlemen I understand are pleasant and sociable. Your old Acquaintance Mr Macleod of Colbecks and his Lady are come to Ickenham. The Neighbourhood are all in Love with them. Enough of the Green.

Your Letters of the 1st and 7th Instant are I believe unacknowledged. As I have not since heard from you I conclude that Mr Bell and you are set out to make the Tour of Switzerland according to the Plan mentioned in your late Letters and I hope you will this Tour among the rude and hardy Sons of Freedom as pleasant and improving, as that among the more polished Italians. Your Companion will I am told assist much in observing the Genius and Manners of People you meet with. The Duke of Dorset[241] is lately returned here to be present at his favourite

[241] The Duke, who was the Ambassador in Paris, attempted to introduce cricket to France, but was frustrated by the outbreak of the Revolution without which perhaps France would have become a great cricketing nation!. While there however he did from

Amusement – some great Cricket Matches – but I understand he goes back again to Paris. Mr Eden I am afraid makes but slow Progress in the Commercial Treaty. Did you see his French Secretary Mr Gibert? You seemed surprized at the King's Birthday being celebrated on the 5th of June. It was celebrated here on the same day, the 4th falling on a Sunday. The Cardinal de Rohan I suppose is considered as having got well off. It is dangerous meddling with such edged Tools as he did. Our Parliament is still sitting, but the Sessions is winding up. Mr Hastings's Business stands over till next Sessions under a Bill for the Purpose, Mr Burke having substituted one Charge leaves Mr Hastings in an unpleasant Situation. He has purchased Beaumont Lodge near Old Windsor in the Neighbourhood of the Summer Court. This Business seems to have drawn the Attention of all Parties more than the Fortifications at Cherburg. What do you think of their being obliged after next War to demolish them by Treaty, as those at Dunkirk on a former Occasion? My wish however is for Peace.

I am very happy to hear Mr Potts is so well and so well pleased. Lord Massarene's[242] Business, as giving him something to do in his own Way, would assist both his Health and Spirits. He is not expected here till August after all Law Business is over. He will be in good time to undertake Mr Hastings Defence before the Lord's. Richard left us Tuesday Morning early. He is very busy settling in his mercantile apartments in Salvadore House Bishopsgate Street.

Your Mother and all the Family send their kindest love and best wishes. Let me hear from you on your Progress. Adieu I am My dear Robert

Your very Affectionate Father Robert Cooper Lee.

John Lee to Robert Cooper Lee

Leipzig, 24th July 1786

Dear Uncle,

By the lively style in which you wrote to me last, I am in hopes you are in good health and spirits. I am sorry to find by your letter that Mrs Lee has

time to time offer a place in his coach to a young English school girl called Fanny Dashwood who would soon play a significant, indeed fatal, part in the Lee family story.

242 Clotworthy Skeffington, 2nd Earl of Massereene, 6th Viscount Massereene (1743–1805)

been indisposed, but Shredding Green will be more salutary prescription than any which Dr anyone could give. When I wrote you last, I was in the determination to stay here in Germany another year. But the inactivity and shameful behaviour of my Agent Thompson, I fear, will oblige me to return to England sooner than I had wish'd. For which reason I must beg your pardon for having given you so much trouble in procuring letters from Mr Herries, which it is probable I shall not be able to make use of. I shall not be glad to go so soon, but –

My late illness was a cold caught from sleeping under the Featherbeds of the Country, which falling in with my poor old unfortunate B. and L. complications, play'd terrible havoc with the Lieutenant, it affected my eyes very much, but nothing lost except a few Louis d'ors which I gave to the Doctor.

In a month from the date of this letter, I shall set out from Berlin. You mention the report you have in England of Old Frederic's being 'in a dangerous way'. I believe you take my word for the truth of it, for he is in the way to his grave. Not all the Uncle Tobys in the Universe could make him march this Autumn to the Silesian Reviews he'll be engaged. His new coat which he had made for that purpose will serve for his burying coat. Not many tears will flow for him. He is more fear'd than loved. It is almost a proverb among the German authors that the fate of Prussia depends upon its King. Now, the dear Heir to the Crown, is rather fat headed. At least that is the general opinion, for the King has given him very few opportunities of showing his abilities in any line. That comes from Jealousy. The Prince however is supposed to be a good general; he has shewn himself so upon an occasion. Before I leave off journalyzing let me tell you something of Leipzig. The Inhabitants of Leipzig may be divided into three classes viz: Children, Cripples, and Students. Of all the poor unfortunate places I ever was in, I never saw such a number of crooked and deformed people as here, they have a particular breed of Hunchback, another of bow legs, another of – in short they are the most miserable beings I ever saw. Children therefore are not to be distinguish'd from the cripples, so that there are properly only two classes Cripples and Students for the students come chiefly from other parts to study, and it is not common to see a crippled student. I will not trouble you any longer, but will refer you to the "description of Leipzig".

I sent over to England just before I left Cassell, a box with a few books in it; but have not heard any thing of it since. I wrote to Richard to beg him to keep it for me unopen'd 'till I came over. Pray be so good and let me know if Books are contraband in England. I beg to have my Duty presented to my Aunt, and hope to hear by the next letter that Shredding

Green has given health again. Do me the favor to remember me kindly to all my friends. If you should hear any thing of Mr Thompson, put it in your Postscript.

I have taken the liberty to enclose a letter to Mama. Brother's letter is already answer'd.

John Lee to Robert Cooper Lee

Leipzig, 13th August 1786

My dear Uncle,

I have disposed of the last £100 and have been obliged to draw upon you for £150 more, in order to help me at Berlin and on my way to England. The Bill is drawn upon M.M.Berman of Cassell. For I applied to the same man from whom I had money last at this place, but was refused, unless I would consent to his sending it over to England first, as he had done before. These Merchants are the most insolent ill bred fellows I ever met with. Messrs Reichenbachs are one of the true Leipziger breed; imagine to yourself a flash of lightning, and you will have a good idea of them. Zig, Zag. Zig,Zag.

Will you be so good as to direct your next letter to Berlin. I would give your compliments to Captain Thomas. (There is a strong report that the King is dead.) Compliments to Compliments to (sic) Captain Thomas, if I knew where he was, the last time I heard of him he was at Brunswick.

John Lee to Robert Cooper Lee

Leipzig, 22nd August 1786

My Dear Uncle,

The King is dead; he died last Thursday the 17th at 7 O'Clock in great pain. I shall go to Berlin the [day] after tomorrow. I am just returned from a visit I made to Baron von Wintzingerode a Captain in the Prussian Service, he is forced to join immediately on the King's death. I spent a week at his Estate 'tis a very snug little Farm, 'tis great pity that the land is divided in the Family, for the wood lands alone for burning and building on his Estate amount to 80,000 acres. They have five villages, where they may exercise their power even to hanging.

I will write to you again from Berlin. I have not heard anything of Mr Thompson my Agent, therefore I am afraid I must absolutely go to England after the Reviews. . . . .

Charles Richard to Robert Cooper Lee

Winchester, 30th August 1786

Sir,

I think it requisite to inform you that Master Lee's cough is rather more troublesome to him the constant attention has been paid to his diet. He has also taken something recommended by our Apothecary, but without any material effect. If you know of any medicine which you found serviceable to him, it shall be instantly made use of. I find him a pleasing little Boy, perfectly good tempered and assiduous.

I am Sir your obliged and honourable servant Charles Richard.

Note by Robert Cooper Lee relating to the treatment of Scudamore's cough

Master L. should live very regularly and avoid the Night Air. He ought to drink Barley Water with Lemon Juice and a little Honey or Syrup of Caguillaise for common Drink. He should take thirty Grains of Polychrest Salt dissolved in a Cup of Barley Water as above three times a day. It is most probable this Plan will relieve and cure Master L. in a week or ten days. If he should have any Pain in his Breast with the least difficulty breathing attended with Heat upon his Skin he should lose six or seven Ounces of Blood and the next day take a Dose of Salts.

1 Sept. '86

The polychrest salts were a purgative sometimes administered with rhubarb or calomel (mercurous chloride) to relieve constipation and in the belief that repeated, frequent purging helped to rid the body of infection. You had to be tough to survive eighteenth century medical treatment!

John Lee to Robert Cooper Lee

Jermyn Street, Thursday Morning [28th December 1786]

Sir,

I have spoken with Mr Thompson, and find every thing in train to compleat the Exchange. I shall therefore be much obliged to you if you will deliver into the hands of Mr Thompson the sum of £271.15.0 for the Exchange. I am Sir

Your most Obedient Humble Servant John Lee.

On the 23rd of December 1786 Richard Lee turned twenty-one and came into his inheritance from his uncle Joseph and from Scudamore Winde. He had moved into his own offices in Salvadore House Bishopsgate Street six months earlier, in July he became a director of Royal Exchange Assurance, and at the end of December he drew up a balance sheet for the first half-year he had spent in business.

He had handled sugar carried on the *Justina*, *Caroline* and *Amity Hall* ships and done business with Thomas Wynter, John Bourke, Thomas Vardon, Samuel S.Truman, Gordon & Co., John Anderson, Keeling and Reid, John Munt, R.R. and E. Maitland, Timothy and William Curtis, George Neuemburgh, Allen and Green, and Tyers & Co. He had bought a lottery ticket for £14.19 shillings, and he had balanced his books. It was a strong indicator of things to come.

John Lee to Robert Cooper Lee

Huberston, 18th July 1787

Dear Sir,

My passage has been delayed much longer than I could have imagined, and I am not yet in a fair way, on account of the foul weather we have here continually.

I slept at Bath on Friday Night. I call'd at Mr Wynter's the next morning, but he was gone. I left my Card of congé and proceeded to Bristol, where I waited a day in expectation of a Ship for Ireland, but there was not the least chance of one. From there I was obliged to make a tour of more than 120 miles to come to Huberston, where I have a better chance of getting over. I could have had a passage in the Packet Boat, but I saw actually fourteen passengers get into the boat, and seeing that there are cribs for twelve only, they must be stowed tolerably thick. I would not have gone with them if I was to have a Regiment on landing. I have since that time agreed for a passage in a Merchant ship (in the coal trade). I give two guineas for Myself, my Baggage and my servant. I am the only passenger, and shall have the State Room to myself, the Captain says. As soon as I get on-board I shall go to bed, and not get up again till we come to the Quay of Cork. I shall write to you on my Arrival. Pray present my best Respects to Mrs Lee and remember me kindly to Mrs Lee, Richard, Matt and all friends.

I am, Your affectionate Nephew John Lee.

John Lee to Robert Cooper Lee

Cork, 30th July 1787

Dear Sir

Since I wrote you last I have undergone a great deal of fatigue both by Sea and Land. After waiting some days at Milford in expectation of having a passage in the Collier, and finding that the Master would not go but in fair weather, I took my passage in the Packet Boat on Sunday the 22nd and arrived at Waterford on Wednesday Evening. My Shipmates were Mr Smith of Waterford, Merchant, Mr Heron Excise Officer, Mr Leigh MP for Wicklow, two Irish Beggars and an English one, Mr Fitzgerald and Parson Grimston, Travellers. Our passage was [illegible] long. I was not at all affected by the Sea. I arrived here just one day before the expiration of my leave of absence. I waited upon Lord Suffolk immediately, he has been here a month or six weeks. We seem to have come here more on the Plan of œconomy than anything else, for he has nothing to do with the Regiment. Nobody sees him except at the Mess where he is a pretty constant guest. I am not yet perfectly recover'd from the rocking of the Ship.

The small part of the country I have come thro' has not given me a very favourable opinion of Ireland. The misery of the common people is worth examining. I never saw such wretched objects in my life. Tho' the Pigs do live in the same [illegible] with the men and women, yet they are very badly lodged.

Cork is a large town and dirty in proportion, the streets are narrow and ill paved, the materials with which their houses are built are so bad that they very soon look old, and fall to ruins.

Lord Suffolk, or they call him here Colonel Suffolk, is not thought much of here. He has no money to throw away. Lieutenant-Colonel St George is in greater favor, both with the Civil and Military.

This day the Assizes begin. They call it their gay time because they have for this week a Ball and a Play alternately and at every other time a man must find amusement in himself.

Pray present my best respects to Mrs Lee, whose health I hope is re-established and kind remembrance to Miss Lee, Richard, Matt and all friends.

I am your affectionate Nephew John Lee.

PS Pray address your letters to Lieutenant Lee 70th Regiment Cork.

Frances Lee to Priscilla Lee

Shreeding green, 13th September 1787

Dear Madam,

I know it will be a gratification to you to hear of us tho' I have little more to say than that we are as you left us. Our kind Neighbour Mrs Mainwaring called here before she went to Mrs Bulkeley's yesterday evening and invited me and Favell to spend the Day with her either To-day or Tomorrow, as I hope for the pleasure of your return Tomorrow I have promised to be with Mrs M by 12 o'Clock To-day. She said she would send her Carriage but I told her I should prefer walking if the Weather permitted. She will send us Home in the Evening. Mrs Browne has left her little Girl behind. Lady Young's and Miss Young's answer is that 'they are sorry they cannot have the pleasure of waiting on Mr and Mrs Lee on Tuesday as they expect two Friends to make some stay with them'. The Hilliards were from Home. I sent Cards for the Evening to the Missses Bulkeleys and Turners, the latter sent verbal Message that they could come, the two former were out. The Butcher waits for this scrawl, I shall therefore conclude with Favell's and my kind Love to you and my Father etc etc

I am Dear Madam Your affectionate Daughter Frances Lee.

Robert Cooper Lee to Priscilla Lee

Bedford Square, 30th September 1787

I am afraid it will be Saturday before I can return to the Green. I have not seen Mr Wynter. Our Friends in Portman Square are well, I have an invitation to dine there. Matt Scott is in high Spirits upon the Rumour of War, he thinks of nothing less than being a Post Captain in a few Years. I wish him well but at the same time I wish for Peace. The Pacquet from Jamaica is in, no news. The Nectarines in the Book Case must eat, or thrown away. You may take my last Night's Earnings, I left the five shillings in my Waistcoat Pocket, my dressing Waistcoat I believe. Remember me kindly to Frances and Favell. It is possible yet I may have the Pleasure of joining the Circle tomorrow. I am

Your ever Affectionate Robert Cooper Lee.

Robert Cooper Lee to Scudamore Cooper Lee

Bedford Square, 15th October 1787

Dear Scud,

It was a great disappointment to Mr Bowes as well as to me that he did not see you in his return through Winchester. Matthew tells me that he received the Cash safe. I believe it is nearly all spent by this time. I will send you a small Parcel in the Course of this Week. I desire you will write to me. You may write in Latin if you chuse it. Tell me how you are, and how you are employed. Be sure to spell every Word right. Favell begins to work very well, and she is learning the French Grammar. Mr Wynter desires to be kindly remembered to you. If the Weather continues good he and I intend to pay you a Visit before the End of this Month. Your Mother and Sisters send their kindest Love to you. I am My dear Scud

Your very affectionate Father Robert Cooper Lee.

Dr William Rutherford to Scudamore Cooper Lee

Bentinck Street No. 13, Thursday morning [January 1788]

My Dear Scudamore,

I send you a Book which I wrote principally for the Improvement of my young friends among which number I must ever consider you. I hope you will take the trouble to read it with care and attention, as it will be paying me the Complement and making yourself acquainted with those subjects which gentleman ought to be ignorant of, besides as all your friends expect you to be a good Classical Scholar you will find yourself much assisted in reading the Greek and Latin Authors by having a previous knowledge of the Countries they describe, and an Acquaintance with their History. If this Volume should afford you either Instruction or Amusement I shall be happy to present you next Christmas with the second, and as a Map of all the Countries described in the work will accompany the next volume you might profitably employ a little time every day in acquiring knowledge of Geography which is a study every young man must be pleased and delighted with. Wishing you not only to become a good scholar but a good Man

I am My Dear Sir Your Sincere friend William Rutherford.

John Lee to Robert Cooper Lee

Cork, 5th January 1788

Dear Sir,

The benefit of the purchase is in such forwardness, that I took the liberty this morning to draw upon you for £2000 which I have desired Mr Piersey to deposit in the Hands of Messrs La Touche Bankers at Dublin. It has proved by far more troublesome business than I could have imagined and had I known as much of it as I now do, I should still have remained a jolly Lieutenant, rather than give myself such a devilish deal of trouble about it. I must go up to Dublin to see Mr Fitzherbert otherwise the affair will probably miscarry.

The Lord Lieutenant is a great man of business, and sees into everything himself, very different from the late Duke. There has [been] great change among his Aide de Camps, and is likely to make more both in the Civil as well as the Military Department. The next letter you receive from me will inform you of the event of this weighty affair.

Pray give my best respects to Mrs Lee and all the family.

I am Dear Sir Your Dutiful Nephew John Lee.

Charles Richard to Robert Cooper Lee

Winchester, 24th November 1788

Sir,

I propose sending my Pupil to you on Monday the 15th of December by the usual conveyance, and trust that you will order a proper Person to receive him at the New White Horse Cellar. His advancement in literature will be deserving of your approbation and I can truly affirm that he has behaved on all occasions with perfect regularity and good nature.

I can not omit acknowledging my obligations to you for the repeated favours my young friend Mr Slater has received from Mr Erskine of Nevis, in consequence of your recommendations. Enclosed is a letter for that gentleman containing my acknowledgements to him for his [illegible] which I must beg you will direct to him as I do not know his proper address. I am Sir your obliged and humble servant C. Richard.

John Lee to Robert Cooper Lee

Bristol, Sunday, 21st December 1788

Dear Sir,

I am just arrived at Bristol, where I may probably remain some time, as there is not a Ship in the River at present. I must wait with resignation. I call'd upon my Brother at Hungerford, and found him confined to his house with a severe cold, he is however getting better. I spoke with Mr Church about the Partnership, but he had not yet come to a resolution he seem'd to wish earnestly for it to take place, but to use his own words, he did not know whether you would think it worth while for your nephew to accept it. All that my Brother can expect is a share, and Mr Church surely will not make that too inconsiderable to be accepted.

I shall wait here for a Ship, and hope soon to acquaint you with my having taken my passage. Pray present my best respects to Mrs Lee and all the Family in Bedford Square.

I am Dear Sir Your most Obedient Servant John Lee.

John Lee to Robert Cooper Lee

Youghall, 3rd February 1789

Dear Sir,

Since I had the pleasure of writing to you last, my quarters have been frequently chang'd. I have been ordered from Cork to the Cove, and from thence back again to Youghall. I have not however left the Army Agents unemploy'd for I have all the papers ready to bring before the new Lord-Lieutenant immediately on his arrival.

On account of the Regimental Agent not having remitted my money at the time appointed, I was obliged to draw upon Mr Richard Lee for £50. I shall remain at this place till I have completed my business and will not to stir before that time as I have been fortunate enough to obtain the ill will of all the Officers for coming into the Regiment over their heads.

Our Lieutenant-Colonel Campbell will be in a few weeks out of the Corps he exchanges into the Guards with Colonel Worneck. The Major too leaves us about the same time, and there will be many an exchange among the Captains before the Regiment goes abroad.

Pray give my best respects to Mrs Lee and Compliments to all the Family.

I am Dear Sir Your most Obedient Servant John Lee.

Charles Richard to Robert Cooper Lee

Winchester, 24th May 1789

Sir,

My Pupil will return to you on Monday next for the Vacation by the usual conveyance. His advancement in literature will I believe merit your approbation and I flatter myself from his having collected an adequate knowledge of the Latin Language that he will soon be able to favour you with a specimen of Latin Versification. I have found him on all occasions of a docile and obliging disposition, sufficiently attentive to his studies, tho' he possesses great vivacity.

I am dear Sir your much obliged and honourable servant Charles Richard.

Charles Richard to Robert Cooper Lee

Winchester, 6th December 1789

Sir,

My Pupil will return to you on Monday the 14th Inst. And I will trouble you to order a servant to meet him at the new White Horse Cellar. His literary improvement will be the best testimony of his application. In composition he has already acquired a facility that convinces me of his possessing very good ability. Have desired him once or twice to convey to you a few specimens of his productions, which tho' they may be short and perhaps inelegant, may not be unacceptable to you.

I am Sir your most obliged and humble servant Charles Richard.

John Lee to Robert Cooper Lee

Youghall, 3rd June 1789

Dear Sir,

I receiv'd your letter of the 14th of March about a month after the date, and I daresay many of my letters are carried to wrong places, or mislaid in these Irish Port Offices. Every thing is very dull in this little corner, and having no news of our own, we are always impatient for the English Packets. The late affair between the Duke of York and Colonel Lenox has spread as far as this country, hardly any thing else is spoken of[243]. For my part, I think it rather a bad precedent. The old King of Prussia would not have let Colonel Lenox off so easy. I was glad to hear that the King had given up his plan of going to Hanover this year, he would have made a fine exhibition in the countries thro' which he was to pass, tho' perhaps the people might think a mad King no such uncommon sight.

I have lately met with an Officer who wishes to exchange with me, but as the Marquis has, for a long time past, been out of favour with the Army, I almost despair of the success of the business. If it miscarries, I must prepare my warm cloaths for Nova Scotia and Canada. I have written very often to the Counsellor and the Merchant[244], but have not had an answer from either of them.

The Weather here has been very unseasonable, we have had nothing but heavy rains, and violent storms of wind. I hope you will not remain so long in town this year as you did the last, for we may yet have a very hot Summer. Pray give my best Respects to Mrs Lee and Compliments to all the Family.

I am Dear Sir Your most Obedient Servant John Lee.

John Lee to Robert Cooper Lee

Youghall, 24th September 1789

Dear Sir,

Tho' it is such a long time since I have seen your hand, that I do not know who is the Debtor and who the Creditor, yet I should not have delay'd writing to you so long, if I had not been engaged in matters of state. I am just return'd from Charles Fort[245], where I have been for some

243 Charles Lennox, later 4th Duke of Richmond, fought a duel with Frederick Duke of York who had expressed the opinion that "Colonel Lennox had heard words spoken to him at Daughbigny's, to which no gentleman ought to have submitted". Lennox fired, but did not wound the Duke, who did not fire. Later the same year he fought another duel, wounding his opponent. His wife, Lady Charlotte Gordon, is famous for hosting the glittering ball in Brussels on the night before the Battle of Waterloo.

244 Robert and Richard Lee respectively.

245 A star shaped fort built in the reign of Charles II near Summer Cove, Kinsale, by the eighteenth century mainly used as a barracks.

time past on a General Court Marshall trying criminals. More than a hundred have been sentenced, and are waiting for Ships to transport them to different parts of the world, from whence few of them I suppose will ever return[246]. My tender feelings were tortured, when I beheld these unfortunate objects, but seeing that the public good was concerned, I steel'd my heart against the nicer feelings, and punished these miscreants according to their deserts.

I have been endeavouring, but hitherto without success, to avoid going to Canada. General Pitt is afraid of granting me a favor after the Marquis refused it. I have, however, sent a Memorial to him (on the report of the Marquis not returning) and he says that he will write to Mr Lewis respecting my business and doubts not that it will be done. If you should see Mr Lewis, I shall be oblig'd to you if you will repeat to him on the subject.

The season here has been very unhealthy, owing to the sudden changes from heat and cold. But it has not affected me in the least. All the Partridges have been destroyed by the rains, and there is very little sport of any kind this year.

Pray give my best respects to Mrs Lee, and compliments to all the family,

I am Dear Sir your most obedient Servant John Lee.

John Lee's brother William Robert Lee is a curiously shadowy character. Born in about 1767, he was sent to England to be educated after the death of his father and like John was a ward of his uncle Robert Cooper Lee who managed his trust fund. There are very few references to him in his brother's letters, and none in any written by other members of the family. He seems to have been articled to a Mr Church in Hungerford in a profession his brother felt not ambitious enough. Marchant Tubb had connections with Hungerford and he may have recommended Mr Church who may have been George Church, a mercer and draper who was buried at St Lawrence Hungerford on 16 March 1797 and whose wife then sold his business. William Robert (who always signs himself Robert) died three months after Mr Church, in June 1797.

---

[246] In May 1789 the first transport of convicts was sent to Australia from England, and within four years legislation was in place to transport convicts from Ireland. Before this transportation was mainly to North America and the Caribbean.

William Robert Lee to Robert Cooper Lee

Hungerford, 12th June 1790

Sir,

It being my custom to pay my Bill half Yearly - the people do expect me to keep good my Word and Credit, if you will please to remit the under mentioned sum by first conveyance it will be most thankfully receive, and the Bills punctually discharged.

Washing	3	7	11
Shoes and Boots	2	4	4
Hatter	1	5	
Hair Dresser	2	2	
Taylor	1	14	3
Draper	8	11	1
	19	4	7

I hope Mrs Lee and the Family are in perfect Health and my Brother when you saw him last please to make my respects.

I remain your Obedient Servant R Lee.

The diffident manner in which Willian Robert approached his uncle for the payment of his modest bills contrasted starkly with those being run up by his cousins Robert and Matthew. The latter had left school with a reasonable education but a taste for nothing so much as sport, and social life. He joined his brother Robert and Cousin William Lee Antonie on the London scene and as a member of the *ton* became a part with them of the Prince of Wales set. Financially, it was ruinous requiring a level of expenditure not available to Matthew. Whereas Frances and Robert had independent legacies from Scudamore Winde and Richard was building his business as a merchant and commission agent for West Indian sugar interests, Matthew had only what his father could allow him during his lifetime.

Robert Cooper Lee to Matthew Lee (draft for a letter)

9th August 1790

Dear Matthew,

Engagements I am under preclude the possibility of my assisting you, was that not the case I should observe to you that this anticipation of your income and that with me would naturally bring on that kind of money negotiation which considering our relation situation must be avoided particularly as I have always found you so bad a calculator. You recollect what passed between us the last time I made a payment to you. I then delivered to you as ~~I had on former occasion~~ (sic) however I have all along done my sentiments with regard to your income and your expenses. You know how in proportion the one is to the other and I did not expect after that conversation that although you might chuse to persist in such expenses, that you would again apply to me to sustain the burthen. The fact most undisguisedly is that your income is very small, that it requires all the oeconomy in the world necessary to bear you thro' with it, and that being exerted to the fullest extent I should feel it my duty as I am sure it would be my inclination to assist you by every means in my power, but when I see you at your time of Life going on without either plan or arrangement you must abide the consequences, the fatal consequences, arising from such conduct should you reach beyond yourself.

It is painful to write these things but more painful to conceal what I feel and I only wish it could have any effect.

William Robert Lee to Robert Cooper Lee

Hungerford, 26th September 1791

Sir,

At the arrival of your Letter I was absent from Hungerford and am sorry I was not present to have answered it before but the Letter not being sent to my Friends House where I was, I could not possibly answer it until my return. The above is a fair statement of my negligence and I'll give you a further Account of my Lodgings according to your desire. I give thirty Pounds a Year and when I am absent which is a few Months in the Year there is something allow'd. The Note you last sent me for which I'm exceedingly thankful has discharged all my Accounts. I shall now thank you for a remittance to discharge some small accounts and my Lodgings at the end of this Month as I have made an agreement. You will please to forward this Letter to my Mother and I beg my respects to Mrs Lee and Family the sooner your kind remittance is received it will much oblige your obedient Servant Robert Lee.

John Lee to Richard Lee

Kilkenny, 5th April 1792

Dear Richard,

I am sorry to be so troublesome correspondence to view, but a sudden change in my establishment obliges me to send a few lines, to request that you will receive a Draft for £30 which you will soon have presented to you by my late servant Osterman, who has lately dismiss'd me, thinking the Service of an Officer too low, and £60 per annum too small. The Pay master of this Regiment is now in Scotland, so that I have drawn for £21 on you. I am glad to find that you agree with me in respect to my military affairs. I expected to hear soon from an Army agent in Dublin, and make no doubt I shall soon find an opportunity of purchasing more reasonable than I mentioned to you last. I was much shock'd to find by your letter, the danger your father had been in, and I most sincerely hope he is by this time quite stout again. You must look to our poor Friend Bob Gordon, or he will certainly die of melancholy in his Fir groves. Remember me to all in the Square and believe me ever

Yours most sincerely John Lee.

John Lee to Richard Lee

New Geneva, 28th July 1792

Dear Richard,

You are the last of my correspondents from whom I should have expected such terrible neglect. I have repeatedly written to you, and have not heard a syllable from you since some time before I left Kilkenny. I console myself, however, with the idea that you are passing your time very pleasantly. If you should happen to visit "Le Coq's gay hotel" this summer, you will see a very fine girl there a Miss Dawson. I shall envy you all your excursions. I might as well be in Arabia as at this place, and yet they will not let us rest even in our misery, but are in hourly expectation of being order'd to Dublin to satisfy the flame of acursed Lieutenant-Colonel who thinks of selling his Commission to more advantage there. I made a party the other day to go to Cork and your favourite place Youghall. I called upon Waggets at Cork, and got £25 from him, with which I purchased a horse, and got drunk with the remainder, so that I must be under the disagreeable necessity of drawing for about the same sum at Waterford. I don't know if I ever mentioned to you that your Friend Jack Enery lives at Kilkenny with his Wife and children. He was frequently asking after you. Sneyd has asked me to pay him a visit at Ballyconnel, county Cavan, but I'm afraid it will be too far. Do for heaven's sake let me hear from you and Believe me

yours very sincerely John Lee.

Robert Cooper Lee to Richard Lee

Brighton, 20th August 1792

Dear Richard,

Your Statement of Mr Polson's Account was very satisfactory. Mr Portis tells me the Settlement will take Place the 28th and that the next continuation for October will not do more than give five per cent. I must take what I can get, and I will speak to Portis about it in the Course of the Week.

The Pacquet from Dieppe ought to have been in yesterday, but is not yet arrived. We expect some interesting Intelligence by her.

The Prince is down here, he graced the Rooms last Night, they were full of Company. The Duke and Duchess of York are to pay a Visit at the Pavilion on Wednesday, to stay till Saturday. Mr Wade's Ball on Friday is to be honoured with their Company. Grand Cricket Match is now playing, to last most part of the week.

Your Mother talks of going to Town on Wednesday with Favell, under the Escort of Scud, this will put off our Hampton Jaunt another week. Our kind regards to you and your Brother, and to our friend Embo. I am

Your truly Affectionate Robert Cooper Lee.

John Lee to Richard Lee

Dublin, 3rd March 1793

Dear Richard,

You have, I suppose, been so much taken up with business for some time past that you have not had time to answer any of the letters I have been continually writing to you since I arrived here. We have been in a state of confusion in this country, and I fear, are likely to be in a more disagreeable situation before long. The cursed Presbyterians are wishing to stir up the people of the North. Mr Butler and Mr Bond went to the House of Commons to be examined at the bar, on a charge of having publish'd seditious handbills etc. On the fact being clearly proved, they were both sent to prison. I hope they will be hanged. They talk much here of another Lord-Lieutenant being sent over. Is there any truth in it? We will now pass from Matters of State, to those of more private concerns. I am most terribly annoy'd at seeing the cursed fall of the Stocks, at a time when I should wish to make the most of it, on account of an opportunity of purchasing which I have some reason to expect soon. I don't know how I can manage. Those rascally 5 percents will never get up again. I was obliged to draw upon you for £25 on Wybrants. I shall take it as a particular favour if you will pay Punch Gregory for the Newspapers he was so good as to order over to me, and tell him that instead of the daily, it is become a monthly paper, owing to the negligence of the Newspaperman. I heard from Bob the other day, for the first time since I have been in Ireland. Let me hear from you. Remember me to all in Bedford Square and believe me

Yours sincerely John Lee.

The next letter, written to Richard on a short business trip to Holland and routed back to Bedford Square having missed him there, demonstrates that catastrophic banking failures are nothing new.

Robert Cooper Lee to Richard Lee

Bedford Square, 22 March 1793

My dear Richard,

You timed it exactly in getting to Helvoet the Day before the French retired from Williamstadt, so that you would be at Liberty to proceed immediately to view the Scene of Action and the glorious Effects of War. We flatter ourselves the Invasion of Holland is at an End, and that Breda and the other Places will be forthwith evacuated or retaken. The Report of a new Victory near Louvain wants Confirmation but I hope it is only a little premature. The French fleet sent out from Brest five Ships of the Line and eight Frigates; they were seen by the *Edgar* and *Bedford;* the former returned into Port, and there was some Fear for the *Bedford,* but she is now considered safe. Monsieur Marmel has received the French Premiers Assassination.

It is I think very well that you are only a small Merchant. The House of Burton Forbes and Gregory[247] stopped last Saturday, for more than a Million, they are since in the Gazette as Bankrupts, their Concession with Caldwell Smith and Cox's Bank at Liverpool is said to be the Cause. Gregson's Bank at Liverpool has also stopped. Heywoods is supported by poor Joe Denison and is likely to go on. Mr Watt brought up to Town with him from the former Banks one Bill for twenty thousand and the other for thirty thousand Pounds, to pay for Sir John Rushout's Estate at Harrow that he was about purchasing, both Bills refused. The Hull Bank and Harrisons their Banking House here stopped two days ago, likewise Mr Yeldam a Bank Director, Mr Willock, and Francis Willock (I suppose the Son) both in the Gazette. I wish the mischief may go no further. It is worse in Liverpool than at Bristol.

I am concerned to tell you our good Friend Mr Allen has been dangerously ill, with a violent Asthmatic Complaint. I had a Line from Mrs Allen yesterday dictated by himself. I trust the Danger is over. Mr William Gregory will forward this under cover to his Brother. Let us know when we may expect to see you. Mr May is in Town but I have not heard anything from him more than his Card. Macleod is come to Town to buy an Estate in Hampshire. Lord Mansfield died on Wednesday Evening.

All the Family are well and join in affectionate Regards to Gordon and yourself. Remember us all to Friends Dutch and English. I will make the Chairman's apology today, George Scott accompanys me.

Your truly Affectionate Robert Cooper Lee.

Robert Cooper Lee to Priscilla Lee

Castle Brighton, 24th June 1793

It is rather warmer here than in Town. We dined yesterday at Reigate and got here before nine o'clock, without the least Fatigue. The Castle was quite full with Families, but Mr Tilt very obligingly procured us Lodgings at Mr *Tilson's* North Street, where we found excellent Beds. In order to encourage the *Apothecary* Richard employed him for some Gargle, having made rather too much use of his Throat in eating a hearty Dinner. Our Habitation of last Year and likewise that General Townsend had are pre-

---

[247] Of Aldermanbury, London.

occupied, but there are plenty of Bills upon the Steyne. I have been with Mrs Piercy (the General's Landlady) over three of her Houses No.2 South Parade and No.11 North Parade, there is great Room in each the Price six Guineas till August, eight Guineas for August and September. No.12 North Parade is on a less Scale, like Mr Lee's No.9 which is inhabited. I leave it for you to determine. It rains a little now from the Westward, but I will look at some other Houses before we go. The Ellis Family is gone from hence to Worthing. Mr Douglas I saw this Morning he is in the Rockhouse. Mr and Mrs E. Clarke are in Russell's House where Mr R E Beckford was last Year. I see on Crawford's List Lord and Lady Cardigan, Lord Westcote, Mr Hume, General Dalrymple and many others. Richard has ordered plenty of Fish for Dinner. I am not determined what Route we shall take in our Return, but I hope for the Pleasure of finding you well, and recovered from the Fatigue of moving on Wednesday Morning, as I think we shall sleep somewhere on the Road tomorrow. Richard joins me in most affectionate Regards to you, and the Girls. I ever am Most truly Yours Robert Cooper Lee.

PS No News of the Prince's coming down to stay.

Robert Cooper Lee to Richard Lee

Brighton, 18th August 1793

Dear Richard,

The Cash Supply I desired will be in very good time on Thursday. Mr Plett's Excursion to Town is doubtful. I understood you by a former Letter that the settling day was to be the 15th or rather when the Mail arrived after that Day. Mr Bowes lodged yesterday my Power of Attorney to you for the Bank Stock. Pray bring with you from Lombard Street Mr Ross's India [illegible] Receipts, he having desired them to be sold and it is necessary I should disclose them. You have had a great deal of Trouble about Barnett's Bill on Jacks. He ought to have no Objection to depositing the Bill of Lading in the Hands of a third good Person of his own Nomination, in order to pay Mr Barnett's Bill in the first Instance, but I think he may insist on a literal Performance of the Indorsement.

I should have postponed our Matters of Business till we met, but for an unexpected Application from your Brother Robert 'to enable him to pay Bills delivered and unpaid amounting to nearly five hundred Pounds, for the greatest part of which he has given his Notes that become due almost immediately'. You have my answer herewith, and you will let your Brother have the Money.

We shall be happy to see you on Thursday; bring us good News. All join in kindest regards to you I am Dear Richard

Your truly affectionate Robert Cooper Lee.

Copy of Letter to your Brother

I wish it was convenient and right for me to send you the money you desire, without doing any more. Indeed your own Reflections will suggest every thing I can say upon the subject, yet I cannot but remind you how much this Mode of Anticipation must be ruinous to yourself, or injurious to the Rest of the Family. I trust there will be no Occasion for repeating it; there would be some Comfort in having Reason to think so. Your Brother who take the Trouble of my Matters while I am from town will do the necessary.

Bearing in mind that £500 in 1793 would have the purchasing power of over £45,000 now, Robert seems to have shown remarkable restraint.

John Lee to Richard Lee

Dublin, 15th September 1793

Dear Richard,

It is so long since I heard from you, that I begin to be apprehensive lest the Turtle should have disagreed with you. I think I can give the tolerably good guess at your amusements and occupations at this season of the year. I frequently regret that I am not of your parties, rather than lounge about the gloomy streets of Dublin. We have just received an order to march from this place in a few days to some country quarter, to relieve the Regiments under orders for embarkation. You shall hear from me when we march, and in the mean time I will trouble you to beg Punch Gregory to stop the Newspapers.

There are a great many about to be raised in England. I had the offer of a Majority in one of them, but the conditions were much above the standard of my finances. I was to give up the purchase money of my Company and £2000 in addition. All these new corps will certainly be reduced the end of the war. Lewis will have fifty opportunities of serving anyone he chooses to speak for, and I have a great mind to mention the circumstance to your father. The Stocks wear a very pleasing aspect at present. Every thing goes on very quietly here. The Militia is getting on very fast. I am question'd almost every day about Gregory's selling out, and obliged to confess myself as much in the dark as everyone here. How soon does he mean to come to this country? Remember me to all Friends and believe me ever

Yours very sincerely John Lee.

Until reforms instituted by the Duke of York in 1795 which brought in minimum periods of service required before progressing to the next rank, officers purchased their promotions the cost of which varied according to the regiment in question. The money for the purchase was usually lodged with the Regimental Agent together with initial Letters of Recommendation. For someone to progress to Major it was necessary for his rank of Lieutenant to be sold on to someone else (who could be in a different regiment). The new Major then paid the difference between what he had first paid and the cost of a majority in that particular regiment. The soldier whose rank was being purchased did not receive the money directly as it was all held by the Agents until he either sold out or was pensioned off. Abuses and inefficiencies in the purchase system resulted in the quality of officers depending not on ability but on wealth and influence. John Lee was not completely without either, but neither was he ideally placed for promotion. As a result his next correspondence comes from the force being sent to capture Martinique from the French.

John Lee to Robert Cooper Lee

Carlisle Bay, Barbadoes, 10th January 1794

Dear Sir,

I arrived at this place the day before yesterday after a very pleasant voyage of six weeks and three days. Our passage would have been much shorter (at least by five or six days) if we had not been obliged to go a great way out of our course, and stand in, as near as we could, for the coast of Portugal, in order to see the 12th Light Dragoons safe off the Straits of Gibraltar in their way to Toulon. Our fleet, which consisted of 40 sail of Transports, one seventy four, and one frigate were entirely dispersed in the night by a heavy gale of wind, in about the latitude of the Azores, the gale continuing for two days after, our ships were so scattered that from that time we never saw them till our arrival here, where we found only three vessels in before us. We were fortunate in meeting the Trade winds much sooner than is normally the case, from about a degree to the northward of Madeira we steer'd a direct course for this island, and never had occasion to shift a sale during the whole passage. The only occurrence that happened was our falling in with a vessel off Palma, when both of us feeling bold, we immediately clear'd for action, but were happy to find on coming nearer that we were friends. She was an armed Ship of Greenock bound for Jamaica. On my arrival here, going on board the *Bayne* to wait on Sir Charles Grey, I was much surprised to meet Matt Scott the first person I saw on the quarterdeck. He is now first Lieutenant, the Lieutenant above him having been appointed to the command of the Frigate on this station, the yellow fever having made a vacancy for him. Matt Scott it is expected will very soon be promoted to the command of the *Sans culottes* a French privateer mounting 20 guns lately taken by the *Blanche* Frigate. I was advised, on leaving Ireland, to wear flannel under waistcoats in this country, and tho' I find them the most disagreeable things in the world, I still keep them on. We are fortunate in the season, for I have not found the heat by any means so great as I expected. I daresay I shall form another opinion when we land at Martinique. Sir Charles Grey is much hurt at part of the Army destined for this expedition, being sent to St Malo. But he says that we have still enough to do everything required of us. The young Count Mochambeau, the Governor of Martinique gives out that he is perfectly prepared for us. As our ships are coming in very fast, we shall soon put him to the trial. You have before this, I daresay, have heard that the Jamaica expedition against Santa Domingo has been very successful. General Williamson has taken several places, and is well supported by the Royalists. The Fleet here, I make no doubt, will be equal to that which the French have in these seas. Captain Scott, of the *Sans culottes*, will not be the last to distinguish himself. Our land force consists of about 8 or 9000 men besides a strong Detachment of Artillery.

I left Ireland at a time very favourable for promotion, but, I trust, I shall be able to succeed in my absence.

I hope to inform you more of the situation of our affairs and our prospects, when we arrive at Martinique.

Pray present my best respects to Mrs Lee and kindest remembrances to all at Bedford Square, and believe me Dear Sir

Yours very sincerely John Lee.

While John was fighting for his country in flannel waistcoat in the Caribbean, his cousin Matthew precipitated a family crisis that would reverberate down the next decade and a half.

Some time in 1793 he had met Fanny Dashwood. Rachael Frances Antonina Dashwood was the illegitimate daughter of Sir Francis Dashwood (he of the Hellfire Club) and the actress Mrs Fanny Barry. Together with her brother Francis, two years older than her, she had enjoyed an idyllic early childhood at West Wycombe Park, the much loved and spoiled only daughter of her father. He died when she was seven and on the 27th of May 1784 two and a half years after the death of Sir Francis Dashwood, Fanny Barry married Sir Archibald Murray at St Marylebone. Interestingly in the parish register Fanny Barry is referred to as a 'spinster' rather than a widow suggesting that either she was never married to Mr Barry or she was air-brushing her past.

According to her daughter the new husband was an honest man placed by circumstance in a rather 'obscure situation' and was related in some way to the Duke of Atholl. In all her references to her mother's marriage Fanny was disparaging about her drop in social status and hinted that as 'she had precipitately placed herself in a worldly situation that was beneath that in which she hoped to see R.F.A. her pride and wounded feelings might sometimes urge her to speak and act harshly'[248] Whether this was true or whether her mother was simply exasperated by her daughter's attitude to her new stepfather is not clear. Fanny's later claims to a legitimate position in society were to some extent frustrated by her mother's refusal ever to discuss her own background and family with her daughter, who apparently never knew who her mother really was. The refusal to acknowledge her more humble origins and her career on the stage may have been intended to protect her daughter from worldly censure but the absence of information on the subject led young Fanny to fantasise mysterious aristocratic origins for her mother for which there is no evidence. She even hinted that there might be a connection with the Duke of Marlborough.[249] She also wasted much time and effort in later years attempting to prove that her parents had been married.

For a short time Fanny lived with her mother and stepfather near Edgware, until at the age of about ten she was sent to France to continue her education in a convent. She later wrote with great affection of the woman who befriended her there and 'devoted what time she could steal

---

248 *Memoirs of R.F.A.*, 1812, p.11
249 Ibid, p.10

from the duties of her situation, to the cultivation of my mind'. From her she learned a liberality of thought, and history, philosophy and Latin. She also encountered someone who was willing to meet Fanny's religious scepticism calmly and to provide her with reading material designed to enable her to form her own opinions. Fanny conceived a desire to learn from 'reflection and experience' rather than by rote, which perhaps indicates a rather undisciplined side to her character. There is no doubt that she had considerable intelligence (she taught herself Hebrew) and she was also very musical, capable of dramatic improvisations on the organ.

With the outbreak of the French Revolution Fanny returned to England and for a time boarded with the Honourable Mrs Gordon, a well-connected widow, in Kensington Square. There is no doubt that Fanny was a great beauty like her mother and at the age of fifteen while staying in Bath she became 'entangled' with a Mr F. described by her as a 'son of Lord F.' and brother to the Duchess of Athol.[250]. Her mother broke off this intended marriage on the grounds of her youth and took Fanny away to Hastings. Here she similarly prevented an unsuitable alliance with a Mr B. 'son of the Judge'[251]. Perhaps her mother found Fanny too much of a handful or perhaps Sir Archibald was already ill, at any event after her brother's marriage in July 1793 Fanny went to live with Francis and his wife Lady Isabel Anne Maitland.

The most likely explanation for what happened next lies in the desire of both Fanny Dashwood and Matthew Lee for financial independence. Matthew was very good looking, but without fortune and tired of constant rows with his father over money, Fanny was beautiful and believed to be heir to a considerable fortune that she felt she should be able to access.

In February 1794 Matthew and Fanny eloped to Scotland.

---

[250] Marjory Forbes was the second wife of the Duke of Atholl and sister to the four sons of the sixteenth Lord Forbes, this suggests that the young man in question was Robert, Andrew or William Forbes, two of whom were dead by 1807.

[251] Probably a son of Sir William Blackstone (1723-80) author of *Commentaries on the Laws of England*..

Robert Cooper Lee to Matthew Allen Lee

Bedford Square, 7th February 1794

Dear Matthew,

It is only a few Days ago that I heard you were living at Limmer's Hotel. Your Brother initimated to the Family your Intention of appearing in Bedford Square the 22nd of last Month. We expected you, but were disappointed. I am quite at a Loss to judge what can have induced you to desert your Family and your Father's House. I can say nothing new on this very unpleasant Subject. The sooner you return Home the better let me know what Money you want. Your Brother or myself will furnish you with any thing reasonable. Have I ever refused you any thing? I am still

Your Affectionate Robert Cooper Lee

John Lee, campaigning in Martinique, was unaware of the drama unfolding in London.

John Lee to Robert Cooper Lee

Martinique, Camp Sourier, 3rd March 1794

Dear Sir,

I have been long waiting for an opportunity of writing to you, but only two ships have sail'd to England since I wrote last, and I did not hear of them till after their departure. The best chance we stand is by sending by the Frigate which will go with dispatches.

We left Barbadoes on the 3rd of February in 3 Divisions and had a very short and safe passage to this island. Matt Scott being made Master and Commander a few days before, and commanding a Ship of War, was appointed Major of one of the 3 Battalions of Sailors, which were formed to act on this occasion. Sir Charles Grey with the greater part of the Army landed near St Etienne without the smallest opposition. I was with that division under the command of General Dundas. We landed at Trinity, and after a slight action with Bellegarde, the Negro chief, in which he was put to flight, we took possession of the town and Fort of La Trinité. Mr Bellegarde however, had left two or three Negroes in the town with orders to set fire to some matches and trains he had left in his own house, if the English should take the place, so that in the middle of the night we discover'd the town in flames, and before any kind of assistance could be given, three fourths of the town was in ashes. We still pursued him in his flight, and did not stop till we came within three miles of Fort Bourbon, or Fort de la Constitution as they call it. They made a sortie in the night and attacked a post of ours, but were soon repulsed. Their army consists of Negroes and gens de couleurs who as soon as they find themselves hard-pressed, have always thrown down their arms and fled to the woods. Our whole Army have been provided with flannel shirts and drawers, both men and officers, and I am persuaded it has been of infinite advantage in preserving the health of the troops in keeping off the cold and damps of the night after a long march in the heat of the day. I have not had the slightest illness and bear the heat much better than I expected. We traversed the island without seeing any white person scarcely. They are all driven from the country and are gone to Dominica and other islands.

We went next to St Pierre, the largest and most flourishing town in the island. They made some stand here, and might if they had the least courage have kept us out a long time. But we were fortunate in our guides and came upon them when they did not expect us. After staying a day before the place the town surrender'd and the black troops under Bellegarde and Grandmaison retreated to Fort Bourbon. We remain'd three days in St Pierre, and I never was more pleased with the appearance of any place. After a little fighting we have driven them all into Fort Bourbon, and we have opened our batteries upon them this morning at six O'Clock. From all appearances the siege will prove a short one. Prince Edward arrived here three days ago, and took the command of a part of the army. I hope I may be as successful in Europe, as we have been in these parts. I have not yet heard from the commanding Officer of the 44th respecting the Majority in that corps, but should I fail in that quarter, I think I may hope for success in another part. If we, who are abroad, have all the glory, then officers who remained at home have the profit and advantages.

I hope soon to write to you from Fort Royal, and to give you an account of the riches of this island.

Pray present my best respects to Mrs Lee, who I hope has had her health perfectly well, and kindest remembrances to all in Bedford Square. I am Dear Sir

yours very sincerely John Lee.

The next letter, written when news of the elopement had reached Bedford Square, is a moving testament to the loving marriage that Robert Cooper Lee had himself experienced.

Robert Cooper Lee to Matthew Allen Lee

Bedford Square, 4th March 1794

My dear Matthew,

I hope for the satisfaction of hearing from you by to morrow's Post, to say how far you are got, and the Road you take and I shall anxiously expect the glad Tidings of your perfect Happiness by the indissoluble Knot. May you both long enjoy the pleasing Society of each other. Your first Duty as well as Inclination will I trust be ever in your Mind, to make the Object of your Affection happy by Affection and Constancy without giving the least Cause or appearance of Cause for Jealousy. I recommend you not to say anything to anyone of the Rise and Progress of the happy Connexion. It will be enough to say you have had the Happiness of gaining the Lady's Hand and Heart, with the perfect Approbation of her near Relations. Make the most Affectionate Respects of your Mother Sister and myself to your fair betrothed, and assure her of our constant and sincerest Regard. We all join in kindest Love to you. I am My dear Matthew

Your truly affectionate Robert Cooper Lee.

Robert Cooper Lee to Matthew Allen Lee

Bedford Square, 7th March 1794

My dear Matthew,

You will I am sure anticipate our most cordial Congratulations to your amiable Bride and yourself upon the happy Union that we conclude has before this time taken Place, and our warmest Wishes that you long, very long enjoy together the most perfect happiness.

I have had the Pleasure to receive your letters from Stilton and from Durham. I can hardly wish you have been so expeditious as to reach Edinburgh on Thursday; it would be too fatiguing. I flatter myself Mr Allen would be ready to receive you with his usual Kindness, and that he would be present at the Ceremony. He will introduce you to Sir James [Stirling] Mr James Wedderburn and other Friends. Mrs Grant you know, and I believe her Brother Mr MacLeod Bannatyne – Colbecks and his Lady will not be backward in their attentions.

Your Mother and Frances desire their affectionate Regards with mine to our new Relation, whom we cannot sufficiently express how highly we esteem for her attachment to you, and how desirous we are of being personally known to her. I ever am My dear Matthew

Your truly affectionate Robert Cooper Lee.

PS Your Letters to Gordon and Richard will be highly acceptable; the latter is still at Colworth House[252]. I wish you to drop two Lines to W. Gregory. Our constant Toast is our Friends in the North.

John Lee to Richard Lee

Heights of Sourier, Martinique, 8th March 1794

Dear Richard,

I have this instant heard of the Packett sailing to England, which is the first opportunity I've had of writing since I have been in this island.

We made two different landings at the same time, one at St Etienne and the other La Trinité with scarcely any opposition. We were very fortunate in our guides, especially Mr Soter, who had been at the head of the Royalist party before we came to the Island and had beat them in several encounters. We came upon them unawares in their strongest holds, and drove them before us. The great rival in command of Mr Rochambeau, is a Negro chief, Bellegarde and 'tis said that just before we landed, there was Plan formed by the blacks and gens de couleur to murder all the whites in the island. They have so much the upper hand, that they do any thing with them they choose. They attack'd us at an out post near Fort Bourbon in the night, but were repulsed with loss. They attempted to make a stand at St Pierre but were soon obliged to leave the town to surrender at discretion and fled in the greatest confusion to Fort Royal, leaving behind very considerable stores of all kinds, and a quantity of shipping.

During the three weeks or months we have been on shore, we have not once slept under cover, yet I never knew troops in better health, which I think is to be attributed entirely to the flannel cloathing which was given out to the whole Army on their coming to the West Indies.

---

252 Home of William Lee Antonie

Prince Edward arrived here the day before yesterday and went immediately to Care Navires to take the command of the division of the Army there. Our batteries open'd this morning at 6 o'clock, and in 12 hours nearly destroy'd an advanced work. The explosion of one of their magazines by the falling of a shell was the occasion of it. We have had very little loss on our side. An unlucky 24 pounder killed 3 men and wounded 2 more last night, which is, I think, the most considerable loss we have had since we broke ground.

Have you heard from Ireland respecting the Majority? I have seen some of the new promotions in the English papers. If I don't succeed in the 44th Regiment I hope we shall be able to accomplish the business [torn] I would give any sum that I have [torn] this opportunity.

After my bearing the heat of this climate so well, I think Bob Gordon may venture to Jamaica. I will write to him from Fort Bourbon. Remember me to Friends and believe me ever

Yours very sincerely John Lee.

Robert Cooper Lee to Matthew Allen Lee

Bedford Square, 13th March 1794

My dear Matthew,

Your very interesting and welcome Letter of Monday last gives me again Occasion to express my sincere Joy, and congratulation upon your present happy Situation. Say every thing kind and affectionate for us to your beloved Partner, and may it ever be your greatest Pleasure to make her truly happy.

Mr Allen would soon be with you after your Arrival, having he writes Mee being upon my Watch, in consequence of my Letters to him. I have written to Mr Dashwood and shall pay my Compliments and Thanks in Leicester Square to morrow on Saturday I go for Bath from thence to Burton on Trent and so home. I shall be absent a tour 10 days. On my Return I will consult on the speediest Means for adjusting Matthew, and smoothing the Way for your return to this Kingdom, and in which I think there will be little difficulty. My Letters for you under Mr Allen's Cover you will have received. With our most tender and kindest Regards to both I am

Your truly affectionate Robert Cooper Lee

PS the Cheeses came safe. One of them in your name to your Godmother.

On the reverse of this letter Frances had written

Accept my dear Matthew of the *heartfelt* Congratulations and best Wishes of Your affectionate Sister and faithful Friend Frances Lee.

Robert Cooper Lee to Matthew Allen Lee

Bedford Square, 17th March 1794

My dear Matthew,

Your Letter of the 10th is the last I have had the Pleasure of receiving. Mr Allen wrote to me the next Day. I know you would have many Letters to write. Your mother and Sister paid their Respects to Lady Murray yesterday, having previously exchanged Cards and Notes. I should have been of the Party, but was prevented by an Attack of the Gout that began on Thursday Evening; it promises to be slight and regular the same Cause disappointed my Intention of waiting on Lord Lauderdale and Major Maitland[253]. Lady Murray mentioned that the latter and Mr Dashwood are gone North. Mr Dashwood may possibly have called here and I not know it. I hope to be out in three or four Days. Make our kindest regards to our justly esteemed Daughter, and be assured that I ever am her's and

Your truly affectionate Robert Cooper Lee.

On the reverse of this letter Matthew wrote: '17 March '94 My dearest Father's last Letter to me'.

In the early hours of the 20th of March 1794 Robert Cooper Lee suddenly died.

His obituary notice in *The Times* read:

On Thursday morning, in Bedford-square, Robert Cooper Lee Esq. He had lately a slight attack of the gout, from which he thought himself recovering, but was seized with a fit in the night, which carried him off in a few hours.

---

[253] Brothers of Francis Dashwood's wife.

He was buried with his brother Joseph in the vault he had created at St Mary's, Barnes.

He had probably not received any of the letters describing John's exploits, and John would not hear of his death until sometime afterwards.

John Lee to Robert Cooper Lee

Fort Royal, Martinique, 24th March 1794

Dear Sir,

Our labours in this island ended yesterday. A Flag of Truce was sent in, and the Patriots surrendered themselves prisoners of war. They are to march out of Fort Bourbon tomorrow, from there proceed on board ships, which have been provided for them, and sent to Europe, it is supposed.

Fort Royal was taken possession of the day before, and Prince Edward had the command of 4 Battalions who took possession of the Gates of the Fortress yesterday. I never saw such complete ruins as the buildings in Fort Louis. The Stores of different kinds, but particularly military stores, were found in very great abundance in this Fort, and 'tis said that Fort Bourbon is equally well supplied. The latter place is universally allowed to be by far the strongest place in these parts and inferior to very few in Europe. I never saw such a beautiful country, as I have, throughout the whole of this island. The climate is much milder than I could have imagined, and if I was to remain in the West Indies, I would not go further than this Island to seek for habitation. In the course of a few days it is expected, we shall sail to Guadeloupe and St Lucie which I believe will terminate our campaign.

The sailors have had a great share in this expedition by assisting in bringing up our Artillery. We should have had great trouble and inconvenience without them. Our cannon were brought over hills, where the French thought it almost impossible for them to march. Our bad success at Toulon and other parts on the Continent put the Patriots here in spirits for a short time, but they soon found it necessary to think of their own safety. The greater part of the troops in the Fort were blacks, who were absolutely chain'd to the Guns they were working against us. The most inveterate part are the gens de couleur, and I am persuaded that if proper steps had not been taken to transport them to Europe, they would make this a very disagreeable quarter, even after the conquest is completed.

I hope to date my next letter from another island and I trust we shall be as successful as we have been here as this has been considered as the great strength of the French in this quarter.

Pray present my best respects to Mrs Lee who, I hope is perfectly well, and my best compliments to all the Family. I am Dear Sir

Yours very sincerely John Lee.

The 70th Regiment did successfully take the islands they had been sent to capture, but despite their flannel underwear they lost more men to yellow fever than to the campaign. By October 1794 only nine men in the whole regiment were fit for duty[254]. John returned with the regiment to England and in early 1795 was briefly back in London.

His cousin Richard meanwhile was enduring one of the most difficult years of his life. The whole burden of the family now fell on his shoulders notwithstanding that his older brother Robert might have been expected to take charge.

Robert Cooper Lee's Will was written just under a year before he died and was proved on the 10th of April 1794 giving administration to Richard and John Allen as executors. Robert's first care had been for Priscilla to whom he left all his personal effects, furniture, plate, jewels, trinkets, books, linen, clothes, liquors, carriages and horses and an immediate payment of three hundred pounds so that she would not be without ready cash. She was then provided with an annuity of five hundred pounds a year for life payable half yearly. Frances was left two thousand pounds invested at four percent and secured free from the control of any husband she might subsequently marry, but inheritable by any of her children (becoming increasingly unlikely as she was now thirty-five and still unmarried), and a further three thousand to be invested for her by the executors. Over and above this Robert had been managing another fifteen hundred pounds for Frances that was now to be given over to her. Robert Lee 'now chiefly residing in the County of Leicester' was left four thousand pounds invested at four percent and a further thousand on the death of his mother. Richard received the same amounts with the additional injunction that, as his father's business partner, any money owing to or by Robert's estate should be properly accounted for and settled up.

---

[254] http://www.queensroyalsurreys.org.uk/1661to1966/martinique/martinique.html

Matthew was to receive three thousand pounds invested in the four percents and a further thousand on Priscilla's death. The dreadful irony of this of course was that if Matthew *had* just married Fanny Dashwood for her money, he now had much less need of it. Scudamore was still a minor and so his three thousand pounds was held in trust, with money provided for his education and maintenance, and he too was to receive a further thousand on Priscilla's death when the principal would no longer be needed to fund her annuity. Fourteen year old Favell was still at school at the Misses Olier in Bloomsbury Square and she was left two thousand pounds, with a further three thousand set aside for her education and maintenance. As with Frances this inheritance was to be given to Favell on her majority for her sole use 'free from the debts or contract of any husband' – the experience of poor Mary Charlotte Lee had cast a long shadow.

Among the minor legatees John Lee and his brother William Robert each received a hundred pounds, Mary Charlotte Morley (now Mrs Isaac Parmenter) and her sister Frances received lifetime annuities of thirty pounds a year, and Robert's widowed cousin Sophia Sayer who was living in St Albans was given fifty pounds. Mary Powell Royall, John Allen, Robert Home Gordon and Charles Causton were each given twenty guineas to buy mourning rings and his clerk James Bowes received fifty guineas. Elizabeth Harrison 'who has lived in my family for many years' was given twenty pounds a year for life (worth about £20,000 compared with average wages today).

Robert still owned property in Jamaica and he left instructions that 'all and every my messuages plantations lands tenements slaves and hereditaments and parts and shares of messuages plantations lands tenements slaves and hereditaments situate and being in the said Island of Jamaica' should be left in trust to Richard Lee and John Allen to sell as and when they thought proper, with the result added to his estate and from which all debts should be paid. Half the residue was to be divided equally between Frances, Robert and Richard with the other half of the residue invested and on the first of February 1801, when Favell came of age, divided equally between Matthew, Scudamore and Favell. Scudamore Winde's estate at Fencott[255] in Herefordshire also formed part of the inheritance of the three older Lees. Richard and John Allen were

[255] Now called Fencote

appointed as guardians of Scudamore and Favell, and in addition Priscilla and Frances were also made guardians of Favell. Robert Cooper Lee had done everything he could to provide for Priscilla during her lifetime and to deal equably with his children.

In a codicil Robert had added legacies of three hundred pounds each for Scudamore Winde's grandchildren, the children of Robert Winde of Botolph Lane East Cheap, and of Penelope Steel, payable if and when they reached the age of twenty one.

For the young boy who had left England with only a parcel of ribbons forty-five years earlier Robert Cooper Lee had done well - his estate was worth something over £30,000, equivalent to about two and three quarter million now, using the retail price index, or over thirty one million compared with average wages.

However his optimism that Matthew's hasty marriage, which had taken place at Haddington on the 9th of March, could be smoothed over both socially and legally was to prove unfounded.

Matthew Allen Lee to Richard Lee

York, 6th April 1794

My dear Richard,

Your very kind Letter I received this Morning together with the copy of one to Mr Allen. I am sorry our Affairs wear so unfavourable an Appearance, as I had hoped little difficulty would have arisen in the Arrangement, and that the Opinion was strengthened by Mr A's Concurrence together with that of my beloved fathers. In a Letter from him he says 'I will consult on the speediest Means of adjusting Matters and smoothing the Wafer your Return to this Kingdom and in which I think there will be little difficulty'.

You may well conceive the Suspense I am under occasioned by the different Opinion of Mr Halliday and Dashwood.

The Agreement I sent you was drawn up by my poor Father and is in his Writing. There evidently I stand as Tenant for Life, but I fear Dashwood has not thoroughly comprehended what Mr A. suggested, he thinks a certain sum of money should *not* be in Trust. The Meaning as I conceive it is simply this "That tho' the Money is not absolutely in Trust, nevertheless *I should consider myself bound to account for its Expenditure*" did it strike you so?

Till I hear further from you or Dashwood I know not how to proceed therefore as I have stated every thing I could, I cannot now think of trespassing on your patience unnecessarily.

Heaven preserve you My dear Richard. Pray make my kindest Love at home and tell them how I long to embrace them. Adieu and believe me

Your Affectionate and obliged Brother MA Lee.

PS the tender Letters of Fanny and Miss Dickson I will acknowledge tomorrow. They have penetrated my very soul.

I am writing to Dashwood.

William Robert Lee to Richard Lee

Hungerford, 10th April 1794

Dear Sir,

Receiving a letter from Mr Thomas he inform'd me you wished to know my situation, I am in lodgings and board which cost thirty five Pounds per Year, the business I served my time to, there is scarce enough for the Master to do in the Country. I should have been in Mourning but not hearing from any of the Family I did not know until Mr Thomas inform'd me, my situation in another point I assure you is very bad, I hired a Horse and going on the Turnpike Road it started threw me off broke his nees and injured him in several places, the Man is going out of the Town in a few Days and wishes to have the remainder of the Money which is eight Guineas if you will please to except a Draft drawn in a Day or two as the Man is going away shall be very thankful least I should be punished by any confinement or other troubles, my Doctors Bill is between fourteen and fifteen, and Mr Church for Shirts and Clothes is near thirteen, besides something to Shoemaker and Taylor, if you will be obliging to settle it I shall be very thankful, for it has been dew some little time. Possibly the Person might it tomorrow or next Day I beg you will please to except the Draft if I should draw for that Sum for I assure you I dreaded [illegible] the matter I have received many expensive misfortunes by Horse and Doctors bills and thank God I hope never to have more. I cannot help mentioning that I trust you will be so friendly as to except the Draft, for there might not be time for me to have your answer. Dear Sir I hope the Family are pretty well.

Your Obedient Servant Robert Lee.

Although John Allen was a co-executor and joint guardian, he was mainly living in Scotland and also he was not well. In August 1794 he wrote to Richard from Harrogate, for on their return from Scotland Matthew had found himself clapped up in the Fleet prison for marrying an under age heiress without the permission of her trustees!

John Allen to Richard Lee

Queen's Head, Harrogate, 30 August 1794

It was with Concern my dear Richard that in the newspaper the other Day I observed the Commitment of our Friend Matthew, but from the Circumstance of its being, not to the Fleet, but only "to the Custody of the Warden of the Fleet", I am hopefull that the Matter has been nothing very serious, probably some slight Fine and commitment till paid in, deformity with the Rules of Court, be so kind as explained to me this Affair and let us know how all our Friends your way are especially the Ladies at Ramsgate and what is become of, or is to be done with Scudamore for the ensuing Winter etc. I am sorry to observe the great Fall of Sugars, which must affect many of our Friends. Pray are the Papers respecting Rose Hall gone to Jamaica with full Instructions?

Since I last wrote you I have made some considerable Progress in the Way of Recovery, tho' still but poorly. I have been at this Place about a Week only, so cannot form any decided Opinion how far the Waters are likely to have any salutary Effect upon me, the Weather is now begun to be wet and likely I fear to continue rather unfavourable so that I think we shall not be here beyond Eight or Ten Days further. Mean while direct for me Queen's Head Harrowgate. My Course from hence will be strait Home, should you not be able to write within the time I have mention'd

Mrs Allen joins me in best Wishes, and I am very truly yours J Allen.

A bundle of bills incurred by his brother Robert have been preserved with the letters and it seems that Richard, as executor, had also asked his elder brother for an account of his financial position. With the bills is a settlement account for Robert in relation to his father's estate which shows a large number of outstanding debts paid out of the estate and the interest due to Robert on the remainder of his investments between March 1794 and March 1795. From this point onwards, particularly as he spent much time out of town, presumably living partly at the expense of others, Robert seems to have controlled his expenditure rather better.

It is obvious that Robert was not someone who paid his bills as soon as he received them. An account from T.Mobbs at his 'Hatt, Hose and Glove Manufactory', No.373 Oxford Street, listed items from the end of 1786 to the middle of 1791. They included dress silk hose (never fewer than two pairs and often as many as twelve at a time) pattent (sic) silk hose, black silk hose, best coloured silk hose, white ribbed silk hose, real pattent worsted hose, two pair sox (sic), two pair doeskin gloves and a 'round Hat for Groom'. Several of the orders were for 'outsize' hose, though whether these were for Robert who we know was tall, or possibly his servant, is not clear. The total outstanding came to nearly fifty pounds.

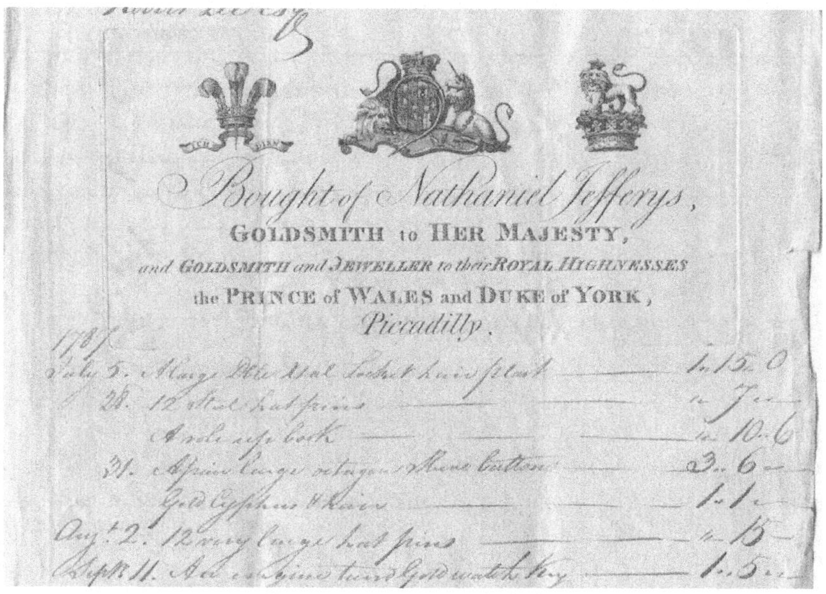

Bought of Nathaniel Jefferys,
GOLDSMITH to HER MAJESTY,
and GOLDSMITH and JEWELLER to their ROYAL HIGHNESSES
the PRINCE of WALES and DUKE of YORK,
Piccadilly.

Bill from Nathaniel Jefferys

The unpaid account with Nathaniel Jefferys[256], the royal jeweller, also ran from 1787 and included numerous lavish items not all of which it can safely be assumed were for Robert himself – a large Double Crystal Locket with plait Hair (we don't know whose!) was presumably a gift for a

[256] Robert was not the only customer of Nathaniel Jefferys to run up large bills on account, and in 1806 Jefferys published 'A Review of the Conduct of the Prince of Wales in His Various Transactions with Mr. Jefferys, During a Period of More Than Twenty Years' an exposé of the Prince and Princess of Wales and Mrs Fitzherbert and a decade of unpaid bills. Jefferys was very nearly ruined by his royal patrons.

lady as perhaps was a 'role up red Book with Silver lock'. The two large octagonal crystal sleeve buttons cost £3 6s and there was 'An Engine Turned Gold Watch Key' at £1 5s and repairs to a Gold Watch Chain – which implies that he had lost the former and broken the latter. Judging by the number of repairs to Robert's clothes and various other items he was somewhat careless of his possessions.

A pair of neat silver boot buckles cost 9s 6d, and an ivory lip salve box 2s 6d. There were numerous ornamental buttons and buckles, and a further purchase of a double crystal locket in 1788. Repairs to jet buckles cost him 6s and he bought a 'Sandal Wood Almanack mounted with Gold' for £3 10s. A Sandal Wood Pincushion with steel ornaments, costing £2 18s might have been a present for a lady, but men did use pins too[257].

A steel sword cost Robert eight guineas, and a decorative white sword knot was four shillings with a sword hook and chain at 7s 6d. A pair of large oval gold wires with beads at 8s 6d sounds like another present for a lady, whereas a gold shirt pin was probably for Robert himself. There were several more repairs to buckles to be paid for, and a sandalwood toothpick case which cost 18s on the 18th of March 1790 went in for repairs less than ten days later at a cost of two shillings. A 'Gold Box 2 Openings lin'd with Ivory' cost four guineas and even more expensive was a pair of buckles that cost £4 18s. The total outstanding on this bill was £47 8s, but there was a note to indicate that credit was given for 10 buttons which reduced the amount by twelve shillings.

A smaller bill covering the period 1785 to 1790 was for the cleaning and re-lining of hats and the renewing of hatbands by James Sack. It is no wonder this was required since the use of powder and pomatum[258] on the hair must have rapidly rendered hats quite unpleasant. Pomades were worn by both sexes, and it is clear that Robert Lee was a liberal user, although he also wore his hair powdered, a fashion that was about to come to an end. His account with the Perfumer William Walker, which ran from 1788 to 1793, included both superfine hair powder, and plain and rose scented pomatum. Mr Walker also sold Robert tooth brushes by the dozen, a tongue scraper, a nail brush, a French Wash Ball, hair ribbon

[257] Steel pins rusted easily so when not in use they were pushed into a pincushion filled with emery powder, bran or wool to keep them shiny.

[258] Pomatum, or pomade, was the hair gel of its day, so called because the original recipes often included pulped apples, which must indeed have left the wearer smelling ripe. By the eighteenth century it was made of bear or other animal fat, lard or wax and was often perfumed.

and hair pins, a pair of French Irons (presumably for hair curling), and a fine silk puff. Moreover he was also a hairdresser and there are repeated entries for hair cutting at five shillings a time and hair dressing costing two shillings and sixpence. The total outstanding on this account was £33 9s 6d.

It is when we come to the bills of John Bray, the tailor, however that we see Robert in all his finery. Two scarlet Tambour (embroidered) waistcoats lappelled; a superfine mixed cloth Frock coat; a pair of best fine sage colour kerseymere[259] breeches unlined with covered buttons; a white velvet collar to a mixed cloth Frock; a superfine brown cloth Frock lappelled; a Tambour kerseymere waistcoat lappelled and single breasted; superfine green breeches unlined with covered buttons; a superfine green cloth Frock; superfine Buff breeches unlined with covered buttons.

Unlike the three quarter length coats of his father's youth with their wide cuffs, huge pockets and heavy pleats at the back, these frock coats for Robert were lighter and had wide lapels and high collars dipping to a point at the back, with the coat cut away at the front and narrower pleats at the back. It is clear from these bills however, that the most colourful expression of fashion was the waistcoat. A double-breasted waistcoat would fasten with two rows of buttons covered in the same fabric as the garment, or perhaps expensive polished steel or crystal buttons and might be laced or tied at the back for a tighter fit. Bright colours, elaborate weaves, and embroidery all featured - the days of Beau Brummell's trousers, plain dark coats, and white shirts had not yet arrived. Breeches would have reached to just below the knee where they fastened over the stockings with buckles or perhaps half a dozen buttons on the outside seam and were decorated with a bunch of lace or ribbon ties at the bottom of the fastening, sometimes elaborated with 'puffs'. The breeches were becoming increasingly close fitting and fastened at the front with a buttoned flap. During the day boots were worn and for evening wear leather shoes with decorative buckles or softer dancing pumps. Hats were essential, gloves were always carried if not worn, and swords could be worn for decoration rather than function.

Occasionally items were repaired rather than discarded, such as the repair of a brown cloth frock coat and seven buttons, and repairs and sewing on two and a half dozen buttons to twelve different waistcoats, and for

---

[259] Kerseymere was a fine woollen cloth with a fancy twill weave originating from Kersey in Suffolk.

repairs and ten buttons for kerseymere breeches. How ever did he manage to lose so many buttons?

There were orders for waistcoats in striped muslin and brown silk tambour, two pairs of fine Nankeen breeches lined and with strings at the knee. To protect his clothes when his hair was being powdered there was a fine printed cotton powdering wrapper. There were corduroy breeches lined with leather; a livery drab surtout coat double breasted and faced with the same, with double capes and a collar; unlined breeches with plated buttons, green puffs and strings – and so it goes on with more than thirty items for the year 1788 alone totalling £68 18s. In 1789 there are coats in green, maroon and mottled silk, more waistcoats in striped Baggatelle and spotted kerseymere, breeches in buff and dark green kerseymere, a fustian jacket and a fine linen dressing apron, and rich silk Florentine breeches faced with silk. Possibly Robert was putting on a little weight since one item is for 'letting out and making the back to lace of a dress waistcoat', and another for repairing and letting out a figured tambour waistcoat. For the colder weather there was 'a fine Callicoe Waistct. To wer under the shirt'.

There were also a fustian jacket and printed fabric waistcoat for his servant M.C.Neal, and a blue livery frock coat with blue velvet collar for his smartly turned out groom! And so it goes on and on - a best scarlet second cloth hunting coat, a pair of fine green thickset breeches with strings and puff at the knees and covered buttons. 1789 ends with a superfine dark green cloth coat faced with the same, with silk sleeve linings and covered buttons costing £3 15s, the total for the year being £94 8s 4d.

Intriguingly a later bill also included a pair of 'black ladies cloth breeches', but who they were for and when she wore them is not recorded.

Of course these items only formed a part of Robert's wardrobe which must also have included many shirts, neckcloths, nightshirts and nightcaps, hats, gloves, boots, shoes, slippers and pumps for dancing, not to mention the gold watch that must have accompanied the repaired watch chain, and other items of jewellery.

The final bill in the collection for this period suggests that Robert rarely ate at home. John Westbrook[260] kept the highly fashionable Mount

---

[260] Westbrook, who made a comfortable fortune out of his business, was the father of the unfortunate Harriet Westbrook who eloped with the poet Shelley and eventually drowned herself in the Serpentine after he had left her for Mary Godwin.

Coffee House in Grosvenor Street, where between the 11th and the 25th of September 1787 Robert ate breakfast almost every day costing a shilling, and a four shilling supper on the 27th. Once he paid a shilling for lemonade, occasionally he had supper there but most of the tab he ran up was for breakfasts for one, or sometimes for two people. The total by the end of January 1789 was £10 5s or getting on for two hundred breakfasts. While Robert was running up these huge bills for clothes he was also paying at least two servants (including servant tax), feeding and clothing them, and keeping one or more horses in town, where fodder and stabling was always expensive. In addition, since he was no longer living at home, he had to pay for his rooms in town or accommodation in Brighton when he followed the fashionable set to the rapidly developing fishing village of Brighthelmstone. The advantage of staying with friends in large country houses of course was that food and accommodation came free!

Tall and good looking, the three older Lee brothers were known in Society as the Triumvirate. Illustrating that social circle, fragments of notes exist from Beau Brummell to Bob; from the Duchess of Bedford to the Duchess of Manchester asking 'Do you ever see Bob Lee? The first time you do would you ask him to send me some rouge No. 10 – not pale – from Madame Ste Margueritte: if you will pay him I will refund him immediately'; and from the Duchess of Manchester to Bob who wrote: 'Two females arrived last night from the Country and were already wishing themselves out of this dull place and unless the Kangarou has Charity enough to come and visit them, there is the greatest danger of their attacking him in his den.' Rosalie Duthé, celebrated French royal courtesan, and later the mistress of William Lee Antonie was reported to have said of Bob and Lee Antonie, 'L'un c'est mon Lit de Parade, et l'autre mon Lit de Repos!'[261] Another great courtesan, Harriette Wilson mentions a conversation with Matthew Lee in her memoirs[262].

As the Lee brothers moved in the best, and most expensive, circles it is perhaps no wonder that Matthew felt the need for a rich wife. The problem was that neither Matthew nor his new wife seems to have taken into account the fact that not only was she under age, but that if she married without the permission of her trustees they could prevent her accessing any of her money.

---

261 Gamble, op.cit. p.79.

262 Harriette Wilson's Memoirs, p.137-139.

On 9th of August 1794 Matthew wrote to his sister Favell. 'I trust my confinement will not be of long duration; the late season of the year will probably not enable us to settle matters now agreeable to the Court of Chancery. I therefore mean on Wednesday to apply to be discharged on giving security on my Wife, that the Court in the ensuing Term shall think it proper to direct.'[263]

Matthew was duly freed, and Richard and the lawyers hammered out a retrospective marriage settlement, Fanny's family having accepted her marriage as a fait accompli. On the death of Sir Francis Dashwood his estates had gone by entail to Sir John Dashwood. Fanny and her brother Francis were both beneficiaries under their father's Will with their inheritance being managed by four trustees. By 1795 when the marriage settlement was completed the only surviving executor of Sir Francis Dashwood's Will was Daniel Macnamara. In order to determine the amount of the marriage settlement it was necessary to value both Fanny's share of her inheritance, which included a further legacy from her Aunt Austen, and also Matthew's fortune. In Matthew's case his father's Will had left him £3000 to be paid a year after Robert Cooper Lee's death, a further £1000 would be due on the death of his mother, and half of his father's Jamaican property was to be allowed to accrue interest until February 1801 and the proceeds divided equally between the three youngest Lees. Therefore much of Matthew's fortune still consisted of 'expectations'. In Fanny's case a large part of her income derived from a mortgage her father had granted to Sir Lucius O'Brien in 1775 when he had lent him £25,000 to enable his friend to consolidate the debts on his Irish estates. Repayments on this mortgage were expected to bring Fanny £1000 a year, and in addition there were various other smaller mortgages, over £15,000 invested in 3% consols and bank annuities, two East India Bonds and about £2400 in cash.

In the end it was agreed that Matthew would be allowed £2000 immediately in order to provide and furnish a house for the couple, with any money remaining repaid to the trustees. While Fanny was still under twenty-one she would receive an income of £500 a year to be paid to her quarterly by the trust, and she was not to be liable for any of Matthew's debts. The new trustees created under the marriage settlement were Fanny's brother Francis Dashwood, Anthony Parkin a Grays Inn lawyer, the Rev. Hugh Moises[264] Fellow of University College Oxford and

---

263 Gamble, op.cit. p.85.

264 Son of the much esteemed Headmaster of the Royal Grammar School, Newcastle.

Richard Lee. Agreement was finally reached a year after the elopement on the 13th of February 1795.

Matthew and Fanny moved into a house in fashionable Grosvenor Square considerably above their means, but certainly not above Fanny's expectations, and she proceeded to run up debts at an alarming rate.

While Richard was spending time running his own business, sorting out his father's estate and trying to achieve a fair settlement for Matthew, he was also trying to settle his youngest brother's future. Robert Cooper Lee had expressed the hope in his Will that Scudamore would go to Oxford University. Whether Scudamore objected or Richard felt it would be too expensive, Richard instead looked about for a place in a merchant house where Scudamore could learn to follow business similar to his own. In November he wrote to Hercules Ross, now settled with his wife Henrietta Parish, and legitimate family[265] at Rossie.

Hercules Ross to Richard Lee

Rossie, 19th December 1794

Dear Sir,

I have hitherto delayed acknowledging your favour of the 21st ult., In hopes of being able to find out some way of being of Service, to my friend Scudamore, in his proposed plan of going to Glasgow; but upon enquiry the whole of my acquaintance which were of any consideration in that City, are either dead or retired from business. Should you think of persevering in the plan I shall make a point, through the medium of some friends in Edinburgh probably the Bankers Messrs Mansfield Ramsay and Co. to obtain the best information as to Houses of repute, their terms, etc. But to tell you the truth, I am exceedingly doubtful as to Glasgow being a proper place. It was used to be replete with Drunkenness, and low debauchery. What the state of manners may be now I am totally un-acquainted; our distance from the place being very great, and no kind of intercourse with it.

---

[265] Hercules Ross had a family in Jamaica with Elizabeth Foord, a free quadroon who owned property in her own right. Of their seven children five survived and were provided for by their father. Two daughters ran a school at Ramsgate, Hercules was Captain of the Brig *Malacca* and was murdered by pirates in the East Indies, Daniel had a very distinguished career as a Naval Hydrographer, and little is known of David.

Have you turn'd your attention to either Liverpool or Bristol? These in point of Merchants, I apprehend surpass Glasgow which of late has rather become a great Manufactory.

However as I have already suggested, should you think it eligible, to persist in the plan I shall with great pleasure go to Glasgow and there upon *the spot* do everything in my power, to fix our Young friend in the best manner; therefore speak out what you would wish to be done, without a moments hesitation.

On Sunday next which day is too often my post day I propose to trouble you with a letter under cover to Mr D. Scott, New Broad Street about my demand against Sir J. Dalling[266].

I am My dear Sir Most truly Yours H. Ross

As if family problems were not enough for Richard to have to deal with, in the autumn of 1794 he became reluctantly involved in a court case on behalf of Robert Home Gordon who was being sued for ten thousand pounds by Joseph Biscoe for Gordon's adultery with his wife Susanna.

Joseph Seymour Biscoe, who had been at school with Richard and Robert Gordon, had married Susanna Harriot Hope in 1786 when he was twenty-six and she was eighteen. He was the wealthy grandson of Lady Somerset and she was the daughter of a well respected Derby vicar, and had been painted on at least two occasions by Joseph Wright of Derby. Their only child Mary was born in September 1787. The marriage was apparently perfectly happy and in due course the couple moved to Shoreham in Kent where they took a house belonging to Robert Gordon. Richard, as the friend of both, was responsible for reintroducing Biscoe to Gordon who rapidly fell madly in love with Biscoe's wife and spent every possible moment in her company.

What was developing seems to have been evident to everyone except Joseph Biscoe, who was either too diffident or too uncaring to intervene, although there was a suggestion that the marriage had been troubled since a trip to Hastings the previous summer. The servants noticed it, Richard noticed it, but Biscoe went out shooting with Richard leaving Robert and Susanna alone and either failed to notice it, didn't care or didn't know what to do about it. When all four were out riding and Richard suggested the group should keep together Biscoe apparently told him to leave

266 General Sir John Dalling (c.1731-1798), Governor of Jamaica from 1777-1782.

Robert and Susanna alone as they were 'made for each other'. On the 21st of October 1794 Robert and Susanna eloped while her husband was in London on business. Susanna's brothers had arrived to try to reason with her, drank a lot of Biscoe's wine and left. The servants heard raised voices, the sound of weeping and Susanna saying 'How can I think of leaving my child?' All the evidence suggests that everyone except Biscoe knew what was about to happen.

Susanna moved into Albemarle Street with Robert Gordon. Joseph's sister collected poor little Mary who seems for the moment to have been the chief loser in all this, and on the 8th of December Susanna's husband sued Gordon for damages of ten thousand pounds. Richard was called as an extremely reluctant witness, both as a friend of the two men and as the consignee of Robert's West Indian estates, to give testimony about his income. About the latter he was uncharacteristically vague, perhaps hoping not to represent Robert as being so wealthy that £10,000 would be considered a trifling fine. Richard had a rough time of it and was painted as 'an accomplice in this abominable conspiracy' by the prosecution. When asked why he had not intervened he told the court that 'I was apt to think that the Plaintiff had winked at the business; and I repeat it, that I did not think it my duty to speak to either party'. The Judge, Lord Justice Kenyon, who had succeeded Lord Mansfield as Lord Chief Justice, also gave Richard a hard time. He had known Robert Cooper Lee and told Richard 'I am very sorry to find the son has not inherited the virtues of the father. One would have thought that he would have endeavoured to rescue the wife and his friend from seduction, and the husband from misery.'

Impressive legal teams appeared for both sides with Gordon represented by Thomas Erskine (who had defended Lord George Gordon after the riots) and the up and coming William Garrow. Their effectiveness, in the face of an admitted adultery, may account for the jury awarding only half the damages sought in spite of strong direction from Kenyon to award the full amount.

Throughout the following year Matthew was struggling financially and repeatedly turned to Richard for advice and financial help.

Matthew Allen Lee to Richard Lee

[Monday Morning, undated 1795]

Dear Richard,

Freeman's answer to my Proposition is this "that on Account of so considerable share of all Housekeepers Income being required for Taxes and Contributions, it will be most inconvenient he thinks for him to wait for the £500 till 1801, but he is willing to take an Acceptance payable in March next, and if at that expiration, he can make it in the least convenient to renew it for the time I first proposed, he will do it"

To this I can only say, if you will give me the Acceptance (and in failure of renewal on the part of F.) I will undertake to furnish the Money in March let it be at the greatest Inconvenience possible.

This has cut me up more than twenty Pounds.

Affectionately yours Matt Lee

Other more distant relations also sought Richard's help and advice. Isaac Parmenter had married Mary Charlotte Morley, the eldest daughter of Charlotte Lee, in 1777 and by the time of this next letter they had produced twelve of thirteen children, the eldest of whom was disabled.

Isaac Parmenter to Richard Lee

Thundersley Hall, 4th January 1795

Dear Sir,

Since I had the pleasure of seeing you in Town I have minutely considered my Affairs and as I find it Improbable I should have it in my Power to pay you the Sum I am Indebted for a very Considerable Time if I continue in this Extensive line of Business. Through that consideration I am induced (with the Approbation of my good Friend Mr Morley) to dispose of it, which will enable me to Repay you the whole Sum and I hope secure to me and mine the Future Friendship and Protection of yourself and kind Family, to whom I shall always be proud of Acknowledging the favour I have Received. As I shall not be out of Business till Michaelmas I hope in the interim to procure another Situation as I by no means wish to be unemploy'd. Mrs Parmenter beg to unite with me in the kindest Respects to Mrs Lee Miss Lee self and Family.

I am Dear Sir Your Obliged Honourable Servant I. Parmenter

January also brought news of the death of the family's close friend John Allen who left behind a widow and two young sons.

Margaret Grant to Richard Lee

Edinburgh, 9th January 1795

Dear Sir,

With the deepest concern I take up my pen to inform you, that our dear friend Mr Allen is no more. They returned from a short excursion they had made to Glasgow on Saturday last; that night he was seized with a severe attack of the Astmah which though alleviated by medical aid did not yield to it and joined to some internal malady, which the force of medicine, or human skill could not reach, at ¼ past eleven yesterday morning proved fatal.

His disconsolate Widow and her dear Boys are with me, she wonderfully calm and collected under her severe loss, the more so as so unexpected, at least by her. May the Almighty support and protect her and her Boys. She herself requested I should write to you that you might communicate this sad intelligence in the least alarming way to our good friends Mrs and Miss Lee: who with myself have sustained a loss that we must long feel and lament. Nothing that the tenderest friendship can suggest to asswage or alleviate the distress of our Afflicted friend shall be omitted on my part.

With the offer of kind regards to you Mrs and Miss Lee and your family I remain Dear Sir

Your most honourable Servant Margaret Grant.

John Morley, who since his separation from Mary Charlotte Lee in 1769 appears to have been living on Morley family charity, wrote a begging letter to Richard in 1795. There is no indication as to whether he replied.

John Morley to Richard Lee

Hedingham, 26th January 1795

Sir,

I hope this letter is not wrote through any sinister view, you will excuse my addressing you, but am sensible the loss that have befell your worthy family must have taken your attention up too much, even to think upon such an unworthy Person as I am. But Sir my Good uncle for this six years past has allowed me £5 per annum which hope and trust will be allowed to me for this last year, which is all I can ever expect, and if I am so fortunate as to receive it will be of essential service to me, this severe weather. I am now settl'd at this place as determin'd the peace of none of my family shall never more be disturbed by me, if you should wish to enquire, sir, into my conduct I think Mr Parmenter will do me that justice, in saying that had my conduct been as good in the early part of my life, should not have been under the necessity of troubling your worthy family, in the manner I have done, but might have been a great support to my own, but alas it is now too late. I was at Thundersley Hall during Mrs Parmenter's illness and officiated for him and was the unwelcome messenger who brought the letter from the office of my Dear Uncle's Death.

Now Sir shall conclude In hopes you will forgive me in addressing you in so doing you will oblige your unworthy Relation John Morley.

PS if i have the honour of hearing from you Please to Direct to me at Mr Smiths, Sible Hedingham, Essex.

Amidst all this Richard was still struggling to find a suitable placement for his youngest brother.

Richard Lee to William Mitchell

Bedford Square, 11th February 1795

My Dear Sir,

I shall not trouble you with Apologies for this abrupt Address, knowing that your friendly character and wish to oblige will deem them superfluous and that they would not add to the Energy of your good Offices in what I am about to propose. I have been endeavouring for some Months past to fix my Brother Scudamore either at Liverpool or Glasgow but my wish of procuring him *a residence* in the some Merchants House has been a bar to carrying the plan into Execution, so much time has been now lost that not to procrastinate matters longer I desire at once to get him into a Compting House in London for two or three Years, and to lodge and board him in a Situation contiguous to where he follows business; if this had been my original intention our mutual friends Messrs Milligan and Mitchell would have immediately occurred to me, as a House I should have been highly gratified to place him in, and it has struck me that a recent melancholy Event may occasion a vacancy, that may render my present wish not impracticable. I should therefore be extremely obliged to you at some fit and convenient Opportunity to mention the Subject whatever may be the Success of the Application I shall rest fully satisfied with your kind Endeavours on the Occasion.

The Ladies join me in respects to Mrs Mitchell and your Fire-side.

Believe me always My Dear Sir Your Much Obliged and Obedient servant Richard Lee

In March 1795, to reduce the family's expenditure, they removed from the big house in Bedford Square back to number 26 Berners Street, which they had first occupied on their return from Jamaica. On the 25th of March an inventory was made of the contents of the wine cellar.

143 Dozen Red Port

45 Do. Cherry

24 Do. New Madeira

11 Do. Old Madeira

16 Do. Claret

32 Do. Rum

13 Do. Vandregra

8 Do. Burgundy

3 Do. Marmse Madeira

4 Do. Old Hook

3 Do. Renish

1 Do. Champane

4 Do. Sundrys

26 Do. Cyder

6 Do. Burton Ale

This came to a total of 338 Dozen bottles!

Matthew Allen Lee to Richard Lee

8th July 1795

Dear Richard,

I am most grievously disappointed about the Money. My Friend writes me Word, that the ready Money he had by, he meant to lay out in the purchase of an Estate, that Land was now very low and that he had heard of an Estate that came about his Mark. He then goes on to say that *he still would keep his Promise to me if I required it.* I have answered him and released him most compleatly.

I apprehend this to be the entire Work of the Lawyer whose Fees for drawing up Deeds inspecting the Title etc etc are a great deal more profitable than my Matter would have been.

For Heaven's sake what am I to do now?

Parkin and Arnold[267] must be paid my House and several other Matters and exclusive of about £400 which becomes due from the Trust this Month no prospect do I see of touching a settling. I do not wish to inconvenience you. Will you give me your Acceptances at whatever date you please or advise me about getting the Money.

Mrs Matt dined in Town yesterday. I did not see her but find a most pathetic Effusion from her.

I am resolved upon Separation. Lauderdale and Dashwood propose an equal division and Moises comes to Town tomorrow about it.

Froggatt had the Insolence to stop me in the Street and begged me to ask you for the Act of Assembly in Jamaica relative to Emblements 25th Goe.3rd pray [lick?] him or send it him.

What time can I see you *tomorrow* early?

Ever Yours Affectionately Mat Lee.

Matthew Allen Lee to Messrs Lee and Moises

14th July 1795

You have my Instructions to bring about an immediate Separation between Mrs Lee and myself.

Matthew Allen Lee

---

267 Lawyers for Fanny Dashwood

At about the same time, Fanny Dashwood wrote to Richard from her brother's house Hall Place at Dartford.

Frances Dashwood Lee to Richard Lee

Hall Place Dartford, Monday [ ] July 1795

Sir,

I understand you are to be the principle agent in settling the present business between your brother and myself. I shall not advert to his word which may be doubted because not *proved* – or to the laws of equity – which are so *rarely* listened to but I shall simply appeal to the *circumstances* of my marriage with your brother which ought to prove to every just mind that no measures derogatory to my interest should be adopted on the present occasion. I hope and believe that he will reject any offers which are inimical to my welfare – he has promised to deal nobly by me (as the injustice of fate has put me in his power). Sorry I shall be if he disgraces the little he has given himself of a *disinterested* friend.

Time will show whether I can rely upon his honor or your impartiality. As my brother is too much indisposed to attend I must submit to be judged by my enemies. God knows what their decision may be! If I am reduced to beggary by the plausible arguments of those who wish my ruin, I can only say that I shall have recourse to a life which I inwardly abhor, but your brother's words almost preclude the possibility of so cruel a fate he can never bear to see me living upon the bounty of others while he is enjoying my *lawful property* – if he is advised to so vile a measure may the stings of a guilty conscience be his eternal punishment – excuse my warmth of expressions, consider that I have *none* to protect me or to plead my cause and that I am obliged to rely upon *you who are my enemy* – yet there is such a thing as generosity even in an enemy – may I find it in you is my sincere wish! F.D.Lee

The letter is typical of Fanny's exaggerated style, yet it was true that she was in a fairly difficult position. Apart from her brother, who seems to have been very little help to her, she was alone. Her widowed mother had died the previous month. As a married woman all her property belonged to her husband, although the marriage settlement had attempted to ensure it was divided equally. Moreover her main income derived from the interest on the mortgage her father had granted his friend Sir Lucius

O'Brien whose son Sir Edward O'Brien would spend the next forty years attempting to avoid payment.

Matthew Allen Lee to Richard Lee

Wednesday morning [November 1795]

Dear Richard,

It grieves me again to trouble you on an unpleasant subject.

You know my Situation about money and how anxious I have been that you should not be a Sufferer on my Account.

I have tried everywhere to raise it and have at last succeeded provided I have your Acceptance - for that purpose I send you the enclosed, assuring you that no Exertion on my part shall be wanting to raise the Money already advanced by you and provide for the payment of this Bill when due. I am obliged by a Friend and consequently have [ ] Sum total.

I am in great Hopes Sir Edward O'Brien will pay up Arrears. We saw him at Petworth and I shall desire Arnold to wait on Stewart in Aldermanbury to be fully informed on the Matter.

I shall receive the Money this Morning if you would be good enough to return me the Bill accepted.

Most Affectionately Yours Mat Lee

Matthew Allen Lee to Richard Lee

St Maries, Southampton, 3rd November [1795]

Dear Richard,

Have you heard from Parkin? I left particular directions with him to pay the Money to you and I trust he has done it.

The Society here has been much clouded by the death of Mrs R Streatfeild all the Horses would have performed very pleasantly. We have been to Lymington and the Isle of Wight twice in Ogle's Cutter and I yesterday shook hands with Matt Scott at Portsmouth. His Ship is not yet paid off but he expects it daily. He has fixed his Eye on the *Tribune* a very beautiful Frigate.

I propose remaining in Hampshire a Week or 10 days longer. Tomorrow I am going to Stockbridge where I shall be happy to hear from you – to remain till Sunday.

My Mother I hope is in good Spirits. Remember me to her and my Sisters and believe me

Your truly affectionate Brother Matt Lee.

Matthew Allen Lee to Richard Lee

Deanery Winchester, 20th November 1795

Dear Richard,

I inclose you Mr Parkin's Answer to my Remonstrance and shall feel infinitely obliged to you if you would see him previous to receiving the Money. Upon the simple account stated, the Trustees were indebted to me Two Hundred and odd Pounds after Payments were made to Mrs Lee and myself in July last, namely £155.5.0 which I contend is improperly charged against me being positively my Right previous to the Separation and not by any means invalidated by the Deed of Separation and the Error in Mr Parkin's Account relative to the £100 I am debited with, when that Sum was equally divided between Mrs L. and myself by our respective drafts on Sikes and Co for £90.

You will observe that £152 has been laid out in the Funds out of the £250 lately received from Sir Edward O'Brien which is perfectly right, all arrears being paid now up to July 1794 from which time the Marriage Settlement takes Effect therefore I surely am entitled to one whole year's Interest from Sir E.B. from July 94 to July 95, before any division can take place – I claim £500 on that account.

One Word more. Like Charles Fox and lesser Heroes I must *repeat July* again and again.

Mr Parkin in July 95 receives the Dividend pays Mrs Lee her Pin Money and retains the Remainder to discharge His Bill. This is not included in the account though decidedly analogous to the other matters. 'Shame Shame upon them' and could they dare put in an Answer to a Bill of Complaint?

Arnold who drew the Deed is with me upon every point and perfectly convinced Mr Parkin, though he appears to act now completely (though a Trustee and in conscience ought to follow his own opinion) under the direction of their Modern Lawgivers, Mr Dashwood and Mrs Lee.

Depend upon it they are satisfied of the truly quiet and gentlemanly manner you have displayed and one Word from you could not fail of having great effect, but I leave this to your own Feelings and Judgement.

What think you of my Promises? Dashwood says it is perfectly right as far as it goes, but is nothing to the purpose – Oh most wrong headed !!!

In addition to the Uneasiness my own Misfortunes occasion me, the Situation of this Family has caused me much concern. Mrs Streatfeild, Lady Ogle (the Dean's Wife's Sister)[268] and the Bishop of Exeter[269] all dying in one week and allied in Friendship as well as blood.

What a World it is!

I intend getting to Chichester tomorrow Evening and will thank you to let me hear from you there at your Leisure.

Remember me most affectionately to my Mother and Sisters and believe me

Yours most sincerely Mat Lee.

Richard Lee eventually abandoned any attempt to get his youngest brother into training as a merchant and eighteen year-old Scudamore got his wish to go into the army, where he found himself serving in Ireland as an Ensign in the 6th Foot.

Scudamore Cooper Lee to Richard Lee

Waterford, 12th March 1796

My dear Brother,

I am sorry I have delay'd so long a time in addressing you from Ireland where I have been some time. I cannot say I admire this Country as much as my own but I believe it is a very pleasant Country as we have receiv'd during our Short Stay at Waterford much Civility. I think however it is most probable we shall soon leave this Quarter, and by what I can understand, we are to be remov'd to Barracks at or near Ross some

---

268 The Dean of Winchester was Newton Ogle, whose daughter Hester had married the playwright Sheridan earlier the same year. The latter couple sailed on the Solent in a Cutter called the *Phaedria*, possibly the same as the one sailed in by Matthew. The Dean's brother was Admiral Chaloner Ogle of the West Indies Squadron who was married to Hester Thomas, sister of the Dean's wife Susanna. The Streatfeild and Ogle families were connected by the marriage of Elizabeth Catherine Ogle, daughter of Newton, to Henry Streatfeild of Chiddingstone in 1782.

269 The Bishop of Exeter, William Buller, was married to Anne Thomas, sister to Hester and Susanna.

small distance from Hence. I wish some settlement with regard to our either remaining or going on actual service would take place for our present unsettled Manner is very far from being pleasant.

Believe S.C.Lee

Scudamore Cooper Lee to Richard Lee

Waterford, 1st May 1796

My dear Brother,

I am sorry I have delay'd answering your kind Favor but as I expected daily to have heard particulars about my expected Lieutenancy I have procrastinated addressing you till this late period, however no Advices having been receiv'd at the Regiment about many Expected Promotions so I am still ignorant *where* the Provision for Purchase ought to be lodg'd and *when* it will be required. I think most probably something decisive must take place soon and then I shall hasten to communicate to you the proper Measures that ought to be pursued. Accept my sincere Thanks for your Countenance in this Business as well as in manifold others. I am very much oblig'd to for paying such strict Attention to the Letter I enclos'd you in my last and Believe me the Settlement of the Affair has given me infinite Satisfaction. I trust I shall never commit such an Error for the future.

I perceive with Regret in the Papers the Captures of several Jamaica Ships. I hope you are not greatly concern'd in them. I should ever wish you were not at all but that I fear would be entertaining false Hope, for in Business of all Kinds the Bitters must be mix'd with the Sweets. I wish the loss you may have sustained is trivial. It appears from Papers of both Sides of the Question that the War will be still pursued, it is the general Idea [illegible] that this Campaign must make an End to the War. Both Countries seem to groan for a Peace and as it would be a salutary Object I truly desire a Termination to Hostilities will crown the mutual Wish of all Countries involved in the Contest.

The Regiment will quit this Place in the Course of a fortnight and we move to Kilkenny Barracks there to remain till the Corps musters stronger and then I suppose we shall be sent on some foreign Service in the Fall of the year, it is expected, will be time of our quitting this Country our Conjectures here on the Subject are merely Ideal so the Regiments may yet remain in the Country.

As I have no Agent in London now I must take the Liberty of drawing on you for Twenty Pounds which I believe I shall be necessitated to do in a few days. Requesting you will [give] my Duty to my Mother and kind [torn] to all the Family

I am Your affectionate Brother Scudamore Cooper Lee.

Left to his own devices, among brother officers with deeper pockets than his own, Scudamore seems rapidly to have found himself in financial trouble, a habit he never lost, while Matthew was still struggling with his wife's debts and her Trustees.

By the time the separation document was signed on the 4th of January 1796 Fanny was twenty-one and entitled to possession of her fortune, albeit managed by trustees on her behalf. It was agreed that Fanny should have her £500 a year guaranteed and that she was to have the right to live freely wherever she should choose. Matthew further guaranteed not to take her to court for living apart from him, nor to sue anyone she was living with for encouraging her to leave the matrimonial home. Fanny was to be entitled to enjoy her property as if she were a 'feme sole and unmarried' and to be free to will her property to anyone she wished to.

Matthew in turn was guaranteed sole possession of his own £3000 (and in due course his further inheritances) and was to have the residual income from the investments after Fanny was paid her £500. In a key provision he was not to be considered responsible for Fanny's debts.

Fanny was not one to go quietly. She complained that her share of the china that she received from the matrimonial home had arrived broken. She would continue to complain for years to anyone who would listen, about her treatment, about Matthew and especially about her trustees. Despite the settlement it took some time for Matthew to extricate himself from serious debt, and for several years he continued to apply at intervals to be rescued by Richard.

Matthew Allen Lee to Richard Lee

Tuesday [undated 1797]

Dear Richard,

The agony I feel at the Moment is not to be described and to you and you alone can I apply in this Hour of distress. By a false Calculation of my income I have involved myself very deeply and without you can assist me with £400 I am a ruined man. Having paid the greatest part of the Debts contracted by Mrs Lee and during our Residence in Berkeley Square, I rely'd upon the Promise of the Tradesmen for Time to discharge the remainder and knowing that no more Debts had been made since that period I imagined my affairs in very good order. But the People have near all come upon me and press very severely for Payment of the demands – to many I have given my Acceptance and I know the chief Part of the Sum I mentioned to pay this day. It is impossible for me to combat any Argument that you may bring against me but when I tell you I am willing to quit London discharge my Groom and Horses and live infinitely within my Income, I trust you will credit me as a man and not attribute it to violence of Passions at this moment. I throw myself upon your Mercy and remain the

Your truly affectionate Brother Matthew Allen Lee.

Scudamore also applied repeatedly for money and John Lee, whose advice was sought by Richard, worried that of all the Lee brothers he was the only one to succumb to gambling.

John Lee to Richard Lee

Stafford Street, Wednesday morning, [undated] 1797

Dear Richard,

I am sorry that your last letter has had so little effect on Scudamore. He seems to think that he is unkindly used because he cannot have whatever money he chooses to draw for.

You have, I make no doubt, come to a determination of whether or not you will allow him to continue his present expense and whether his finances and your family arrangements will permit any advance of income.

I think you should be informed, that his own representation of the expense of his present situation in the Army, made it absolutely necessary that he should consider employing his time and his fortune to more advantage and not continue a line of life which must only lead to ruin.

There is a thing which strikes me on reading his letter, and which, however I hope I may be deceived in. I feel very much both from the general tenor of his letter as well as from the date, that he has been losing money at play or Billiards or some other game. Read his letter again and consider it.

Yours sincerely John Lee.

The tenor of Richard's letters to both Matthew and Scudamore became ever more like letters written by his father to Robert and Matthew.

Richard Lee to Scudamore Cooper Lee (draft)

10th January 1799

Dear Scudamore,

Your last letter was duly received by me advising your farther bills on me for £12.12 and£36.15. After having so lately come forward and exceeded to the utmost extent of your wishes in relieving you from your difficulties, this last piece of conduct I consider such a breach of all confidence, that I should become an accomplice in your follies, were I not now to take a decided line of conduct. As to your promises I am ashamed for your sake to say a word respecting them! It must be only from real distress I fear that an amendment can be worked. The bills are honoured you must not from henceforward on any account whatsoever presence to draw a Draft on me. On the 20th of March I shall pay in £25 to your Agent and so on every succeeding three months.

On this footing must ever remain our money transactions. Weigh with the consequences.

Richard Lee

Matthew Allen Lee

Favell Bourke Lee

David Bevan

Marchant Tubb

General John Lee

Epilogue

Priscilla Lee did not live to see the worst of her sons' excesses. She died at Berners Street after a short illness on the 18th of October 1797 and was buried in the family vault at Barnes. The following May Favell married the up and coming banker David Bevan. She was just eighteen and probably pressed to accept him by Frances and Richard, anxious to secure her future.

Following the sale of the Berners Street house in 1802 Frances moved to 53 Devonshire Street, off Portland Place with Betty Harrison. Richard shared his new house at Weymouth Street (just around the corner from Frances) with a mistress, referred to in letters from John only as Charlotte.

On the 24th of April 1805 at Chester Scudamore Cooper Lee shot himself, apparently seeing no solution to his debts and no way of providing for his illegitimate daughter and her mother.

Three years later at Colworth Park Matthew Allen Lee also ended his own life.

Robert Lee, after several years of declining health, was finally persuaded to seek warmer climes and set off with William Lee Antonie's nephew John Fiott for a tour of the Mediterranean. From Gibraltar he wrote what seems to have been a quite unforgiveable letter to his cousin John, blaming him for all his ills, and he then decided to return to England. He got as far as Lisbon where he died in June 1810, probably of liver disease.

Frances never married, a letter with her Will requested Favell to destroy 'a most precious packet', which hints at unrequited love. She settled comfortably into the role of aunt, intermittently laid low by her illness and treating her pain with Kendal Black Drop[270]. Independently wealthy she inherited further property at Wheelersfield in Jamaica from Mary Powell Royall.

---

270 'I owe much for the little rest I get to the black drop, but that is not *infallible* as pain very frequently predominates & an increased quantity to my usual (equivalent to 40 Drops of Laudanum) even to one hundred daily is not always successful as my latter nights bear witness, as well I hope as my patience.'
Black Drop was a painkiller composed of opium, vinegar, sugar and spices, and it is likely that after many years use Frances had become dependent on it.

Betty Harrison, who at some point became Mrs William Pack, lived with Frances until her death on the 10th of January 1820 aged about seventy. She was buried at Barnes close to the family she had served for nearly sixty years. Despite her ill health Frances Lee lived to be eighty-one, dying at 53 Devonshire Place on the 7th of December 1839 with her sister Favell at her side.

Favell and David Bevan had eight children, and also brought up Scudamore's daughter Marian Farmer. Their first son died at birth and was followed by three daughters before the arrival of an heir, Robert Cooper Lee Bevan, whose son would go on to become the first Chairman of Barclays Bank. Favell sought consolation in evangelical Christianity and her daughter Favell Lee Mortimer found fame as the author of simple Christian books for children. By the end of the nineteenth century the descendants of Favell and David Bevan included fifty two grandchildren and numerous great grandchildren. Writing to Favell in 1806 Mrs Boyd, an old Jamaica family friend said, 'How happy would your Father and Mother have been to see their grandchildren; Mr Lee was the best male nurse I ever saw and would never have been without one of your trio in his arms. Mrs Lee would have indulged them more than she did Matt. *He* was only permitted to paw the Sugar Dish, but *Louisa* might wash her hands in the Cream Ewer!'[271]

John Lee continued his career in the Army, and after a period on half pay he went back on the active list when he was made Lieutenant General in 1814. He died at his home in Clifton, Bristol in December 1821 leaving a comfortable legacy to Elizabeth Hobbs of Charlotte Street, London. He left books to Robert Home Gordon, his curios to Richard Lee (who was residuary legatee) and made Matt Scott one of his executors.

Matt Scott ended his Naval career as Vice Admiral of the White Squadron. He had married a fellow child of the Plantocracy Mary Pinnock with whom he had thirteen children. His brother George married Euphine Cussens and settled in Hampshire. Jack Scott returned to Jamaica to manage the family plantations at the Retreat and Clarendon Park, where he fathered numerous children by several mothers, became President of the Council and incurred the displeasure of Governor Nugent who described him as 'a silly, vain, chattering blockhead...not to be trusted with anything confidential'. He returned to England in 1806

[271] Gamble op. cit. P.99

and married Matt's sister-in-law Elizabeth Favell Pinnock; their sixth child was born posthumously in June 1814.

Of all the Jamaica generation of the mid-eighteenth century Richard Lee lived the longest. Already closely allied with the West Indian interests in London, in 1802 he joined the board of the West India Dock Company, having previously subscribed for £2000, and in 1806 he became Deputy Chairman. He was also closely connected with its spin-off company the Imperial Insurance Company and he still had interests in the estates of Rosehall in the parish of St Thomas in the Vale, and Wheelersfield in the parish of St Thomas in the East, Jamaica.

After a life-long career in business Richard died at his home 14 Calverley Park, Tunbridge Wells on the 16th of January 1857 at the age of ninety-one, an age only trumped by his great uncle Thomas Marlton who had lived to be ninety-three.

At his death Richard was worth about £600,000[272] a fortune divided mainly between his Bevan nieces and nephews. However he fulfilled the promise of his father to look after the descendants of Mary Charlotte Lee, and there were minor legacies to five of her grandchildren and their children, and provision for the care of Robert Lee Parmenter (one of the sons of Isaac Parmenter and Mary Charlotte Morley) who having worked for some years for Richard spent thirty years in Kensington Asylum.

Mysteriously, the largest legacy apart from those to his sister's children was £6500 to Sarah Nichols of Lambeth who also received an annuity of £300. The Nichols family had been neighbours in Berners Street many years before, but what other connection there was remains obscure although Sarah and her niece Frances Richmond (also a legatee) were staying with Richard when the census was taken in 1851.

One of the minor legatees under Richard's Will was Mary Charlotte Lee's great granddaughter whose grandchildren remembered her telling of an ancestor who was an Indian Princess. Decoding the story led not to an Indian Princess but to a West Indian called Priscy. By living beyond the 1851 census, which listed his birthplace as Jamaica, Richard Lee provided the thread that led to the disentangling of the parcel of ribbons.

---

[272] Equivalent in 2012 to about £446 million using the retail price index or £3,830 million using average earnings. Source: measuringworth.com

Family of Joseph Lee

Joseph Lee
b. abt 1692 St Michael Bassishaw, London, England
d. 1750/51 London

Frances Jaques
b. 1698 Angel Court, Snow Hill, parish of St Sepulchre, London
d. 1748 Islington, Middlesex, England

Joseph Lee
b. abt 1721 St Michael Bassishaw, London, England
d. abt 1721 St Michael Bassishaw, London, England

William Lee
b. abt 1723 London
d. 1735 St Michael Bassishaw, London, England

Frances Lee
b. 1729 St Vedast Foster Lane and St Michael le Querne, London, England
d. abt 1751 Turnagain Lane, London

John Lee
b. 1730 St Michael Bassishaw, London, England
d. 1761 Spanish Town, Jamaica

Sarah Maria Lee
b. 1731 St Michael Bassishaw, London, England
d. 1732

Joseph Lee
b. 1732/33 St Michael Bassishaw, London, England
d. 1732/33 London, England

Mary Charlotte Lee
b. 1734 St Michael Bassishaw, London, England
d. 1782 Sible Hedingham, Essex, England

Robert Cooper Lee
b. 1735 St Michael Bassishaw, London, England
d. 1794 30 Bedford Square, London

Joseph Lee
b. 1737 St Michael Bassishaw, London, England
d. abt 1772 Spanish Town, Jamaica

Family of Robert Cooper Lee

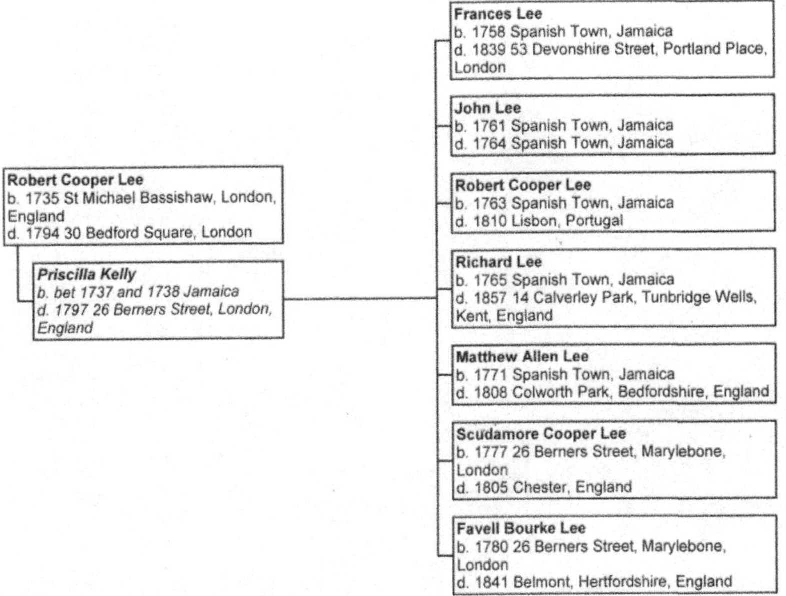
Robert Cooper Lee
b. 1735 St Michael Bassishaw, London, England
d. 1794 30 Bedford Square, London
Priscilla Kelly
b. bet 1737 and 1738 Jamaica
d. 1797 26 Berners Street, London, England
Frances Lee
b. 1758 Spanish Town, Jamaica
d. 1839 53 Devonshire Street, Portland Place, London
John Lee
b. 1761 Spanish Town, Jamaica
d. 1764 Spanish Town, Jamaica
Robert Cooper Lee
b. 1763 Spanish Town, Jamaica
d. 1810 Lisbon, Portugal
Richard Lee
b. 1765 Spanish Town, Jamaica
d. 1857 14 Calverley Park, Tunbridge Wells, Kent, England
Matthew Allen Lee
b. 1771 Spanish Town, Jamaica
d. 1808 Colworth Park, Bedfordshire, England
Scudamore Cooper Lee
b. 1777 26 Berners Street, Marylebone, London
d. 1805 Chester, England
Favell Bourke Lee
b. 1780 26 Berners Street, Marylebone, London
d. 1841 Belmont, Hertfordshire, England

The Lee family tomb at St Mary's, Barnes.

Originally the tomb stood further from the church, but following a disastrous fire in 1978 the church was rebuilt and extended bringing it closer to the tomb. The Lee monuments inside the church were destroyed in the fire but had previously been recorded. No record exists of the exact burial place of Frances Lee, and her infant daughter Sarah Maria. Nor is there any marker for the grave of Betty Harrison.

Bibliography

Ackrill, Margaret and Hannah, Leslie, *Barclays, The Business of Banking 1690-1996*, Cambridge University Press, 2007.

Armitage, Philip and McCarthy Colin, *Turtle Remains from a late 18th century well at Leadenhall Buildings*, London Archaeologist, Vol. 4, No.1 pp 8-16, 1980.

Bevan, Edwyn, *Peep of Day A Lawgiver in the Nursery, The Long Reign of Miss Bevan*, The Times, London, 27 June 1933.

Black, Clinton V., *History of Jamaica*, Longman Group UK Ltd., 1991.

Brathwaite, Kamau, *The Development of Creole Society in Jamaica 1770-1820*, Ian Randle Publishers, Kingston, Jamaica, 2005.

Briant-Evans, Amanda, *A Portrait of the Rossie Estate and its Owners* in *Flowing Past – More Historical Highlights from Montrose Basin*, Montrose Basin Heritage Society, PrintMatters, Brechin, Angus, 2008, pp.47-100.

Brooks, E. St John, *Sir Hans Sloane: The Great Collecter and His Circle*, The Batchworth Press, London, 1954.

Buisseret, David, *Historic Jamaica from the Air*, Ian Randle Publishers, Kingston, 1996.

Burnard, Trevor, *A Failed Settler Society: Marriage and Demographic Failure in Early Jamaica*, Journal of Social History, Vol..28, No.1(Autumn 1994) pp.63-82.

Burnard, Trevor, *European Migration to Jamaica,1655-1780*, The William and Mary Quarterly, Third Series, Vol.53, No.4,(Oct.1996), pp.769-796.

Burnard, Trevor, *'The Countrie Continues Sickly':White Mortality in Jamaica, 1655-1780*, Social History of Medicine, Vol.12, No.1 pp.45-72, 1999.

Burnard, Trevor, *Mastery, Tyranny and Desire: Thomas Thistlewood and his Slaves in the Anglo-Jamaican World*, University of North Carolina Press, Chapel Hill and London, 2004.

Burnard, Trevor, *Kingston Merchants and the Atlantic Slave Trade in the Eighteenth Century*, BGEAH, Stirling, 3 September 2009.

Burnard, Trevor and Morgan, Kenneth, *The Dynamics of the Slave Market and Slave Purchasing Patterns in Jamaica, 1655–1788*, The William and Mary Quarterly, Vol. 58, No.1, January 2001.

Burney, Frances, *Journals and Letters*, Penguin Classics, London, 2001.

Bush, Barbara, *Slave Women in Caribbean Society 1650-1838*, Heinemann Publishers (Caribbean), Kingston, Indiana University Press, Bloomington and Indianapolis, James Currey, London, 1990.

Campbell, Patrick, *Trent Park: A History*, Middlesex University Press, 1997.

Clarke, Colin G., *Kingston Jamaica: Urban Development and Social Change, 1692-2002*, Ian Randle, Kingston and Miami, 2006.

Clarke, John, *George III*, Weidenfeld and Nicholson & Book Club Associates, London 1972.

Constable, Rosalind, *Department of Amplification*, The New Yorker, 04 March 1950.

Craton, Michael and Walvin, James, *A Jamaican Plantation: The History of Worthy Park 1670-1970*, W.H.Allen & Co. London, 1970.

Cripps, Ernest C., *Plough Court: The Story of a Notable Pharmacy 1715-1927*, Allen and Hanburys, London 1927.

Curl, James Stevens, *Spas, Wells and Pleasure Gardens of London*, Historical Publications Ltd, London 2010

Dashwood, Sir Francis, *The Dashwoods of West Wycombe*, Aurum Press, London, 1987.

Delap, Francis, An Account of the Trial of Francis Delap Esq., London 1755, ECCO Digital Reprint.

Delle, James A., Hauser, Mark W., Armstrong, Douglas V. eds, *Out of Many One People, The Historical Archaeology of Jamaica,* University of Alabama Press, Tuscaloosa, 2011.

Dobson, David, *Scots in the West Indies 1707-1857, Volume 1*, Clearfield, Baltimore, 2006.

Dobson, David, *Scots in Jamaica 1655-1855,* Clearfield, Baltimore, 2011.

Dunn, Richard S., *Sugar and Slaves: The Rise of the Planter Class in the English West Indies 1624-1713*, University of North Carolina Press, 1972.

Edwards, Bryan, The History Civil and Commercial of the British West Indies, 1819, AMS Press Inc.,New York, 1966.

Eveleigh, David J. *Firegrates and Kitchen Ranges*, Shire Publications Ltd., Oxford, 2008.

Fildes, Valerie, *Wet Nursing: A History from Antiquity to the Present*, Basil Blackwell Ltd, Oxford, 1988.

Foot, Constance, *In and Around London*, T.C. & E.C.Jack, London, 1923.

Foreman, Amanda, *Georgiana Duchess of Devonshire*, HarperCollins, London, 1998.

Gamble, Audrey Nona, *A History of the Bevan Family*, Headley Brothers, London. 1923.

Gensel, Lisa, *The Medical World of Benjamin Franklin,* Journal of the Royal Society of Medicine, Vol. 98, No 12, pp. 534-538.

George, Dorothy, *London Life in the Eighteenth Century,* 1925, reprinted LSE, London 1951.

Grannum, Guy, *Tracing Your West Indian Ancestors,* Public Record Office, Kew, England, 2002.

Gravette, Andrew, *Architectural Heritage of the Caribbean,* Ian Randle Publishers, Kingston, Jamaica, 2000.

Gwynn, Robin, *The Huguenots of London*, The Alpha Press, Brighton, 1998.

Hanson, Neil, *The Dreadful Judgement, The True Story of the Great Fire of London*, Corgi, London 2002.

Hamilton, Douglas J., *Scotland, the Caribbean and the Atlantic World 1750-1820*, Manchester University Press, 2005.

Harrison, Michelle, *King Sugar, Jamaica, the Caribbean and the World Sugar Economy*, Latin America Bureau, London 2001.

Hart, Avril and North, Susan, *Seventeenth and Eighteenth Century Fashion in Detail*, V&A Publishing, London, 2009.

Hostettler, John and Braby, Richard, *Sir William Garrow His Life, Times and Fight for Justice,* Waterside Press Ltd, Hook, UK, 2010.

Howard, David, Kingston, *A Cultural and Literary History*, Signal Books, Oxford, 2005.

Hennessy, Elizabeth, *Coffee House to Cyber Market, 200 Years of the London Stock Exchange,* Ebury Press, London, 2001.

Higman, B.W., *Montpelier Jamaica: A Plantation Community in Slavery and Freedom 1739-1912,* The Press University of the West Indies, Barbados, Jamaica, Trinidad and Tobago,1998.

Hurwitz,Samuel J. And Hurwitz, Edith F., *A Token of Freedom: Private Bill Legislation for Free Negroes in Eighteenth-Century Jamaica*, The William and Mary Quarterly, Third Series, Vol. 24, No.3, (July 1967), pp.423-431.

Inglis, Lucy, *'A Blaze of Loyalty': The illuminations of Georgian London,* www.georgianlondon.com, 2010.

Ingram, Kenneth E.N., *Manuscript Sources for the History of the West Indies*, University of the West Indies Press, limited edition.

Jamaican Assembly, *The Laws of Jamaica*, Vols. 1 & 2, 1782, Google Books.

Kelly, Ian, *Beau Brummell, The Ultimate Man of Style*, Free Press, New York, 2006.

Kemp, Betty, *Sir Francis Dashwood An Eighteenth Century Independent*, Macmillan, London, 1967.

Lawrence-Archer, J.H., *Monumental Inscriptions of the British West Indies*, London 1875, Nabu Digital On-Demand Reprint.

Lee, Rachael Fanny Antonina, *Memoirs of R.F.A.*, 1812.

Lewis, Samuel ed., *A Topographical Dictionary of England*, 1848, http://www.british-history.ac.uk

Livesay, Daniel A., *Children of Uncertain Fortune: Mixed-Race Migration from the West Indies to Britain*, unpublished PhD thesis, University of Michigan, 2010 (in preparation, University of North Carolina Press).

Livingston, Noel B., *Sketch Pedigrees of some of the Early Settlers in Jamaica*, Jamaica 1909, reprinted Clearfield, Baltimore, 1992.

London Record Society, *London Inhabitants within the Walls 1695*, London, 1966, http://www.british-history.ac.uk

Long, Edward, *The History of Jamaica*, 3 vols, London 1774, reprinted by Frank Cass & Co Ltd, London 1970.

Mackenzie, Alexander, *History of the Mackenzies*, A&W Mackenzie, Inverness, 1894, reprinted Dodo Press.

Mackenzie, Alexander, *History of the Munros of Fowlis*, A&W Mackenzie, Inverness, 1898.

Mair, Lucille Mathurin, edited by Beckles, Hilary McD. And Shepherd, Verene A., *A Historical Study of Women in Jamaica*, University of the West Indies Press, Barbados, Jamaica, Trinidad and Tobago, 2006.

Matthews, P.W. and Tuke, Anthony W., *History of Barclays Bank Limited*, London, 1926.

McLynn, Frank, *1759 The Year Britain Became Master of the World*, Vintage Books, London, 2004.

Meyer, Mrs (Louisa), *The Author of the Peep of Day Being the Life Story of Mrs Mortimer by her niece Mrs Meyer*, The Religious Tract Society, London, 1901.

Mintz, Sidney W., *Sweetness and Power: The Place of Sugar in Modern History*, Penguin Books, London, 1986.

Monteith, Kathleen E.A. and Richards, Glen, *Jamaica in Slavery and Freedom*, University of the West Indies Press, Barbados, Jamaica, Trinidad and Tobago, 2002.

Mortimer, Favell Lee, *The Peep of Day*, Longmans, Green and Co., London 1900.

Mulcahy, Matthew, Hurricanes and Society in the British Greater Caribbean, 1624-1783, The Johns Hopkins University Press, Baltimore, 2008.

Neale, J.A., *The Case of William Jaques*, Antiquarian Horology, Volume 20, No.4, Winter 1992, pp.340-355.

Nugent, Maria, *Lady Nugent's Journal of her residence in Jamaica from 1802-1805*, edited by Philip Wright, Institute of Jamaica, Kingston, 4th revised edn. 1966.

Nuki, George and Simkin, Peter A., *A concise history of gout and hyperuricemia and their treatment,* Arthritis Research and Therapy 2006, 8 (Suppl.1):S1, 2006.

Parker, Matthew, *The Sugar Barons: Family, Corruption, Empire and War*, Hutchinson, London, 2011.

Picard, Liza, *Dr Johnson's London*, Weidenfeld and Nicolson, London, 2000.

Pierce, Patricia, *Old London Bridge: The Story of the Longest Inhabited Bridge in Europe, Headline Book Publishing*, London, 2001.

Price, F.G.Hilton, *A Handbook of London Bankers, with some account of their predecessors The Early Goldsmiths,* Burt Franklin, New York, 1876, reprinted 1970.

Robertson, James, *Gone is the Ancient Glory, Spanish Town Jamaica 1534-2000*, Ian Randle Publishers, Kingston, Jamaica, 2005.

Rolls, Roger, *Spa Therapy through the Ages,* Bath and North East Somerset Council.

Ryden, David Beck, *West Indian Slavery and British Abolition 1783-1807*, Cambridge University Press, 2010.

Shepherd, Verene A.(ed.), *Women in Caribbean History*, Ian Randle, Kingston, James Currey Ltd., Oxford, Markus Wiener, Princeton, 1999.

Sheridan, Richard B., *Simon Taylor, Sugar Tycoon of Jamaica, 1740-1813*, Agricultural History, Vol. 45, No.4 (Oct. 1971) pp.285-296.

Sheridan, Richard B., *Doctors and Slaves: A medical and demographic history of slavery in the British West Indies, 1680-1834*, Cambridge University Press, 2009.

Sheridan, Richard B., *Sugar and Slavery: An Economic History of the British West Indies, 1623-1775*, Canoe Press, University of the West Indies, Barbados, Jamaica, Trinidad and Tobago, reprinted 2007.

Sloane, Hans, *A Letter from Hans Sloane MD and SRS with Several Accounts of the Earthquakes in Peru October the 20th 1687. And at Jamaica, February 19th 1687/8 and June 7th 1692*, Philosophical Transaction of the Royal Society, 1694 18, 78-100.

Smith, D.J.M, *A Dictionary of Horse-Drawn Vehicles*, J.A.Allen and Co. London, 1988.

Smith, F.Andrew, *An 'Arch-Villain' to be rehabilitated?* Borneo Research Bulletin vol.38, 2007. p.101.

Smith, Raymond, T., *Kinship and Class in the West Indies: A Genealogical Study of Jamaica and Guyana*, Cambridge University Press, 1988.

Stead, Jennifer, *Georgian Cooker Recipes and History*, English Heritage, revised edition 2003.

Sturtz, Linda L., *The 'Dim Duke' and the Duchess of Chandos: Gender and Power in Jamaican Plantation Management -- A Case Study,* Revista/Review Interamericana 29, 1999.

Sturtz, Linda L., *Mary Rose: "White" African Jamaican Woman? Race and Gender in Eighteenth Century Jamaica,* in *Gendering the African Diaspora:Women, Culture, and Historical Change in the Caribbean and Nigerian Hinterland* edited by Judith A. Byfield, LaRay Denzer and Anthea Morrison, Indiana University Press, Bloomington and Indianapolis, 2010.

Towers, Eric, *Dashwood the Man and the Myth*, Crucible, UK, 1986.

White, Jerry, *London in the Eighteenth Century: A Great and Monstrous Thing*, The Bodley Head, London, 2012.

Willeett, C. And Cunnington, Phillis, *The History of Underclothes*, Dover Publications Inc., New York, 1992.

Wilson, Harriette, ed. Blanch, Lesley, *Harriette Wilson's Memoirs The Greatest Courtesan of her Age*, Phoenix Press, London, 2003.

Wood, Betty ed., *The Letters of Simon Taylor of Jamaica to Chaloner Arcedeckne 1765-1775,* in *Travel Trade and Power in the Atlantic 1765-1884* Camden Miscellany XXXV, vol.19, Cambridge University Press, 2002.

Index